The Destruction of the Zulu Kingdom

The Destruction of the Zulu Kingdom

The Civil War in Zululand, 1879–1884

Jeff Guy

Longman

LONGMAN GROUP LIMITED
LONDON
Associated companies, branches and
representatives throughout the world

© Longman Group Ltd 1979

First published 1979

ISBN 0 582 64686 3

Printed in Great Britain by
Western Printing Services Ltd, Bristol

For my Mother and Father

Contents

List of Illustrations

Maps

Figures

Plates

Abbreviations

APS	Aborigines Protection Society
AS	Anti-Slavery papers, Rhodes House, Oxford
BM	British Museum
BPP	British Parliamentary Papers
CO	Colonial Office, London
GH	Government House, Natal, papers in Natal Archives
GHZ	Government House, Zululand, papers in Natal Archives
KC	Killie Campbell Africana Library, Durban
NA	Natal Archives (South African Archives, Pietermaritzburg Depot)
SNA	Secretary for Native Affairs, Natal
ZA	Zululand Archives, part of the collection in the Natal Archives

Acknowledgements

The author and publishers are grateful for permission to reproduce photographs from the following:
Natal Archives (plates 1, 2, 3, 5, 8, 10, 12, 13, 16, 17, 18, 20, 21, 22, 23, 26); Africana Museum, Johannesburg Public Library (plates 6, 7, 9); Killie Campbell Africana Library (plates 11 and 15); the National Army Museum (plates 24 and 25); Bassano and Vandyk Studios, London (plate 19, also shown on jacket). Plate 14 is taken from F. E. Colenso, *The Ruin of Zululand*, Ridgway, London, 1884-5.

Preface

This book tells the story of the destruction of the material strength and political independence of an African society in southern Africa in the late nineteenth century. While comparable events occurred in many parts of Africa at this time the contemporary records are usually dominated by the viewpoints of those who initiated the process of conquest. In the case of the destruction of the Zulu kingdom, however, one major protagonist – the Zulu royal house – found literate allies who left a detailed record of their actions and their interpretation of events. These spokesmen were led by the Bishop of Natal, John William Colenso, and members of his family, all intelligent, energetic, Zulu-speaking, political allies who worked for the perpetuation of the authority of the royal house. Their public attack on colonial policy provoked a counter-attack from the officials connected with Zulu affairs, and the record of this dispute is to be found in the documentary sources of the period.

It is upon these sources that much of this book is based. They give opposing interpretations of events, and the tales they tell are contradictory. I have tried to resolve or explain some of these contradictions by close empirical analysis and to construct a narrative which moves from the homesteads of the Zulu kingdom to colonial Natal and the Cape, to Victorian London, and back to the battlefields of Zululand. Where possible I have allowed the African actors in this tragedy to speak for themselves; they were eloquent, well aware of the attempts to suppress their voice, and deeply concerned about the judgement of history. At the same time I have attempted to go beyond the prejudice and ideologies of the time and reveal something of the deeper historical forces which provided the context in which these events occurred – the inexorable drive to divert the surplus supporting one society and use it to serve the interests of another intrusive one.

Details of the official records, and the writings and researches of the Colenso family which have been used here, can be found in the bibliography. Two other sources should be mentioned: firstly, the remarkable collection of historical and cultural information gathered by James Stuart from Zulu informants at the turn of the century and now housed in the Killie Campbell Africana Library of the University of Natal;[1] secondly the account given in Zulu by one of the participants in these events, Maphelu kaMkhosana of the Zungu clan, taken down by the Zulu Society probably in the 1940s, which is also in the Killie Campbell Africana Library.

The use of Zulu words and names in an English text raises many problems. The English language itself in Africa still reflects structures of dominance and it is difficult to free oneself of this and remain comprehensible, or without entering lengthy debate. Even such basic terms as father, mother, brother and marriage are inadequate, and an *umuzi* for example is more than a homestead, and an *indlu* is not merely a 'hut'. At the same time the use of Zulu equivalents is clumsy and does not solve the problem of definition. I have tried to use sensible forms of Zulu words, according to modern orthography; at the same time I have had to temper pedantry with common sense and on occasion follow popular usage, particularly with place names. Some of my decisions are, I know, debatable. I should like to draw the reader's attention to the Biographical Notes in the Appendix (p. 248). These have been included for reference during the reading of the text.

It was Colin Webb's teaching at the University of Natal that first made me, together with many others, aware of the fascination and the importance of the study of southern African history, and who introduced me to the history of Natal and Zululand. Shula Marks of the University of London has given me encouragement, support and friendship. To both these fine historians I am deeply grateful.

This book, and the dissertation upon which it is based, was written while I was working in the History Department of the Lesotho campus of the University of Botswana, Lesotho and Swaziland, which in 1975 became the National University of Lesotho. I must acknowledge not only the assistance I have received from the University authorities, the Research and Publications Committee in particular, my colleagues and students, but also the practical commitment of the University to the ideals of academic freedom. This has created an educational institution in the heart of southern Africa where teaching and research can be carried out without formal interference – a unique and valuable achievement. The Library staff have been of special assistance and I would like to thank Nana Tau, Monty Mareletse, and Michael Walpole for their help over the years. Jeremiah and Estelle Dlamini, Njabulo Ndebele, Joe Sithole, Sipho Nhlabathi, and Agatha Shange, while they were students, assisted in the translation of documents and problems of spelling and orthography. Charles Perrings, Lucas Smits, Njabulo Ndebele, Brendon Hughes, David and Spaña Hirschmann have always been ready to discuss issues raised in this book and to help, and Benedicta Melato and Linus Majoro made the task of writing much easier.

It is eight years since I did my initial research in Natal and what is now called kwaZulu. At that time I received hospitality and assistance from many people including Chief Mangosuthu Gatsha Buthelezi, his wife Irene Buthelezi, Princess Constance Magogo, and the present king, Goodwill Zwelithini. Since then Chief Buthelezi has become a controversial figure of international repute, Chief Minister of kwaZulu, and President of Inkatha, a 'national cultural liberation movement'. It is therefore important that I state that the responsibility for the facts and interpretations in this book are my own: it would be ungracious of me to fail to acknowledge the help and kindness I received in Zululand in 1970 and at the same time unjust if those who assisted me should in any way be identified with my opinions.

Also in Zululand at that time were Anthony and Maggie Barker of the Charles Johnson Memorial Hospital and I would like to thank them, and the staff of the hospital, for their assistance and company, together with staff of Ceza Hospital and the many other residents of Zululand who put me up, and who were prepared to talk about Zulu history.

I must acknowledge a grant from the Ernest Oppenheimer Memorial Trust upon which I depended in the initial stages of research.

Naimi and Heli have willingly made many sacrifices: they know what this has meant for me.

Roma, Lesotho   JEFF GUY
July 1978

Notes

1 A selection from this collection is in the process of being published. See C. de B. Webb, and J. B. Wright (eds), *The James Stuart Archive*, Pietermaritzburg and Durban, 1976, i.

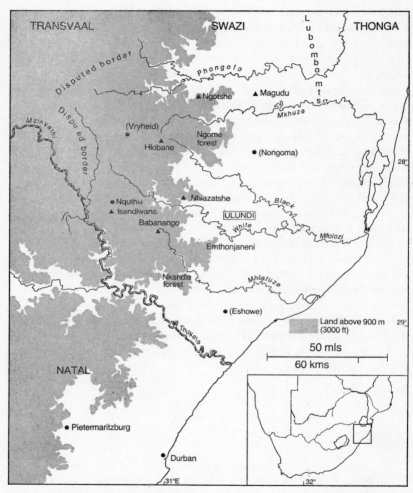

Map I Zululand and surrounding territories

Introduction

Any analysis of those people who have at different times considered themselves, or have been considered by others, as 'Zulu' would necessitate an examination of some of the major themes of South African history. In its strict sense Zulu is a clan name, referring to the descendants of Zulu, a man who lived perhaps three hundred years ago in the vicinity of the middle reaches of the White Mfolozi river. His descendant, Shaka kaSenzangakhona, extended the use of the name considerably when he incorporated the members of different clans into the Zulu kingdom which he founded early in the nineteenth century. Towards the end of that century many Africans in the neighbouring Colony of Natal, who spoke the same language, and who had shared a common history until the disruption of the Mfecane and the establishment of colonial rule, were calling themselves Zulu. And this trend has been extended until now over 4 000 000 Africans in southern Africa are considered to be Zulu.

In this book, however, I use the word in a more restricted sense: by Zulu I mean those people who gave their allegiance to the Zulu kings, who lived and worked land granted them by the kings, and whose menfolk served in the state army until 1879. It might be argued that I should extend this definition and use the locative formation – kwaZulu – when referring to the area in which the Zulu lived. KwaZulu, however, has contemporary connotations with the apartheid policy of the South African Government and I use the word 'Zululand' to describe the territory in which the Zulu lived. When I refer specifically to the Zulu clan, the Zulu lineage, or the Zulu royal house, the context should make this clear. I must stress that these are not rigid definitions but convenient descriptive terms.

The story of Shaka, the son of Senzangakhona and founder of the Zulu kingdom, has been told many times and, although the literature has still to rid itself of ethnocentricity, exaggeration and sensationalism, the outlines of the narrative are well-known. Shaka was born in about 1787 and after an unhappy and insecure early life, succeeded to the chieftainship of the Zulu clan in 1816. The first quarter of the nineteenth century was a period of great violence and disruption in south-east Africa as rival chiefdoms fought for territory and the extension of political control. Using his exceptional military talents Shaka successfully asserted the supremacy of the comparatively small Zulu chiefdom over its major rivals. In the process he absorbed many of the other groups in the area into the new Zulu military kingdom, annihilated some and dispersed others, initiating a chain of violence which left few parts of the sub-continent untouched and caused basic alterations in the demographic and political patterns of the region. By the mid-1820s the Zulu kingdom, centred on what is now Natal and kwaZulu, and dominating the surrounding area, was the most formidable power in south-east Africa. But even as it reached the moment of its greatest strength, there appeared in Shaka's kingdom the first white traders and adventurers, representatives of the forces that Shaka's successors would have to confront and which finally overthrew his kingdom.

In 1828 Shaka was assassinated by his brother, Dingane, who then became king. During Dingane's reign a permanent trading settlement was established on the coast, the first missionaries arrived, and at the end of the 1830s the waggons of the Voortrekkers crossed the passes of the Drakensberg in search of fertile land between the mountains and the Indian ocean. Dingane first attempted to accommodate the Trekkers, and then to annihilate them. He failed, however, and in the aftermath of a major defeat in battle, the kingdom split when Mpande, Dingane's brother, went over to the Trekkers and with their assistance drove Dingane out of the country to his death on the Lubombo mountains.

Mpande came to the Zulu throne in 1840 and was to rule the Zulu kingdom for over thirty years. The borders of the kingdom were now reduced but he established his rule over its core, sharing a boundary with the Colony of Natal, which was established in the mid-1840s, and disputing a border with the Transvaal in the north-west. To the north and north-east the direct rule of Mpande was replaced by that of the Swazi king and the Thonga chiefdoms. During his long reign Mpande was to deal successfully with civil war, pressure on his borders and the attempts of traders, missionaries and neighbouring governments to undermine his authority and to bring about change in Zululand. But unlike so many nearby African societies the Zulu kingdom, protected by astute rulers and a large army, retained its essential autonomy and self-sufficiency. When Mpande's son, Cetshwayo, succeeded to the throne in 1872 he became the ruler of a powerful, independent African kingdom, that was looked upon with fear, and acquisitiveness, by neighbouring settler communities.

Cetshwayo kaMpande was to rule for only eight years. Important changes were taking place in southern Africa at the time, and the Zulu kingdom was seen as an obstacle hindering progress and peaceful development in the region. Thus, in 1879, the kingdom was invaded by the British army supported by colonial forces. The Zulu king was exiled and the Zulu military system terminated, but the intensity of Zulu resistance persuaded the British to leave the Zulu in possession of most of their land, and they escaped annexation. The external forces of change, having failed in a direct assault, then started to erode Zulu independence. Divisions within Zulu society were exploited and the material strength of the Zulu undermined; partition was attempted, unsuccessfully in 1883 and successfully in 1887, when political authority was divided between the Transvaal and Britain. Zulu were now beginning to leave their homesteads in large numbers to work on the farms, railways, mines and in the homes of neighbouring colonies. In 1897 British Zululand was handed over to the Colony of Natal which, in the early years of the twentieth century, appropriated much of Zulu land for white settlement. A despairing rising in 1906 was unsuccessful and the areas of Zulu occupation became 'Native Reserves' to be administered in much the same way as those which had already existed in Natal for half a century. The Native Land Act of 1913, passed by the government of the Union of South Africa, confirmed this land distribution pattern, and with a few insubstantial changes made in terms of the 1936 Native Trust and Land Act, this pattern can still be discerned in the present-day kwaZulu. This 'homeland' is without historical basis, unable to support its own population, fragmented, penetrated by areas of white settlement and white corridors which dominate the most important areas of development, the resources, ports, and communication routes.

I have already mentioned that to understand the different ways in which the name Zulu has been used in South Africa it would be necessary to examine some of the major themes in South African history. A discussion of what the name 'Zulu' has meant to foreign audiences would be equally interesting. In 1879, when British troops, supported by colonial forces, invaded the Zulu kingdom, the Zulu people resisted this assault on their independence with such vigour that they not only inflicted on the invaders one of the greatest defeats in the history of Britain's colonial wars, but they also impressed the name Zulu indelibly on the popular imagination of Europe and America.

At one level this can be seen in the way in which the name Zulu has entered popular speech and writing over the last century and has become widely identified with an idea of traditional African savagery, bravery and a barbarous nobility. It has been used to name, and to sell, an extra-ordinary range of commodities, particularly when such qualities as speed, vigour or blackness need to be emphasised. A successful film, purporting to be about the British invasion, was called simply 'Zulu', and as I write another film of this genre, inexplicably named 'Zulu Dawn', is being made. 'Zulu' musicals still fill London theatres.

At a more complex level the nature of the Zulu people and their history has been transformed to fulfil particular needs among widely differing groups of people, thousands of miles away from Zululand. For example, it can be found in accounts of the birth of jazz in the red-light district of New Orleans at the turn of the century where

> The whites had an idea of a real king – he came in on Canal Street. The coloured people had the King of the Zulus and he came in on Basin Street – dressed in funny feathers and straw – boy, that was something.[1]

The Zulu and their kings have undergone a different, but no less radical, transformation in the minds of the English reading public. The outlines of the process can be traced from the first missionary and traveller accounts to the 1860s when Bishop Colenso caught the public's attention by writing of the 'intelligent Zulu' whose penetrating questions were the origin of Colenso's notorious biblical criticism. In 1879 the Zulu came suddenly and dramatically before the world with the news of the British defeat at Isandlwana, the defence of Rorke's Drift, the killing of the Prince Imperial, and Disraeli's famous comment on the remarkable Zulu people who convert our bishops, defeat our generals, and put an end to a great European dynasty. All this was intensified by the grotesque imagin-ation of Rider Haggard who became the great popular writer of his time by showing the Zulu 'as they were, in all their superstitious madness and bloodstained grandeur',[2] and who successfully confused in his readers' minds campfire anecdotes about the rise of Shaka with the later history of the kingdom.

From all this the myth of the Zulu as the noblest of savages emerged – significantly only after their independent power had been broken. And it can still be found in the many books which tell and retell the stories of Isandlwana, Rorke's Drift, the death of Louis Napoleon, their authors re-working essentially the same source material with a greater or lesser degree of accuracy. And the centenary of the invasion will no doubt be followed by a sustained attempt to capitalise on the reading public's apparently insatiable appetite for stories of the 'glamour and tragedy' of the invasion of Zululand.

This approach is conveyed most immediately by C. E. Fripp's popular painting of the last stand of the 24th Regiment at Isandlwana, part of which is shown on the jacket of this book. It depicts the battle as an episode in the great imperial adventure, and sets staunch redcoats, short of ammunition and on badly chosen ground, against the massed charge of the Zulu, with both sides going gloriously to their deaths. The shortcomings of this view should be obvious and would not need discussion if it were not for the fact that this approach still pervades accounts of the war and, as a result, continues to obstruct any serious understanding of the events which took place. The brutality of the war is dimmed in a haze of nostalgia evoked by stirring stories of reckless bravery in far-off lands for Queen and Country. The emphasis placed on the set battles draws attention away from the fact that the invasion was an assault on a people's way of life and took suffering and tragedy far beyond the battle-field. Moreover the social forces which brought about the invasion are obscured, together with the intentions of the men who planned the war, and the motives of those who fought in it. For Zululand was invaded in 1879 to facilitate the absorption of the Zulu people into the developing southern African capitalist system by the forcible acquisition of Zulu land and Zulu labour. The majority of the men who died in the war were either the enlisted soldiers of the British army, 'recruited', we are told, 'mostly from the very poorest and most ignorant'[3] in Britain, or the Zulu soldiers, fighting to save themselves and their children from becoming 'the very poorest and most ignorant' in southern Africa.

One hundred years after the event all this should be clear enough. Not so obvious perhaps is the connected point which this book takes as its starting position: this is that the conventional view, which equates the end of Zulu power and independence with the British military victory at Ulundi in July 1879, is a misleading oversimplification. It is an interpretation which ignores the fact that, by the time the battle was fought, the intensity of Zulu resistance had already persuaded London that the cost of ending Zulu independence by force of arms would be too high, that the officials who had brought about the war had been checked, and that orders had been given that Zululand should not be annexed. Nevertheless Isandlwana could not go unavenged; Britain's colonial peoples had to be convinced of the Queen's military superiority, and the 'stain' on Britain's honour had to be wiped out. To achieve this the battle of Ulundi was promoted to the rank of a major military victory. Peace was in fact attained in the weeks that followed Ulundi by promising the Zulu people that they would retain possession of their land if they laid down their arms.

This is not to say that the imperatives which had brought war to Zululand disappeared with the discredited statesmen who had planned it. They changed their form, however, no longer manifesting themselves as obviously and directly as the drum-rolls and ranked volley-firing of an invading imperial army, but nonetheless discernible if one examines the official dispatches and minutes on events which followed the war, reads the letters of local officials concerned with Zulu affairs, and analyses Zulu petitions, protests and praise-poems, land grants and hut tax registers.

The intention of those who planned the invasion of 1879 was to terminate Zulu political independence and free Zulu labour by means of a decisive military victory. The Zulu army thwarted this and as a result the war became merely the first stage in a prolonged process during which metropolitan and colonial forces undermined the strength of the Zulu by exploiting divisions within their society, and brought about a civil war which left the country and its people open to political subjugation and economic exploitation.

It is the story of this civil war with which this book is concerned.

Notes

1 Kid Ory in N. Shapiro and N. Hentoff (eds), *Hear me talkin' to ya. The story of Jazz by the men who made it*, London, 1955, p. 28.
2 Quoted in M. Cohen, *Rider Haggard. His life and work*, London, 1968, p. 227.
3 C. Barnett, *Britain and Her Army, 1509–1970*, London, 1970, p. 313.

Glossary

ibandla	the highest council of state
isibongo	the praise poem
induna/*izinduna*	official in the service of the Zulu state
ikhanda/*amakhanda*	royal homestead, and barracks for the army
ikhohlo	the people who make up the left hand side of the homestead or lineage
isikhulu/*izikhulu*	the great ones of the kingdom: the hereditary chiefs of the clans: members of the *ibandla*
imbongi	the declaimer of praise-poems
impi	an armed force
inceku	personal attendant and confidential adviser
umntwana/*abantwana*	princes – the children of the king
umnumzana/*abanumzana*	homestead-heads
umuzi/*imizi*	the homestead – the physical structure of its occupants, or a lineage (cf. English – the royal house)
Sobantu	Father of the People (J. W. Colenso's Zulu name)
Somtsewu	Father of Whiteness (Sir Theophilus Shepstone's Zulu name)
Malimathe	Derived from Melmoth Osborn's name

PART I

Invasion

Had Cetywayo's thirty thousand warriors been in time changed to labourers working for wages, Zululand would have been a prosperous peaceful country instead of what it now is, a source of perpetual danger to itself and its neighbours.

Sir Theophilus Shepstone, 1878

[If the Zulu agree to the demand that they abandon restrictions on marriage, and disband their military system] they would lower their country to the debased level of amaKafula . . . [Africans in the Colony of Natal], to be *isangcobe* (spoiled maize out of the holes in the cattle-fold) instead of *umbila ong'umzanzato* (maize which is sound, dry, and hard); therefore, they will fight rather than give in on those points.

Reported reaction of the Zulu who received Frere's Ultimatum to the Zulu king

CHAPTER ONE

The Zulu Kingdom

Foundations

Early in the 1880s when Cetshwayo kaMpande, the last of the Zulu kings, was in exile he was asked what he knew of the diamond fields around Kimberley. It was believed that, when he was king, Cetshwayo had been planning a black rising in southern Africa and that he had his spies in all parts of the region, and his captors were therefore surprised to discover that the king knew little about the diamond fields. Visiting traders had spoken about the mines but Cetshwayo was not even sure where they were situated for, as he said, 'the Zulu people never went to the Diamond Fields; the Natal Zulus did'.[1]

This statement tells us much about the nature of the kingdom which Cetshwayo ruled from 1872, and also suggests why it was invaded by the British in 1879. The discovery of diamonds in the southern African interior in the late 1860s had brought the first stirring of economic revolution to most communities between the Cape and the Zambezi. One of its effects was to attract to the mines Africans from all parts of the sub-continent. The Zulu, however, seem to have been an exception to this. There was as yet no need for them to labour outside their territory for cash or firearms because the expanding forces of colonialism had not penetrated the structure of the Zulu social formation. While other African communities had been forcibly driven from their land, or had lost their self-sufficiency as their surplus products and labour were drawn beyond their borders, the Zulu remained in possession of their land, and their labour was still expended within the kingdom.

The Zulu of Cetshwayo's kingdom were very aware of these differences between their way of life and that of most of their African neighbours; they were proud of their political and economic independence and the manner in which they had resisted change, as befitted the descendants of Shaka kaSenzangakhona, the founder of the kingdom.

The social strength and resilience of the kingdom and the independence of its members had its origins in the particular qualities of the physical environment in which it had developed. Labour within this environment produced the food, the basic materials, and the instruments of production upon which the inhabitants depended. Consequently the links between man and the land were direct and intimate, and an understanding of the nature of the physical environment and its productive potential is fundamental to an understanding of the Zulu people's history.

Zululand's boundaries changed greatly during the years between the rule of its founder, Shaka (*c.* 1816–28), and his nephew, the last Zulu king, Cetshwayo (1872–9), but what might be called the 'core' of the kingdom lay between the Phongolo and Thukela river valleys in the north and south, and the valley of the Mzinyathi (Buffalo) river in the west. It is a region of high relief; rivers and streams have cut deep valleys as they retreated westwards leaving huge spurs of more resistant material jutting towards the sea. Thus the five major river systems – the Thukela, Mhlatuze, Mfolozi, Mkhuze and Phongolo – are separated by high-lying ground, at times 1 000 m above the adjacent river-valley floors, and the sides of the valleys are deeply incised by feeder streams creating much broken country (see Map II).

This high relief leads to great variations in rainfall and temperature over short distances. Thus the coastal area is hot and sub-tropical while in the highlands the climate is far more temperate with warm, wet summers and cold, dry winters. Rain-bearing winds come off the Indian ocean and deposit over 1 000 mm a year on the coast, but the rainfall decreases as the distance from the sea increases. However, the rainfall does not decrease uniformly, as the high ground receives far more than the major river valleys which lie in rain-shadow areas where precipitation can be less than 600 mm a year (see Map III).

Variations in rainfall create differences in vegetation, and Zululand contains a number of different vegetation types interlacing through the country. Any description of vegetation has to take into account the fact that plant communities are never static and are constantly being altered by the effects of human activity. The vegetation of Zululand has been changed radically in the course of human history. Botanical research suggests that before the coming of the first farmers to the region it was heavily wooded.[2] The higher rainfall areas, like the coastal plain and much of the country over 500 m, were covered with dense bush and forest. The deep river valleys and the area in the north-east, lying in the rain-shadow of the Lubombo range, where the rainfall is low, tended to produce types of 'savanna' vegetation – that is, scattered trees with a grass understorey.

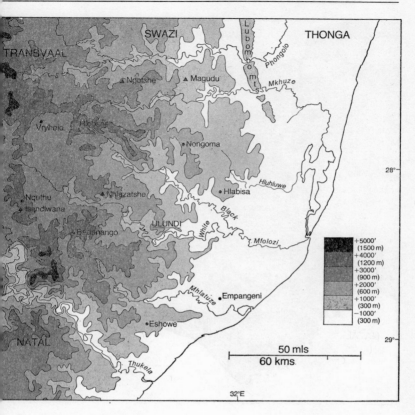

Map II   Zululand: Topography

Fire, the iron hoe and the axe in the hands of man, and the grazing patterns of his stock had, over a period of perhaps 1500 years, slowly altered these vegetational patterns. The forest was driven back to the crests of the high ridges, and the bush to the wettest slopes and along water-courses, and it was replaced by grassland. In the dry valleys burning and grazing reduced the wooded element of the savanna, opening it up and favouring the grasses. Indeed some botanists believe that this vegetation type can only be maintained by the constant activity of man and his stock.

By the beginning of the nineteenth century, when the Zulu kingdom came into being, the region contained a great variety of vegetation types. The coastal strip with its high rainfall and hot, sub-tropical climate was still covered with extensive tracts of bush. Away from the coast, as the rainfall decreased, the density of the bush was reduced and the resultant

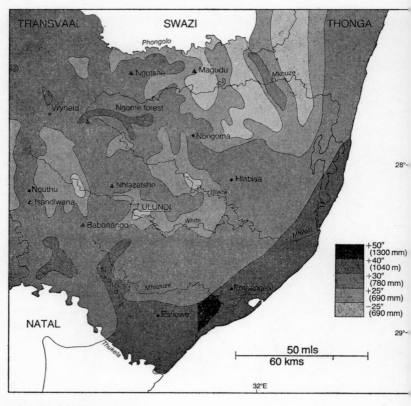

Map III   Zululand: Rainfall

grassy areas were well-suited to occupation by man, once his cattle were immune to the diseases transmitted by the ticks which thrived in the rank grasses.

The river valleys penetrate far into the interior of Zululand. The rainfall in these valleys is low, the temperature range wide, and the various types of savanna – commonly known as *ihlanze*, Thornveld, Lowveld or Bushveld – follow the rivers and spread beneath the forest-crowned highlands. The grasses which form the understorey in these areas are 'sweet', that is they provide nutritious and palatable grazing throughout the dry winter. In most parts of Africa it is the dry winter months which makes stock-keeping so hazardous; during this time the quality of the grass deteriorates, stock loses condition, and if the spring rains are late, stock losses can be high. In sweetveld regions, however, the grass retains its nutritive qualities and cattle thrive. While there were vast tracts of sweetveld in southern Africa in pre-colonial times they tended to be associated with tsetse-infected belts, or they were situated in regions where there was insufficient surface water to support a high density of stock. In Zululand, however, tsetse was confined to the borders of the country or the deepest river valleys and, although sweetveld only occurs where rainfall is low, the Zululand sweetveld regions were well watered by the streams and rivers rising in the surrounding hills and ranges.

Sourveld occurs in the high rainfall regions. It is nutritious and pala-table after the spring rains in the growing season, but once it has matured it loses these attributes. In Zululand it occurred on the coast and in the highlands, in areas once covered by forest and bush. And between the sour and sweet grazing regions were belts of mixed veld; the intermediate type which can be profitably grazed for about six months in the year (see Map IV)[3].

These different types of grazing, occurring over a comparatively small area, made Zululand an excellent region for stock. As long as the Zulu herder could move his animals freely he could take advantage of the spring grazing in the high country and, as the summer advanced, move them down the valley sides to the sweet grasses of the valley floors in the winter.

The wide range in climate allowed the Zulu cultivator to choose between the types of environment best suited to the different requirements of sorghum, millets and maize. Maize cultivation appears to have become established in the country by the eighteenth century and was probably the most important food crop by the nineteenth century. It has a number of advantages, being comparatively high-yielding when grown in suitable areas; it requires far less labour to produce, as it is resistant to the depre-dations of most birds, and needs neither winnowing nor threshing. Cereals, mixed with dairy products, formed the basis of the Zulu diet.

Most of the other materials essential to the Zulu way of life were produced in the environment in which they lived. Except for the western highlands the country was well-wooded, providing fuel as well as the materials from which the homesteads were constructed. Basic items of clothing were made from the hides of slaughtered cattle, and cooking and eating receptacles were made from grass, wood and clay. Iron for weapons and agricultural implements was mined, smelted and forged within the country, at least until iron became more readily available through external trade.

Taken as a whole the physical environment of Zululand was particularly well suited to the needs of these pre-colonial farmers. Lying between the tropical and temperate regions it possessed the fertility and fecundity, but

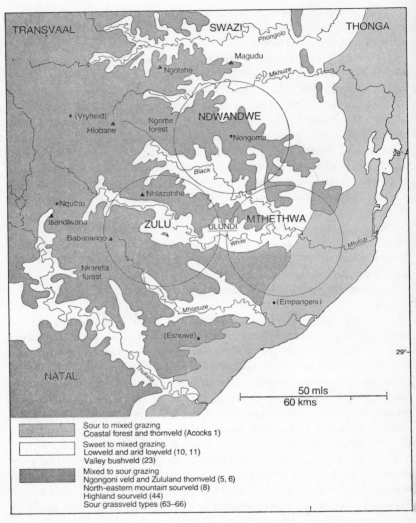

Map IV   Zululand: Grazing

not the debilitating diseases, of the tropics, and the grazing potential of its grasses was perhaps unrivalled in southern Africa under existing methods of stock-keeping.

At the same time it must be remembered that the productive potential of any environment is not static. The prolonged activity of man and his stock had done much to create Zululand's qualities as an excellent region for production by stock-keeping cultivators, but human activity had also initiated a process of environmental degeneration. The grasses of Zululand are easily damaged: over-stocking leads to the destruction of the grass-cover, soil erosion and bush encroachment; sweetveld is particularly vulnerable, and even under-stocking can lead to pasture deterioration because selective grazing favours unpalatable grasses which eventually come to dominate the plant community. It seems impossible that the pre-colonial peoples of south-eastern Africa could have established a long-term ecological equilibrium with their environment; a society without scientific knowledge of plant life and nutrition, or the means to control grazing and cattle movements by fencing, or to store and pump water, could not avert pasture degeneration.

Once population density in the sub-continent made migration to new areas difficult, and when it was no longer possible to convert forest and bush to grass and arable land, then there were definite limits on the rate of increase of production and of population density, limits imposed by the changing productive capacity of the environment under existing modes of exploitation. As these limits were approached a probable outcome would have been increasing violence between social groups living in the area as they struggled for access to diminishing resources. And there is evidence which suggests that such a struggle was an important factor in the conflict which occurred in the region at the end of the eighteenth and the beginning of the nineteenth centuries, out of which Shaka and the Zulu kingdom emerged. The geographical situation and the direction of expansion of the major groups contending for dominance, like the Mthethwa, the Ndwandwe and the Zulu, suggest that their leaders were concerned with gaining access to a wide variety of grazing types.[4] There was a major famine in the region during the early years of the nineteenth century during which starving marauders tried to seize food-stores, and settlement patterns were changed with the object of protecting such stores more effectively.[5] A feature of the struggles at this time was the increase in the area controlled by a single political unit. This gave members of the unit access to a wider range of grazing, enabling them to avoid the effects of local drought and shortage, and making for more effective control of the environment. And of course the rise of Shaka was characterised by a substantial reduction in the population of the region by warfare.

But perhaps the strongest indication that the struggle out of which the Zulu kingdom emerged was created in part by an imbalance between population density and existing resources can be discerned by considering the structure of the kingdom itself. An examination of production within the kingdom, and the manner in which it was organised, does suggest that an important factor in its emergence was the need to alter social relations in order to solve problems that hitherto existing modes of exploitation and social organisation could not answer.

Production in Zululand took place in the tens of thousands of homesteads (*imizi*) which were scattered over the hills and ridges of the country.[6] These were the homesteads of the 'common man', consisting of a circle of huts (*izindlu*) around a cattle kraal. In these huts lived the homestead-head (*umnumzana*) and perhaps two or three wives and their children. To a large degree the homestead was materially self-sufficient, its inhabitants subsisting almost entirely on the products of their own labour. There was a rigid sexual division of labour within the homestead: the men worked with livestock and the women in the production of cereals. Supporting activities, like the manufacture of the instruments of production, clothing, and handicrafts, were also allocated according to sex, but the task undertaken usually depended on an individual's particular talents, and the local availability of the necessary raw materials. It was the day-to-day labour within these homesteads, and in the lands associated with them, which, from the time of Shaka to Cetshwayo, provided the subsistence and the surplus upon which the continued existence of the kingdom depended.

But although it has been estimated that 90 per cent of the people of Zululand lived in such homesteads[7] it must be remembered that the kingdom was highly stratified and that the king and his officials exercised authority over these homesteads, extracting surplus from them, and uniting them politically into one large centralised polity. The homesteads of men of rank within the kingdom were far larger than those of the men living under their authority but the essential principles by which they were organised, and by which production took place, were the same. And these principles can also be perceived in the manner in which the king's homesteads were organised, although in these royal homesteads there were also important differences, the most significant relating to the king's position as head of the Zulu army.

The royal homesteads – the *amakhanda* – were not only production communities, supported by the labour of the relatives and retainers of the king living within them, but they were also barracks which housed members of the Zulu army while serving the king. Under the Zulu military system all men and women in the country, on reaching the age of puberty, were gathered into age-sets, *amabutho*. Members of the female age-sets did not give direct service to the king and remained within their fathers' homesteads, but they were not allowed to marry until the king had given his permission. As members of the regiments of the Zulu army, men served the king directly, raiding beyond Zululand's borders, acting as a coercive force within the kingdom, and, while they were living in the royal homesteads, they laboured for the king. Here the sexual division of labour did not apply and the regiments' work included crop production. The importance of the Zulu army as a raiding force declined after the death of Shaka although of course the threat posed by the army, even when it was inactive, was of the greatest importance in securing the country's independence.

Although, while in service, the regiments received a certain amount of food from the king, most of their subsistence was derived from their own labour and they were also heavily dependent on supplies brought from their fathers' homesteads. Thus the Zulu army was supported, in the main, by the homesteads from which its members originated; and its strength, upon which the king's power and the nation's independence was based, depended ultimately on the surplus labour drawn from every homestead within the country.

When the men of a regiment were well into their thirties, and the women of the age-sets associated with them perhaps ten years younger, the king gave them permission to marry and set up homesteads of their own.[8] These restrictions on the age of marriage have led many writers on Zulu history into confusion. There has been a tendency to ascribe these features of Zulu society as innovations introduced by Shaka for reasons directly related to his own personality. Thus a well-known social anthropologist has written recently that 'the extreme development of the military system, with its long-term celibacy' was the consequence of Shaka's own 'disturbed psychosexuality'.[9] And it is frequently supposed that the restriction on the age of marriage led to an accumulation of sexual energy which was somehow transmuted into military vigour.

These misconceptions are based on a crude Freudian approach which is frequently overlaid by transpositions of bourgeois concepts of marriage to Zulu society. In fact marriage in Zulu society did not signal the onset of sexual relations; these had been taking place long before, although they were a of kind which did not lead to conception. Moreover marriage in the Zulu kingdom meant far more than 'taking a wife' for when a man married he also left his father's homestead and established a new production community, served by tracts of arable and grazing land, supported by its own cattle, and which was soon augmented by more wives and their offspring. Thus by controlling marriage in the kingdom through the military system the king in fact controlled the rate and the direction of the fundamental social processes within the kingdom – those of production and reproduction.

In the case of women the delay in marriage reduced their fertile span, which necessarily reduced the potential rate of population increase.[10] When men are subjected to delays of this kind it does not have a marked effect on population increase; however, in Zulu society, where marriage was linked with the creation of new production communities, the king's authority to hold back marriage gave him a significant degree of control over the rate at which production communities were formed and therefore over the intensity with which the environment was exploited.

Thus a study of the physical environment of Zululand indicates that there were definite limits to the productive capacity of the region, and there are suggestions that these limits were being approached in the eighteenth century. Furthermore the structure of the Zulu kingdom founded in the early nineteenth century was such that it gave the king the power to control, to a significant degree, the rate of population increase and the rate at which the basic production processes of the kingdom expanded. While it would be an over-simplification to argue that the environmental crisis of the late eighteenth century led to the creation of the nineteenth-century kingdom which solved this problem, the evidence does suggest that we should study the early history of the kingdom within the context of the effect of existing production techniques on the physical environment and the problems caused in such an environment by the pressure of population on existing resources.

However, whatever the exact causes of Shaka's rise to power were, we do know that he left a form of social organisation which survived for half a century after his death, in the face of continual threats from the expanding forces of colonialism. There were of course many changes; nonetheless the fundamental structure of Zulu society remained substantially unaltered, maintaining a continuity between the kingdom Shaka founded and that ruled by Cetshwayo sixty years later.

Zulu independence and the Zulu kings

Shaka was assassinated in 1828 by his brother Dingane. It was Dingane's misfortune to have to deal with the arrival of the Voortrekkers in the region in 1837. He attempted to overcome the threat they posed by a surprise attack. This was only partially successful and the Voortrekkers had their revenge at Blood River in 1838 when they demonstrated the effect of concentrated fire-power from a defensive position on the massed charge of the Zulu army by killing three thousand Zulu without loss to themselves. Dingane's power was weakened by this defeat and another brother, Mpande, took the opportunity to ally himself with the Boers and overthrow Dingane in 1840.

The Zulu avoided paying the full price of this alliance when in 1842 the British terminated the existence of the Boer Republic of Natalia and in the following year recognised Mpande as the independent ruler of the territory to the north of the Thukela and east of the Mzinyathi rivers. In 1845 the Colony of Natal was founded. Its history and that of the neighbouring Zulu kingdom were to be closely connected.

Mpande ruled the kingdom for thirty-two years, that is for more than half the time it was in existence, and he was the only Zulu king to die peacefully in old age. By adopting a mask of lethargic stupidity he had escaped the attentions of his brothers, Shaka and Dingane, and he continued to use the same device to mislead his contemporaries. He did so with such effect that even today he is generally regarded as an indolent incompetent, a judgement belied by any serious attempt to assess his achievements in securing both his own power, and the independence of the kingdom.

Unlike Shaka and Dingane, Mpande married and allowed his children to survive. Two of the oldest were Mbulazi and Cetshwayo who were born in the early 1830s[11] Cetshwayo was the son of Ngqumbazi, a daughter of the dominant lineage of the Zungu clan, and Mbulazi was the son of Monase, a favourite wife of Mpande. The two princes were recruited into the Thulwana regiment and received their first military experience against the Swazi in the early 1850s in the last of the great Zulu raids. By this time factions had begun to gather around the young men: Mbulazi's followers were known as the Gqoza; Cetshwayo's were the Usuthu, a name derived from a drinking boast among the young men associated with him at the Ekubazeni homestead and which referred to the prodigious capacity of the huge 'Suthu' cattle raided from the Pedi.[12]

Rivalry began to develop between the two factions and in 1856 the Gqoza tried to cross into Natal. The Usuthu intercepted them on the banks of the Thukela river and defeated them at the battle of Ndondakusuka. Six of Mpande's sons were killed and others sought refuge among the colonists in Natal and the Boers of the Transvaal. Zulu tradition has it that Mpande had brought on the fight between the most powerful of his sons, and that he had a third, more malleable, candidate for succession to the Zulu throne in mind.[13]

However, Cetshwayo, by his victory over Mbulazi, had taken the first steps towards the Zulu throne. But his position was still far from secure.

There was still opposition to him within the kingdom, and both the neighbouring settler communities had possible successors to the kingship living among them and Cetshwayo feared an attack on the kingdom in the name of one of these exiled sons of Mpande. These fears were increased by the steadily increasing pressure of the Transvaal Boers on the north-eastern boundaries of the kingdom. Cetshwayo began to develop an external policy whereby he tried to gain the support of the Colony of Natal both for his claim to the Zulu throne, and against the threat posed by the Transvaal. As a result of this, the Secretary for Native Affairs in Natal, Theophilus Shepstone, came to Zululand in 1861 and, during a tense meeting, recognised Cetshwayo as successor to Mpande.

During the 1860s the Boer encroachments intensified and the Zulu made a number of appeals to Natal for support. They even suggested that Natal occupy a buffer zone between the two parties. The matter was still unresolved when, in October 1872, Mpande died. In the following year Shepstone was invited to Zululand again and this time he formally recognised Cetshwayo as successor to Mpande, and king of the Zulu.

These diplomatic links established by Cetshwayo and Shepstone between the Zulu kingdom and Natal must not obscure the kingdom's essential independence. The spread of colonialism in southern Africa in the nineteenth century had of course affected the Zulu. They had suffered a major defeat at the hands of the Boers in 1838, and although Mpande had managed to retrieve the situation and retain the core of the kingdom, the outlying regions once traversed by the Zulu army were now under white rule. Missionaries and traders had been active in the kingdom from its earliest years and the Zulu sought the assistance of their white neighbours in both internal and external disputes. Nonetheless, these factors had caused only marginal changes within the kingdom: while other African societies in the region had lost their independence by direct conquest, or had been transformed by the adaptations they had to make to the new situation, it does not appear as if the changes the Zulu had to make caused any fundamental alteration to social relations within the kingdom. At the same time, however, the changes which were occurring did gain significance later, eventually providing the lines of cleavage used by external forces to gain access to the kingdom's resources.

Living in a fertile, well-watered region, ideal for cattle-raising, largely free of debilitating tropical diseases and protected by a formidable military organisation, the population of perhaps a quarter of a million Zulu seems to have prospered during Mpande's long reign. There had been severe internal dissension but, when Mpande died, Cetshwayo succeeded him without dividing the kingdom. Like most pre-industrial societies without forms of storeable wealth, the people of Zululand were especially vulnerable to adverse climatic conditions; but it is noteworthy that Zulu people have said that the great famine of Mpande's reign was neither as severe nor as widespread as the famine which occurred in the early years of the century.[14]

Exotic diseases had entered the kingdom, but in spite of human and animal losses, the Zulu had overcome the worst of their effects. Lung-sickness (bovine pleuro-pneumonia) was introduced to the Cape in 1854 and had infected Zulu herds by the end of the decade; although it was always a problem in the kingdom a degree of immunity was developed by Zulu cattle. The Zulu had suffered from smallpox in Shaka's time but the serious epidemic of 1863 was 'stamped out by means of vaccination, which was introduced by Europeans and carried out by the people themselves'.[15]

Missionary enterprise in Zululand was intense but conspicuous for its lack of success. The Africans living on the mission stations were usually brought into the kingdom from other communities by the missionaries who found it extremely difficult to prise the Zulu from their way of life.[16]

The activities of traders from neighbouring territories seem to have had only a superficial effect on the way of life of the people of Zululand. In view of the fact that traders had operated energetically in the kingdom for a long period of time this point needs further explanation.

Traders from Delagoa Bay appear in the earliest documentary records of the kingdom, and the 'Zululand trader' was a feature of colonial life from Natal's earliest years. These traders carried blankets, hoes, picks, knives, metal cooking utensils, cloth, beads and trinkets into the country to exchange for hides and the small, hardy Sanga cattle of Zululand which were highly prized in neighbouring territories.

While these commodities imported into Zululand were extremely useful, or at least decorative, they were not unique, being, with the exception of firearms, for the most part industrially manufactured versions of products which were made by the Zulu craftsman or artisan. They were exchanged for cattle or hides, procured by the trader who travelled from homestead to homestead within the kingdom. The general impression one gains is that the Zulu were well aware of the advantages of acquiring some of the commodities in the visiting trader's waggon, and that many possessed the useful blanket, lengths of cloth, and an assortment of metal utensils and tools. At the same time the impact of colonial trade of this kind was slight, for the trader in Zululand was not able to introduce any product which came to be seen as essential to the Zulu way of life and which could not be manufactured within the country. Moreover, because he acquired cattle, the trader gained possession of the surplus commodity already produced in the country and thus demanded no alteration to the process of production.

At the same time there were white traders living in the Zulu kingdom, and some Zulu had themselves made contact with the colonial world and adopted certain of its ways, including trading. They were few in number, and perhaps, because their ways of life were so different from that of the average Zulu, they stand out misleadingly in the records. Nonetheless they were often men of note and figured prominently in the events with which this book is primarily concerned.

Dabulamanzi, son of Mpande, the best shot in the country and an aggressive, rowdy man, was one of these. He was feared by the Zulu and disliked by most of the whites who knew him.[17] Sihayo, chief of the Qungebe, and an especial favourite of Cetshwayo, ate at table with local missionaries, dressed in European clothes and was considered by the Bishop of Zululand to be perhaps the most 'advanced' man in the country. His territory was on the Natal border and a waggon track passed through it. He was involved in trade through Swaziland to Delagoa Bay, used oxen as draught animals and ploughed his fields.[18] Hamu, genealogically the son of Nzibe, Mpande's deceased brother, although biologically the son of Mpande himself, allowed a white, Herbert Nunn, to take up residence with him in the early 1860s. Nunn married Zulu wives, set himself up as a trader, and exploited the timber resources in the nearby Ngome forest.[19] Hamu was an alcoholic, addicted to European spirits,[20] and was the only Zulu of note to defect to the British at the time of the 1879 invasion.

The best known of the white traders living in Zululand was John Dunn.[21] As a young man he had hunted and traded in Zululand and had attracted Cetshwayo's attention in 1856 when he had fought as a mercenary for Mbulazi in the civil war. Needing a literate and bilingual adviser and secretary, Cetshwayo invited Dunn to live in Zululand. Dunn adopted the way of life of a Zulu chief, married Zulu women, and set up homesteads along the southern coastal strip between the Thukela and Mhlatuze, through which passed the waggon track to the northern districts. He collected a large following, employed African hunters, traded stock with settlers in Natal and entertained members of the British aristocracy, guiding their hunting parties into the Zululand coastal belt. Working in conjunction with Natal merchant houses, he imported thousands of obsolete muzzle-loaders into Zululand through Delagoa Bay, paying the Natal firms with livestock driven south across the Thukela.[22] In 1873 Dunn was appointed by the Natal authorities to recruit Thonga labourers living to the north-east of Zululand and to arrange for their safe passage through the kingdom to the colony. On occasion the king himself assisted in recruiting labour for Natal and was paid well for it.[23]

Dunn's trading route had to pass through the territory under the control of Zibhebhu. He was chief of the Mandlakazi lineage of the Zulu clan and appears to have been the most active Zulu trader in the country. The Mandlakazi chiefs were said to have special responsibility over the Thonga people living to the east of the Lubombo mountains,[24] as well as the people of the Lubombo range itself, whose allegiance was often ambiguous as a result of their proximity to the centre of Swazi power. The high-lying country of the Lubombo range rose above the fever-ridden, tsetse-fly infested country around it, and formed a bridge between Zululand and the northern parts of south-eastern Africa. Zibhebhu is said to have sent

> his agents through Swaziland, the Eastern Transvaal and even Portuguese East Africa, with merchandise such as beads, blankets, Salampore cloth and brass-wire to be exchanged for leopard, civet cat and nsimango monkey-skins which were greatly in demand among the Zulus. Zibhebhu paid for his trading goods in cattle. . . .[25]

The fact that there was a huge demand for wild animal skins in the Zulu kingdom is confirmed in traders' inventories and hunters' journals,[26] and in a lengthy statement made by a member of Cetshwayo's tribute-collecting parties who travelled to Thongaland, the 'great supplying country for Zululand'.[27] Genet skins were needed for the ceremonial dancing dress, samango monkey pelts for the warriors' headdress, leopard and otter skins formed part of the chief's attire and were greatly valued, as were lion claws, rhino horn for snuff boxes, and crane, secretary bird and ostrich feathers. The spread of settler communities and the resultant destruction of African wild life had made it necessary for the Zulu to look to the north for items they considered necessary for their rituals, cere-monies and the martial display which was still an essential part of their way of life. And it is surely significant that the Zulu most deeply involved in trading, Zibhebhu, used cattle to obtain manufactured goods of exotic origin, which were then used to obtain the articles of African origin which were so much in demand in the kingdom. The importance of imported European trade goods for the Zulu seems to have been matched, if not surpassed, by the importance of articles indigenous to Africa.

Further evidence of the economic independence of the Zulu kingdom lies in the fact that members of the Zulu kingdom were not considered as wage-labourers by nearby settlers. The demand for labourers was intense, and workers were obtained from territories adjoining and beyond the kingdom, and from overseas; but the Zulu, on Natal's borders, were 'too strongly attached to their military organisation for the planters of Natal to hope for a direct supply of labour from the unemployed population of Zululand'.[28] Although individuals crossed the boundary to work in Natal[29] and the Transvaal, and the price Zulu paid for political asylum in Natal was a period of forced labour, the vast majority of Zulu grew up, worked and died within the kingdom. They held in contempt their African neighbours who sold their labour to the whites, calling them *amakhafula*, a name derived from 'kaffir', a derogatory term as used by whites, but which gained added meaning among the Zulu because of its similarity to 'khafula', meaning to eject or spit out.

The image is an apposite one. The majority of the Zulu were still held firmly in the different production communities of the kingdom, moving from one type to another as they grew older and their status altered. The boys worked in their fathers' homesteads, the young men in the military homesteads before establishing homesteads of their own, while the girls worked in their fathers' homesteads before establishing their own production units within their husbands' homesteads. Of course external forces had affected the Zulu increasingly as settler communities became established on the borders of the kingdom. Nevertheless throughout the reigns of the kings Zulu labour expended within the commoners' homesteads continued to support the bulk of the population, and the surplus which was drawn from them by the king through the military system created the basis for his material power and authority, together with that of the officials with and through whom he ruled. Despite this extraction of surplus the autonomy of the commoner's homestead was considerable; here the Zulu men and women consumed the products of their own labour, which provided the means of subsistence and reproduction of the homestead. To the Zulu men and their wives in the homesteads of the kingdom their way of life contrasted strongly with that of the African in colonial Natal across the border who, as he became increasingly free and alienated from the means of production, indeed seemed to be a man 'spat out'.

Notes

1 Reply to question 285, Supplementary Minutes of Evidence, *Cape Native Laws and Customs Commission*, Cape Town, 1883, p. 529. There are many references to 'Zulus' at the diamond fields in the 1870s but as the king asserts here they seem to refer to Africans from Natal. See also the statement, based on information supplied by Cetshwayo, that 'No Zulus (proper) work there. There are no Zulus in Zululand who have ever been there', on p. 723 of

'Cetshwayo's story of the Zulu nation and the war', reprinted from *Macmillan's Magazine*, Feb. 1880, in Colenso, series 1 (Bishopstowe papers).

2 For a much more detailed discussion of the nature of the changing physical environment of Zululand see my paper, 'Ecological factors in the rise of Shaka and the Zulu kingdom', presented to the Conference on Southern African history at the National University of Lesotho, Aug. 1977.

3 Map IV gives a rough idea of the possible distribution of these grazing types, according to the reconstruction of veld types in J. P. H. Acocks, *Veld Types of South Africa*, Pretoria, 1953, and his map *Veld Types of South Africa*, Pretoria, 1951.

4 See J. B. McI. Daniel, 'A Geographical Study of pre-Shakan Zululand', *South African Geographical Journal*, lv, 1 (1973).

5 C. de B. Webb and J. B. Wright (eds), *The James Stuart Archive*, Pietermaritzburg and Durban, 1976, i, Evidence of Jantshi, p. 201; D. McK. Malcolm, 'The Bantu', transcripts of broadcast talks (KC); A. T. Bryant, *Olden Times in Zululand and Natal*, London, 1929, pp. 63 and 88.

6 This section is based on my paper, 'Production and Exchange in the Zulu kingdom', *Mohlomi: Journal of Southern African Studies*, ii, 1978.

7 A. T. Bryant, *The Zulu People, as they were before the white man came*, Pietermaritzburg, 1967, p. 438.

8 The age of the Zulu at marriage no doubt differed at various points in Zulu history. The very rough estimates given here are based on Bryant, *The Zulu People*, p. 188; Bryant, *Olden Times*, p. 645; E. J. Krige, *The Social System of the Zulus*, Pietermaritzburg, 1957, p. 38; O. H. Spohr (ed.), *The Natal Diaries of Dr W. H. I. Bleek, 1855–1856*, Cape Town, 1965, p. 67; BPP, C.1137: I, enc. 1, T. Shepstone, Report of the expedition to install Cetshwayo, p. 21; among other sources.

9 M. Gluckman, 'The Individual in a Social Framework: the rise of King Shaka of Zululand', *Journal of African Studies*, i, 2, 1974.

10 E. A. Wrigley, *Population and History*, London, 1969, p. 116.

11 It is frequently stated that Cetshwayo was born in 1826; however this date appears to be derived from an incorrect assumption made by R. C. A. Samuelson in *Long, Long Ago*, Durban, 1929, p. 213. Cetshwayo was probably born towards the end of 1832.

12 Colenso, series 2, pp. 525–6.

13 KC, Stuart papers: Evidence of Makuza, 5 March 1921, and Evidence of Mangati; Colenso, series 1, p. 783.

14 Webb and Wright (eds), *James Stuart Archive*, i, p. 201.

15 J. Y. Gibson, *The Story of the Zulus*, London, 1911, p. 108.

16 N. A. Etherington, 'The Rise of the Kholwa in Southeastern Africa: African Christian Communities in Natal, Pondoland and Zululand, 1835–1880', (PhD thesis, Yale University, 1971), pp. 181–200.

17 For some white opinions of Dabulamanzi see F. B. Fynney, *The Zulu Army, and Zulu Headmen*, Pietermaritzburg, 1879, and B. Mitford, *Through the Zulu country, its battlefields and its people*, London, 1883, pp. 178–84. For Zulu attitudes to his 'quarrelsome habits' see Colenso, series 1, p. 740.

18 Etherington, 'The Rise of the Kholwa', p. 190, n. 52; and SNA 1/1/26, two statements dated 19 Jan. 1875 and 25 March 1875.

19 Colenso, series 2, p. 45 and p. 864.

20 According to Cetshwayo the only other Zulu of importance similarly addicted was Mfanawendlela of the Zungu.

21 For Dunn see D. C. F. Moodie (ed.), *John Dunn, Cetwayo and the three generals*, Pietermaritzburg, 1886, and C. S. Shields, 'The Life of John Dunn, with special reference to Zululand, 1879–1897' (MA thesis, University of South Africa, 1939).

22 For more details see J. J. Guy, 'A note on firearms in the Zulu kingdom with special reference to the Anglo-Zulu war, 1879', *Journal of African History*, xii, 4 (1971), pp. 559–60.

23 CO 879 14, 162: no. 185, Bulwer to Hicks Beach, 23 Aug. 1878.

24 KC, Stuart papers: Evidence of Ndukwana, 20 Oct. 1900.

25 B. H. Kemp, 'Johan William Colenbrander: A history of his times and the people and events with which he was associated, 1879–1896' (PhD thesis, University of Natal, 1962), i, pp. 30–1.

26 See Dalgado to SNA, 3 June 1863 in SNA 1/1/13, and the 700 monkey and 'cat' skins in the list of goods in SNA 1/1/10. For monkey hunters see *Private Journal of Guy C. Dawnay, 1872–4* (privately printed), i, pp. 200–1.

27 Webb and Wright (eds), *James Stuart Archive*, i, p. 68, Evidence of Bikwayo ka Noziwawa.

28 BPP, C.1137: 1, enc.1, T. Shepstone, Report of expedition to install Cetshwayo, p. 20.

29 There is evidence that there was some movement of labour between Zululand and Natal, but until we can identify exactly where these workers originated, or unless fresh information is discovered, we must accept the view that the vast majority of Zulu laboured within the kingdom.

CHAPTER TWO

The political structure of the Zulu Kingdom during the reign of Cetshwayo kaMpande

Clan, chiefdom and kingdom

When Cetshwayo kaMpande succeeded his father in 1872 at the age of forty he became ruler of some 300 000 people, most of them concentrated between the Thukela and Mzinyathi rivers and the valley of the Phongolo. The Colony of Natal and the Transvaal were situated on the kingdom's southern and western borders while to the north lay the Swazi kingdom, and in the north-east the direct authority of the Zulu king shaded into the tribute areas of the Thonga chiefdoms.

Only half a century separated Shaka's rule from that of Cetshwayo and many of the features of Shaka's kingdom could still be discerned in the kingdom ruled by his nephew. As successor to the founder of the kingdom Cetshwayo was held to own the land on which his people lived. Those who gave their allegiance to the king were given the right to occupy and work the land, and they could retain a substantial part of the fruits of their labour. Surplus was still extracted, largely through the labour all men gave in the royal army. There had of course been many changes; the area directly controlled by the king had been reduced and although the collection of tribute continued this was restricted and raiding had ceased. Kinship ties were closely linked to the productive system and the people of the kingdom still saw themselves as members of clans and lineages whose origins could be traced to pre-Shakan times. This continuity was a reflection of the fact that the productive forces had not undergone radical changes in this period.

The Zulu kingdom can be seen as the social integration of two systems, which although they must be analysed separately can only be understood in their interaction. On the one hand there was social power based on production, coming from the production units – the homesteads (*umuzi/ imizi*) – and expressed in terms of kinship and the clan: on the other hand there was the power of the state coming from above, and based on the

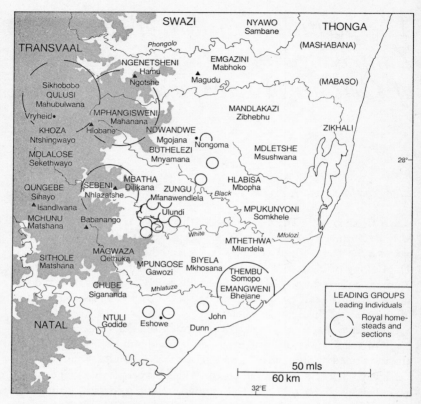

Map V The Zulu Kingdom during the reign of Cetshwayo: a schematic representation

extraction of surplus, mainly in labour through the military system.[1]

In the first chapter we saw how production in the Zulu kingdom took place in the tens of thousands of homesteads scattered through the country. These *imizi* were of different sizes, according to an individual's status and wealth, but it has been estimated that 90 per cent of them were commoners' homesteads consisting of a man (the homestead-head, *umnumzana*), two or three wives, their offspring, cattle and smallstock, grazing and agricultural land. The men worked with the livestock, the women in agriculture, the two fundamental branches of production and there was a clear sexual division of labour in the many supporting tasks. The wives were ranked and housed separately within the homestead. Schematically the homestead can be portrayed as in Fig. 1.[2]

On the death of the homestead-head or, in special cases of men of status,

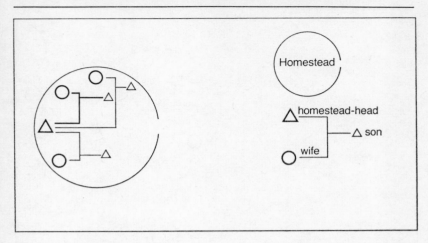

Fig. 1 The homestead

when his children matured, the homestead would break up (segment) and the sons of each house would establish homesteads of their own (Fig. 2).

These basic principles of production and reproduction were expressed in terms of kinship. Anthropologists looking at this and similar social processes called it a patrilineal, segmentary, lineage system. The total unit is called a clan; that is, a social unit made up men and women who believe they have descended from a common ancestor, through the male line, and which can be depicted as in Fig. 3.

Note, however, that at another level of analysis these kinship relations can also be seen in terms of production and reproduction – the male triangle representing the productive unit, the homestead.

Two further points of great importance must be made here. First, marriage within the clan was prohibited and wives had therefore to be drawn from other clans. This transaction was marked by the movement of cattle: cattle were given to a wife's father on marriage or, in other words, cattle were received by a daughter's father when she left his homestead to marry. Secondly, the lineages and homesteads within the clan were not egalitarian units. The chief son of a homestead inherited the bulk of his father's property, most of it in cattle, and he could therefore obtain more wives and, through this, increase the size of his particular lineage. There was thus a concentration of wealth within the chiefly lineage, and the members of the chiefly house could trace their dominant position back to the original clan-founder. The material basis of the status of the chief was the large number of cattle he possessed which he could exchange for wives and transform into more lineages, that is, more

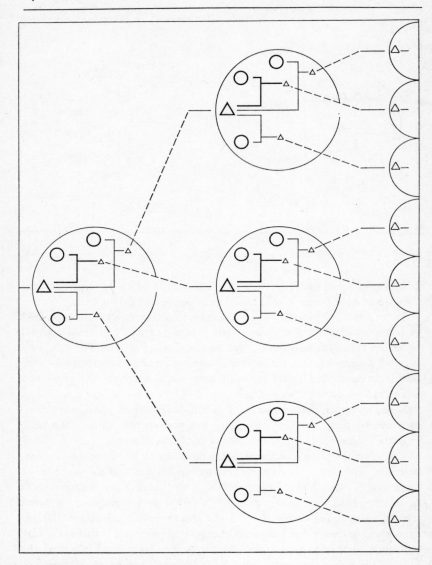

Fig. 2 Homestead segmentation

productive workers to support the homestead. The process can be depicted as in Fig. 4.

At some time in the past the clan was possibly a discrete unit – it certainly appears to be a social form suited to an increasing population in

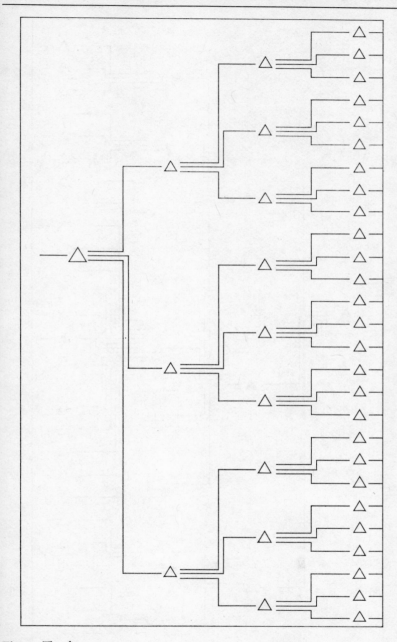

Fig. 3   The clan

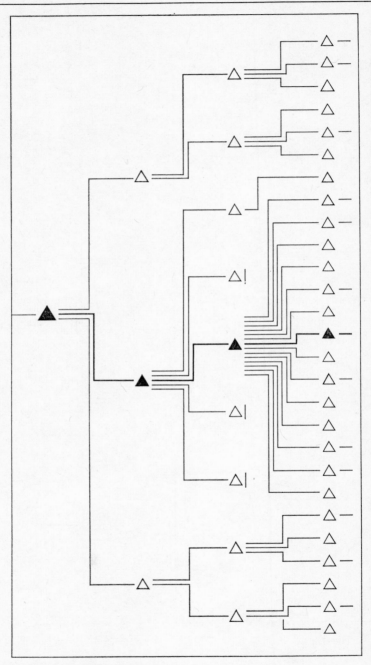

Fig. 4 The dominant lineage of the clan

a favourable environment which offers no great obstacles to expansion. However we have no records of autonomous clans in south-east Africa and by the eighteenth century they formed only a part of the major political unit – the chiefdom.[3] The chiefdom consisted of members of different clans, one of which was politically dominant and can be depicted schematically as in Fig. 5.

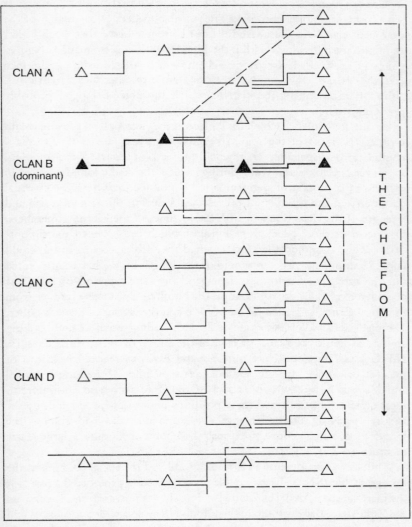

Fig. 5   The chiefdom

The wars of the late eighteenth and early nineteenth centuries were struggles between large chiefdoms like the Ngwane, the Ndwandwe, and the Mthethwa, whose leaders were attempting to increase their power by the forcible acquisition of land and the incorporation of different peoples into their chiefdoms. Out of this violence the Zulu chiefdom under Shaka emerged victorious. Shaka built up a society of a scale hitherto unknown in the region and the chiefdoms which survived the struggle became units within the kingdom, becoming known to outsiders by the name of the dominant clan – the Zulu. And it must be remembered that when I refer to important individuals within the kingdom – like Mnyamana kaNgqengelele of the Buthelezi clan, or Sekethwayo of the Mdlalose – the men directly under them were drawn from a large number of different clans, although members of the clan to which the chief belonged probably predominated.

During the violence which took place in the early part of the nineteenth century the clans of the region suffered the same fate as the people – annihilation, dispersion, fragmentation, and of course incorporation. However, in the sixty years during which the Zulu kingdom was in existence the process of clan formation continued, reflecting the essential continuity of the production process. And during this time the size and strength of the clans changed with the fortunes of their leading members. Over two or three generations lineages which had retained the support of the Zulu king, and therefore ensured they had access to cattle, could come to dominate large areas within the kingdom. As has been pointed out the capacity of a lineage to expand in a short period of time was considerable.[4] Consider for example the Ntuli. Sompisi was a refugee from the Ntuli clan who gained the protection and the favour of Shaka's father. Sompisi's son, Ndlela, was one of Shaka's leading warriors and his king appointed him over a tract of land in the southern parts of the country. Ndlela was Dingane's chief minister and his sons reached positions of great status under Mpande. Godide was a member of the king's council and Mavumengwana a commander of the Zulu army and an important local official. They retained these positions under Cetshwayo and, by the 1870s, the Ntuli descendants of the wanderer who had entered the kingdom two generations previously had come to dominate large tracts of southern Zululand.[5]

While it was production in the homestead and the social strength of the lineage within the clan based on this production that provided the basis for the material strength of the Zulu kingdom, it was power from above, from the Zulu state, that identified which individuals and which groups would achieve status within the kingdom. Zulu state power was based ultimately on the surplus labour drawn from every homestead in the land. While various forms of tribute passed up through the social hierarchy it was labour in the military homesteads of the royal house – the *amakhanda* – which formed the most important basis of state power. From the age of puberty until their late thirties most Zulu men worked in the *amakhanda* for considerable periods of time. Here the sexual division of labour of the conventional homestead broke down and the men were occupied, as the king said, in 'Building military kraals, planting, reaping, and making gardens for the king. These are the men who look after the king.'[6]

When Cetshwayo came to the Zulu throne there were about a dozen royal residences on the Mahlabathini plain and they served as barracks for the men attending the king. Cetshwayo built Ulundi there as his chief homestead and it became the political and administrative centre of the kingdom, where meetings of state and national ceremonies took place. State power thus spread outwards from the geographical heart of the kingdom and, as one of Stuart's informants said, 'all paths ultimately found their way to the king's kraal'.

The king ruled with the *izikhulu* – the great ones – of the kingdom. The *izikhulu* represented the great pre-Shakan chiefdoms, incorporated by the founder into the kingdom, although in fact their relative size and status had changed during the half century since Shaka's death, reflecting to a large degree the changing fortunes of leading individuals within the kingdom. The king with the *izikhulu* comprised the *ibandla,* the highest council of state, and without the *izikhulu* the king could make no decisions of national importance. The status of the *izikhulu* depended primarily on birth and they were seen as the living representatives of the dominant lineages of the chiefdoms of the kingdom. In reality the dominant lineages had frequently been 'raised up' by the interference of the Zulu kings in the affairs of the clan. Furthermore birth was not the only factor; the *izikhulu* had to show political acumen as well, and not all men of the highest hereditary rank – the *izilomo* – were members of the *ibandla*. And not all *izikhulu* were members of a dominant lineage: for example, Mbopha kaWolizibi of the Hlabisa was an *isikhulu* as a result of his kinship links with the royal house (his father was the brother of Mpande's mother) and because he was a great favourite of Mpande. And, in spite of his youth, Zibhebhu, a relative of Cetshwayo, was also an *isikhulu*, probably because of his independent power in the north-eastern corner of the kingdom and his aggressive self-confidence.

Most of the *izikhulu* within the kingdom were in fact older than the king, Cetshwayo, having reached their positions during the reign of his father.[7] And there is evidence that there was tension between the younger monarch and these older men, and that they probably obstructed the appointment of Cetshwayo's contemporaries.[8] Sihayo of the Qungebe, a favourite of the king, was excluded from the council. Also younger chiefs, who had lived under the shadow of an ageing parent of great status, like Msushwana of the Mdletshe, Sokwetshata of the Mthethwa, Mkhosana of the Biyela, and Ndabankulu of the Ntombela, seem, despite their large followings in the country and their importance in the political matters of the land, not to have been members of the highest council of the land.

While the *ibandla* represented the authority of the state at its highest level, state meetings were frequently much more widely based and included the younger chiefs, men of note within the kingdom, the large number of officers in charge of the homesteads and the regiments of the state, and the confidential advisers to the king. The control and administration of the kingdom depended on the work of a vast number of state officials of differing rank and status. These were the *izinduna* (sing. *induna*) of the kingdom, the army commanders, regimental officers, personal attendants to the king, messengers, tribute collectors, and so on.

State power was devolved from the king to the *izikhulu*, to the heads of the administrative areas within the kingdom, with local affairs being the responsibility of the resident homestead-heads. These *abanumzana* were responsible for the allocation of land, the implementation of the law and the resolution of disputes in their areas. They were also the channels connecting the people under them to higher authorities.

The integration of state authority and the productive base within the kingdom is well illustrated if we consider the terms *induna* and *umnumzana*: they do not refer to a group of officials and another of homestead-heads, but to an individual's functions within the state. All married men in the kingdom were homestead-heads (*abanumzana*) and many of these men were also state officials. As the king expressed it, 'An induna is called a headman [*umnumzana*] when he is in his own district, and an induna when he is at the military kraal.'[9] And it is this integration which is the crucial point to grasp: administrative authority was related to productive capacity, the extent of the chiefdom to the strength of the clan, the size of the lineage within the clan to access to political power.

The distribution of political power[10]

The centre of royal authority was situated on the Mahlabathini plain. From a point just north of this (see Map V on page 22 and refer throughout this section) the homesteads of the most powerful man in the country

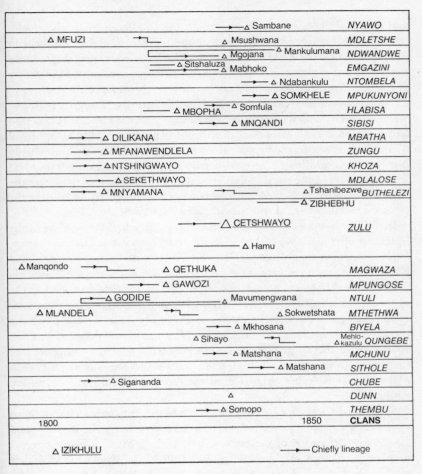

Fig. 6   Some leading figures in the Zulu kingdom

next to Cetshwayo were to be found. He was Mnyamana kaNgqengelele of the Buthelezi clan, the king's chief minister. Mnyamana's father had achieved his position under Shaka, and Mnyamana had been a man of importance under Mpande. He succeeded to the post of chief minister when Cetshwayo came to the throne. His personal homestead was near the Sikhwebezi river but he had homesteads in the Black Mfolozi valley and his territory stretched from the area just north of the Mahlabathini plain, through the middle reaches of the Black Mfolozi, to the Phongolo river and beyond. He was an exceptionally intelligent and shrewd man, and his tragic history is summed up in the line from his praise poem, 'He who succeeds when there is no hope of success'.[11] He was held in great respect by the Zulu people; when Mpande's sons were drafted into the Thulwana regiment it was Mnyamana who was appointed chief *induna* as the only man who the Thulwana 'would stand in awe of'.[12]

To the north and north-west of Ulundi were the Zungu of Mfana-wendlela, an *isikhulu* whose father had been assassinated by Shaka and who had lived on the Mahlabathini plain until Mpande established the royal homesteads there. In the vicinity lived many of the Mbatha whose chiefly line had been terminated by Shaka, who had then raised up another line which had served the royal house faithfully. The foremost of these was the *isikhulu* Dilikana, in Cetshwayo's time a very old man. He lived near the Nhlazatshe mountain, as did the *isikhulu* Mnqandi of the Sibisi.

In the north-western parts of the country lived Sekethwayo, chief of the Mdlalose clan and *isikhulu* to Mpande and Cetshwayo. His neighbour, Ntshingwayo, was commander of the Zulu army and *isikhulu* of the Khoza. In the mountains near the present-day Vryheid lived the Ntombela under Ndabankulu kaLukwazi whose father, an *isikhulu*, had died in the 1870s. Eastwards near where Nongoma stands today, lived the remainder of the once great Ndwandwe chiefdom under Mgojana. To the north the powerful Emgazini clan,[13] built up by Mnyamana's predecessor as chief councillor to the king, Masiphula. His successor was too young to take the chieftainship and Sitshaluza, Masiphula's brother was regent, with Mabhoko, Masiphula's eldest son as the most powerful man among the Emgazini.

Situated in a great arc running down the Nongoma ridge to its southern spurs, then swinging in a south-easterly direction along the high ground on the northern edge of the tsetse-infested Black Mfolozi valley, were a number of groups established by the Zulu kings. Some of Mpande's closest associates had their homesteads here, including Mbopha of the Hlabisa, whose status within the state structure of the kingdom over-shadowed the heir to the Hlabisa chieftainship, Somfula.[14] To the east again were the Mdletshe under Mfuzi who died late in the 1870s and was succeeded by Msushwana.

Moving back to the central parts of the kingdom, Sihayo of the Qungebe, the 'progressive' chief[15] whose sons' escapades provided one of the pretexts for the British invasion, lived east of Ulundi, on the western borders of the kingdom. He was popular with Cetshwayo but unpopular with older men.

South of Mahlabathini lived the Mpungose under the *isikhulu* Gawozi. They had supported the Zulu kings from Shaka's time and the lineage had

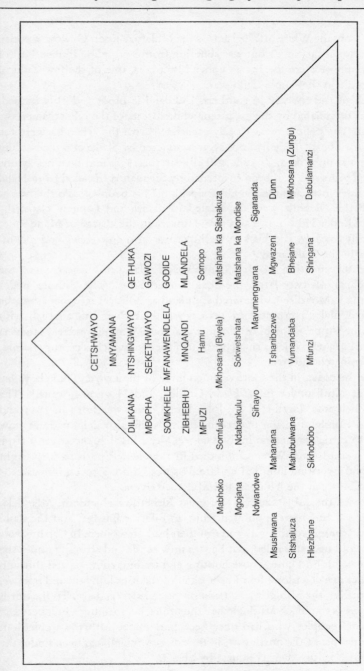

Fig. 7   Some members of the political hierarchy in Zululand

spread from the White Mfolozi across the Mhlatuze river. Gawozi was also a favourite of the king's but was suffering from a crippling illness. East of the Mpungose were the Biyela under Mkhosana, one of the few Zulu of note to die in the Anglo-Zulu war.

Much of the country in southern Zululand is broken, deeply incised, and was dominated by the great temperate forests of the Nkandla and the Qudeni. The people most closely associated with the Nkandla were the Chube (or Shezi). They had not been conquered by Shaka and their ruling lineage was unbroken. Zokufa, still alive in the 1870s and then nearly one hundred years old, had been succeeded by Sigananda, recalled from Natal by Cetshwayo to assume the chieftainship of his people.[16] To the north-west of the Nkandla were the related Magwaza and Langeni clans, the Langeni under Ndwandwe and the Magwaza in the charge of Manqondo, an elderly *isikhulu*, and his son Qethuka was also an *isikhulu* and a commander in the Zulu army.[17]

Near the junction of the Thukela and Mzinyathi rivers were the descendants of two large pre-Shakan chiefdoms. The Sithole under Matshana kaMondise had entered Zululand as political refugees from the Natal colonial government in 1858 when their chief had a brush with John Shepstone. North of them were the Mchunu under Matshana kaSitshakuza who ruled a small portion of the clan which, a century before, had dominated the area.

Near the coast, in the more open country of the Lower Thukela valley lived the Ntuli under the *isikhulu*, Godide, and Mavumengwana.[18] The coastal belt was dominated by John Dunn, who was born in 1833 and came to Zululand in the mid-1850s. Dunn's life also demonstrates how access to cattle enabled an individual to spread his influence over a large area in a short time. When Dunn died in 1895 he left perhaps forty-eight wives and over one hundred children[19] spread among seven homesteads situated between the Thukela and Mhlatuze rivers.

North of the Mhlatuze was the great Mthethwa chiefdom. Mlandela, the *isikhulu*, had been appointed from an inferior lineage, and the Zulu kings had presented him with some of their leading women. In Cetshwayo's time the old man still ruled, but he was now senile and strongly under the influence of John Dunn whose hunting and trading route passed through the Mthethwa chiefdom. Somkhele, chief of the Mpukunyoni and *isikhulu*, lived north of the Mthethwa and east of the St Lucia estuary. To the north again, across the Black Mfolozi were the Mdletshe, forming a link between the coastal peoples who had once been part of the Mthethwa chiefdom and the people of the north-east, in the country which had been under the Ndwandwe before their conquest by Shaka.

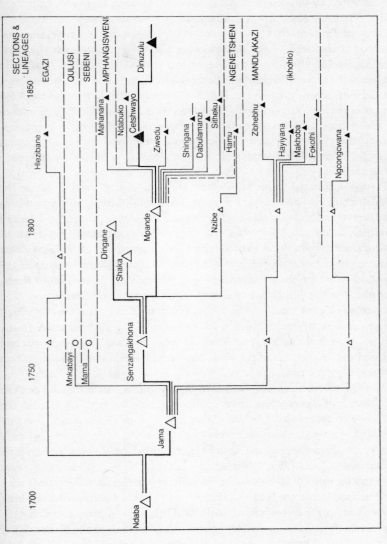

Fig. 8 Some leading members of the Zulu clan

Spread among these different clans and chiefdoms were the lineages of the royal clan itself.[20] The homesteads of the king, the *amakhanda*, were concentrated around his personal homestead, Ulundi, on the Mahlabathini plain. The size and physical structure of the *amakhanda* reflected the enormous amount of social power concentrated in the royal lineage. Situated at the head of the *ikhanda*, opposite the entrance, was the royal area containing the king's private house, that of the female relative in charge of the *ikhanda*, who might be an elderly member of the royal lineage, a widow of Mpande, or one of the king's wives. Also living and working here was the *umdlunkulu* – girls presented to the king by the leading men of the nation, and his servants and retainers. Stretching in huge arcs around the cattle kraal and parade ground were the hundreds of houses used by the soldiers attached to the *ikhanda* when they were in residence.

It was estimated that there were about a dozen *amakhanda* in the Mahlabathini area and about the same number in outlying districts where they served as local centres of influence and recruiting points.[21] Some had originally been the homesteads of Cetshwayo's ancestors, although of course their geographical situation and the composition of their residents and regiments had changed over the years. Others in different parts of the kingdom were originally homesteads of Mpande or created from these, according to the principles of lineage segmentation, by Cetshwayo. The district *amakhanda* were served by people drawn from the area in which they were situated and their *izinduna* were usually local dignitaries. In the case of some of the oldest *amakhanda* the importance of the *amakhanda* had eclipsed the importance of the clan in so far as the relations of its members to the state were concerned.

The Qulusi people were the best example of this. After driving out the inhabitants of the region around Hlobane, Shaka sent Ntlaka of the Mdlalose to establish an *ikhanda* known as Qulusi in the area. The first two Zulu kings did not take wives so it was placed in the charge of a senior, female member of the Zulu lineage, Mnkabayi, daughter of Shaka's grandfather, Jama. The people, of different clan origins, who were attached to this royal homestead as officers tended in time to establish their private homesteads in the vicinity, and others were sent by the king to settle in this area associated with the Qulusi royal homestead. By the time Cetshwayo came to the Zulu throne they numbered thousands. They were not drafted into the conventional regiments but mobilised and fought as a royal section, and they were not represented in the king's council by a chief, because they represented the power of the Zulu royal house, not a pre-Shakan chiefdom. They were in the charge of *izinduna*, the leading ones being important men within the nation, including Sikhobobo and Mahubulwana.

Another important royal section which originated in Shaka's time was the Mphangisweni, situated around the sources of the Black Mfolozi river and in the charge of Mahanana, a son of Mpande.[22] Further south near the Nhlazatshe mountain was the Sebeni, originally under Mama, twin sister of Mnkabayi. The royal sections represented the most radical departure from the pre-Shakan past, and reduced the importance of the independent clan, as is reflected in Mnkabayi's praise-poem in which the lines

> The opener of all the main gates so that people may enter,
> The owners of the home enter by the narrow side gates[23]

have been interpreted to mean that Mnkabayi was 'an avenue of advance for people, regardless of status'.

The same process can be observed happening around the Emangweni homestead[24] of Mpande, where Cetshwayo lived before coming to the throne. It was situated on the waggon road which linked Dunn and Zibhebhu to the north. Somopo, chief of the Thembu clan, lived close by and was in charge of the Emangweni, and Bhejane of the Cebekhulu, personal aide to Cetshwayo, was an *induna.* Their positions within the Emangweni homesteads seemed to overshadow their positions as leading members of their lineages.

Then there were lineages of the Zulu clan which had separated from the chiefly line before the rule of Shaka's father, Senzangakhona. The most important of these was the Mandlakazi under Zibhebhu. Maphitha, Zibhebhu's father, was, like the first three Zulu kings, a grandson of Jama, and had been placed in the north-eastern part of the country in the early years of the kingdom and had built up a large following there. He apparently held a unique position within the kingdom – he is described not only as an *isikhulu* but as an *umntwana,* a child of the king, with *izikhulu* of his own. One of the reasons for this semi-independent position within the kingdom was possibly the distance of the Mandlakazi districts from the centre of power, and its access to the north, particularly towards the Thonga who supplied so much tribute to the Zulu state. Maphitha was said to have particular responsibility for the people living on and beyond the Lubombo range to the north-east of the kingdom. When he died in 1872 he was succeeded by Zibhebhu, the eldest son of Maphitha's great house. As we have seen Zibhebhu was a young man of considerable independence, involved in trading ventures to the north. His father had viewed this with suspicion and there are stories of disputes between him and his son, and also tension between Zibhebhu and his king. He also quarrelled with the *ikhohlo* or left-hand segment of his father's homestead over cattle. The *ikhohlo* was led by Maphitha's eldest son, Hayiyana, and included Fokothi and Makhoba. Other important lineages in the northern districts were the Ngenetsheni of Hamu in the west, and the Egazini of Hlezibane living nearby.

Finally there were the *abantwana*, the children of Mpande, the princes of the kingdom. Among the most important was Dabulamanzi in the south at Ezulwini near Entumeni, Ziwedu on the southern spurs of the Nongoma range, and Sitheku near the Kwamagwaza mission south-east of Emthonjaneni. Shingane had his homestead near Emakhosini, the place of the kings, where the original chiefs of the Zulu clan had lived and were buried. Ndabuko, Cetshwayo's full brother, lived at kwaMinya, in the Ivuna valley.

Even this simplified sketch which serves only to introduce some of the leading personalities and groups within the kingdom shows something of the complexity of the links between the king and his people. From the centre of the polity the Zulu clan, in close association with the military system, spread its influence through the kingdom. To the centre were drawn the people of Zululand represented by their chiefs. The segmentary lineage system, giving social expression to basic productive processes, worked as part of the political system through which authority was delegated from the centre outwards to increasingly smaller units. Cetshwayo's rule was a personal one: the territory was compact and he was well acquainted with it; he knew the officers within the kingdom, their histories and those of the people over whom they ruled; he married their daughters and gave his sisters to them in marriage and he was for the Zulu the living symbol of the mighty Zulu state, its unique history, and was responsible for its continued well-being.

I am not however suggesting that the Zulu kingdom was 'static' or perpetuated by 'a system of checks and balances'. Wealth was concentrated in the hands of the king and his higher officials, and men, until they were close to middle-age, and women spent much of their time labouring for others. At the same time the homestead, and the houses within the homestead, retained considerable autonomy, and all men at some time in their lives could expect to become homestead-heads. But, as one might expect with age determining to a large extent the amount of surplus extracted from an individual, 'inter-generational' conflicts caused Cetshwayo considerable difficulty. The older Thulwana regiment and the younger Ngobomakhosi fought in the central barrack area early in 1878 and some were killed. On another occasion an older regiment was given permission to marry but many of the girls in the female age-sets from which they were supposed to take wives had already taken lovers from the men in the younger regiments. They refused to accept the older men and this led to a number of executions. As I have tried to show, 'marriage' in the Zulu kingdom was closely linked to the availability of resources, growth of population, productivity and political power, and the delay in marriage suggests internal difficulties within the Zulu state.

Nevertheless these tensions and divisions within the kingdom never developed into large-scale internal conflict. In 1879 the British invaded the kingdom and, faced by a severe external threat, the Zulu fought to preserve their independence and way of life. Only one man of importance, Hamu, defected. In the tactics and organisation of the army they sent against the British the Zulu demonstrated the social continuity that existed between the kingdom created by Shaka and the one ruled by Cetshwayo. And perhaps there is no greater indication of the real nature of the Zulu kingdom in 1879 than the fact that when faced with invasion, the Zulu king could put 30 000 men into the field in an attempt to preserve the Zulu state.

Notes

1 Any comprehensive analysis of the structure of the Zulu kingdom raises difficult problems of conceptualisation which deserve more space than I can give here. For a more lengthy discussion see my 'Production and Exchange in the Zulu kingdom' in *Mohlomi: Journal of Southern African Historical Studies*, ii, 1978.

2 It must be stressed that Figs 1–5 are schematic and attempt to convey social principles and not historical actuality.

3 For further discussion on this point see M. Wilson, 'The Nguni People' in M. Wilson and L. Thompson (eds), *The Oxford History of South Africa*, Oxford, 1969, i, pp. 118ff.

4 M. Wilson, 'Changes in social structure in southern Africa: the relevance of kinship studies to the historian' in L. Thompson (ed.), *African Societies in Southern Africa*, London, 1969, pp. 78–9.

5 A. T. Bryant, *Olden Times in Zululand and Natal*, London, 1829, pp. 58–60, and the evidence given to James Stuart by Mangati kaGodide, 12 July 1920 in notebook 37 in the Stuart Papers (KC).

6 Reply to question 44, Supplementary Minutes of Evidence, in *Cape Native Laws and Customs Commission*, Cape Town, 1883, p. 519.

7 I have attempted to depict this in Fig. 6 by placing the leading figures according to their year of birth. It must be remembered however that it is extremely difficult to do more than estimate the age of the various leading Zulu.

8 BPP, C.1137: 1, enc. 1, T. Shepstone, Report of expedition to install Cetshwayo, pp. 9 and 19; KC, Stuart Papers: Evidence of Ndukwana, 2 Dec. 1900.

9 Reply to question 174, Supplementary minutes of evidence, *Cape Native Laws and Customs Commission*, p. 525.

10　The purpose of this section is to introduce some of the leading figures in the Zulu kingdom during Cetshwayo's reign, in the light of the subsequent narrative. The greatest problem in the writing of this section has been to decide on which personalities and which groups to exclude. To clarify the text I have given a number of illustrations. Fig. 6 groups the leaders around the king, according to clan and age. Fig. 7 attempts to place them in a political hierarchy and spatially on Map V. I must stress that I have had to exclude certain important individuals and groups, that I discuss only the highest levels of the political structure, and that the names I have chosen are biased towards the story I want to tell here.

11　J. Stuart, *uBaxoxele*, London, 1924, p. 38 (translation).

12　KC, Stuart Papers: Evidence of Ndukwana, 1 Oct. 1900. In this section the information is drawn from references scattered through the records of the period which followed the invasion of 1879, and in the Stuart papers. The evidence Stuart collected from Ndukwana is of particular importance. Bryant's *Olden Times* is fundamental to any reconstruction of Zulu history, and a pamphlet published by the military authorities at the time of the invasion, based on information collected by F. B. Fynney, *The Zulu Army and Zulu Headmen*, Pietermaritzburg, 1879, is of great importance.

13　J. Y. Gibson, *The Story of the Zulus*, London, 1911, p. 224. The Emgazini clan has been confused on many occasions with the Egazini lineage of the Zulu clan.

14　See above, p. 29.

15　See above, p. 16.

16　KC, Stuart Papers: Sigananda and his Tribe, 23 Dec. 1906.

17　KC, Stuart Papers: Notes on Qethuka, Book of Eulogies, i.

18　See above, p. 28.

19　This is the figure given on p. 3 of the *Natal Regional Survey, Add. Report No. 4, The Dunn Reserve Zululand*, Pietermaritzburg, 1953. For another estimate see n. 2, on p. 8 of S. Marks, *Reluctant Rebellion, the 1906–8 disturbances in Natal*, Oxford, 1970.

20　See Fig. 8 for an illustration of some leading members of the Zulu clan, spaced according to age, and divided among various lineages and homesteads.

21　I have not discussed any specific royal homesteads here. For a fuller description see J. J. Guy, 'The Destruction of the Zulu Kingdom: the Civil War in Zululand, 1879–1884', (PhD thesis, University of London, 1975), pp. 42ff.

22　Ndukwana, one of Stuart's main informants, had been linked to this homestead because his father had been one of the founders. See the life of Ndukwana kaM'mbengwana in notebook 30091 in the Stuart Papers (KC).

23　T. Cope (ed.), *Izibongo, Zulu Praise-poems*, Oxford, 1968, p. 172.

24　There are references to the Emangweni in KC, Stuart Papers: Misc. vol. 29393; and very useful information in the File on Competitions, Zulu essays, 1942, Historical records by C. J. Magwaza (KC).

CHAPTER THREE

The invasion of the Zulu Kingdom

Shepstone and Natal

Theophilus Shepstone, Secretary for Native Affairs in Natal until 1875, was closely associated with the events which culminated in the invasion of the Zulu kingdom. He was born in England in 1817 and had grown up in a missionary family in the Cape Colony. A fluent speaker of Nguni languages, he had had some administrative experience on the Eastern frontier of the Cape before coming to Natal in 1846. First as Diplomatic Agent and then as Secretary for Native Affairs he was the official in charge of African administration in Natal for the first thirty years of the colony's existence.[1]

The basic reasons for Shepstone's interest in the internal affairs of the Zulu kingdom can be understood in the context of the peculiar position and special needs of Natal. It was a poor colony; geographical isolation from commercial centres and markets, a lack of raw materials or the conditions to produce a profitable staple export commodity, the sense of insecurity that large internal and external African populations created among the settlers, discouraged investment and immigration. The economic activities of the colonists were largely commercial, concentrating on the importation of commodities for internal consumption or for transportation and sale in the southern African interior. Capital from these enterprises, supplemented by capital from the Cape and London was invested in land; as a result much of Natal's best agricultural land was acquired by large speculating companies which effectively removed it from the reach of Natal's under-capitalised, settler-farming community.[2]

The inadequacy of internal resources, raw material and land, the large internal black population reluctant to sell its labour at the price settler Natal offered, the dependence on external markets: all these lay at the heart of the aggressive expansionism which characterised the history of colonial Natal in the nineteenth century. Shepstone was often in the forefront of such movements. In the 1850s he attempted to obtain authority to move Africans from Natal to a district south of the colony where he hoped to establish a black chiefdom under his personal rule. He failed in this but continued to support attempts by Natal to extend her control over the territory to the south of the Mzimkhulu river. The Basotho-Boer war of the late 1860s disrupted the 'overberg' trade and intensified the effects of the economic slump in Natal. Shepstone made a vigorous attempt to persuade Britain to annex Lesotho to Natal and was sorely disappointed when this failed. In his attempts to get black labour to the colony Shepstone's agents travelled widely in Mozambique and his emissaries could be found deeply involved in the internal affairs of the Swazi and Ndebele kingdoms. And of course he had a continual interest in the affairs of the fertile and populous Zulu kingdom on his borders.

In spite of Shepstone's efforts to obtain access to more land and labour for Natal, he spent most of the thirty years he held office in dispute with the colony's settlers, for they considered him to be largely responsible for their financial difficulties. His 'native policy', which reserved some 2 000 000 acres of land as African 'locations' was supposed to have 'locked up' the black labour supply. Furthermore his 'gradualist' approach to questions of African administration tended to perpetuate pre-capitalist modes of production, with the homestead as the production community and the social relations which sprang from this. For the settlers it was a policy which perpetuated barbarism and denied them the labour they needed for an economically profitable existence. Moreover those Africans who moved towards peasant production not only resisted selling their labour to whites, at least on the terms the whites were prepared to offer, but also became rivals in agricultural production.

An important reason for Shepstone's 'conservatism' in African administration was that he was more aware of African feelings and attitudes than his fellow-colonists and he realised that a frontal attack on Natal Africans' way of life to produce wage labourers would provoke a reaction which the small white community and the British garrison could never control. This is not to say that Shepstone rose above settler ideology; it was more a question of means than ends. Etherington has argued that his administration was a series of pragmatic improvisations rather than a 'system'.[3] And the anomalies and contradictions which emerged as a result are suggested by de Kiewiet's description of Natal in the mid-1870s, at the end of Shepstone's term of office.[4] Of the colony's 12 000 000 acres, 2 000 000 acres consisted of African locations; but about half of Natal's black population of over 300 000 was involved in agricultural production *outside* these locations and lived on some 5 000 000 acres of land as labour, or rent-paying tenants. The agricultural surplus they produced made vital contributions to the Colony's finances in the form of direct and indirect taxation, and to the income of the land-owners who drew off a portion of the surplus in the form of rentals. It appears that, far from allowing the African to live in slothful, unproductive barbarism, Shepstone's administration saw the development of a class of African agricultural producers who made a major contribution to Natal's finances.

By the 1870s Shepstone was intensely aware of the potential danger of this situation. More than half the black population lived on land to which they had no legal rights; increase in African population could not be indefinitely absorbed by allowing them to move on to 'white' land, and any change in the overall economic situation could lead to wholesale evictions of Africans and a crisis of major proportions. Thus, in 1874, Shepstone wrote:

> Natal . . . with her overwhelming and ever-increasing native population finds herself hemmed in on all sides by Governments anxious to acquire and retain extensions of Territory. The Population per square mile far exceeds that borne by any Territory of equal extent in South Africa. The occupation by natives of farms and Crown lands unoccupied by whites as yet prevents much inconvenient pressure, but should any sudden and considerable accession of white population take place, – a matter beyond the control of any Government, – it is impossible to foresee what solution will be found to so serious and dangerous a problem. A safety valve in the shape of adjoining Territory has always been looked to as the only source of relief. . . .[5]

The land of the Zulu was the most obvious 'safety valve'. It shared the same border with Natal for one hundred miles along the Thukela and Mzinyathi and its continued independence was an economic and psychological affront to settler Natal. At the beginning of the century its armies had devastated the whole region and in the 1830s the Zulu king had attempted to annihilate the first white settlers. Its military organisation was still in existence, new regiments being formed every few years. Disruption within the kingdom caused certain Zulu to seek refuge in Natal, just as Natal Africans sought asylum in Zululand. Black workers travelling overland to the colony had to walk across the kingdom. And Zululand lay between the Transvaal and St Lucia, which was believed to be a potential harbour; from the late 1840s there had been reports that the Transvalers were attempting to move through Zululand to the sea. The Natal settlers believed that their economic ills were largely the result of shortage of land and cheap labour, and yet they lived next to a populous and fertile black kingdom, its land and labour beyond their grasp.

The control, and eventual domination, of Zululand was never far from

Shepstone's mind. He was convinced that he possessed immense influence within the Zulu kingdom. In 1854, when the country was divided over the question of succession, he had said that it was 'in the power of the Government of Natal to annihilate the Zulu Government by a simple order'.[6] Shepstone's confidence was increased by the requests which followed, asking him to recognise Cetshwayo as Mpande's successor and confirmed when he was invited to Zululand to formalise this after Mpande's death in 1872. But where the Zulu were looking for internal stability and external support for their border dispute with the Transvaal, Shepstone was hoping for the opportunity to acquire the land which would 'afford Natal some chance of an outlet for her Native population'.[7]

That opportunity was to come within five years but in circumstances which Shepstone could hardly have foreseen, for it was the result of initiatives coming primarily not from Natal but from London.

Confederation

The invasion of Zululand was the direct result of the 'Confederation Scheme' initiated in 1875 by the British Secretary of State for the Colonies, Lord Carnarvon, and the origins of this policy lay in the consequences of the discovery of diamonds in the southern African interior in the late 1860s.[8] Up to this time the region was, in terms of capitalist development, backward; economic activity centred upon agriculture and the raising of stock, but exports were insubstantial, systems of communication rudimentary, and it was difficult to create capital or attract overseas investment. Beyond the commercial enclaves at the ports, the southern African settler communities tended to be poor, insecure and aggressive when the opportunity arose to obtain land or cheap labour, frequently involving Britain in their disputes with African communities.

Great Britain, as the metropolitan power, was determined to keep control of the southern African coastline and the colonies of the Cape and Natal and their ports, for this was considered essential if she was to maintain her overall position in the increasingly competitive capitalist world.[9] However, her policy towards the interior of the subcontinent was less consistent. As the settlers moved into African territory there were violent clashes which at times threatened the interests of the colonies themselves. Because official British attitudes towards southern Africa were based primarily on the region's strategic position in a world-wide commercial network, rather than any immediately discernible economic interest within the region itself, policy tended to be erratic as different solutions were tried in an effort to solve local problems with the minimum amount of expense.

The discovery of diamonds, however, provided southern Africa with a source of indigenous capital. Within a few years of the opening of the fields the value of diamonds exported dwarfed that of previous export commodities. Between 1871 and 1875 imports through the Cape and Natal doubled. Commercial ventures in the colonies and the Orange Free State began to prosper and local treasuries gained from the increased dues and tariffs. There was a growing market for local agricultural produce and, as the region became more attractive to investors, railway lines began to reach out from the ports towards Kimberley, and the demand for labour increased. African societies in turn began to feel the strain as their surplus produce and labour was diverted in the direction of the diamond fields.

It is in the context of these developments that Carnarvon's confederation scheme has to be seen. The continued political fragmentation of southern Africa hindered further capitalist advance whereas a union of southern African communities would facilitate it. Confederation would establish an administrative structure which would reduce inter-colonial rivalry and allow the implementation of common policies, in particular a common policy towards the control of Africans and the supply of labour. A more effective communication system would enable commodities and labour to move more freely across the sub-continent, and a system of defence could be built up which would give confidence to colonists and investors. By confederation it was hoped that a strong, united, white-dominated southern Africa could be created, one that was suited to the demands of expanding capitalist development and, at the same time, would be able to carry its own administrative and military costs, thereby reducing the direct responsibility of the British Government in the region without harming its interests.

One of the first victims of confederation was the Boer republic of the Transvaal. Unable to take advantage of the diamond discoveries because of its geographical position, in debt and finding it difficult to keep down its African population, the Transvaal, it was felt, could be persuaded if not to accept, then at least not to resist annexation. And the man chosen to carry out the annexation was Theophilus Shepstone.

Shepstone had just completed thirty years' service as Secretary for Native Affairs in Natal. As a colonial official with an intimate knowledge of southern Africa and its inhabitants, long experience, and a reputation for self-reliance, he was considered by Carnarvon to be an ideal choice. He proved, however, to be a failure; his annexation of the Transvaal in

April 1877 was a precipitate action, and the manner in which it was carried out alienated many of the Boers upon whose support, it had been hoped, he could depend.

For the Zulu the transformation of the Secretary for Native Affairs in Natal into the Administrator of the Transvaal was a serious development for it destroyed the diplomatic link forged between Shepstone and Cetshwayo. Shepstone had previously appeared to be sympathetic to the Zulu in their border dispute with the Transvaal but in his new capacity he came under a different set of pressures and, in the words of an official in the Colonial Office, 'he turned his coat in the most shameless manner'.[10] Desperately in need of Boer support for the annexation he tried to win their approval by travelling to the border and using his influence over the Zulu to settle the boundary dispute in a way which would be satisfactory to the Boers.

On 18 October 1877, near the Blood river on the kingdom's western borders, Shepstone met the Zulu deputation.[11] It was headed by Mnyamana kaNgqengelele, chief of the Buthelezi, chief minister to Cetshwayo. Also present was Bhejane, *induna* of the Emangweni royal homestead, and *inceku*, personal attendant to the king. When Shepstone made his idea on the boundary question known, the Zulu accused him of deserting the king and going over to the Boers.

After thirty years of personal, authoritarian rule in Natal, Shepstone was convinced that his influence over Africans was based, not on the office he held and the coercive force this placed at his command, but on his status as the representative of a superior civilisation together with his insight into the native mind. When told by the Zulu that he had acted treacherously towards them and their king he felt this to be an unacceptable insult and was furious. Mnyamana accused him of not speaking frankly. Sigcwelegcwele asked Shepstone how he, as a friend of the dead king Mpande, could now turn against Mpande's son:

> 'Is it so, then, Somtseu,[12] that after two men have been friends, and then one of them dies and leaves his son fatherless, the one who lives on ought to be harsh to the son of the deceased? This Cetshwayo, whom you have come to trouble and not to help, is Mpande's son, and Mpande used to be your friend.'[13]

Shepstone tried to avoid the accusation:

> 'I have only come to talk about the boundary of the country; but the English Nation will come and settle matters for you. Go and tell my child these words, because I know that he will understand me.' Bejana then stood up and said 'Somtseu, we do not understand you.'[14]

The mask of the imperturbable Great White Chief fell away:

Somtseu then became very angry and said 'Who is that calling me by my name and not addressing me as "Inkosi" (Chief, King)?' The Chiefs then said 'There is no "Inkosi" in our country; although a man be an "Inkosi", we Chiefs call him by his name.'[15]

According to one report Mnyamana struck his shield with his assegai and left the meeting with the other chiefs.[16] Another alleged that Shepstone postponed the meeting to the next day but left before this without explanation.[17] Rumour had it that he 'was quite demoralised & apparently lost his head' and wanted to march a detachment of troops into Zululand for a show of force.[18] Certainly he was not to forget the incident nor the men who had dared to question his integrity. For Cetshwayo it had shown that Shepstone was 'no more a father, but a firebrand',[19] and the Zulu were later to see the incident as the event which heralded their destruction.

A significant change in Shepstone's official attitude to the Zulu can be discerned after this event. On 2 January 1878 he informed his superiors that he had discovered 'the most incontrovertible, overwhelming and clear' evidence, of which he had been previously unaware, which supported the Boer claims to Zulu territory.[20] Shepstone did not produce this new evidence and its nature has never been ascertained; it seems doubtful if it ever existed.[21] Three days after this he wrote another dispatch expounding on the dangers to southern Africa of the Zulu military system. He portrayed Zulu society as a vicious military despotism in which every male had been taught from childhood that the 'sole object of his life was fighting and war'. This system had served a bloody purpose in the time of Shaka, but was now a dangerous anachronism. Using an extended mechanistic metaphor, a device to which he frequently turned when describing African societies, Shepstone wrote of 'this organisation' which

> must be looked upon as an engine constructed and used to generate power, the accumulation of which is now kept pent up in this machine, while the process that produces that power is as actively going on as ever . . . the engine has not ceased to exist or generate its forces, although the reason or excuse for its existence has died away; those forces have continued to accumulate and are daily accumulating without safety valve or outlet. . . .
>
> Had Cetywayo's thirty thousand warriors been in time changed to labourers working for wages, Zululand would have been a prosperous peaceful country instead of what it now is, a source of perpetual danger to itself and its neighbours.[22]

Statements such as these were eagerly accepted by the new High Commissioner, Sir Bartle Frere. Frere had recently retired from the Indian Civil Service, and had been appointed to supervise confederation as the crowning achievement of a long and distinguished career. He was quick to realise that a powerful independent African kingdom had no place in the proposed southern African union. Combining Shepstone's views with those of neighbouring colonists, and the attacks made on Cetshwayo by disappointed Zululand missionaries, he used them in official dispatches to persuade the British Government that peace in southern Africa was seriously threatened by Cetshwayo and his army.

Frere had the reputation, and it is a reputation that persists, of being 'An English Christian gentleman of a very high type'. But, as Bishop Colenso was to reveal in his researches, Frere's attacks on Cetshwayo and the kingdom, and the persistence with which he pursued a policy which would inevitably lead to war in spite of the evidence before him that Cetshwayo was doing what he could to avoid war, suggest a fanaticism and an utter disregard for the lives of those who, he believed, were obstructing the ends he wanted to achieve. His social evolutionism enabled him to argue that, in so far as the border dispute was concerned,

> The Boers had force of their own, and every right of conquest; but they had also what they seriously believed to be a higher title, in the old commands they found in parts of their Bible to exterminate the Gentiles, and take their land in possession. We may freely admit that they misinterpreted the text, and were utterly mistaken in its application. But they had at least a sincere belief in the Divine authority for what they did, and therefore a far higher title than the Zulus could claim for all they acquired.[23]

His prejudice against Cetshwayo was overwhelming. He spoke of a general feeling among Africans

> that the time was come for them all to join to resist the flood of new ideas and ways which threatened to sweep away the idle, sensuous elysium of Kaffir-dom. . . .[24]

At the head of this movement was the Zulu king, whose 'history had been written in characters of blood' and who was trying to reconstruct the 'brutalizing system of Chaka'.[25]

Towards the end of 1877 Cetshwayo was convinced that the diplomatic understanding he had reached with Natal, through Shepstone, was in ruins and needed to be reconstructed. As a result he turned to Natal's Lieutenant Governor, Sir Henry Bulwer. Bulwer had become increasingly disturbed by the attitude of Shepstone and Frere towards the Zulu and was already considering some form of mediation. He therefore appointed a Boundary Commission to inquire into the dispute between the Boers and the Zulu. Its findings substantially supported the Zulu position.

Though Frere was informed of this in July 1878, he chose not to make the findings public for five months. Meanwhile he made political capital out of minor border incidents and the rising tension within Zululand and appealed for British troops to be sent to southern Africa in the light of the deteriorating situation.

Deeply worried at the inexplicable change in the British attitude towards him, Cetshwayo appealed for moderation and peace, and asked for an explanation:

> What have I done or said to the Great House of England, which placed my father, Panda, over the Zulu Nation, and after his death put me in power? What have I done to the Great White Chief? I hear from all parts that the soldiers are around me, and the Zulu Nation ask me this day what I have said to the white people. I hear that British troops are now in Swaziland, and that they are there for the purpose of fighting the Zulu Nation, and that these troops crossed through Zulu Territory. . . . I hear that there is war intended, and the reason for it is that I said I was as great as the Queen of England – that 'Somtseu' . . . was only as great as my Chief Mnyamana, and that 'Tshela' (Mr. Rudolph) only of the same rank as my Chief Bejana.
> I feel the English Chiefs have stopped the rain, and the land is being destroyed.
> The English Chiefs are speaking. They have always told me that a kraal of blood cannot stand, and I wish to sit quietly, according to their orders, and cultivate the land. I do not know anything about war, and want the Great Chiefs to send me the rain.[26]

At the Colonial Office Sir Michael Hicks Beach had taken over from Carnarvon as Secretary of State. He protested mildly at what seemed to be an unnecessarily aggressive approach. But Frere deprived him of information and pursued his goal regardless of Hicks Beach's pleas for caution and his orders that war be avoided. As Hicks Beach wrote to his Prime Minister in November 1878

> I have impressed this view upon Sir B. Frere, both officially and privately, to the best of my power. But I cannot really control him without a telegraph – (I don't know that I could with one) – I feel it is as likely as not that he is at war with the Zulus at the present moment. . . .[27]

In December 1878 Frere made the findings of the Boundary Commission known to the Zulu, but he accompanied this information with an ultimatum demanding not only the payment of fines and the surrender of certain Zulu men to the colonial authorities but also the abolition of the Zulu military system within thirty days. Cetshwayo could not have complied with these demands and Frere knew it.[28]

Frere justified making these demands on the Zulu king by asserting that they would bring peace and security to the kingdom's white neighbours, and free the Zulu people from the tyranny of a bloody despot. He believed that military invasion would enable dissident elements within the kingdom to rise against Cetshwayo. Shepstone was largely responsible for giving the High Commissioner this idea for he asserted that the kingdom was deeply divided and likely to fall to pieces when touched. '. . . It is like a huge ball of sand', Shepstone continued, 'with no larger base than a ball would have, and with only cohesion enough to keep its shape while undisturbed.'[29] Thus, persuaded by the great authority on African affairs of the fragility of the kingdom and confident in the strength of the British troops at his disposal, Frere believed he could crush the Zulu before the British Government had an opportunity to question either the efficacy, or the morality, of the methods he used.

But the High Commissioner was never able to present his superiors with this *fait accompli*. British troops under Lord Chelmsford entered Zululand on 11 January 1879 to enforce the terms of the Ultimatum. Eleven days later they retired in confusion when the Zulu destroyed the headquarter column at Isandlwana. The invasion, instead of fragmenting the kingdom, united the Zulu people in support of Cetshwayo and independence.

Notes

1 There is still no adequate biography of this important figure in southern African history. But for significant assessments of his character and policy see H. J. Simons, *African Women, their legal status in South Africa*, London, 1968, pp. 18–26; S. Marks, *Reluctant Rebellion: the 1906–8 disturbances in Natal*, Oxford, 1970; D. Welsh, *The Roots of Segregation: native policy in colonial Natal, 1845–1910*, Cape Town, 1971; N. Etherington, 'The Rise of the Kholwa in Southeastern Africa: African Christian Communities in Natal, Pondoland and Zululand, 1835–1880' (PhD thesis, Yale University, 1971); R. L. Cope, 'Shepstone and Cetshwayo, 1873–1879' (MA thesis, University of Natal, 1967).

2 Writers on the economic history of Natal in the nineteenth century have still to rely on C. W. de Kiewiet's superb, but necessarily dated, description of the colony in *The Imperial Factor in South Africa: a study in politics and economics*, Cambridge, 1937, pp. 188–206. I have drawn heavily on this and H. Slater's most stimulating article 'Land, labour and capital in Natal: The Natal Land and Colonisation Company 1860–1948', *Journal of African History*, xvi, 2, 1975, pp. 257–83.

3 Etherington, 'The Rise of the Kholwa', Ch. 2.

4 De Kiewiet, *The Imperial Factor*, pp. 188–206.

5 Ibid., p. 34, quoting a letter by T. Shepstone to Carnarvon, 30 Nov. 1874.

6 Quoted in Welsh, *Roots of Segregation*, p. 215.

7 Quoted in C. J. Uys, *In the Era of Shepstone, being a study of British expansion in South Africa (1842–1877)*, Lovedale, 1933, p. 84, from a 'Memorandum and minute by Shepstone', 15 Jan. and 28 Feb. 1874.

8 For the Confederation Scheme see de Kiewiet, *The Imperial Factor*; C. F. Goodfellow, *Great Britain and South African Confederation, 1870–1881*, Cape

Town, 1966; and a useful chapter on the prelude to the invasion in E. H. Brookes and C. de B. Webb, *A History of Natal*, Pietermaritzburg, 1965. I have made extensive use of an important article by A. Atmore and S. Marks, 'The Imperial Factor in South Africa in the Nineteenth Century: Towards a Reassessment', reprinted in E. F. Penrose (ed.), *European Imperialism and the Partition of Africa*, London, 1975.

9 R. Robinson and J. Gallagher, *Africa and the Victorians. The Official Mind of Imperialism*, London, 1961, pp. 53–63.

10 CO 179/162: 7267, minute by E. Fairfield, 25 April 1885, on State Sec. to S.A.R., to Derby, 16 March 1885.

11 For accounts of this very important meeting, differing in detail, but confirming one another in substance, see BPP, C.2950: 42, Robinson to Kimberley, 19 April 1881, enc. 2, Cetshwayo to Robinson, 29 March 1881, p. 133; KC, Stuart Papers: Evidence of Lazarus Xaba, 1 May 1910 and 6–9 May 1910, in Notebooks on the Life of T. Shepstone; Colenso, series 1, pp. 74–5, p. 633 (where references to the meeting published in British Parliamentary Papers are reprinted) and pp. 834–55.

12 Somtsewu – Shepstone's name to the Zulu. Notwithstanding much speculation on its meaning along the lines of 'mighty hunter' it is a word of Sesotho origin meaning 'Father of Whiteness'.

13 Colenso, series 1, Cetshwayo's own statement of the origin and progress of the Zulu War, p. 842, a version of the account published as enc. 2, Cetshwayo to Robinson, 29 March 1881, in BPP, C.2950: 42.

14 Ibid., pp. 842–3.

15 Ibid., p. 843.

16 Colenso, series 1, p. 633, reprinting extract from BPP, C.2367.

17 Colenso, series 1, p. 843.

18 *The South African Journal of Sir Garnet Wolseley, 1879–1880* (ed. A. Preston), Cape Town, 1973, p. 150.

19 Colenso, series 1, p. 81, reprinting a message from Cetshwayo to Bulwer in BPP, C.2000.

20 BPP, C.2079: 38, T. Shepstone to Carnarvon, 2 Jan. 1879.

21 Cope, 'Shepstone and Cetshwayo', pp. 247ff.

22 BPP, C.2079: 39, T. Shepstone to Carnarvon, 5 Jan. 1878, p. 55.

23 Quoted in F. E. Colenso and E. Durnford, *History of the Zulu War and its origin*, London, 1880, p. 135.

24 J. Martineau, *The Life and Correspondence of the Right Hon. Sir Bartle Frere*, London, 1895, Frere to R. W. Herbert, 18 March 1878, ii, p. 224.

25 BPP, C.2252: 18, Frere to Hicks Beach, 24 Jan. 1879.

26 Colenso, series 1, p. 263, reprinted from BPP, C.2308.

27 V. Hicks Beach, *Life of Sir Michael Hicks Beach (Earl St Aldwyn)*, London, 1932, i, Hicks Beach to Beaconsfield, 3 Nov. 1878, p. 103.

28 See Martineau, *Life of Frere*, ii, pp. 253–4 and 263; and KC, Stuart Papers, Evidence of J. W. Shepstone, 8 March 1912, Life of Sir T. Shepstone.

29 Cope, 'Shepstone and Cetshwayo', quoting T. Shepstone to Frere, 30 Nov. 1878, p. 369.

CHAPTER FOUR

The Anglo-Zulu war

Isandlwana

Direct telegraphic links between southern Africa and London had not been completed in 1879 and it was only on 11 February that the news of the battle of Isandlwana reached London. The Cabinet met that afternoon and arrangements were made to send reinforcements to Chelmsford without delay.

For Disraeli, Prime Minister of the Conservative government, the reverse at Isandlwana was a serious blow. It forced him to divert troops urgently needed elsewhere, and he felt it seriously weakened his international bargaining position. The added expenditure, coming at a time of economic recession, made the government particularly vulnerable to attack. He was thus 'greatly stricken. . . . Everybody was congratulating me on being the most fortunate of Ministers, when there comes this horrible disaster!'[1]

The British Government, with good reason, held Frere and Chelmsford directly responsible for its predicament: the High Commissioner for depriving it of information and committing British troops to war without proper authority, and Chelmsford for failing to achieve the one thing which might have excused Frere's insubordination – a decisive, inexpensive British victory over the Zulu.

The Opposition in Parliament, backed by a vocal section of the public, expressed its outrage at the Conservatives' forward policy overseas, of which the disaster at Isandlwana was a logical outcome, and Frere's recall was demanded. This the government refused to do, but tried to dampen the attacks by writing Frere a letter of censure, and stressing that confederation did not necessarily imply annexation. As far as the Zulu were concerned Frere was reminded forcefully that neither he nor Chelmsford had 'authority either to accept a cession of territory or to proclaim the Queen's sovereignty over any part of the country'.[2] And later Frere was told that

Her Majesty's Government, though desirous by every legitimate means in their power to promote the civilization of the Zulus, are not prepared to sanction any further interference with the internal government of the country than may be necessary for securing the peace and safety of the adjacent Colonies.[3]

Thus the Zulu, by their victory at Isandlwana, had successfully destroyed the High Commissioner's plans to absorb the kingdom into the proposed political union. In his dispatches Frere had avoided, when he could, discussing in detail his plans for a conquered Zulu kingdom, being content with reassuring the home government of the future tractability of the Zulu once the king was removed. But only hours before the battle of Isandlwana he wrote privately to Chelmsford:

Acting as Glyn's and Wood's columns are now doing, you will virtually annex and settle the country, as you proceed, and greatly simplify proceedings when Cetywayo is disposed of. I have no idea of recommending any revival of a paramount chief or king or of any separate Zulu nationality. An active and absolute Military Administrator with a firm grip of the country, by means of the pick of your Native Regiments or Sepoys and Police, and supported by a backbone of H.M. Troops, will keep order among the chiefs who submit and obey, and will after putting down opposition govern directly, through headmen, the subjects of those who resist – all as subjects of Queen Victoria. . . . I am not reckoning my chickens before they are hatched. . . .[4]

But the Zulu put an end to all such plans for annexation and a military dictatorship. After giving Frere his head, and being landed in a very difficult situation as a result, the British Government now checked him at every turn. His activities were closely scrutinised and any suggestion of expansionist intentions was firmly refused.

Frere's position was made even more difficult by Chelmsford's inability to devise a method of attacking the Zulu again without reinforcements, and even after they had arrived, by the painstakingly slow pace at which he prosecuted the war and the steadily mounting costs of an already disastrously expensive campaign. And although the British Government was to pay lip service to the policy of confederation for some time, it never recovered from the setback it received at Isandlwana which

marks a definite turning point in British South African policy. A policy that in straining after confederation had not hesitated to annex an independent republic, and that would certainly have annexed Zululand and other territories, now turned about and began to slip down the arduous path it had steeply trodden, back again finally to abandonment and non-interference.[5]

But, regardless of overall policy, there was no debate over the fact that the Zulu had to be punished for daring to defend their independence so effectively. Thus operations against them were to drag on till July, at terrible cost to the Zulu people. But by their resistance at Isandlwana the Zulu had not only put an end to plans to force them into the proposed southern African union, but they had damaged irreparably the confederation scheme itself. Capitalist development in southern Africa had caused major changes in the region, but the intensity of the resistance to the attempt to speed up the process persuaded the metropolitan government that the price it would have to pay for destroying non-capitalist social formations by force of arms was too high.

Ulundi

Lord Chelmsford had based his strategy on the assumption that the Zulu would fight in their traditional manner; that is by mounting a massed frontal charge, supported by flanking and encircling movements, in order to reach the enemy with their stabbing spears. For this reason the British did not attempt a war of manoeuvre and every effort was made to entice the Zulu into a position where they would be exposed to concentrated rifle, rocket and artillery fire.[6]

Three columns were sent into Zululand and it was intended that they should converge on the royal residence at Ulundi in the centre of Zululand. The swiftness of the Zulu attack at Isandlwana caught the central headquarter column spread over a wide front, and the Zulu, after suffering terrible losses, managed to break through the British lines and annihilate the defenders at close quarters.

The loss of the central column halted the invasion while reinforcements were awaited. The left-flank column was forced to withdraw to the border areas and mount harassing raids into Zululand from there. The right-flank column was besieged at Eshowe. In March the left-flank column, after suffering a reverse at Hlobane, had its revenge when it decimated the Zulu army which had rashly attacked the heavily-defended British position commanded by Sir Evelyn Wood at Khambula. Chelmsford raised the siege of Eshowe in April, and then, with reinforcements, began the slow crawl into Zululand once again (losing the Prince Imperial on the way). On 4 July, Chelmsford was able to march a huge square towards the royal homestead, Ulundi, where the Zulu attacked for about half an hour. They were unable to reach the square and cavalry put them to flight. After burning the royal homesteads Chelmsford withdrew his troops from Zululand and resigned his command.

Few of Britain's wars against African states have attracted so much attention as the Anglo-Zulu war of 1879. For nearly a century journalists, military men, and historians have excited their readers with accounts of the formal battles, emphasising the suicidal bravery of the Zulu, the imperturbable courage of the redcoats, the ineffectiveness of the assegai when matched with the breech-loading rifle and the Gatling. The victory at Isandlwana is seen as an historical accident; the consequence of inept leadership and absence of the screwdrivers needed to open ammunition boxes. But at Ulundi the inevitable victory was won when British firepower finally persuaded the Zulu of the futility of resistance, breaking the Zulu army and with it the power of the Zulu dynasty.

However this approach, by removing the war from the social and political context in which it was fought and concentrating on the pitched battles, misinterprets the invasion's place and significance in Zulu, and southern African, history.[7]

After the battle of Isandlwana both sides were faced with serious problems springing largely from logistic difficulties. In the case of the Zulu there had been little change in the organisation and structure of the army since Shaka's day. The British invasion of 1879 exposed its weaknesses as a defending force. Traditionally the Zulu were raiders; although boys followed the army carrying sleeping mats and small supplies of food, and a number of cattle were driven with the force, it was assumed that the army's main source of supply would come from the plundered property of the enemy. In 1879 however the Zulu had to fight a defensive war on their own soil. Where possible, food stores and cattle had been moved from the areas of conflict; thus when concentrations of 20 000 men moved through these districts they were unable to obtain sufficient food.

If Zulu soldiers had been able to carry adequate stores with them this would have destroyed the army's greatest advantage – its mobility. In later years Zulu men who had fought in the campaign spoke of the sufferings of the starving troops.[8] After the battle at Khambula, Zulu dead were found with their mouths stuffed with porridge from abandoned cooking pots,[9] and, a year after the war, areas through which the Zulu army had marched were still suffering from food shortages.[10]

This failure to supply the Zulu army adequately while it was in the field was only one reason why, after every battle, the soldiers dispersed and returned to their homes. There were certain rituals which had to be carried out after killing in battle. And, as Bishop Colenso pointed out, the Zulu 'were merely an *armed people,* not a "standing army" '.[11] The implications of this distinction are important. A standing army of specialists can operate without seriously affecting the continuity of the essential functions of the society to which it belongs, whereas with an 'armed people' the mobilisation of able-bodied males causes disruption which in turn reduces the efficiency of the fighting force.

With the men on active service, the Zulu women and children together with their herds of cattle were in danger, not only from British troops, but also from the Zulu army when it traversed the area.[12] Thus the Zulu soldier returned home after the battles not only to regain his strength, but also to protect his property. A Zulu deserter told his new allies that the soldiers 'found that, instead of getting plenty of booty in the shape of cattle, stores, arms and ammunition, they were the losers, as during their absence with the army the English attacked their kraals, and carried off their oxen, sheep and goats'.[13]

The dispersal of the Zulu army after every engagement made it extremely difficult for the commanders to implement an overall strategy, and Cetshwayo protested strongly against his soldiers' failure to remain in the field. As it was, Cetshwayo's approach to the war placed the army at a great disadvantage. Fully aware of the might of the forces ranged against him, the Zulu king fought a defensive war, hoping for a peaceful settlement. He therefore did not take advantage of his victory at Isandlwana when Natal lay at his mercy, and even offered the besieged troops at Eshowe a safe passage back to Natal. While Chelmsford was inching his way towards Ulundi the king held back his soldiers and tried, as he had done throughout the invasion, to negotiate a peaceful settlement. The British approach to the war was clear cut; initially, the Zulu power had to be destroyed by force of arms for reasons of imperial policy, and when this failed the defeat at Isandlwana had to be avenged. Cetshwayo, however, hesitated in his prosecution of the war, and in trying to gain diplomatic advantages he lost military ones.

If the Zulu had avoided pitched battles and concentrated on attacking supply lines from defensive positions the British would have had to alter their strategy completely. Cetshwayo realised this and tried to take advantage of British weaknesses, but a breakdown in discipline in the Zulu army (partly the consequence of the inadequate supply system) frustrated the king's attempts to avoid massed charges on heavily defended positions. The attack on the camp at Isandlwana was provoked by British scouting patrols which blundered on the Zulu when their commanders were still under orders to negotiate with their counterparts. Using the argument that they had disobeyed orders at Isandlwana and won, the Zulu attacked the camp at Khambula without waiting for the flanking sections, and against the orders of the king. It was reported that

When the King heard of the lost battle and of the many men who had fallen, he was exceedingly angry, and asked, 'Who had given the word for his people

...es for change in Zululand: Dabulamanzi kaMpande and John Dunn, 1873 (above);
...a Dunn and his *izinduna*, 1873 (below)

Forces for change in Zululand: Zibhebhu kaMaphitha of the Mandlakazi (above); Ham̄
kaNzibe of the Ngenetsheni (below)

The imperial factor: the High Commissioner, Sir Bartle Frere, and his staff in Natal, 1873

Lord Chelmsford

Sir Garnet Wolseley

to be allowed to fight against Whites who had already entrenched themselves, since even in the open field one Whiteman was nearly as good as ten Zulus?' ... For the King's plan had always been, whenever the Whites . . . entrenched themselves, to make his army pass by them, in order thus to bring the Whites into the open field, or else to surround them from a distance, and make them die of hunger. But his people had not patience enough for all this; and, each time they fought, they must go and rest again for two or three months before beginning another fight.[14]

If the Zulu army had been able to carry out these instructions the effect on the British force would have been disastrous, for the white commanders also found it extremely difficult to support their troops in Zululand. Stores and equipment upon which the soldiers depended were carried in ox-waggons and the rough tracks of Zululand and Natal soon broke down under the strain; drifts collapsed, tracks became waterlogged, grazing along the line of march was destroyed, overwork and disease killed the oxen, and the cost of the war mounted. At the head of the long, limping train of waggons moving slowly back and forth across the country were the soldiers it supported, unable to break free from their inadequate lifeline. Any attempt by the Zulu to break these supply lines would have crippled the British force. The Zulu had to be provoked into attacking the army itself for, as Chelmsford wrote soon after the British had lost their great opportunity of inflicting a defeat at Isandlwana:

> Unless the Swazies come down and help us I do not see how we are to make any impression in Zululand. The country is quite impractical for a force which must take ox-waggons about with it and it is not possible to guard properly the line of communications.
> We might all march straight through the country taking a month's provisions with us, but having done so, what should we have gained?[15]

Chelmsford also faced political difficulties. The Lieutenant Governor of Natal, Sir Henry Bulwer, had signed the Ultimatum to the Zulu only under strong pressure from Frere. After the invasion had begun he was determined that, as far as it was possible, the ultimate aim of the war – peace and security in the region – should be taken seriously. Chelmsford in his eagerness to gain a victory, however, felt he should be getting strong support from Natal and if this was not forthcoming then it should be obtained by the declaration of martial law. Bulwer resisted this and obstructed Chelmsford's attempts to get Natal Africans to harass the Zulu by making raids across the border, an action which Bulwer felt would create long-standing resentment between peoples who had hitherto lived on peaceful terms with each other.

These differences of opinion between the civil and military authorities, coming at a time when the cost of the invasion was already damagingly high, and Frere's political dependability and Chelmsford's military ability were doubted, persuaded the British Government to take drastic action.[16] In May 1879 both Frere and Chelmsford were superseded when Sir Garnet Wolseley was appointed supreme military and civil authority in south-east Africa.

When Wolseley arrived in Natal in late June, Chelmsford's position was precarious. He had managed to get his troops to the edge of the valley of the White Mfolozi but his supply line was extended close to its limit and it would soon be necessary to fall back for stores. He knew that the only way to save the shreds of his military reputation was to defeat the Zulu army in battle using the tactics he had decided upon when he mounted the invasion. Once Wolseley arrived in Zululand that opportunity would be lost. On 3 July Wolseley attempted to land on the Zululand coast but the sea was too high and he had to return to Durban to make the journey overland. On 4 July Chelmsford marched the huge square of 5 000 men on to the Mahlabathini plain where the royal homestead Ulundi was built. The Zulu attacked but did not reach the square and the cavalry was then released and put the survivors to flight. Chelmsford burnt the royal homestead and retired with his troops to Natal and resigned his command.

The battle of Ulundi is conventionally held to be the engagement which avenged the defeat at Isandlwana, vindicated Chelmsford's overall strategy and broke the power of the Zulu, 'the House of Shaka never to rise again'.

However, closer examination shows that this view is a distorted one. Bishop Colenso suspected this at the time when he asked:

> But was it a *political success,* or any more than a bloody but barren victory? . . . The burning of Ulundi & other kraals means nothing in Zulu eyes, as I hear from natives. And there is no clear evidence as yet that the loss of so many warriors . . . has broken the spirit of the natives.[17]

Seen in terms of the original aims of the invasion, the battle of Ulundi, like the campaign itself, was a failure; by their resistance the Zulu had escaped annexation and severely damaged the policy which brought the war. Furthermore there is evidence which suggests that the battle was not the crushing military victory it was made out to be. Wood, who had seen the Zulu attack at Khambula, said he 'could not believe they would make so half-hearted an attack'.[18] Estimates give the time the battle lasted as between twenty-five and forty-five minutes. The riflemen fired an average of 6·4 rounds each. Even considering their numbers, and the support given by Gatling and artillery fire, this cannot be called a high rate of fire, and yet no Zulu reached the square. The number of casualties on the Zulu side is usually given as 1 500, based it would seem on Chelmsford's 'estimate' as there was no body-count after the battle. Wolseley, when he visited the battle field, said that he did not believe Zulu casualties could have exceeded four hundred.[19] Pockets of resistance continued after Ulundi. Skirmishes took place between Zulu and British patrols till late August; Wolseley was informed on 24 August that the Qulusi sent 'defiant messages & say they want to fight',[20] and it was on the night of 28 August that the king gave instructions for the last of the Zulu fighting bands to lay down their arms.[21]

By the time that the battle of Ulundi was fought both sides wished to end hostilities. The Zulu needed peace: they had been under arms for six months and suffered severely; it was now midwinter, and many had lost their foodstocks and cattle, and unless some form of settlement was reached before the spring rains when planting began, they faced famine. An attempt to extract a war indemnity, or open up the country to white settlement, might well have persuaded certain groups to retire to de-fensive positions and adopt harassing tactics at a local level – as indeed the Qulusi and Mdlalose did after Ulundi. But the Zulu did not have to make this choice between subjugation and resistance, because the British, on their side, had no wish to prolong hostilities. A victory in formal battle was needed to protect political reputations by giving British policy a veneer of continuity, and as an example to colonial subjects both in southern Africa and elsewhere in the Empire.[22] At the same time, for reasons of economy, military commitments elsewhere and the political capital being made out of the war, the Conservative government wanted to end this embarrassing example of imperial ineptitude. Thus it was far easier to follow Chelmsford's example and elevate the battle of Ulundi to the rank of a crushing military victory than create the force of mobile fighting units which would have been needed to defeat the Zulu con-vincingly.

For this reason when Wolseley entered Zululand immediately after Ulundi, he announced that Britain had not been fighting the Zulu people, but the Zulu king; Cetshwayo's reign was therefore to be terminated once he was captured, but his people would be left in full possession of their land and their property if they submitted. Under the threat of further hostilities, social disruption and eventual starvation, the Zulu did not call Wolseley's bluff. We must not give credit solely to the battle of Ulundi for the cessation of hostilities in Zululand in 1879; a far more important factor was the promise Wolseley made to the Zulu that, if they laid down their arms, they would remain in possession of their means of production.

The capture of Cetshwayo

Sir Garnet Wolseley had just turned forty-six years of age when he arrived in Zululand and he was probably at the height of his popular reputation at the time. He had wide military experience gained in the Crimea, India, the Far East, North America and Africa. To the British public he was a modernising young general whose dash and efficiency, and desire for military reform, had made him the enemy of the Victorian military establishment. This reputation was reinforced by the activities of the energetic officers on his staff who made sure that the exploits of their general reached the public through the press and their own publications. In 1875 they had been sent to Natal where, as a prelude to confederation, their task had been to cajole the settlers into accepting a reduction in their political independence.

Wolseley's private diaries, however, reveal that behind the calm, efficient exterior lay an insecure, desperately ambitious man, with an obsession for public recognition. He believed himself to be surrounded by enemies determined to destroy his career, while his prejudices were those of the imperial era, but exaggerated to a grotesque degree. While most of these characteristics were kept out of the public eye, his egotism appalled a number of his contemporaries, including Queen Victoria. But to Disraeli and his Cabinet, his southern African experience, his reputed military ability and his brash self-confidence were what was needed to bring the war to a speedy end and to resist any plans Sir Bartle Frere might have to extend British responsibility in the region.

On this latter point Disraeli was quite correct. The High Commissioner continued to object strongly to the instruction that, after the defeat of the Zulu, Britain should not intervene in Zulu affairs, writing that 'in the interests of the Zulus themselves we have no right to leave them to their fate'.[23] However, although Wolseley was personally attracted by what he saw as Frere's dream of establishing a 'great African Empire'[24] he had no difficulty in obeying instructions and ruthlessly obstructing all Frere's intentions in this direction.

It was from Sir Henry Bulwer that Wolseley received advice on the tactics he adopted to 'settle' Zululand. Although they approached the question from different standpoints their views were not incompatible: Wolseley had instructions not to devise any scheme which might imply annexation; Bulwer opposed annexation on the grounds that the war had been fought for the Zulu people, to free them from Cetshwayo's tyranny, and not to dispossess them of their land. Bulwer advised Wolseley to do all he could to convince the Zulu people of our good intentions and to shew them that we desire nothing from them but a proper security for peace; that we desire nothing but this and the welfare of the Zulu people; that we do not desire any portion of their territory; that our quarrel was with the King, and not with them; that Zululand is for the Zulu people, and that we only desire that there shall be security for peace, and that the people shall live safely and shall prosper. The Zulu Nation, once it gets fully to understand this, can scarcely fail to be on our side in accepting and securing those arrangements which take away nothing from them, but which, on the contrary, are for their good.[25]

Wolseley seized on these expressions of British goodwill and used them at his meeting with the Zulu. They were, of course, without foundation; the division between the tyrannical king and an oppressed people did not exist – as the war had shown – and the Zulu people were allowed to retain their land, not as a result of British magnanimity, but to put a stop to an expensive and politically damaging campaign.

And the adoption of this tactic necessarily implied the deposition of Cetshwayo. This was necessary to maintain the fiction that it was Cetshwayo's excesses which had persuaded Britain to invade the kingdom, and to cover up the failure of the invasion, for the British could hardly withdraw from Zululand after six months of war and leave untouched the man whose actions had been its ostensible cause.

Wolseley travelled first to the coastal districts and there, with the help of John Dunn, attempted to persuade the inhabitants to formally give their submission. His announcements must have sounded strange to the people who had just experienced the horror of the war. Wolseley told them that the British

were not & had never been at war with the Zulu people: our dispute was with Cetewayo who had been guilty of cruelties to his people: that he took life without trial & that under his rule neither life nor property were even [ever] safe. That by the military system he maintained, he prevented the men from marrying & from working & so kept them poor. That he should never again be King of Zululand. . . . In future all men should be allowed to marry & to come & go when they liked, so that they might become rich & prosperous as we wished them to be. That the Great Queen who ruled in South Africa desired to see the Zulu people rich and happy as the Zulus were who resided in Natal.[26]

Understandably the Zulu treated such statements with scepticism. Wolseley spent two weeks on the coast and, despite Dunn's assistance, few Zulu leaders came in to submit. Then reports reached Sir Garnet that Cetshwayo was gathering armed men around him in the northern districts of the country and he decided that he should move out of the coastal districts, to the centre of the country, and reoccupy Ulundi and direct operations from there.

After the battle of Ulundi Cetshwayo had moved to northern Zululand to the homesteads of his first minister, Mnyamana. From there he tried to open negotiations with Wolseley, but the British general would not promise the king anything except good treatment if he surrendered. Cetshwayo refused to do this and it was reported to Wolseley that 'All the Natives . . . [in Natal] think we shall have another fight for it, as the young men do not yet consider themselves as beaten' and that Cetshwayo was preparing for further resistance. Wolseley wrote in his journal:

> Perhaps I am brutal, but I think it important to punish these northern tribes severely as a warning to all others in South Africa as to what they may expect should they ever be fools enough to make war upon the English. Up to the present beyond shooting & wounding some 10,000 men, we have not really punished the people as a nation, and our leniency in now allowing all the people to return to their Kraals, retaining all their cattle, may possibly be mistaken for fear. I should therefore like to let loose the Swazies upon these northern tribes at once, but I have to think of the howling Societies at home who have sympathy with all black men whilst they care nothing for the miseries & cruelties inflicted upon their own kith & kin who have the misfortune to be located near these interesting niggers.[27]

Ulundi was occupied on 10 August and Wolseley began sending patrols north of the Black Mfolozi to try to discover the king's whereabouts, and threatened the people of the Nkandla and Qudeni with force if they did not surrender. In the north the Qulusi were still in their strongholds and fired on messengers. Wolseley refused to be provoked, hoping that once Cetshwayo was captured this resistance would cease.

On 14 August three of the most important chiefs under Cetshwayo – Mnyamana, Ntshingwayo and Sitshaluza came to Wolseley with a large number of cattle, hoping to be able to negotiate a peace which would secure the king's safety and his continued residence in the country. Wolseley refused either to negotiate or let them leave the camp and they were horrified to find themselves detained, to all intents and purposes, as hostages.[28] This action only confirmed Zulu suspicions. Cetshwayo moved to more inaccessible territory and was passed from homestead to homestead to avoid patrols.

On 20 August Wolseley gave orders 'to burn Kraals & carry off cattle where the King is known to be & to be concealed by the inhabitants'.[29] His patrols began to torture Zulu they found in the vicinity of the homesteads in which they suspected the king was hiding. The chief Mbopha of the Hlabisa, one of the most important councillors in the land and a particular favourite of the royal house, was kicked to the ground and burnt with firebrands in an unsuccessful attempt to make him reveal Cetshwayo's whereabouts.[30]

Systematic terrorism eventually revealed Cetshwayo's hiding place. Early on the morning of 28 August the king was in a homestead on the margins of the Ngome forest. He had with him a number of his followers, including Mkhosana of the Zungu, a confidential adviser, Mkhosana's son, Maphelu, who in his old age left a detailed account of what happened, and female attendants and bearers.[31] Early in the morning the king gave orders for a beast to be slaughtered. After holding a discussion with the men accompanying him on the problems of feeding his party while in hiding, he retired into a hut to eat. Suddenly there was a shout of 'Impi' from the gate of the homestead and the Zulu looked up to find that they had been surrounded by troops. Someone panicked and began to call out hysterically 'Arm! Arm!', but the majority of those within the homestead remained quiet, while Cetshwayo's female attendants moved into the hut in which the king was. Black soldiers from Natal attached to the patrol entered the homestead and began looting. In Cetshwayo's hut they were berated by the girls with him and the king intervened saying, 'Get out of my home, go and fetch your chief and bring him here.' Martin Oftebro, a Zululand missionary's son, was acting as interpreter to the British soldiers. He knew Cetshwayo and was sent to identify him. Mkhosana, as senior councillor, positioned himself at the gate, told Oftebro to identify himself and took him to the king. Cetshwayo recognised the young man and said, 'Was your father a friend of mine for so long that you should do this to me?'[32] He then surrendered.

Under close guard Cetshwayo was marched to Ulundi. A number of followers remained with him, including Mkhosana and Maphelu. That night Cetshwayo discharged the last of his duties as king of Zululand. Permission was obtained from the guard for Maphelu and another young man to leave the camp on the grounds that they had been inadvertently captured in the homestead and had not been members of the royal entourage. They left the camp carrying secret instructions to Mahubulwana, *induna* of the Qulusi, and to Sekethwayo, chief of the Mdlalose, ordering them to disband the men still under arms in the north-western districts.[33]

Cetshwayo arrived in the British camp on 31 August. He was refused permission to consult with his *izinduna* and neither Wolseley nor Dunn was prepared to have any direct dealings with him. A reluctant John Shepstone was ordered to inform the king that he was to be sent into exile. The king's pleas to be allowed to stay in his country were rejected. On the same day he was marched towards Port Durnford where he boarded the *Natal* which then sailed for Cape Town.

On 1 September Wolseley assembled the Zulu at Ulundi for the meeting at which he announced the arrangements he had decided upon for the future government of Zululand.

Notes

1 G. E. Buckle, *The Life of Benjamin Disraeli, Earl of Beaconsfield*, London, 1920, vi, p. 424.

2 BPP, C.2260: 7, Hicks Beach to Frere, 6 March 1879, p. 60.

3 BPP, C.2260: 16, Hicks Beach to Frere, 20 March 1879, p. 110.

4 E. G. French, *Lord Chelmsford and the Zulu War*, London, 1939, p. 83.

5 C. W. de Kiewiet, *The Imperial Factor in South Africa: a study in politics and economics*, Cambridge, 1937, pp. 234–5.

6 There are many books on the invasion of Zululand, virtually all badly flawed. By far the best is D. R. Morris, *The Washing of the Spears: a History of the Rise of the Zulu nation under Shaka and Its Fall in the Zulu War of 1879*, London, 1966, which includes a critical bibliography.

7 The following section is based on my article 'A note on firearms in the Zulu kingdom with special reference to the Anglo-Zulu war, 1879', *Journal of African History*, xii, 4, 1971.

8 J. Y. Gibson. *The Story of the Zulus*, London, 1911, pp. 175–6.

9 Morris, *Washing of the Spears*, p. 496.

10 BPP, C.2695: 43, Colley to Kimberley, 9 Aug. 1880, enc., Osborn to Colley, 4 Aug. 1880, p. 87.

11 C. Vijn, *Cetshwayo's Dutchman, being the private journal of a white trader in Zululand during the British Invasion*, translated, edited, annotated by J. W. Colenso, London, 1880, p. 142.

12 See G. H. Swinny (translator), *A Zulu Boy's recollections of the Zulu War and of Cetshwayo's return*, London, 1884.

13 W. Ashe and E. V. Wyatt-Edgell, *The Story of the Zulu Campaign*, London, 1880, p. 134.

14 Vijn, *Cetshwayo's Dutchman*, pp. 38–9.

15 NA, Sir Evelyn Wood Collection: II, 2/2, Chelmsford to Wood, 27 Jan. 1879.

16 V. Hicks Beach, *Life of Sir Michael Hicks Beach (Earl St Aldwyn)*, London, 1932, i, pp. 133–7.

17 KC, Colenso papers, folio 26, 2. 24, J. W. Colenso to Chesson, 25 July 1879.

18 E. Wood, *From Midshipman to Field Marshal*, London, 1906, ii, p. 81.

19 A. Preston (ed.), *The South African Journal of Sir Garnet Wolseley, 1879–80*, Cape Town, 1973, p. 93, entry for 21 Aug. 1879. Wolseley made a number of references to the inconclusive nature to the battle of Ulundi, although it could be argued that he was only trying to emphasise his role in Zululand, which began when the battle was over.

20 Ibid., p. 95, entry for 24 Aug. 1879.

21 See below, p. 63.

22 Like 'King Theebaw of Burma' who on hearing of Isandlwana 'wanted to order a march on Rangoon forthwith'. Quoted in V. G. Kiernan, *The Lords of Human Kind: European Attitudes towards the Outside World in the Imperial Age*, Great Britain, 1972, p. 334.

23 BPP, C.2318: 12, Frere to Hicks Beach, 18 April 1879, p. 51.

24 *Wolseley's Journal*, pp. 39 and 72–3.
25 GH 1401: 'Further Memorandum on the subject of the settlement of Zulu difficulty', 5 July 1879.
26 *Wolseley's Journal*, p. 59, entry for 19 July 1879.
27 Ibid., p. 71, entry for 4 Aug. 1879.
28 See Vijn, *Cetshwayo's Dutchman*, pp. 156–60 and Colenso, series 1, p. 728.
29 *Wolseley's Journal*, p. 92, entry for 20 Aug. 1879.
30 Colenso, series 1, pp. 628 and 745; Vijn, *Cetshwayo's Dutchman*, pp. 169–75.
31 KC, Maphelu, pp. 5–6.
32 KC, Zulu war reminiscences, II, 'Reminiscences of Martin Oftebro'.
33 KC, Maphelu, pp. 7–8.

PART II

Civil War

... of this be sure, that the source and spring of all this that you hear of, and of all this which is being done, is that which I have mentioned; you will not find any other whatever. That kind of action is what we call 'knocking people's heads together'. He is knocking their heads together, setting them across with each other that they may dislike one another, and then he may enter in among them and make an end of them. . . . I quite hope that now you know that the Zulus are set at loggerheads by the cunning of white men, who want to eat up their land. My heart is very full of grief, I cannot find words to express it, for this splendid old Zulu people.

William Ngidi, 1883

CHAPTER FIVE

The 'settlement' of Zululand

Wolseley's plan

On the afternoon of 1 September 1879 Wolseley addressed some two hundred Zulu who had gathered at the British camp. Through John Shepstone, the Acting Secretary for Native Affairs in Natal, and brother of Sir Theophilus, they were told that Cetshwayo had been sent into exile and was never to return to Zululand. The Zulu were to be ruled by thirteen independent chiefs appointed by the British.

Only four of these appointed chiefs were present in person and they signed an agreement which bound them to respect their new boundaries, to abolish the Zulu military system, and not to obstruct any of their people who might wish to work in neighbouring territories. They were forbidden to import firearms or become involved in any form of trade which did not reach them through Natal or the Transvaal. Capital punishment without trial was disallowed, land could not be alienated, and they were to keep the peace and apply the law according to the 'ancient laws and customs' of their people.[1]

A British Resident was appointed but he would not have administrative or legislative authority, exercising diplomatic duties only. Wolseley wrote:

> I have been . . . careful to make it clear that we intend to exercise no administrative authority over the country, and that we wish to disturb the existing conditions of life and government only where, as in the cases of the military system and the barbarous practices of witchcraft, these conditions were irreconcilable with the safety of British subjects in South Africa, or with the peace and prosperity of the country itself.[2]

The Resident was to report to the High Commissioner, or the Lieutenant Governor of Natal. While he could offer advice to the chiefs if they requested it and could remonstrate if they departed from the terms of their appointment, the Resident was instructed not to involve himself in the internal administration of the chiefdoms. It proved extremely difficult to find a suitable official who would accept the post, but eventually Melmoth Osborn, an ex-Natal official and close friend of Theophilus Shepstone, then serving in the Transvaal, was appointed.[3]

Wolseley based his settlement on information and advice gained from a number of sources. Sir Henry Bulwer had provided the initial framework early in July, but during Wolseley's stay in Zululand awaiting the capture of the king he had come under the influence of several other men. As a result Bulwer's original suggestion that Zululand be divided into four independent chiefdoms each with a British adviser was slowly altered. Traders, missionaries and local officials all gave their advice to Sir Garnet who worked

> them all separately as far as possible in obtaining news for me & [I] then compare their statements: I have a horror of being in the hands of any one man especially if that one be not an English officer.[4]

Of all these men only one gained Wolseley's unqualified confidence and that was John Dunn. Dunn had left Zululand with his followers just before the war and, turning against his friend and benefactor, the Zulu king, he had joined the invading forces' Intelligence department. After the war he joined Wolseley in Zululand, and Sir Garnet wrote:

> . . . he is a power in Zululand and I intend making as much use of him as possible. My idea is to increase his powers by making him paramount Chief over the District of Zululand lying along the Tegula [Thukela] & Buffalo Rivers frontiers of Natal. I shall thus secure the civilizing influence of a White man over the district of Zululand nearest to us, and he and his people will be a buffer between us and the barbarous districts of Zululand beyond. He is at heart more a Zulu than an Englishman, but he has none of the blood-thirsty and conquering instincts of the Zulu people.[5]

But as Wolseley got to know Dunn better so his opinion changed and his admiration for him increased. Dunn's knowledge of Zululand was of great use to Wolseley, and he was increasingly attracted by Dunn's self-assurance and independence. From a man who was 'at heart more a Zulu than an Englishman' Dunn became for Wolseley an English Gentleman – and to someone who was not a British officer Wolseley could give no higher accolade.

> I have never met a man who was more of a puzzle to me than Dunn. He has never been in England & most of his life he has passed in Zululand without any English or civilized society, and yet in his manners he is in every way the Gentleman. He is quiet, self-possessed and respectful without any servility whatever, and his voice is soft and pleasant. He is much more of the English Gentleman than any of the self opinionated & stuck up people who profess to be 'our leading citizens' in Natal. . . . He leads a curiously solitary life, but he says he enjoys it thoroughly, being in every way his own King, without any

policeman in his dominions to serve him with a writ or lay rough hands on him for taking the law into his own hands. . . . He has as many wives & concubines as he wishes to keep & he has a clan about him who are all ready to obey his slightest nod. He pays periodical visits to Natal & has his books, letters & newspapers sent to him regularly. I wish I dared make [him] King of Zululand, for he [would] make an admirable ruler: however I am giving him the largest District in the country, an arrangement that I believe will be the small end of the wedge [of] civilization inserted into it.[6]

The other local adviser who strongly influenced Wolseley was John Shepstone, Acting Secretary for Native Affairs in Natal.[7] Although Wolseley felt that John Shepstone was a 'stupid man', associated in the Zulu mind with treachery, it was he who suggested the names of most of the appointed chiefs and who, in his discussions with Wolseley on Zulu customs and history, gave him the rationale with which he justified the settlement.[8] According to this interpretation, which Theophilus Shepstone shared and perhaps originated, the majority of the members of the kingdom saw the Zulu royal house as a band of conquering oppressors who had destroyed the independent and peaceful rule of the pre-Shakan chiefdoms by imposing over them the ruthless Zulu system. Thus Wolseley wrote:

> In the country now known as Zululand, there were, before the setting out of Chaka upon his scheme of conquest, besides others of lesser account, three powerful and respected tribes enjoying independence, the Ndwandwe, the Umtetwa, and the Zungu tribes. In the redistribution of territory which I have now made, I have given a place to the representatives of these subjugated people, who, though to a large extent amalgamated, after this lapse of time, with the Zulus, are I am assured, mindful of their ancient and independent origin, and proud of their distinct traditions. Such breaking up of the cohesion of the country will, I firmly believe, preclude for the future all, or almost all, possibility of any reunion of its inhabitants under one rule.[9]

From Wolseley's settlement came a disastrous civil war through which the Zulu lost all they had secured by their resistance to the invasion. While the invasion caused tremendous disruption and loss of life, and of course the centralised political system was disbanded, it must not be forgotten that the Zulu had retained most of their land and that only a handful of the kingdom's leaders had lost their lives. There is a continuity between events before and after the war, and any assessment of Wolseley's settlement and the civil war which followed must be based on an understanding of the Zulu political structure as it existed before the war of 1879. In Chapter 2 we saw something of the complexity of the distribution of political power and authority in Zululand, with the royal lineage extending its direct influence through the royal homesteads of the kingdom but intermixed with large areas inhabited by people who came under powerful local chiefs. Wolseley's settlement, however, ignored the fact that the royal house had inextricably penetrated all aspects of Zulu social life and divided the country internally in a manner which bore virtually no relation to the existing distribution of authority.

The thirteen appointed chiefs

Wolseley appointed a Boundary Commission to demarcate the external border of Zululand and the internal boundaries of the thirteen chiefdoms.[10] As far as the external border was concerned Wolseley failed to implement his pledge that the Zulu would be left in full possession of their land. The northern limit of the kingdom was moved southwards so that it coincided with the Phongolo river, thereby excluding many of the Qulusi and Emgazini people, together with followers of Hamu and Mnyamana. Wolseley chose to ignore the findings of the 1878 Boundary Commission and moved the western boundary, which Zululand shared with the Transvaal, to the east. In the north-east a line was drawn which followed the Lubombo mountains; beyond it lay territory and people intimately linked with the political and economic life of the Zulu, which Wolseley labelled the 'country which it is proposed to give back to the Tongas'.[11]

After the king had been captured and the Zulu had turned to the vital tasks of planting for the coming season, Wolseley's confidence increased. He ordered the Boundary Commission to lay down the borders of the chiefdoms following, where possible, natural physical features. He ordered the Commission to inform

> the Chiefs that Zululand, having been conquered by us, according to Zulu law, really belongs to Her Majesty the Queen, but as Her Majesty has no wish to increase her dominions in South Africa, as an act of grace to the Zulu people, she has now parcelled out the country into independent chieftainships. It is, therefore, for her officers, on her behalf, to decide the extent of territory that is by her favour to be allotted to each Chief. This was a right freely exercised by Cetywayo, as well as by his predecessors, and it is a right which devolves upon the Great Queen by right of conquest, and that must not be disputed.[12]

Even if we assume that it was possible to ignore the effect of sixty years of Zulu rule and to resuscitate the pre-Shakan chiefdoms, the majority of the chiefs appointed failed to reflect the pre-Shakan system. Two of the appointed chiefs were aliens. John Dunn was the most important of these and, in return for his services to the British in the war and as a

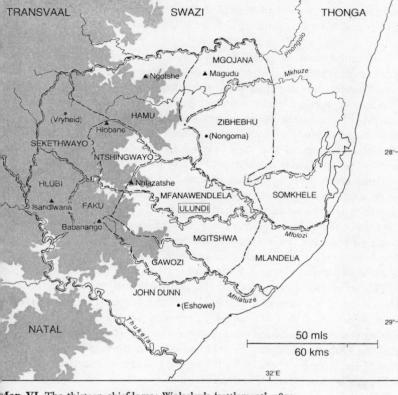

Map VI The thirteen chiefdoms: Wolseley's 'settlement' 1879,

esult of the confidence Wolseley had gained in him, he was awarded the
argest chieftainship in Zululand. It was situated between the Mhlatuze
und Thukela rivers, occupying most of southern Zululand and comprised
ubout one-fifth of the total area of Zululand. It included both the Nkandla
und Qudeni forests, and portions of the Mpungose and Biyela, as well as
he Ntuli, Chube, Mchunu and Sithole and Sibiya peoples together with
he homestead of Dabulamanzi and his followers.[13]

On Dunn's north-western border, in the vicinity of Babanango,
Wolseley created a small chiefdom under Faku, a member of an inferior
ineage of the Ntombela. Further west, the other alien was awarded a
chiefdom. He was Hlubi, a member of a Sotho group, the Tlokoa, who
had distinguished themselves serving as mercenaries for the Natal
government, and during the invasion. Hlubi was appointed over the

district previously dominated by Sihayo of the Qungebe, whose sons' incursion into Natal had provided Frere with one of the pretexts for invasion. Sihayo was ordered to leave his district, with his son Mehloka-zulu.

The appointment of Mlandela over the Mthethwa in the coastal district was the most successful attempt to revive a pre-Shakan chiefdom. However Mlandela was now too old to rule effectively and the existence of the Emangweni section in the southern portions of this area meant that a number of important people directly attached to the royal house now came under Mlandela's jurisdiction. North of Mlandela was Somkhele's district and most of the Mpukunyoni he ruled appear to have fallen within the boundaries marked out for him by the Commission.

Three chiefs were appointed in Zululand north of the Black Mfolozi river. One was Mgojana, representative of the once great Ndwandwe chiefdom but whose territory had been greatly encroached upon during the rule of the Zulu kings. However, the expressed aim of the settlement was to encourage the revival of the pre-Shakan chiefdoms; as a result Mgojana was awarded a district between the Mkhuze and Phongolo, dominated by the powerful Emagazini.

The other two chiefs north of the Black Mfolozi were Zibhebhu and Hamu – both members of the Zulu clan. Hamu acquired his large territory in recognition of the services he gave when he defected to the British during the war. It included not only his followers – the Ngenetsheni – but also the Qulusi and Mphangisweni sections, the dominant lineage of the Ntombela, large numbers of the Buthelezi, and also Mnyamana's personal homesteads about the Sikhwebezi river.

Mnyamana himself was offered a territory but refused to accept it. Various interpretaions are given for this; Wolseley believed it a result of his inflated opinion of himself and desire for greater recognition, while many Zulu assert it was out of loyalty to the exiled king.[14] His own explanation to the Boundary Commission was

> that he honestly considered that he was going to be given a tract of country which, though amply large enough for his extensive following, yet . . . it did not include one-third of the land where his kraals were situated; he also considered that Oham [Hamu] would, by the settlement, get most of the country formerly owned by him. For these reasons he refused to sign the paper as he did not see his way to govern a people that did not own him in any way as their Chief, and that he would only get into trouble by attempting to do so.[15]

Mnyamana's chiefdom was therefore given to Ntshingwayo, and Cetshwayo's chief councillor, the most powerful man in the land, was excluded from the settlement. Ntshingwayo in turn was reluctant to accept the district because it contained so many Buthelezi and Mdlalose, as well as Sekethwayo's personal homestead. Sekethwayo himself was appointed over a district further to the west.

To the east of Hamu and Mgojana, was the chiefdom of Zibhebhu. In his south-western districts there lived important groups of people whose power was linked directly with that of the royal house; these included homesteads of Ndabuko and Ziwedu, the people attached to the Gqikazi homestead and its offshoots. Within his western borders were members of Zibhebhu's father's *ikhohlo* who had quarrelled with him before the war and now came under his rule by the settlement. Although a number of Zibhebhu's Mandlakazi were included in Mgojana's territory, he was more than compensated by the fact that his southern boundary was extended to the Black Mfolozi river. This placed under the Mandlakazi chief a number of groups with close links to the royal house, or with considerable autonomy within the kingdom. They included the Hlabisa, and Mdletshe, and the homesteads of Mfinyeli and Mgamule.

The triangle formed by the Black and White Mfolozi, up to the vicinity of the Nhlazatshe mountain, was awarded to Mfanawendlela of the Zungu who moved back to the Mahlabathini plain from where they had moved when Mpande established the centre of Zulu government there.

Two chiefdoms were marked out between the White Mfolozi river and the Mhlatuze. One was given to Mgitshwa of the Biyela. The chief of the Biyela, Mkhosana, had been killed at Isandlwana and Mgitshwa's appointment (probably made at Dunn's suggestion) excluded Somhlolo of the great house of the Biyela.[16] The Biyela were spread north and south of the Mhlatuze; thus many came under Dunn's jurisdiction, and the same was true of the Mpungose who were placed under their chief Gawozi, and both Gawozi and Mgitshwa had their chief homesteads in Dunn's territory. Gawozi died soon after his appointment, and although many believed that the chieftainship should pass to Gawozi's son, the British Resident followed the advice of a missionary and appointed his brother Siyunguza.[17]

It has been argued that historians have failed to emphasise the 'Machiavellian quality' of Wolseley's settlement; that 'no more astute device could have been found for setting Zulu against Zulu and thus consummating the military victory without further cost or responsibility'.[18] This interpretation, however, credits Wolseley with an understanding of the Zulu which he did not possess. While it is true that the 1879 settlement set Zulu against Zulu, and initiated a civil war which finally destroyed Zulu independence, this did not occur in a manner, nor for the reasons, that Wolseley intended. The settlement can only be characterised as invalid, both in conception and in implementation, and it cannot be understood in the terms in which it was defended by its creators. Wolseley and his adviser John Shepstone believed they had created thirteen autonomous chiefdoms which gave expression to real forces within the Zulu political structure, and whose chiefs would jealously guard their authority and independence from internal and external threats. In less than two years events in Zululand were to show that this was not so, and the Colonial Office was preparing to abandon the arrangement as unworkable and a potential threat to British interests. Political expediency, cultural arrogance and ignorance played a far more important part in the planning of the settlement than did conscious political manipulation.

Wolseley saw his southern African commission as just one step on the ladder to higher office and he soon became impatient at having to remain in this remote part of the world. His political superiors moreover urgently needed an apparent solution to their difficulties in the region, the better to defend themselves against Liberal attacks on their policies. Once the terms of the settlement had been announced Wolseley moved hastily to the Transvaal and was most reluctant to reconsider any aspect of the settlement. When the Boundary Commissioners informed him that many of the appointed chiefs were unsuitable,[19] Wolseley responded by suppressing that portion of their report. And when some of the settlement's more severe shortcomings became apparent Wolseley argued that the fault lay, not in the settlement itself, but in the unwillingness of Zulu and officials to adhere to its terms.[20]

In many ways the terms and strictures imposed on the appointed chiefs were irrelevant, for they failed to reflect the realities of the social and political structure of Zululand. As shown above, the new borders of the country and the boundaries of the chiefdoms cut indiscriminately across the social and political groupings which had developed during the reigns of the Zulu kings. Members of the same political unit were now placed under different political authorities. Long-standing rivals came under the same appointed chief. In a number of instances, the homesteads of the appointed chiefs lay outside the territories over which they were instructed to rule, and in the case of Mgojana he was appointed over a district occupied not by his followers but by the powerful Emgazini.

Wolseley was not unaware that the settlement would create anomalies of this kind, and for this reason the Boundary Commission was instructed to inform the Zulu that, if they had reason to object to the chief appointed over them, then they should move to another chief's territory. The Commissioners, however, were soon to discover that the 'people we questioned in the kraals seem to prefer an unwelcome ruler to changing their abode'.[21] Economic necessity and emotional and religious links tied the Zulu to the districts their ancestors had won by sacrifice, political skill and force of arms; time and again in the coming years the Zulu were to demonstrate that they moved from their districts only as a last resort, not to satisfy white attempts at social manipulation.

Furthermore, although the king had been removed, nearly all other members of the Zulu political hierarchy had survived the war; in every part of the country there were men of status and authority, with large followings, whose power was not recognised by the settlement. Some of them were heads of chiefdoms which Shaka has incorporated into the kingdom, and who had enjoyed the support of Shaka's successors. Others were members of the royal lineage or powerful supporters of the royal house and leaders of royal sections. Many of these men found themselves under appointed chiefs whom they considered their inferiors, and who soon became rivals when they chose to exercise the authority Wolseley had given them.

One of Wolseley's instructions was that members of the royal house should abandon their homes and move into Dunn's territory. This order was simply ignored and no one had the power to enforce it. Wolseley also laid the basis for bitter and bloody disputes in the coming years when he instructed the appointed chiefs to collect royal cattle and firearms and deliver them to the Resident. Sir Garnet wrote that the royal herds were 'not in themselves of any great value, and I regard their delivery to us only as a symbol of the submission' which will practically be shown in a more significant way.[22] He was of course wrong. Cattle were crucial to the operation of the Zulu economy and polity. The king was the most powerful and therefore the wealthiest man in the kingdom, with access to most cattle. There were certain royal herds immediately recognisable as the king's, often as the result of certain physical characteristics developed by selective breeding. There were the cattle attached to the *amakhanda* and homesteads of the royal lineage. Moreover the king, like all wealthy Zulu, practised *ukusisa*, by which cattle were 'lent out' to Zulu who could use them as breeding stock and for the milk they produced. It is fruitless trying to decide whether these cattle, together with their offspring over a number of generations, were 'royal cattle' which 'belonged to the king'; clearly defined personal ownership rights did not apply. Wolseley's injunction merely gave those appointed chiefs who felt sufficiently confident an opportunity to take cattle from those Zulu who had been attached to the royal house.

Wolseley's settlement was a hurried and pragmatic arrangement devised to satisfy the immediate needs of the Conservative government in a moment of crisis. The defences with which Wolseley surrounded the settlement are easy to penetrate; they were provided by his prejudice and ignorance and that of his colonial advisers. The talk of destroying the Zulu tyranny by reviving the pre-Shakan chiefdoms was there to make the settlement more palatable and persuade the public that the lives and treasure spent in the war had not been wasted. But with all his short-comings Wolseley had keen insight into matters which affected his own political advancement and, after all, he had attended the special meeting of the Cabinet where all the Ministers were 'emphatic on the point of avoiding any annexation of territory which should thereby increase our national responsibilities'[23] in Zululand.

This is not to say that the settlement was not of great significance to Zulu history. The Zulu people had retained possession of most of their land, but, when they lost the king and the state army by the settlement, they lost the means to defend it. And, although Britain was no longer prepared to facilitate the development of capitalism by using military force, the overall situation which had brought about confederation was still in existence. In particular colonial Natal still looked at Zulu land and labour, perhaps even more enviously than before, because Wolseley's settlement had seemingly removed Zululand even further from the colony's grasp. In Zululand itself three of the appointed chiefs, Dunn, Hamu, and Zibhebhu were self-seeking, individualistic and had direct connections with the colonial world: Zibhebhu and Hamu were leading members of the Zulu royal house; Dunn and Zibhebhu were deeply involved in trading and labour recruiting. On the other hand the settlement excluded from positions of authority, and undermined the power of, many Zulu of great status and influence as representatives of the old Zulu order. In the conjunction of these elements lay the origins of the Zulu civil war.

Notes

1   CO 879/16, 204: no. 123, Wolseley to Hicks Beach, 27 Aug. 1879, enc., Agreement to be signed by Chiefs receiving territories in Zululand.
2   Ibid.
3   C. A. Wheelwright, another Natal official, filled the post for a few months before Osborn took it up.
4   A. Preston (ed.), *The South African Journal of Sir Garnet Wolseley, 1879–80*, Cape Town, 1973, p. 56, entry for 14 July 1879.
5   Ibid., p. 53, entry for 8 July 1879.
6   Ibid., pp. 93–4, entry for 22 Aug. 1879.
7   John Wesley Shepstone (1827–1916) was a brother of Theophilus and throughout his life his elder brother appears to have been successful in keep-

ing him employed, first in the Cape, then in the Natal administrations. He was Resident Magistrate in Natal before becoming Acting Secretary for Native Affairs in 1876, a post he held until 1884 when he became Judge of the Native High Court. Bulwer had pressed John Shepstone on Wolseley, but the latter had refused to have him until an accident incapacitated his adviser, Fred Fynney. The 'treachery' to which Wolseley alluded was a reference to the 'Matshana affair' when John Shepstone lured a Natal chief to a peaceful meeting, and then produced a hidden pistol. In the ensuing fracas some thirty Africans were killed (see above, p. 34).

8 See *Wolseley's Journal*, pp. 78–9, entry for 8 Aug. 1879, and p. 97, entry for 25 Aug. 1879; and SNA 1/7/12: J. W. Shepstone, Report of Acting Secretary for Native Affairs on report of the Zulu Boundary Commission, 9 Jan. 1880.

9 BPP, C.2482: 87, p. 257, Wolseley to Hicks Beach, 3 Sept. 1879.

10 CO 879/16, 204: no. 151, Wolseley to Hicks Beach, 9 Sept. 1879, enc. 1, and enc. 2.

11 BPP, C.3466: Map, 'Zululand: Showing the thirteen Chieftainships into which the country is divided', p, 338.

12 CO 879/16, 204: no. 151, enc. 2, Instructions for the guidance of the Zululand Boundary Commission.

13 The following section on the territories awarded to the appointed chiefs is based on information drawn from dispatches from Wolseley to Hicks Beach in CO 879/16, 204: nos. 151, 253, 294, and encs. written between 9 Sept. 1879 and 11 Nov. 1879; and letters from the British Resident in GHZ 677 and GH 844 and SNA 1/1/36: The reader is also referred to Map VI, p. 73.

14 KC, Stuart Papers: Evidence of Ndukwana, 1 Oct. 1900. This view is also put forward by Mnyamana's descendants.

15 CO 879/17, 215: no. 49, Report of the Zulu Boundary Commission, enc. (e).

16 Colenso, series 2: Letter from Fynney to Editor, *The Natal Mercury,* 3 April 1882, p. 174; *The Court of Special Commissioners for Zululand: November 15th 1888 to April 27th 1889*, London, 1889, p. 14.

17 ZA 1: R. Robertson to J. Shepstone, 9 Jan. 1880; Wheelwright to Bulwer, 12 Jan. 1880; Report by H. Shepstone, 22 Jan. 1880; Bulwer to Wheelwright, 23 Jan. 1880; Wheelwright to Bulwer, 29 Jan. 1880; minute by Bulwer to Wolseley, 5 Feb. 1880.

18 M. Wilson and L. Thompson (eds), *The Oxford History of South Africa*, Oxford, 1971, ii, p. 265.

19 See *Wolseley's Journal*, p. 201, entry for 4 Jan. 1880, where he writes that 'all except that young villain Ussibebu [Zibhebhu] are said to be either imbeciles or cripples'.

20 See, for example, GHZ 677: Wolseley to Bulwer, 12 Dec. 1879.

21 CO 879/16, 204: no. 253, enc. 6, President of the Zulu Boundary Commission to Bulwer, 25 Sept. 1879, p. 507

22 CO 879/16, 204: no. 39, Wolseley to Hicks Beach, 19 July 1879, p. 67.

23 *Wolseley's Journal*, p. 131, entry for 9 Oct. 1879.

CHAPTER SIX

The origins of the civil war

The Shepstone clique

From the time of its inception Wolseley's settlement was attacked from all sides. Natal settlers argued that the terrible sacrifices demanded of the colony by Britain during the war had been for nothing. Zululand should have been annexed and opened to white settlement, its people taxed and brought under white rule, or arrangements made to facilitate the movement of Africans from Natal to Zululand thereby relieving the pressure on land in the colony. The Zululand missionaries were especially critical when they discovered that the settlement did not recognise the 'land grants' made to them by the Zulu kings. Most critics made the obvious point that there was no coercive force in Zululand to ensure that the chiefs would keep the terms by which they were appointed; Cetshwayo had been removed but the authority he had exercised was replaced by that of thirteen other tyrants.

The most significant criticisms of the settlement came from Sir Theophilus Shepstone. The ex-Secretary for Native Affairs for Natal and Administrator of the Transvaal had now been retired and, as a leading figure in a disastrous political experiment, was under something of a cloud. His long career had ended ignominiously, one of his sons and those of many of his friends had died at Isandlwana, and the Zulu saw him as a traitor to the king and largely responsible for the war. He exulted in Cetshwayo's capture, an event which he felt had shown 'the world and especially . . . the black South African world that we are the dominant race when we choose to assert our supremacy and maintain it by force.'[1]

The Colonial Office had not allowed Shepstone to play a part in the Zulu settlement but they did ask him to comment on Wolseley's plans. In two extremely critical memoranda he expressed the view that the settlement was 'too feeble'; Cetshwayo's government should be replaced by one 'less barbarous . . . but equally strong'. How could it be ensured that the chiefs kept the terms of their appointment if the British Resident had only diplomatic powers? Shepstone asked. What obligations did the British have towards the chiefs they had appointed, and what were the 'ancient laws' the chiefs had to apply?

> We cannot rid ourselves of the responsibilities which the results of the war, and which the frank acceptance of those results by the Zulu people have placed upon us, by the simple device of practically leaving them to themselves, after we have taken away their head, and advising them not to hurt each other.[2]

What should have been established after the war, Sir Theophilus argued, was 'effective control' over Zululand by white agents of the Natal government placed with the appointed chiefs, all under a Chief Resident. They could be supported by a sum of money raised by the appointed chiefs themselves from their people.[3]

Shepstone's views impressed the officials at the Colonial Office and they were sent to the Cabinet and to Wolseley for consideration.[4] When he read the first memorandum Wolseley was shocked.[5] He wrote an aggressive dispatch to Hicks Beach, pointing out that he had been instructed by the Cabinet to devise an arrangement which avoided making Britain responsible for the future government of Zululand, and yet annexation was just what Shepstone's criticisms implied.[6] Hicks Beach capitulated and Wolseley was sent an apologetic dispatch which officially confirmed the terms of the settlement.[7]

Although Shepstone's comments on the settlement failed to have any impact on imperial policy on this occasion, they are still of importance for they demonstrate the significant difference in attitude towards Zululand between Britain and colonial Natal. In the coming years Shepstone was to write more memoranda, many of which were accepted by the Colonial Office and were to have a significant bearing on events in Zululand.

In late 1879, however, neither the Conservative government, under attack for reckless expansionism, nor the Liberal government which followed it into power early in 1880, felt that direct control over Zululand was in Britain's interests; and to hand the country over to avaricious but impoverished Natal would be hazardous as long as Britain was ultimately responsible for the colony's defence. The maintenance of British supremacy in southern Africa was necessary primarily to secure the vital trade route from Europe to India, the Far East and Australasia. Out of this arose the need to exclude foreign powers from southern Africa's coastline and to deny access to the sea to the Boers of the interior.[8] Once the military strength of the Zulu had been terminated, and as long as the Zulu people remained divided and powerless, there was no need for Zululand to be included within the formal boundaries of the Empire; the Zulu served imperial interests sufficiently merely by occupying their territory, thereby blocking Boer expansion to the south-east, and possible foreign occupation of the coast.

However, from Natal came the demand that Zululand be subordinated to the colony's economic interests. Various factions among the settlers had different ideas on how this could best be achieved. But it was the views held by Sir Theophilus Shepstone and the group of officials who identi-fied themselves with him which eventually succeeded in influencing metropolitan attitudes and policy towards Zululand.

This was an intricate process, often informal and therefore not recorded overtly in official documents, but of greatest significance to the develop-ment of the civil war, and much of the subsequent narrative will be concerned with bringing it to the surface.

The most influential figure next to Shepstone himself was Melmoth Osborn. He was described as Shepstone's 'greatest friend'[9] and for twenty years had been employed in the Natal civil service. He was Chief Magis-trate at Newcastle when he joined Shepstone's staff in the Transvaal, from where he moved to take up the post of British Resident in Zululand in March 1880, and he remained the most important colonial official in Zululand throughout the decade.[10]

Osborn had grown up in a settler community, gained his administrative experience in Natal, and was closely associated with Sir Theophilus Shepstone. He brought with him to Zululand the prejudices and short-comings which can be expected of a man of his background. He was convinced of the superiority of the white race and he had reached maturity and worked in a system which held that the acquisition of African land and the exploitation of African labour were signs of civilisation and progress. By accepting the post of British Resident in Zululand Osborn placed himself in an invidious position. Wolseley's settlement purported to set up a viable administrative and political system which needed only guidance from the Resident to operate smoothly. This was an invalid assumption however, and Osborn found himself under pressure to intervene actively in Zulu affairs although he did not have authority to do so. Moreover, as a result of his settler background and his continuing links with the officials in Natal, in particular his private correspondence with Theophilus Shepstone, this interference took a form which attempted to ensure that the divisive system forced on the Zulu by Wolseley was perpetuated. Any attempt by the royal house to assert itself was seen as a threat to the Zulu people as a whole and to the security of their neighbours.

As British Resident, Osborn was responsible at first to the High

Commissioner and later to the Governor of Natal who was also Special Commissioner for Zululand.[11] These men were directly responsible to the Secretary of State for the Colonies. After Wolseley left, his successors depended heavily on the counsel of Sir Theophilus Shepstone,[12] none of them feeling they could risk acting without the advice of this famous native administrator. He lived a short distance from Government House in Pietermaritzburg and in the coming years was to give informal advice and submit memoranda and reports which were used officially to explain, recommend and justify policy adopted by the government towards the Zulu.

Theophilus Shepstone had other means of influencing events in Zululand. Natal's Secretary for Native Affairs, although not formally connected with Zululand, was continually called upon for advice, to meet deputations from Zululand and to handle Zulu matters in the colony. Until 1884 the Acting SNA was Sir Theophilus' brother, John; he was succeeded by Henrique Shepstone, Sir Theophilus' son.

The influence that these Natal officials brought to bear on the Special Commissioner for Zululand was, on a number of crucial occasions, profound. As a result this imperial officer tended to reflect colonial interests, and this brought him into conflict with his superiors in London. These differences in approach to Zulu affairs between settler Natal and metropolitan Britain were soon detected by the Zulu and became an important factor in the development of their political strategy. For these reasons the civil war which broke out in Zululand in the 1880s can only partly be understood in terms of forces which had their origin in Zulu society, for these forces were affected fundamentally by others originating both in Natal and in Britain.

Zibhebhu, Dunn and Hamu

After Wolseley and the last British troops left Zululand in September 1879 the Zulu occupied themselves with reorganising their social life and concentrated on the urgent tasks of rehabilitation so that they might take full advantage of the spring rains and sow the coming year's harvest. There was of course much confusion: the British withdrawal after the war which had cost so much seemed inexplicable and many doubted that the settlement, which was obviously so inadequate, could possibly be a permanent arrangement.[13]

Traders, adventurers, border farmers, Natal Africans and officials took advantage of the disruption in Zululand and played on Zulu fears that the

British intended to seize their cattle or, by posing as officials, persuaded many Zulu to part with their stock.[14] Jantjie, a favoured 'induna' attached to the office of the SNA in Natal, drove into the colony over four hundred head of cattle which he had collected from Zulu chiefs as 'thank offerings' to the 'government'. The Lieutentant Governor in Natal, Sir Henry Bulwer, investigated this piece of extortion and discovered that John Shepstone, acting SNA and adviser to Wolseley in Zululand, was implicated, and the matter was dealt with privately. It delayed but did not stop John Shepstone from becoming Judge of the Native High Court in Natal in 1884.[15]

However, if most of the Zulu were left confused at the end of the war by Britain's apparent retreat from their country, three of the appointed chiefs – Zibhebhu, Hamu and John Dunn – realised quite clearly how to use the authority that had been granted them by the settlement to their own advantage.

As he moved back to re-establish himself in Zululand after the war, Hamu began making good the losses he had suffered as a result of his defection, his people looting 'whenever they had an opportunity'.[16] Dunn secured the tremendous advantages his new position had given him as the leading trader in Zululand by demanding a £25 licence fee[17] from any trader entering the country thus forcing rivals to avoid all the Thukela drifts and to enter the country to the north of his territory through Rorke's Drift. And both Dunn and Zibhebhu moved quickly into the area to the north-east of the country, now labelled by Wolseley as the country to be 'handed back' to the 'Tongas'.

By running the northern and north-eastern border of Zululand along the Phongolo and down the Lubombo, Wolseley excluded a large number of people who, although not as closely integrated into the social and political life of the Zulu as those living to the south-west, were nonetheless considered to be members of the kingdom. Through this area passed the trade route to the north over which travelled goods, tribute to the Zulu kings, cattle, firearms and labourers on their way to Natal. As we have seen, both Dunn and Zibhebhu were actively involved in this area before the invasion. During the war this district gained an added significance as herds of cattle, many of them belonging to the royal house, were sent there for safety. Wolseley's exclusion of this area from any form of British authority, and the withdrawal of the authority of the Zulu royal house, had the effect of throwing it open to economic exploitation, and Dunn and Zibhebhu led the scramble for the spoils, their task facilitated by Wolseley's injunction that appointed chiefs were to collect royal cattle and firearms.

Before he had even been visited by the Boundary Commission, Zibhebhu had seized cattle from the important Nyawo, under Sambane, who lived on the Lubombo, on the grounds that they were in possession of royal herds.[18] Dunn was later accused of taking Ndabuko's cattle at this time from the same area.[19] Reports from Delagoa Bay suggested that Dunn was demanding tribute from people in the region soon after the war,[20] and Zibhebhu appears to have tried to get control over the labourers passing from Thonga country to Natal.[21]

Before the war a young white from Natal, Johan Colenbrander, had served as a link between Dunn and Zibhebhu. He now took up residence with the Mandlakazi chief and became his adviser, secretary, resident trader and gun-runner. He also began training a mounted squadron recruited from Zibhebhu's followers.[22] Reports reached Natal that Zibhebhu and Colenbrander were forcing people from the area to the north-east of Zibhebhu's territory to take up contracts in Natal and then demanding half their wages and seizing cattle.[23] One of Zibhebhu's Thonga victims tried to persuade a colonist to act on his people's behalf but refused to let him pass the complaints to the Natal officials.[24] This wariness was well warranted. It was Dunn who had warned the Acting Secretary for Native Affairs in Natal, John Shepstone, of the activities of Jantjie and in return he received a letter from Shepstone thanking him for writing 'quietly', pledging friendship and promising to keep Dunn 'straight' with the government.[25]

Although the exact nature of Dunn and Zibhebhu's activities after the war in this inaccessible region to the north-east is difficult to ascertain, there is no doubt that they used rough methods to gain control over trade and labour originating or passing through the area, and that they seized for themselves a considerable amount of the property and the cattle hidden there during the war, much of it belonging to the exiled king and his family.

The three appointed chiefs were also very active within their borders in seizing cattle and fining people for the alleged concealment of royal herds. Dunn collected many, handed them over to the authorities and then bought them back at, it was alleged, very low prices. Hamu singled out the Qulusi and Buthelezi as the groups most guilty of retaining royal cattle, and he petitioned the British for support in a claim to the property of the deposed king.[26] Zibhebhu was accused of handing over only a portion of the cattle he took from royal homesteads.[27]

Most of the members of the royal family, their homes and their property, were situated in the region north of the Black Mfolozi, now under Hamu and Zibhebhu. Of all the Zulu they and their followers had suffered most directly as a result of the war and the settlement. Previously the most favoured group in the land, they were now left without authority or recognition; their humiliation was made worse when Zibhebhu and Dunn began collecting their cattle and property, and fining them for failing to hand it over voluntarily. These activities after the war on the part of Hamu, Zibhebhu and Dunn caused long-lasting resentment among the Zulu.

Cetshwayo's immediate family was particularly vulnerable to Zibhebhu. Many of their personal homesteads, including those of Ndabuko and Ziwedu, were situated within his western boundaries. Moreover the king had used the Mandlakazi district as a place of refuge during the war. He sent his *isigodlo* (the royal women) there together with his personal herds from the 'great house' when war broke out.[28] And after the battle of Ulundi Cetshwayo showed even greater trust in Zibhebhu when he placed his only son, Dinuzulu, in the Mandlakazi chief's charge.[29]

Zibhebhu's actions towards Dinuzulu and Cetshwayo's household at this time, and the response of the *abantwana*, have been fiercely debated for it was in these events that participants saw the origins of the civil war. According to Zulu royalists it soon became obvious that Zibhebhu was determined to increase his wealth and status at the expense of the royal family. One of Stuart's informants expressed this point of view in these terms:

> Zibebu was appointed Guardian of Dinuzulu, as the Govt. looked on Ndabuko and Ziwedu as unsuitable. Well, when Dinuzulu saw that Zibebu was 'consuming' property belonging to the Royal House he left him and went to Mnyamana. It was in consequence of this desire of Zibebu to set himself up as practically King in place of Cetshwayo that stirred up the wrath and intriguing of Ndabuko.[30]

Another of Stuart's informants put forward another interpretation. He alleged that after his capture Cetshwayo was asked what he wanted done with his dependants. Cetshwayo then gave them to Zibhebhu and, with official permission, a hundred head of cattle were given to Zibhebhu to support the royal wives and children.

> Zibebu then rode off on horseback towards Banganomo with Dinuzulu. Ndabuko & the other Usutu heads (Ziwedu Mahanana Mnyamana) followed on foot. After going a little way, Ndabuko declared that they being of the house of Senzangakona would not consent to eat off the dishes . . . of the house of Sojiyisa. . . .[31]

Zibhebhu was eventually persuaded to return Dinuzulu and Cetshwayo's wives, but he refused to hand over the hundred head of cattle. The royal brothers objected, retaliated, and fighting broke out.

There are many accounts of these first disputes between the royal brothers, and Zibhebhu and Hamu. Although contradictory, depending which side the informant takes, they do demonstrate that the opposing factions were arguing from different premises. Ndabuko and his brothers saw themselves as the successors of the Zulu royal house; even though they were now denied supreme political power they were still entitled to certain rights and privileges, and they were heirs to the personal property of their ancestors and that of their exiled brother. Zibhebhu and Hamu on the other hand, saw themselves as appointees of the British and part of the new order proclaimed by their conquerors; this gave them authority over the people in their territories, including the other members of the royal house who had been explicitly excluded from authority by the British.

Furthermore, on a personal level, both Hamu and Zibhebhu were aggressive and avaricious men. The Boundary Commissioners saw this. Hamu, they felt, 'has higher aspirations than the government of his own location. Both he and his followers give themselves airs assumed by no others.'[32] Of Zibhebhu they said that he

> is a grasping ambitious man . . . more advanced than any other Zulu we have met, for instance he rides hard if not well, he has some ideas of counting and of time, and in fact made himself very useful to us from his knowledge of the country and his power of getting quickly over the ground.[33]

There are interesting suggestions in this statement. It would appear that the 'grasping ambitious' qualities which the Boundary Commissioners discerned were not just personal foibles. Both Hamu and Zibhebhu were more closely connected with the colonial world than most Zulu. Hamu was addicted to white man's liquor, lived in the company of a white trader, and of course had gone over to the invaders' side during the war. Zibhebhu was the most active and best known Zulu trader, his commercial transactions covered a wide part of south-east Africa and he worked together with the most important trader in the area, John Dunn, also an appointed chief. For Zibhebhu, and probably for Hamu, cash and coin had a significance lacking for most Zulu; cattle were acquired not only for consumption and redistribution in the Zulu social system, but because they had a commercial value in the colonial system as well. And it was Zibhebhu's and Hamu's aggressive exercise of authority, especially the property they seized, which created the animosity which eventually developed into civil war.

The Usuthu³⁴ and Bishopstowe

On 9 February 1880 two Zulu messengers and their attendants arrived at Bishopstowe, the residence of John William Colenso, Bishop of Natal, a few miles outside Pietermaritzburg. They were Mfunzi of the Mpungose, the best-known and most respected royal messenger before the invasion, and Mgwazeni, brother of Cetshwayo's mother, and a member of a segment of the Zungu under Mbopha of the Hlabisa, and now under the authority of Zibhebhu.³⁵

Mfunzi and Mgwazeni informed the Bishop that they had been sent by Ndabuko,³⁶ Shingana, Sitheku and Ziwedu (all sons of Mpande); the king's chief minister, Mnyamana; Qethuka, chief of the Magwaza and leading officer in the Zulu army, from Dunn's district; Sitshaluza, brother of Masiphula, Mpande's chief minister, of the Emgazini now placed under Mgojana; Mahubulwana, *induna* of the Qulusi; the appointed chiefs Ntshingwayo and Sekethwayo, *izikhulu* under Cetshwayo and Mpande; the late Gawozi's brother, Siyunguza of the Mpungose, and other important chiefs in Zululand. They had been instructed to ask the Bishop's advice. The house of Mpande was being oppressed by Zibhebhu; he had 'eaten up' the cattle that had been left to support the king's dependants, and those belonging to Ndabuko; he was also demanding that members of the royal house do menial tasks for him, and threatened to dishonour the memory of both the king and his father, Mpande. They felt that Zibhebhu intended to destroy Cetshwayo's family, and the messengers asked Colenso if he thought that they would be allowed to petition the Governor personally and request that Mpande's children be allowed to occupy a territory of their own, independent of that of Zibhebhu.

Colenso was cautious in his advice. He recommended that the messengers visit the office of the SNA and make their request, and sent a letter to the acting SNA John Shepstone, introducing the Zulu messengers.³⁷

The Zulu messengers had some further questions for the Bishop which concerned the exiled king. They carried with them the presentation copy of the official account of the 'coronation' of Cetshwayo by Sir Theophilus Shepstone and they asked Colenso which of the 'promises' Cetshwayo had made on that occasion he was supposed to have broken, thereby bringing about the invasion of his country and his exile. For their part they knew of none. They also had some medicine which they asked Colenso to forward to the king.

From these questions we can see that members of the royal house and some of their supporters were attempting to obtain information on which

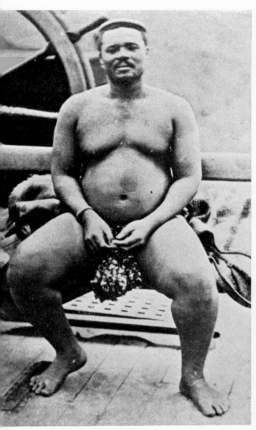

shwayo kaMpande, king of the Zulu, on his way to Cape Town (left); Mkhosana of Zungu, Cetshwayo's friend and confidant, who shared his exile (right)

The local officials: Sir Theophilus
Shepstone, *Somtsewu* (right);
Melmoth Osborn, *Malimathe*
(below)

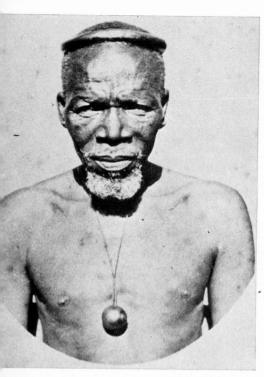

The Usuthu messengers in Natal,
February 1880: Mfunzi of the
Mpungose, confidential messenger
of the Zulu royal house (left);
Mgwazeni kaMbonde of the
Zungu, brother of Cetshwayo's
mother (below)

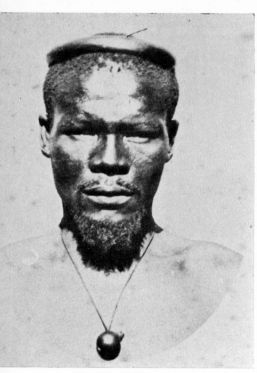

Bishopstowe: John William Colenso,
Bishop of Natal (right), with daughters
Harriette (below left) and Frances (below
right)

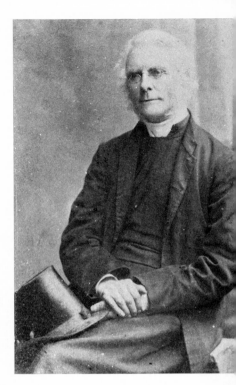

to base a strategy which would give them some means of protecting their interests. They also wanted to make contact if they could with the exiled king. Colenso promised to try to forward the medicine to Cetshwayo, and the messengers replied:

> Now what will those in Zululand say, who insist that he is dead, when we tell them that we have sent Nkomankoma [the medicine] to him? That will show that he's alive![38]

The man whom the Usuthu had chosen to consult, John William Colenso, was born in England in 1814. After an outstanding academic career at Cambridge he married in 1846 and accepted the living at Forncett St Mary, Norfolk. There, four of his five children were born: Harriette, Francis (known as Frank), Frances and Robert. In 1852 Robert Gray, Bishop of Cape Town, asked Colenso to establish the diocese of Natal. Colenso built Bishopstowe near Pietermaritzburg and founded the mission Ekukhunyeni (place of light) close by. Here his fifth child Agnes was born.

For most of the thirty years that this enormously talented man spent in Natal he was involved in bitter disputes, first over theological, constitutional and legal matters, and then in the final decade of his life, over the treatment of Africans in Natal and Zululand.

By attempting to present Christianity to the heathen as a reasoned, universal faith he invoked the wrath of his Metropolitan; and when he wrote a critical study of the Pentateuch in the light of contemporary scientific discoveries he was attacked by his church and finally found guilty of heresy and excommunicated by Bishop Gray. His appeal against this was upheld on legal grounds, a decision not wholly satisfactory to either party. Deprived of funds and clergy, Colenso's work suffered and, although he refused to give up office, his ambitious projects in the field of African education were never fulfilled.

Despite his excommunication and the many attacks made on him, Colenso managed to keep a number of influential friends and supporters in southern Africa and Britain. In Natal his most important ally and most intimate friend was Theophilus Shepstone. But in 1873 Colenso protested against the manner in which Natal put down the alleged rebellion of Langalibalele and his Hlubi people. Convinced that Langalibalele had suffered a terrible wrong at the hands of the Natal government, Colenso broke off relations with Shepstone. This rupture in their relationship was one of the great tragedies of Shepstone's life.

> Good God! [Shepstone wrote to Harriette Colenso] I never could have supposed it possible that the close friendship, aye, love, of 20 years could thus easily have been shaken & wrecked.

In reply Harriette protested at these phrases; there was nothing easy in the decision her father had to make. When he reluctantly came to the conclusion that Shepstone was acting out of 'expediency' and not in the cause of 'Truth and Justice',

> he felt that he had no choice left. And, as once in theological matters he had risked everything – his means of living, his reputation, his early friends – for the sake of what he believed to be the truth, so now for that same conscience sake, although the sacrifice was at least as great, although (as he said to me in the first bitterness of it), 'the light had all gone out from his life in Natal' – he must give up even his dearest friend.[39]

Colenso drew up a defence for Langalibalele, and when that failed he travelled to England to intervene personally on the chief's behalf with the Secretary of State.[40] When Cetshwayo heard of this he sent Mfunzi to Colenso with the following message:

> Cetshwayo rejoices exceedingly to hear that you have gone to the great indunas of the Queen to tell them all the story about the treatment of the black people of Natal, and to say that he prays that you, sir, would fight with all your might, as you have done already, about the matter of Langalibalele. Cetshwayo says that he is in good hope, and, even if you are worsted that is of no consequence, you will have done what becomes a faithful *induna* of the Queen. And you are to remember him continually, as he also remembers you.[41]

Colenso was a social evolutionist and this standpoint linked his ideas on biblical history with his attitude to human societies and the theological and political controversies in which he was involved. The history of mankind to Colenso was the history of man's emergence

> more and more out of darkness into light, out of slavish fears and superstitions into the liberty of God's children, out of confusion and ignorance into the clearer knowledge of the Living God.[42]

The writings of the Old Testament represented the stage knowledge had reached in a more ignorant age, and modern man had to use the God-given insights of the scientific era and apply them critically to these religious works in order that the 'Living Word which speaks in the Book' might be discerned more clearly.

Colenso's attitude to African societies was also evolutionist; but instead of using this philosophical position to emphasise the backwardness of African culture and the superiority of that of nineteenth-century Europe as became common practice, Colenso drew attention to the proximity of human societies on the evolutionary ladder. He believed that

> Wherever we meet with the power of speech with reason and conscience, with human affections we must confess that the owner of such gifts is a man and a brother, – that he has a claim as a member of the great human family; – for in

his heart is beating, even now, however faintly, the Life which we are told, is the Light of men, and lighteth every man that cometh into the world.[43]

Up to the time of the Langalibalele 'rebellion' his confidence in the British Government, both at home and abroad, as the protector of the poor and the weak, and the means by which Justice and Truth might prevail, was hardly questioned. From the time of the Langalibalele affair until Colenso's death a decade later, however, this belief was sorely tested as he saw expediency and force prevail, and the powerless and the weak, over whom God and England had placed him as protector, suffer even further. But the Bishop's energies were absorbed in practical attempts to obtain Justice by discovering and publicising the Truth about affairs in Natal, and he never reached a deeper insight into the nature of colonialism or realised he was observing and protesting against not an aberration, but the essence of the system in which he lived and worked.

Nonetheless Colenso's theological views were unacceptable to the Anglican Church, and his political and social demands were rejected by the Natal settler community. Bishop Colenso and his work suffered when first his church, and then secular Natal, attacked him for his views and his attempts to put them into practice.

The Bishop's ideas and actions had a profound influence on his family, in particular his daughters. They were to spend much of their lives in dispute with the colonial authorities on behalf of the Africans of Natal and Zululand. His eldest daughter, Harriette,[44] was known to the Africans as *Udlwedlwe* – the staff – her father's guide and support. She had her father's intelligence and capacity for work, and was an even better Zulu linguist. Harriette was very close to the youngest member of the Colenso family, the intensely shy Agnes. Frances, Colenso's second daughter, was more confident and outgoing than her sisters. She drew on her father's researches to publish important books on affairs in Natal and Zululand during the 1870s and 1880s.[45] Her publications, however, bear the marks of Frances' personal tragedy. She fell in love with her father's great friend, Major Anthony Durnford, who was to die at Isandlwana, and who many believed was responsible for the disaster. She was also suffering from tuberculosis, and she spent the last years of her life desperately trying to clear Durnford's name, and publicise the injustices which were being inflicted on the Zulu.

In the late 1870s the Colensos' attention was drawn to the aggressive policy which the High Commissioner, Sir Bartle Frere, had adopted towards the Zulu king. The Bishop had little personal knowledge of Cetshwayo at the time,[46] and, although perturbed by Frere's attitude, did not feel that he should oppose his policy. Thus, even after the Ultimatum had been presented to the Zulu, Colenso wrote that he supported Frere, trusting

> that he has spoken and written, as an English gentleman, words of straight-forward simplicity and truth. I should be exceedingly shocked to find that there is anything to be read . . . 'between the lines' of the ultimatum.[47]

By early January, however, Colenso realised that he had been misled and he wrote that it was 'now plain that Sir Bartle Frere came here fully intending to make this invasion of Zululand'.[48] But it was only during the course of the war, when the official documents were published, that Colenso became fully aware of the enormity of Frere's crime against the Zulu people.

Once again Colenso showed great courage. At the time when feeling against the Zulu was highest in Natal the Bishop, from his pulpit, closely analysed the history of events which had brought about the war, questioned the motives of those involved, and prayed for the relatives and friends of those killed on both sides. Taking as his text, 'And what doth the Lord require of thee, but to do justly, and to love mercy, and to walk humbly with thy God?' he applied it to the actions and the motives of those who brought about the war, and found them wanting. He urged his congregation not to compound the sin by demanding vengeance for their losses:

> I repeat the question, Wherein, in our invasion of Zululand, have we shown that we are men who 'love mercy'? Did we not lay upon the people heavily, from the very moment we crossed their border, the terrible scourge of war? Have we not killed already, it is said, 5,000 human beings, and plundered 10,000 head of cattle? It is true that, in that dreadful disaster, on account of which we are this day humbling ourselves before God, we ourselves have lost very many precious lives, and widows and orphans, parents, brothers, sisters, friends are mourning bitterly their sad bereavements. But are there no griefs – no relatives that mourn their dead – in Zululand? Have we not heard how the wail has gone up in all parts of the country for those who have bravely . . . and nobly died in repelling the invader and fighting for their King and fatherland? And shall we kill 10,000 more to avenge the losses of that dreadful day?[49]

When the British Command Papers containing the official dispatches which had preceded the war were published, Colenso reprinted them together with material taken from newspapers and other sources, and his own correspondence with Frere, and distributed them privately in order to expose the machinations of the imperial officials.[50] To reach a wider public he bought the journal of a trader who had been caught in Zululand by the invasion, translated and annotated it, and then used it as a vehicle to put forward his own views of the war.[51]

Cetshwayo's exile and Wolseley's settlement was to Colenso 'the crowning act of infamy to this iniquitous war',[52] and a letter written by Harriette gives an idea of the feeling at Bishopstowe at the time.

It is horrible to see the tone of most of the papers. The Zulu war has been 'a mistake' a 'sad mistake' perhaps, or even 'a most unnecessary & unjust' – but there! its over now, & the least said the soonest mended &c. &c. Over indeed! While the King, who, if the war was unjust & unnecessary, is assuredly a most innocent & injured man, is a prisoner, cut off from all friends, all help, without being allowed to speak a word in his own defence.

It is like a hideous nightmare to us, & I only wish that we could make all our friends as miserable about it as we are.[53]

Two days after this letter was written the Colensos contacted Cetshwayo, now in exile in Cape Town, by sending him a telegram:

Sobantu[54] salutes Cetshwayo: he is grieved for him: he does not forget him.

To which the king replied:

Cetshwayo thanks Sobantu for his message, and is glad to learn that he does not forget him. He hopes Sobantu will speak well for him.[55]

Sobantu was to exceed all Cetshwayo's expectations.

The visit of the Zulu messengers, Mfunzi and Mgwazeni, to the office of the Secretary for Native Affairs was not a success. Their interview with John Shepstone on 10 February 1880 resulted in a slapdash minute to Bulwer. In Shepstone's view:

The message they carry is to beg that Ndabuko . . . be given a district to occupy, in fact to place him in position in Zululand, for it can mean nothing else.

I need scarcely point out that such a step would have the effect of re-establishing the Zulu power under one head, which it is I believe the object of the Government to prevent.[56]

They were told the house of Cetshwayo was now destroyed and Ndabuko would receive no official recognition. However, any complaints they had against their appointed chiefs should be made to the British Resident.[57]

Mfunzi and Mgwazeni returned to Bishopstowe where Colenso had prepared a detailed answer to their request that he inform them of the charges brought against Cetshwayo by Frere. As he read them out the Zulu messengers denied them vigorously, their answers confirming the conclusions that the Bishop had reached through his analyses of the Blue Books. Moreover, far from being hated, they asserted, Cetshwayo was loved by the Zulu people: 'all Zululand' would attend any inquiry into his actions and defend him; indeed they would have done so before now

only that our hearts were dead at first at their taking him over the sea, for people said 'They have killed him and thrown him into the sea!' But now the

Great Chiefs have determined to inquire, if they may be allowed to do so, according to the word which they send to Sobantu about the Book.[58]

Mfunzi and Mgwazeni went back to Zululand and reported to the Usuthu leaders who had sent them. They passed on much important information. They had learnt at Bishopstowe something of the external forces which had brought about the invasion of their country and the exile of their king, and the officials who were responsible for it. Although they had not been received sympathetically at the office of the SNA, they had discovered that in the Colenso family they had sympathetic advisers and perhaps even allies. Moreover they had initiated contact with their exiled leader, Cetshwayo.

But they also had little reason to hope for significant changes. Their request for an independent chiefdom had been turned down without hesitation. Moreover Colenso had advised them to follow John Shepstone's instructions and report their grievances to the British Resident and warned them not to hope for Cetshwayo's return. Sir Garnet Wolseley had declared unequivocally that the king would never return to Zululand.[59]

And yet three months later over two hundred Zulu arrived in Natal to complain of the actions of Zibhebhu and Hamu towards them and to appeal for the return of Cetshwayo to Zululand. The explanation for this lay in changing political circumstances in Britain. The Usuthu, the representatives of the old order in Zululand, who had resisted change in southern Africa so effectively that they had brought the weight of an imperial army against them, were now having to make political calculations which took into consideration the changing fortunes of British political parties.

Notes

1 KC, Shepstone collection: folder f, T. Shepstone to H. Shepstone, 24 Sept. 1879.
2 CO 879/16, 204: no. 168, T. Shepstone, Further memorandum on the Settlement of Zululand, 14 Oct. 1879.
3 CO 879/16, 204: no. 168, T. Shepstone, Memorandum on Wolseley's scheme, 23 Aug. 1879.
4 CO 179/132: 16424, minutes on Shepstone's memos.
5 A. Preston (ed.), *The South African Journal of Sir Garnet Wolseley, 1879–80*, Cape Town, 1973, pp. 130–1, entry for 9 Oct. 1879.
6 CO 879/16, 204: no. 221, Wolseley to Hicks Beach, 9 Oct. 1879.
7 CO 879/16, 204: no. 243, Hicks Beach to Wolseley, 27 Nov. 1879; CO 179/130: 18089, minutes on Wolseley to Hicks Beach, 9 Oct. 1879.
8 R. Robinson and J. Gallagher, *Africa and the Victorians. The Official Mind of Imperialism*, London, 1961, pp. 59–75.

9 *Wolseley's Journal*, p. 270, entry for 13 April 1880.

10 For biographical details see KC, file marked Melmoth Osborn; and H. Rider Haggard, *The Days of My Life*, London, 1906, i, *passim*.

11 They were *High Commissioners*: Sir Garnet Wolseley, June 1879–April 1880; Sir George Pomery Colley, July 1880–Feb. 1881; Sir Evelyn Wood, Feb.–Dec. 1881. *Officer Administering Government of Natal*: C. B. H. Mitchell, Dec. 1881–March 1882. *Governor of Natal and Special Commissioner for Zululand*: Sir Henry Bulwer, March 1882–Oct. 1885: Sir Arthur Havelock, Feb. 1886–May 1887.

12 Although for a time in 1880 Sir Theophilus felt that the administration was slighting him (see KC, Shepstone papers: folder f, T. Shepstone to H. Shepstone, 7 July 1880), Colley soon made amends. See NA, T. Shepstone collection: Colley to T. Shepstone, 15 Sept. 1880.

13 See GHZ 677: Special Border Agent Fannin to Col. Sec., 25 Oct. 1879; CO 879/16, 204: Wolseley to Hicks Beach, 17 Nov. 1879, enc., W. Campbell to SNA, 24 Oct. 1879.

14 Ibid., and GH 844: Wheelwright to Bulwer, 6 Dec. 1879; GHZ 677: Administrator, Pretoria, to Wolseley, 22 April 1880 (teleg.).

15 See J. Shepstone's minute, 27 Oct. 1879 on W. Campbell to SNA, 24 Oct. 1879 cited in n. 13 above, and the minutes on Wood to Kimberley, 17 Oct. 1881, 20002, in CO 179/138. Because they dealt with the case in private any relevant documents do not appear in the official files, but in the Wood collection (NA) there is an unsigned, undated, confidential letter (in III/2/22) written from the office of the Col. Sec. (Natal) to Wood, which states:

> Bulwer was on the point of making John judge of the N.H.C. in the latter part of 1879 but an ugly looking matter – never got to the bottom of but circumstantially strong – respecting certain levies of cattle from Zulu chiefs which accidentally came to the knowledge of Govt. prevented Sir Henry from making the appointment.

16 CO 879/16, 204: no. 253, enc. 2, Villiers to Bulwer, 16 Sept. 1879. See also a number of documents in GH 844, especially Capt. MacLeod to Chief of Staff, 29 Sept. 1879; Bulwer to Wheelwright, 23 Oct. 1879; Wheelwright to Bulwer, 6 Feb. 1880; *A*, statement by Manziyezulu, 9 June 1880; Minute by Osborn, 12 June 1880; also Colenso, series 1, p. 745.

17 BPP, C.2505: 16, enc. 2, Letter by Fynney, 31 Oct. 1879.

18 GH 844; Osborn to Herbert, 22 April 1880; Osborn to Governor, 27 April 1880; and BPP, C.3182: 34, *K*, Inquiry into complaints of Ndabuko, Ziwedu, against Zibhebhu – Ndabuko's statement beginning 'Shortly after the conclusion of the Zulu war . . .', p. 50.

19 Colenso, series 1, p. 691.

20 CO 179/136: 3004, Consul O'Neill to Marquis of Salisbury, 1 Jan. 1880, minutes and enclosures.

21 GH 1402: statement by Kijimana, one of Dunn's men, taken by Fynney, 16 Jan. 1880.

22 B. H. Kemp, 'Johan William Colenbrander: A history of his times and the people and events with which he was associated, 1879–1896' (PhD thesis, University of Natal, 1962), i, p. 33.

23 SNA 1/4/3: 4/80, statement by Unteto of Unmangaliso's tribe, taken by Fynney, 26 March 1880.

24 The information was sent nonetheless. ZA 21: W. Campbell to J. Shepstone, n.d.

25 KC, John Dunn papers: J. Shepstone to Dunn, 8 Oct. 1879.

26 SNA 1/1/35: 1926, Wheelwright to J. Shepstone, 4 Oct. 1879; and the reply in ZA 21: 18 Oct. 1879.

27 BPP, C.3182: 34, *K*, Inquiry into complaints of Ndabuko, Ziwedu, against Zibhebhu, p. 59.

28 KC, Maphelu, p. 9.

29 Ibid.; see also KC, Stuart Papers: Evidence of Mpatshana, 30055, Native habits and customs in war. For a variant of this see C. T. Binns, *Dinuzulu; the death of the House of Shaka*, London, 1968, pp. 2–5. Chief Gatsha Buthelezi in a personal communication has explained this apparent trust in Zibhebhu by saying that, while Zibhebhu was of the royal lineage, he was not close enough genealogically to the king's family to be able to make a claim as Cetshwayo's successor through his guardianship of Dinuzulu.

30 KC, Stuart Papers: Evidence of Mpatshana, 30055, Native habits and customs in war.

31 KC, Stuart Papers: Evidence of Kanisile and Ndabazezwe, 9 July 1921.

32 CO 879/16, 204: no. 294, Villiers to Bulwer, 7 Oct. 1879.

33 ZA 1: Bulwer to Wheelwright, 7 Jan. 1880, extract from Report of the Zulu Boundary Commission. This seems to be the Report that Wolseley suppressed because of its disparaging descriptions of the appointed chiefs; see above, p. 76.

34 Before the civil war of 1856 the name Usuthu was given to Cetshwayo's following within the nation (see above, p. 13). After his accession it became a 'national' cry and after the war it was used to identify the faction which worked to revive the influence of Cetshwayo's lineage in the Zulu clan.

35 This section on the visit to Bishopstowe is based on Colenso, series 1, xxxviii, Message after the War from the great Zulu Chiefs, pp. 69 ff.

36 Ndabuko was known as Maduna at this time.

37 NA, Colenso collection: box 127, J. W. Colenso to J. Shepstone, 9 Feb. 1880.

38 Colenso, series 1, p. 692. Dabulamanzi and Shingana had travelled to the border in Oct. 1879 to try to find out about their brother.

39 KC, Colenso papers: folio 13, T. Shepstone to H. E. Colenso, 15 July 1874 and the reply, 22 [?] July 1874.

40 For a recent account of the Langalibalele affair see N. Herd, *The Bent Pine*, Johannesburg, 1976.

41 G. W. Cox, *The Life of John William Colenso, D.D., Bishop of Natal*, London, 1888, ii, p. 453, n. 2.

42 J. W. Colenso, 'The Missions to the Zulus in Natal & Zululand', reprinted in the *Social Science Review*, June 1864.

43 Ibid.

44 For an assessment of Harriette Colenso see S. Marks, 'Harriette Colenso and the Zulus, 1874–1913', *Journal of African History*, iv, 3 (1963), pp. 403–11.

45 F. E. Colenso and E. Durnford, *History of the Zulu war and its origin*, London, 1880; F. E. Colenso, *The Ruin of Zululand: an account of British doings in Zululand since the invasion of 1879*, 2 vols, London, 1884 and 1885; Atherton Wylde (pseudonym of F. E. Colenso), *My Chief and I: or, six months in Natal after the Langalibalele outbreak*, London, 1880.

46 They had met twenty years before when Colenso visited Mpande in Zulu-land.

47 J. W. Colenso to F. W. Chesson, 19 Dec. 1878, in Cox, *The Life of Colenso*, ii, p. 473. Chesson was Secretary to the Aborigines Protection Society. Colenso made contact with the APS at the time of the Langalibalele affair (ibid., p. 326ff.) and throughout the civil war the Colensos corresponded with Chesson. Until his death in 1888 Chesson proved to be a sympathetic and intelligent correspondent and friend, and the Colensos' most important publicist.

48 Ibid., p. 478, J. W. Colenso to Chesson, 14 Jan. 1879.

49 J. W. Colenso, *What doth the Lord require of us? A sermon preached in the Cathedral Church of St Peter's, Maritzburg, on Wednesday, March 12, 1879*, Pietermaritz-burg, 1879.

50 These were the 'Extracts from the Blue Books', referred to here as Colenso, series 1.

51 C. Vijn, *Cetshwayo's Dutchman, being the private journal of a white trader in Zulu-land during the British invasion*, translated, edited and annotated by J. W. Colenso, London, 1880.

52 KC, Colenso papers: Z30, J. W. Colenso to Chesson, 13 Sept. 1879.

53 KC, Colenso papers: Z244, H. E. Colenso to Chesson, 26 Oct. 1879.

54 'Father of the People', the name by which Colenso was known to Africans.

55 Cox, *The Life of Colenso*, ii, pp. 538–9.

56 ZA 21: SNA 78/80, Minute by J. Shepstone to Bulwer, 10 Feb. 1880.

57 Colenso, series 1, p. 692.

58 Ibid., p. 695. 'The Book' being the presentation copy of the official account of Shepstone's 'installation' of Cetshwayo.

59 Ibid., p. 696.

CHAPTER SEVEN

The Usuthu search for a policy

The Usuthu deputation: May 1880

It is well known that Gladstone's attack on the Conservative policy in southern Africa during his Midlothian campaign, and the subsequent Liberal victory in April 1880, gave strength and encouragement to the Transvaal Boers in their efforts to regain their independence. There can be little doubt that the news of the Liberal victory also had a considerable effect on events in Zululand. Gladstone had exploited the invasion of the kingdom during the election campaign: 'What was the crime of the Zulus?' he asked, 'no other offence than their attempt to defend against your artillery with their naked bodies their hearths and homes, their wives and families. . . .'[1]

At the news of the Liberal victory at the polls the Colensos were exultant.

> Now . . . that the Liberal majority is so magnificent [wrote the Bishop] something will be done, I presume, to rectify the enormous wrongs of the Zulu War & (so-called) Settlement. . . . I cannot but think that the Zulu War, & the revelations made with respect to it, have had considerable weight with the public mind in England – in fact have *fastened* upon it, & helped to generate the feeling which has so unmistakably pronounced itself against the late Government. In short, the Elective Returns seem to show that we were all mistaken in supposing that the English People were drugged and dead to their old principles of truth & justice. The heart of England, I trust, is still beating rightly, & will expect that, now the Liberals are trusted with *predominant* power, they shall do what can be done under existing circumstances to rectify the past.[2]

A week after Colenso wrote this letter Ndabuko appeared before the British Resident in Zululand and asked permission to visit the Governor of Natal to pay him his respects.[3] Once he had obtained his 'pass', Ndabuko used it to lead over two hundred men into Natal to complain to the Governor about their treatment at the hands of Hamu and Zibhebhu, and to ask if Cetshwayo might be allowed to return to Zululand.

It seems unlikely that it was a coincidence that Ndabuko decided to petition the Governor so soon after the news of the Liberal victory reached Natal. And it is quite possible that they received the news from Colenso that there had been a change of government in England and that, if they wished to demonstrate their feelings for the king, the time was now more propitious than it had been in February.[4]

On the evening of 24 May 1880 the large Zulu party arrived at Bishopstowe, a few miles outside Pietermaritzburg the seat of the Natal government. Many of them were servants and carriers, but Colenso counted fifty-three ringed men, of whom twenty were men of rank.[5] The party was in the charge of Cetshwayo's full brother, Ndabuko. It was his close kinship relationship with the king, and the harassment he had suffered from Zibhebhu, which had forced him into the role of leader of the Usuthu. He was a somewhat dour and unimaginative man and perhaps not the best person to have the task of leading the Usuthu thrust upon him. Nevertheless, despite severe personal suffering and loss, he was to lead the royalist faction with tenacity for eight years, until he was sent into exile on St Helena for rebellion against Her Majesty's Government. Ndabuko told Colenso that he represented Cetshwayo's son, Dinuzulu, and most of the followers of Mkhosana, who had been killed at Isandlwana. Mkhosana's successor, Somhlolo, had been excluded from the chieftainship by the appointment of Mgitshwa as chief of the Biyela.[6] Somhlolo was also to stand trial for rebellion eight years later.

Shingana, Cetshwayo's half-brother, was next in rank to Ndabuko as leader of the Usuthu party. He was quicker in mind and body than Ndabuko and not as morose. His presence at Bishopstowe in May 1880 was also the first step on a journey which was to end on St Helena. Then there was Makhoba,[7] Zibhebhu's brother, and a leading member of the *ikhohlo* branch of Maphitha's homestead, which had a long-standing dispute with Zibhebhu. Under threat from Zibhebhu after the war the *ikhohlo* had strengthened its association with the royal groups which lived near them on Zibhebhu's western border.[8] There were members of the Emgazini[9] and *izinduna* from important royal homesteads[10] that had been destroyed, as well as members of the royal lineage,[11] personal attendants of the king, and some of his maternal relatives.[12]

Ndabankulu[13] said he represented the appointed chief Faku, of whose clan the Ntombela, Ndabankulu was the most important member. Nozaza carried Sekethwayo's letter of appointment, and Mfunzi declared that he represented the appointed chief Siyunguza of the Mpungose – the same lineage to which Mfunzi belonged.[14] Mahubulwana,[15] chief *induna* of the Qulusi, was another man of great standing among the Zulu, as the officer-in-charge of this powerful royal section.

An examination of the background of the most important of these men reveals much about their political motives. Most of them came from the northern districts, from the chieftainships of Hamu and Zibhebhu. They had all lost status and authority by the settlement and had either already been victims of their appointed chiefs, or were potential victims should the appointed chiefs choose to exercise their 'legitimate authority'. Ndabuko was the only full brother of the king and was the man responsible, since the king's exile, for Cetshwayo's segment of the Zulu lineage. He had already lost property to Zibhebhu. There were representatives of various lineages closely related to Zibhebhu's, and who before the war had been in dispute with Zibhebhu, and now found themselves under his authority. There were also representatives from powerful clans in this northern region, the Emgazini and Ntombela, and of the most significant royal section, the Qulusi. Then there were leading officials from royal homesteads now under Zibhebhu, and members of the royal family who had held high official posts. The members of the deputation did not represent all groups who might have been expected to oppose Zibhebhu and Hamu; nonetheless, some of the major personalities and groups from the northern districts who had lost authority by the settlement and had been treated harshly by Hamu and Zibhebhu were there.

The decision to participate in the deputation to Natal was a major one that was not taken lightly. Most of the members had never before been out of Zululand, and they did so now with some trepidation, especially as they were visiting a country with which they had been at war so recently. By leaving Zululand they also left their homesteads and their followers at a time of some tension, when their presence was needed to supervise local affairs. This visit to Natal can be seen as the first overt political reaction on any scale to the arrangement which Wolseley had imposed on the Zulu after the war, and to the withdrawal of the political authority of the Zulu royal house. It was a peaceful attempt to bring to the notice of the colonial authorities the anomalies in the settlement and the injustices the Usuthu believed they were suffering under it. It was also a tentative attempt to suggest a possible solution to the problems in the restoration of Cetshwayo.

The Usuthu party had two official meetings with the authorities, walking in to Pietermaritzburg from Bishopstowe. Beyond the fact that they complained of the treatment they had received from Zibhebhu and Hamu, and that they requested that the king be returned to Zululand, it is difficult to discover what transpired at these meetings; no report was forwarded to London. In reply they were told that all complaints had to be made to the British Resident in Zululand.[16]

Before the Usuthu left on their 300 km walk back to their homes, Colenso took the opportunity of questioning them on the allegations made by Frere before the war on the aggressive and cruel nature of Cetshwayo's rule. It was the first meeting the Bishop and his family had with the Usuthu leaders whom they were to support and defend for the rest of their lives.[17] These conversations further confirmed the Bishop's feelings that the king commanded the loyalty of his people and that, given the constraints imposed by Zulu society, he had ruled with justice and humanity and done all he could to avoid war with the British.

The Usuthu left on 5 June. Although they had failed in their objectives, their experience had given them greater insight into the total political situation, and they had confirmed that in the Colensos they had sympathetic white supporters in the colony. In particular they had discovered much about the events which had preceded the war. Even if they received this information only indirectly from Colenso's questioning, there can be no doubt that the Usuthu came to accept the fact that the war had been brought about by the misrepresentations of certain officials in South Africa who had misled the British Government with false reports. Britain's previously inexplicable reversal of policy now made sense to the Usuthu, and they left Bishopstowe promising to answer the charges made against Cetshwayo by Frere.

The authorities react: May 1880 to January 1881

By 22 June Ndabuko and Shingana, joined by Mnyamana, reached Melmoth Osborn, the British Resident, who was living at Nhlazatshe, to make their statement as they had been instructed in Pietermaritzburg. The view that Cetshwayo had been misrepresented and unjustly treated provided the structure of their petition. Ndabuko stressed that good relations had always existed between the English and the Zulu, from the time that Shaka had protected shipwrecked sailors until the 'coronation' of Cetshwayo by Theophilus Shepstone in 1873. These cordial relations, however, had been disrupted by the invasion; but, Ndabuko hinted, ustice could yet be done and the damage repaired:

It often occurs [Ndabuko said] that people belonging to the same house have quarrels and fight. Some of them receive punishment for their conduct, but they are not killed. In this case I ask that Cetywayo may be released from his imprisonment, and allowed to return to Zululand, the land belonging to his father. . . . We do not know what wrongs Cetywayo has done to merit his punishment. . . . Cetywayo was appointed King by Sir T. Shepstone and he therefore belonged to the English house; we do not know of any wrong whatever committed by him.[18]

Ndabuko then linked this request with the complaints he had against Zibhebhu for his oppressive actions against the royal family, the Mandlakazi *ikhohlo*, and the people beyond the Lubombo. Mnyamana complained of the treatment his people had received at the hands of Hamu, and the sufferings of the Qulusi and Sebeni sections were also mentioned, and he once again requested that he be appointed an independent chief over that territory given him by Shaka.

Osborn passed the petition to Colley who was now in charge at Natal. He in turn sent it to John Shepstone who wrote a terse minute which ignored the specific complaints and informed Colley that the 'interference in the Government of Zululand' by Ndabuko 'must tend to unsettle the minds of the people'. The Usuthu should be told they are private individuals under their respective appointed chiefs, he advised Colley, and Mnyamana's claim should be turned down.[19] Three months later Ndabuko was called to Osborn's camp at Nhlazatshe and was informed by the Resident's clerk that Mnyamana had only himself to blame for refusing a chieftainship in 1879, that Ndabuko was now a commoner and that the Resident could not discuss questions of the origins and consequences of the war with him.[20] The Usuthu reported that

we came away quite struck blind and disheartened. And the messengers of Hamu and Zibebu kept coming and saying that it [*sic*] was to hear what tales we had been telling of them in Maritzburg.[21]

Indeed, far more significant than the disappointment of the Usuthu at these refusals, was the encouragement that the official stance gave Zibhebhu and Hamu. As 1880 progressed it had become clearer that there was an identity of interests between them and the officials, and they began to act more openly and with greater confidence against the Usuthu in their territories. Dunn imposed a hut tax of 5 shillings and appointed two white 'magistrates' to supervise the collection of this, and to collect licence fees and fines. Zibhebhu and Hamu imposed a tax of a beast a head. When the news reached Zibhebhu that the petition of the deputation had been rejected he punished those from his territory who had taken part.[22] Ndabuko tried to report this to Osborn but was refused a hearing and told to take his complaints to Zibhebhu his appointed chief. He was then berated by Zibhebhu for travelling to the country of the whites to tell stories against him; he taunted Ndabuko by asking him what he was doing, crossing the water (the Thukela) like little ducks to go to the whites as Mpande had done.[23] Ndabuko and Ziwedu then attempted to approach Zibhebhu privately, but this failed as well. Back Ndabuko went to Osborn but was refused permission to travel to Natal. Nonetheless he began the journey to Pietermaritzburg once again, but this time a Natal official at the border persuaded him not to continue. Secretly, however, Ndabuko sent messengers to Colenso informing him of all that had passed. The Bishop wrote to Chesson saying that, while he could not vouch for the accuracy of the messengers' statements,

> You may judge for yourself what is likely to be in the end the result of such repression of their cries for what they deem – rightly or wrongly – to be justice. . . . it is clear that an unpleasant state of things exists in Zululand which some day or other may end in fighting & revolution.[24]

Zibhebhu himself travelled to Natal in November. He behaved in a manner significantly different from the Usuthu while they were there; while they kept to themselves as far as they could, and concentrated on political matters, Zibhebhu was determined to 'see all there was to be seen' and in particular to travel on the newly opened railway between Pieter-maritzburg and Durban. He had an interview with Sir Theophilus Shepstone and told him that the views expressed by the Usuthu deputation were those of a faction which had no following among the Zulu people. He also

> spoke in very strong terms, but very sensibly of the consequences to them-selves and to the country of the machinations of the disappointed members of Cetywayo's family who, he said, seemed to think that the Government of Zululand of right belonged to them.[25]

Zibhebhu also met Colley, the Governor, who told him that he

> did not recognize any claims to the chieftainship on the part of Cetshwayo's relations but considered them to be under Usibebu, and he to be answerable for them, precisely as in the case of any ordinary native residing in his district.[26]

Statements like these confirmed the appointed chiefs' opinion that they had the authorities' support in any action they took against the Usuthu. Towards the end of November Hamu forcibly removed large numbers of cattle from Mnyamana's personal homestead and that of one of his sons,[27] and the spoiling of grain stocks forced many Buthelezi to seek refuge in other homesteads. At the end of January 1881 Zibhebhu took cattle from a number of people under him on the grounds that they were trying to bewitch him.[28] This, coming so soon after Hamu's action against the Buthelezi, convinced many Usuthu that they were in serious danger from their appointed chiefs and they deserted their homesteads fearing further attacks. It also persuaded the British Resident that, regardless of the terms of his appointment, it was absolutely necessary for him to intervene positively in Zulu affairs to avert a complete breakdown of order in the northern districts.

Ever since he had taken up the post of British Resident in March 1880 Osborn had been dissatisfied with his position. He was without formal authority to intervene in Zulu affairs and yet the Zulu treated him as the representative of the conquering power which had deposed the previous ruler and they brought him requests for mediation and intervention in their disputes. Thus he was unable to act in a situation where he felt that the exercise of authority was absolutely necessary. He wrote to his friend Shepstone that he entirely agreed with his criticism of the settlement[29]

> and do not see how it can possibly stand as it is. More power of control & machinery therefore are necessary. To provide these money must be forth-coming and the question how these ends are to be attained . . . *must soon* come under serious consideration of the Govt. . . . The Zulu people have still the fear of God in them and they will submit quietly & I may say gladly of any change that will ensure them protection against the chiefs who are beginning to eat up right & left without hearing or trial of any kind. Appeals have been made to me but beyond *taking on myself* to warn the chief[s] against oppressing I can do nothing. The people are beginning to see how utterly powerless I am & as a consequence they attach their firm allegiance to the biggest swell & only powerful one – the Chief.[30]

In July 1880 Osborn asked Colley if he might intervene in Zulu disputes but received a sharp reminder of the terms of the settlement.[31] In September, 'quite prepared for a wigging',[32] he proposed that, in order to halt the irresponsible actions of some appointed chiefs towards their people, a hut tax be imposed in Zululand, and white sub-residents be appointed with each chief from the proceeds.[33] This time Colley passed the proposals to Sir Theophilus Shepstone for comment, and, well prepared for this by his private correspondence with Osborn, Shepstone fully endorsed the proposals.[34] The combined opinions of Shepstone and Osborn now persuaded Colley that some form of alteration to the settlement was necessary, and his tentative suggestions were received with some sympathy in London where they were put aside to await further information.[35]

Colley's support gave Osborn a degree of confidence and he began to act with some independence. Thus, after Hamu's attack on Mnyamana's homesteads in November, Osborn decided to ignore the terms of his appointment and intervene between the appointed chief and the leader of the Buthelezi. Firmly believing that, as British representative in Zululand, he could control the situation he informed Hamu and Mnyamana that he would investigate their dispute and pass his findings to the High Commissioner for a decision. Hamu was advised 'to stop seizing cattle and property while this inquiry was in progress'.[36]

When, in January, Zibhebhu fined large numbers of Usuthu in his territory Osborn followed the same procedure. Zibhebhu and Ndabuko and Ziwedu were ordered to attend an inquiry into their disputes and to refrain from further action until the investigation was completed.[37]

The meeting at Nhlazatshe: August 1881

Osborn's intervention between the supporters of the Zulu royal house, and the appointed chiefs, Zibhebhu and Hamu, was a major factor in the development of the civil war. Although his actions at this time have been seen as an attempt by a well-intentioned official, hampered by the terms of his appointment, to avoid violence in Zululand, his intervention was in fact a partisan action in support of the appointed chiefs which only encouraged them to greater violence.

By offering to inquire into their differences with Zibhebhu and Hamu, Osborn raised the hopes of the Usuthu. The Zulu had great faith in the value of public inquiry and litigation. After the removal of the king a continual complaint had been that there was no one to act as supreme arbiter in the land. When Osborn agreed to assume this role the Usuthu felt that they had won a considerable victory.

This can be seen in the great pains they took in presenting their evidence to him. Mnyamana brought forward over sixty witnesses and their evidence, together with Hamu's representatives' replies, fills over ten pages in the Blue Books. He accused Hamu of seizing over 2 870 head of cattle for himself and his people. Twelve witnesses gave accounts of Hamu's actions in November 1880, and they were followed by over fifty witnesses who gave details of a variety of seizures he had made since his appointment in 1879.[38]

Hamu's representatives defended their chief, not by denying that the cattle and property had been taken, but on the grounds that he was merely punishing those Zulu within his territory who had concealed royal cattle and were still in possession of stock taken from Hamu during the war. He was therefore only either carrying out instructions from the British, or collecting his own property.

In his summing up Mnyamana criticised the settlement generally. It was not so much the fact that Hamu seized cattle but that he did so without consultation, notice or trial. Mnyamana declared:

> I wish to hear from the Resident why I and my people have been punished

thus. He must know, and ought to tell me. War was made against the Zulus and against me. At its conclusion, the white chiefs allowed me to live. Why am I oppressed now ? . . . If I was punished for having retained ex-king's cattle, there was no proof of my guilt.[39]

Hamu's *induna* answered:

Uhamu says he is ignored by Umyamana, who is now trying to set himself up as a chief, although he declined to be appointed as one when the country was settled by Government. Uhamu himself joined the English, fought on their side during the Zulu war, and, at the conclusion, was rewarded by being given a territory in Zululand. Now, another man (Umyamana), is trying to usurp his position and authority.[40]

Ndabuko and Ziwedu brought sixty witnesses to give evidence against Zibhebhu. It was alleged that 1 140 head of cattle had been taken, most of them on the grounds that they were royal cattle, or as fines for concealing royal cattle.[41] Accounts were also given of fines and punishments imposed on people on and beyond the Lubombo, a raid on Ziwedu soon after the war, the seizure of cattle from Mpande's widows of the Gqikazi homestead, and the fines imposed on participants in the May deputation to Natal, together with the January 1881 raids. Like Mnyamana, Ndabuko and Ziwedu held the authorities largely responsible. Ziwedu said:

The condition we are now in is caused by the Government. On the downfall of the king, we who are his relations should have been cared for. We ought to have been told together with the principal officers of the ex-king to deliver up all property in the shape of the cattle belonging to him. I know that I am not entitled to inherit those cattle. [but] We never saw that our father (ex-king) had such a number of cattle as are being claimed.[42]

Zibhebhu was also accused of appropriating for himself many of the cattle seized. According to the Usuthu account given to Colenso,

Ndabuko's people counted up the King's cattle which *Zibebu* had seized and said 'Where are they then, *Zibebu,* all these royal cattle ? Have you not kept them yourself ? We have never seen them brought here to Malimati.[43] Were there not four herds, Senzangakona's, and Tshaka's, and Dingane's, and Mpande's, all of which Cetshwayo inherited ? – beside his own herd which he collected from the time he was a boy. Where are they all ?'[44]

Ndabuko also raised the question of the place in the settlement of men who had possessed rank under the king:

Usibebu questions my right to bring up the people to count to the Resident the cattle seized from them. Am I not to do so when they are so extensively eaten up ? I have not understood that I am forbidden to bring to notice of Government acts oppressive against the people of the Government. The people belong to the Government and the country also. Those appointed Chiefs have made the country rotten through their acts, and it is completely rotten.[45]

Zibhebhu's defence was straightforward: he had seized cattle 'because, as Chief of my territory I am responsible to Government for the delivery of all ex-king's cattle'.[46] He then declared to the assembly:

'I am Chief of my territory and give notice plainly here to-day, as these people are in arms against me, I will punish them for it and drive them out of my territory, I will eat them up.' (Exclamations of defiance from Undabuko and party.)[47]

Osborn had only one course to take:

'Now I have heard all about you. Go home and be quiet, all of you. For I have only heard the matter that I may report it to those who can settle it; it is not my place to do so.'
Said Ndabuko 'Yes, Sir, but have you, Sir, given heed to that word of *Zibebu's* that, before this moon is over, he is coming with an *impi* to eat me up? . . .'
Said Malimati 'I command you all, *Zibebu*, Ndabuko, and Ziwedu, to be quiet and keep the peace, while I send on these words to the Authorities. Then I will tell you what they say. But the one who attacks the other will be killed.'[48]

Osborn translated and transcribed the records of the inquiry and was preparing to go to Pietermaritzburg and take the post-cart to Newcastle where he intended to confer with Colley. The meeting never took place. On 28 February 1881 the High Commissioner was killed by the Boers at Majuba.

Colley was succeeded by Sir Evelyn Wood. He was well known in Zululand, because of his activities there during the invasion, and fortunately for Osborn he was persuaded that some form of interference was necessary in Zululand. In April they conferred together in Newcastle where Osborn informed Wood that both factions in Zululand wanted official arbitration in their disputes, and they would abide by whatever decision was arrived at by the officials.[49] Wood asked London for authority for Osborn to 'inquire judicially' into the matter and added a confidential postscript:

Osborn's plan will gain us time and I should like to avoid Zulu questions until the Transvaal is settled but I am uncertain how you will regard any decision shall I do so or let them fight it out. Osborn does not anticipate that they will cross our border.[50]

Put like that the Colonial Office had little choice but to agree, and Osborn received authority to carry out the inquiry[51] he had in fact undertaken four months previously.

By now Osborn, his understanding of the Zulu situation severely limited by the misconceptions and prejudices derived from his Natal background, had placed himself in an impossible situation. He had intervened believing that he could impose his will on the Zulu, that they were still 'like potter's clay & could be brought to do anything required of them'.[52] But the Usuthu had accepted his offer to arbitrate in the belief that proper investigation would expose the injustice they had suffered. As a Natalian and friend of Theophilus Shepstone, however, Osborn could not act impartially. As a colonial official he found that their criticism of a political arrangement made by the representative of the Great White Queen unacceptable insubordination; as an ex-Natal official he could not support the representatives of the faction that had the status and the power to unite Zululand and thereby risk losing whatever had been gained by the war; and as a friend of Shepstone he could not deal fairly with allies and associates of the man, Cetshwayo, who had 'proved himself unfaithful to all – to the British Govt, to his people & to you [Shepstone]. He deserves all the punishment that he can be subjected to in this world.'[53] Thus, when Osborn met Wood in April, he informed him that, when the time came for Wood to announce the results of the inquiry, he should 'support Usibebu and give modified support to Uhamu. . . .'[54]

Osborn returned to Zululand and began to work on the minutes and memoranda with which he intended to justify this decision. These documents reveal clearly Osborn's prejudice in favour of the appointed chiefs. Any serious inquiry would have had to decide, in the first instance, whether the Usuthu charges were correct and if Hamu and Zibhebhu had in fact seized their property. Osborn however made no attempt to assess the large body of evidence on this point, painstakingly led by Mnyamana, Ndabuko and Ziwedu. Instead the Resident concentrated on the question of whether Hamu and Zibhebhu had the *right* to punish those under them. This left it open for Osborn to make judgements in the light of his own, highly subjective interpretation of 'Zulu law', and the 'ancient usages of the Zulu people'.

For example, Osborn argued that Mnyamana and his people had no right to the cattle they took from Hamu during the war because, according to Zulu law, these cattle were classed as loot and therefore the property of the king. However, after the war the king's cattle had been declared the property of the British, and therefore Hamu had no right to the cattle either. Osborn then escaped from this self-devised legal tangle by concluding

> that it would be politic, out of various considerations, that the Government should now abandon its claim to the cattle, and, as an act of grace, allow their restoration to Uhamu direct, Uhamu to be distinctly informed that in doing this the Government does not admit that he possesses any legal claims in the matter.[55]

Osborn went on to state that at the root of the trouble lay Mnyamana's refusal to hand these cattle over to Hamu. Apart from the fact that there is no evidence to support this allegation, it is clear from the records of the inquiry that disputes over cattle lost during the war formed only a small part of the charges against Hamu.

Of the allegations made by the Usuthu against Hamu, Osborn had little more to say than that he believed

> most of the parties punished were more or less guilty of appropriating cattle, to which they must have known they had no title, and of defying Uhamu, the lawful appointed chief of the territory.[56]

Mnyamana's 'real motive' in bringing the case to the Resident, Osborn felt, was 'to obtain for himself a separate and independent territory in Zululand'.[57] But because Hamu had punished his subjects with undue severity he should be ordered to return half of the number of cattle seized; at the same time Hamu's right to punish Mnyamana should be upheld and Mnyamana warned that he must submit to Hamu's authority.

In the case presented by Ndabuko and Ziwedu against Zibhebhu, Osborn ignored the question of the validity of the Usuthu accusations completely.[58] Ndabuko, he asserted, resented the fact that he had been excluded from power by the settlement and had therefore been working to bring about the restoration of the king and the re-establishment of the Zulu dynasty, and of his own appointment as an independent chief. Moreover, Osborn alleged, all the Usuthu complaints dated from the time of their visit to Pietermaritzburg, an action which Zibhebhu justly considered a grievous offence, and for which Ndabuko and Ziwedu were rightfully punished. In fact, Ziwedu had not travelled to Pietermaritzburg with Ndabuko, and Zibhebhu had stated in his own evidence that he had not yet punished the *abantwana* for going to Natal, only some of their followers.

Thus, by false and tortured argument, and by ignoring the spirit in which these cases had been brought before him, Osborn justified his recommendation to Wood that he give support to the appointed chiefs. By any criteria the arguments he presented in support of his decisions were inadequate, and any serious attempt to penetrate the verbiage with which he surrounded his findings or examination of the evidence on record would have revealed this. But the officials in London were always reluctant to debate the mysterious issues raised by native law and justice with the local experts. Moreover, the officials were deeply involved in the major crisis which followed the British defeat in the first Anglo-Boer war; they were not prepared to question the conclusions reached on this comparatively minor faction fight by their experienced man on the spot. Osborn's decisions were accepted without comment.

But a necessary corollary to this attempt to dismiss the grievances of the Usuthu was that they would have to be coerced into accepting the verdict. However, Osborn was on record as saying that the Zulu were tractable, and looked to him with confidence for justice, and would accept whatever decision he came to. He therefore began to argue, not that his original analysis was incorrect, but that the situation was changing and that the Zulu were no longer malleable – indeed the Usuthu, it was alleged, were plotting rebellion. The day after he wrote his minute on the inquiry into the dispute between Ndabuko, Ziwedu, and Zibhebhu, Osborn informed Wood that certain Zulu were becoming defiant and, 'although I have not yet been able to trace the circumstances thereof', this 'defiant attitude' was linked with the actions of Mnyamana and Ndabuko.[59] Consequently, whereas in April he had told Wood that the Zulu people would accept his decision, he now doubted this. As a result, Osborn suggested that Wood, when he announced the conclusions of the investigation, should also expel Ndabuko and Ziwedu from their homes and order them to move to John Dunn's territory.

At this point, Osborn's attention was diverted from the problem in the northern districts when violence broke out in the coastal area of Zululand. An African calling himself Sitimela arrived at Mlandela's homestead, and declared that he was the grandson of Dingiswayo and had returned to claim the Mthethwa inheritance. His claim had considerable appeal among a section of the Mthethwa and a number of leading members of the clan associated themselves with the stranger, putting themselves in opposition to Mlandela's lineage which had been 'raised up' by the Zulu kings.[60] Part of Sitimela's appeal lay in the way in which he appeared to be re-enacting the greatest event in Mthethwa history – the return of Dingiswayo, the wanderer, to claim his father's chieftainship seventy years previously. Whereas Dingiswayo arrived riding a horse and carrying a gun – hitherto unknown in the country and the symbols of the momentous changes which were to overtake southern Africa in the nineteenth century – Sitimela bore in his name the symbol of the changes soon to overtake Zululand, for the name Sitimela means train.[61]

Mlandela, the old chief of the Mthethwa and now an appointed chief under the settlement, fled to John Dunn for protection. Dunn was thus faced by an antagonistic group situated on his trading route to the north, and he armed his men. Skirmishes broke out and in mid-July Osborn moved to the region to attempt to arbitrate. Meanwhile the opposing factions increased in size: Zibhebhu's men, under Colenbrander, joined

Dunn, and Sitimela's forces were supplemented by men from the Mpu-kunyoni and the Emangweni section and, it was later alleged, by members of the Mdletshe and some of Ndabuko's followers.

On 27 July Osborn persuaded Sitimela to come to him for an interview. Sitimela told the Resident that he had no desire to fight but merely claimed his grandfather's property. Osborn pronounced his claim invalid and ordered him to disperse his followers and leave Zululand. The following day Osborn 'advised' the appointed chiefs, Dunn, Zibhebhu, Mgitshwa and Siyunguza 'to render armed aid to Umlandela in re-establishing his authority and to restore order, if applied for. . . .'[62] Osborn then sent a final warning to Sitimela and, believing that he was in danger of assassination,[63] the Resident hurried back to his camp at Nhlazatshe.

On 31 July Dunn attacked Sitimela using 2 000 men divided into three sections. Sitimela's followers made no stand but fled towards the Mfolozi river, and when they crossed they came under attack from Zibhebhu's force, with Colenbrander playing a leading role. Dunn estimated his losses at three or four, and those on Sitimela's side at over two hundred. Of the 2 500 head of cattle which Osborn was informed were captured, Mlandela was said to have retained 1 400 and given all but a few of the rest to Dunn. We will never know the exact figure, but many Zulu believed that Dunn and his allies had acted with harshness and brutality and plundered large numbers of Mthethwa cattle.

An important factor in Dunn's, in Colenbrander's and Zibhebhu's interference in the Sitimela incident was their desire for plunder,[64] but one cannot see it purely as a cattle-lifting incident. Zibhebhu and Dunn obviously felt that it was in their interest to defend the settlement from any threat, and Osborn himself used them to do so. But most important was the fact that if Sitimela had succeeded in taking control over Mlandela's territory he would have formed an obstacle on the line of communication between Dunn and Zibhebhu, and the territories to the north where so many of Dunn's economic activities were concentrated.

All the major groups situated between Dunn and Zibhebhu were drawn into the conflict, or found themselves punished soon afterwards. There was a loose identification in the minds of many Zulu between Sitimela and those who opposed the settlement and were hoping for Cetshwayo's return.[65] At the beginning of August, immediately after Sitimela's defeat, Zibhebhu punished people in his territory for assisting Sitimela or for showing sympathy for the exiled king. Once again they included some of the leading Usuthu: Hayiyana, leader of the Mandlakazi *ikhohlo* whose members now began to move their possessions westwards to the Ivuna and Sikhwebezi valleys for protection among Ndabuko and Mnyamana's homesteads; Ndabuko and Ziwedu lost cattle to Zibhebhu and so did Mbopha and some of his followers; Mgamule and other Ntombela and a son of Mfinyeli of the Xulu all had cattle taken from them; and Msushwana and his Mdletshe lost not only cattle but grain-stores.[66] The reasons for this were said by Zibhebhu to be disloyalty, or a punishment for assistance given to Sitimela. He also demanded that all these disloyal subjects leave his territory. One cannot but suspect that Zibhebhu's sudden increase in confidence and this move against the Usuthu in his territory was the consequence of his having heard about Osborn's decisions in the dispute with the Usuthu.[67]

Osborn had little time to attend to reports of the raids Zibhebhu made in August against those in his territory. On the 3rd of that month the Pretoria Convention was signed between the Boers and the British, and Osborn had to prepare for Sir Evelyn Wood's visit to Zululand where he was to announce the decisions arrived at in the disputes between Mnyamana, Ndabuko and their appointed chiefs.

By now, however, Osborn knew that there was no chance of the Usuthu obeying the decisions he had reached and it was imperative that he acquire the 'authority' he needed to assert himself in Zulu affairs. In August the opportunity seemed to come when the Colonial Office asked Osborn to comment on a set of proposals sent to them by Dunn, which would make Zululand 'self-supporting'.[68] Osborn grasped at this straw and pointed out how closely Dunn's suggestions for a hut tax and white administrators followed those he had made to Colley a year before. If Zululand was not to collapse into 'conflict and anarchy', he said, it was absolutely necessary that a hut tax be introduced, sub-residents with magisterial powers be attached to each appointed chief, and the British Resident 'be vested with some power and authority'.[69]

Osborn's suggestions, however, reached the Colonial Office at a most inopportune moment, for at that time they were considering Wolseley's violent comments on the documents relating to the inquiry. Sir Garnet reminded them how far Osborn and Wood were straying from the original principles of non-interference upon which the settlement was based.[70] It was immediately apparent to the Colonial Office that their local officials were about to carry out a policy which conflicted with that which was considered desirable in London. The response was prompt and unequivocal: no taxes to be imposed, no sub-residents unless appointed by the chiefs themselves, no authority for white officials in Zululand.[71] Wood tried to point out the difficulties that this approach would cause in Zululand,[72] but as Kimberley explained to him in a private letter, Osborn was contemplating 'a new policy, which may or may not be defensible, but it is not that of Wolseley's settlement, to which fair trial must be given'.[73]

Thus Osborn was forced to announce the results of the inquiry to the Zulu without being able to back his findings with an announcement of major changes in the settlement as he had hoped.[74] He did his best to give a show of the authority he lacked. He wrote to Wood asking him to bring an escort of at least a hundred mounted men, 'the dignity attaching to Her Majesty's representative requiring such attendance, in order to ensure for him due respect from the Chiefs and people'.[75] Wood complied with this and brought to Zululand squadrons from the 14th and 15th Hussars, General Buller, and a military band.[76]

On 31 August 1881, after breakfasting at Nhlazatshe, Wood 'departed to his tent to array himself in full pontificals, and shortly after returned so covered with medals as to be almost indistinguishable'.[77] Then the troops, accompanied by two hundred of Hlubi's mounted men and led by the band, marched to the meeting place. Seated beneath the Union Jack were Wood and his staff, Buller, Osborn, Lady Florence Dixie,[78] and Wood's interpreter, G. M. Rudolph.[79] Dunn was placed between the officials and the thousand assembled Zulu.[80]

Only six appointed chiefs attended the meeting, but the Usuthu and their sympathisers who were expecting so much from the judgement to be delivered, were well represented. Five of Cetshwayo's brothers were there, including Ndabuko, Ziwedu, Shingana, and Dabulamanzi, as well as the king's son, Dinuzulu. Mnyamana was also present, as was Dilikana of the Mbatha (who was so old that he was carried to the meeting on an ox hide), and Hayiyana and Msushwana who had both suffered at the hands of Zibhebhu earlier in the month. The *isikhulu* Mnqandi was present, as well as Mavumengwana of the Ntuli, Hlezibane of the Egazini lineage, and Somhlolo, the unrecognised chief of the Biyela.

The meeting opened with a face-saving statement on the retrocession of the Transvaal, and the chiefs were then asked their opinion of the changes suggested originally by Dunn. Discussion on the subject, according to Usuthu accounts, was suddenly interrupted by old Dilikana:

'O Zulus! is it possible that you are wasting the time thus over your separate affairs? Why do you not speak for the King's family? Have they offended you in any way that you do not speak for them in their distress? And your King? I thought that your intention in coming here was to pray for him? What wrong has he ever done?'[81]

This outburst was just what Osborn had feared; Wood had come to Zululand to discourage the movement for the king's return and the pretensions of the royal brothers and their supporters, and Osborn was not prepared to see the meeting used by the Usuthu to express their views. It is possible that Osborn communicated his feelings to the interpreter, Rudolph, who then announced the decisions that had been reached in the inquiry in violent and aggressive language:

> 'You, Maduna, Ziwedu, and Dinuzulu, we give you to John Dunn. . . . [Zibhebhu will have to return one third of the cattle he has taken from you] But this is only on condition that you go to John Dunn.'[82]

The Usuthu were deeply shocked and

> They asked leave to answer, but the White Chiefs refused saying 'What should you answer? We turn you out, Maduna and Dinuzulu and Ziwedu, because you are always saying you want the bone[83] of that scoundrel (*ishinga*)[84] whom we have done away with. You are always saying that you are going to . . . the Authorities about that. We forbid you that road. What business have you there?' They said 'That is just the point on which we wish to speak.' But the White Chiefs forbade it, and they were allowed no reply.[85]

Mnyamana was treated in the same way. He was told that Hamu had to return some of the cattle taken from him, but

> when Mnyamana asked leave to reply, it was said, 'We don't wish you to answer; we are laying down the law to you.'[86]

Dunn and Zibhebhu were then congratulated on putting down Sitimela and, according to the Usuthu, the appointed chiefs were told to follow Dunn's and Zibhebhu's example and 'if any other little *ishinga* (scoundrel) lifts himself up, you appointed Chiefs must join together and break his little neck for him'.[87]

The Usuthu were later to date the start of the civil war from the Nhlazatshe meeting. In spite of every attempt they had made to co-operate with the authorities and solve the difficulties in Zululand by peaceful methods, it was now clear to them that the authorities intended to co-operate with the appointed chiefs in their destruction. They had been betrayed by Osborn, who had promised to inquire into their complaints, but who had in fact ignored them and given unjustifiable support to their oppressors.

The order that Ndabuko, Ziwedu and Dinuzulu should leave their homesteads and move to Dunn's territory was received with the greatest resentment. They had come to Osborn for redress and had been viciously punished for it. And, as Cetshwayo's wives told Osborn when they refused either to be separated from Ndabuko or move to Dunn's territory, Dunn 'is a Kafir. He is not even a Zulu. He is a Kafir who the King made one of his Indunas.'[88] And Mnyamana asked how it was possible that 'the Princes – his own children, whom he has always carried upon his back – are to be taken from him and given to John Dunn, who is by right only one of their servants, and who has been the destruction of the King their brother, when he had protected him and given him everything in kindness. This order that the Princes should go to John Dunn appears to Mnyamana to be simply an order for their destruction, one that sends them to their graves. He cannot reconcile himself to it at all. . . .'[89]

Zibhebhu and Hamu understandably interpreted the meeting as a complete vindication of their actions against the Usuthu, and moved quickly to take advantage of the situation.[90] On the evening of the day of the Nhlazatshe meeting the Mandlakazi *ikhohlo* received a message from Zibhebhu:

'To-day my sores are healed, all my annoyances cleared off. You had better behave yourselves, for I have something to say to you.'[91]

Within forty-eight hours of the meeting Zibhebhu was moving his men towards the western borders of his territory where the Mandlakazi *ikhohlo* had sent many of their cattle to be placed among Ndabuko's people. Skirmishes broke out as the Mandlakazi seized the herds, and Ndabuko and Ziwedu's followers fled across the Ivuna to Mnyamana who gave them protection in his homesteads.

Zibhebhu moved with such speed that Ndabuko, Ziwedu and Dinuzulu had not reached their homes after the Nhlazatshe meeting when they received the order refusing them permission to return to Zibhebhu's territory. Complaints were made to Osborn by the Usuthu but Zibhebhu defended his actions saying that the *ikhohlo* cattle were rightfully his, and by evicting Ndabuko and Ziwedu he 'only adhered to the Governor's decision'.[92]

Hamu tried to follow Zibhebhu's example. Within a few days of the Nhlazatshe meeting he informed Osborn that Mnyamana and his people, and the Qulusi, were hostile to him and should follow Ndabuko into exile.[93] He later extended this demand to include the other royal section in his district, the Mphangisweni.[94] Skirmishes began to break out between the Qulusi and Hamu. Osborn tried to intervene but only made the situation worse.[95] By the end of September the Qulusi had moved their woman and children and their herds into mountain strongholds, or across the Bivane into the Transvaal. Hamu gave his *impi* orders to remove the Qulusi from his territory on 1 October. His force numbered about 3 200 men and was supported by a band of mounted men armed with rifles – probably supplied by Hamu's adviser, Herbert Nunn. The Qulusi were attacked early on the morning of 2 October. They were greatly outnumbered but, supported by rifle fire from defensive positions, they managed to hold off Hamu's Ngenetsheni for a time. But Hamu's mounted men finally broke this resistance and as the Qulusi fled for the Bivane river they were cut to pieces and most of the force of over a thousand were killed.[96]

Northern Zululand mobilised; women, children, stock and grain stores were guarded against possible attack and plunder and the men armed and assembled around their leaders.[97] Some of Zibhebhu's followers living near Mnyamana fled westwards to their leader, pursued by a band of Ndabuko's Usuthu; their cattle were taken and one or two of Zibhebhu's people wounded or killed. Ndabuko said he knew nothing of this, it was not done under his orders and that

> Up to this time, I wish it clearly understood, the man and woman wounded in this boys' retaliatory affray was the only blood shed by the Usutu. We are afraid to touch or go against one placed in authority by the white house.[98]

Zibhebhu retaliated and Colenbrander was nearly killed in an epic hand-to-hand struggle with an Usuthu.[99] It seemed for a few days as if the whole of northern Zululand was to be overtaken by civil war. Osborn was in despair; on 7 October he wrote:

> My Dear General Wood,
>   I shall not be able to go to Usibebu's. The country from within a mile or two of this, right on, is in such a disturbed state, that even native messengers have to make [a] large circuit round to avoid contact with those within the pale of disturbance. I should be able to do but little if any good, even if I did go, the Zulus understand now that I have no authority.[100]

In spite of Osborn's fears, however, full-scale fighting did not break out. Both sides were apparently too aware of the disastrous consequences such violence would have. Osborn was able to persuade Mnyamana to disband his force, and he also called off Hamu. Zibhebhu then removed his forty-one companies of men from their positions on the Ivuna river.[101]

For Osborn, the violence that followed the Nhlazatshe meeting must have been a humiliating defeat, and his credibility as an expert on native affairs suffered, particularly in Wood's eyes. And yet he could not admit, or perhaps his prejudices were so deep-rooted that he did not comprehend, that the explanation for the violence lay in the manner in which he had given Hamu and Zibhebhu confidence by his pronouncements at the Nhlazatshe meeting. Instead he found his explanation in the refusal of the London officials to grant him real authority in Zululand, and his scapegoats in the Usuthu party. In a depressed and confused private letter to Wood he alleged that the Usuthu's idea was to divide the country into two parties viz: Usutu on one side, and those against them on the other. The assegai to be arbiter between the two. . . . Their main object is to reestablish a supreme central authority. . . .

However, Wood dashed the Usuthu's plans at Nhlazatshe when he gave support to the appointed chiefs,

hence the disquiet & disturbances so soon after your visit. But for your words at the meeting showing that the authority of the chiefs was not being interfered with, and especially the presence of your escort which had most beneficial effect in more respects than that apparent on the surface, the assegai would by this be making terrible work in Zululand.[102]

There is no evidence to support this interpretation. Osborn had misinterpreted his influence over the Zulu, and was unable for psychological reasons, and for overtly political ones, to act with any impartiality towards the Usuthu. By casting the blame for the violence on a deep Usuthu plot he obscured his own failure to assess the situation correctly, and gave protection to the appointed chiefs and support for a political arrangement which kept the Zulu divided. To hold the Usuthu responsible for the upheavals at this stage was a particularly perverse interpretation. The assegai had indeed made 'terrible work' in Zululand, but in the hands of Hamu, and to a lesser extent Zibhebhu, not the Usuthu. And Mnyamana himself had played a leading role in averting widespread violence. But for Osborn to admit this publicly would have suggested where real power and influence lay in Zululand.[103]

The Usuthu were still not prepared to confront the appointed chiefs and the officials with rebellion. They were very aware of the tremendous damage internecine conflict on a large scale would inflict on all the country's people. As it was the situation was becoming serious:

Trading is, and has been for months, entirely suspended in this district. The fields are unplanted, no ploughs or Kafir picks at work – all in a state of excitement, not knowing the moment when a collision might take place. Hunger will stare many in the face next year, and all the men are yelling to their Chiefs to be let loose, that an end may be put to the state of uncertainty.[104]

As a result the Usuthu leaders sent those dispossessed by the violence for protection among supporters and relatives, and kept control of the younger members of the party who were calling for retaliation. But if the Usuthu were not yet prepared to upset the settlement by force, they still felt that they had been betrayed by the officials and they began to look around for alternative ways of bringing change to Zululand. In 1880 they had sounded out Colenso on the possibility of the return of Cetshwayo. In 1881, the belief that Osborn and the High Commissioner might consider their grievances impartially and redress them had deflected the movement for restoration to a large extent. But by the end of 1881, after the Nhlazatshe meeting had dashed all hopes that the officials would alter the settlement, the Usuthu turned once again to Bishopstowe, in the hope that the return of Cetshwayo might be the panacea which would solve their difficulties in Zululand.

It was a sensible decision made at the right moment. Cetshwayo had now been in exile for two years during which time he had been working hard to bring his case before the British authorities. The full implications of the abandonment of the confederation policy had just been seen in the retrocession of the Transvaal. And as the reports of the post-Nhlazatshe violence in Zululand arrived at the Colonial Office, and it seemed as if Wolseley's settlement might be breaking down, the officials began wondering whether the exiled king might not yet have a role to play in the government of Zululand.

Notes

1   Quoted on p. 53 of D. M. Schreuder, *Gladstone and Kruger: Liberal Government and Colonial 'Home Rule' 1880–1885*, London and Toronto, 1969.

2   KC, Colenso papers: Z80, J. W. Colenso to Chesson, 24 April 1880.

3   See the Pass signed by M. Osborn, 1 May 1880 and also Osborn to 'His Excellency', 10 June 1880 in GH 844.

4   We have no direct evidence of this, but we know that clandestine contact was made with the Usuthu on at least one other occasion and went unrecorded in Colenso's printed papers on Zulu affairs, and transcripts of the messages were suppressed by the Colensos. Moreover Colenso deliberately tried to avoid contact with the Usuthu party knowing that their case would carry less weight if the officials knew that they were in contact with Bishopstowe. One wonders why Colenso tried to avoid the party if he was ignorant of its purpose.

5   For Colenso's account of the visit see Colenso, series 1, XXXVII. Sequel to the Message after the War from the great Zulu Chiefs, pp. 733 ff.

6   See above, p. 75.

7   See Plate 18 (4).

8   Ndabezimbi, son of a brother of Maphitha and therefore Zibhebhu's 'cousin', was a member of another Mandlakazi lineage hostile to Zibhebhu, (5) in Plate 18.

9   Madlenya (18), Nyosana (6).

10   Magadeni (11), Mhlolo (9), Ngatsha (17).

11   Ngcongcwana (3), Hawana, and of course the members of the Mandlakazi.

12   Mgwazeni (16), Nkungane (7).

13   See Plate 18 (8).

14   See above, p. 75.

15   See Plate 18 (10).

16   The official report of the meeting with the Usuthu was only written ten

months later, in response to questions raised by Colenso; see BPP, C.2950: 25, report by J. Shepstone, 19 March 1881. John Shepstone on 26 May 1880, in GHZ 677, report on the day of the meeting.

17 Colenso, series 1, pp. 733–48.
18 GH 844: Osborn to Officer administering the Government, 23 June 1880, statement by Ndabuko, 22 June 1880. For the Usuthu version of this meeting see Colenso, series 1, pp. 772–4.
19 John Shepstone's minute is dated 12 July 1880 and in GH 844.
20 Colenso, series 1, p. 775.
21 Ibid.
22 Ibid., pp. 776–7: and GHZ 677: Osborn to Colley, 12 Oct. 1880, statement by Ndabuko, 2 Oct. 1880. Among those 'eaten up' at about this time were the followers of Cetshwayo's mother's house, and Ziwedu, Dinuzulu, Ngatsha, Ngcongcwana, Mahubulwana, Mgwazeni, and the Mandlakazi *ikhohlo*.
23 Colenso, series 1, p. 779.
24 KC, Colenso papers: Z114, J. W. Colenso to Chesson, 3 Dec. 1880.
25 GHZ 677: 'Memo. of Sir T. Shepstone's interview on the 9th Novr 1880 with Zibebu. . . .' A further memo. exists in the same file, dated 13 Nov. 1880, in which Shepstone writes that soon after this interview he received a letter which stated that a white man was alleged to have been made Zibhebhu's 'Prime Minister', that he would receive half the fines he imposed, and that his brother was told to stay on the border to collect the cattle raised in this way.
26 GHZ 677: Colley to Osborn, 12 Nov. 1880.
27 See the enclosures in Osborn to Colley, 4 and 7 Dec. 1880 in GHZ 677; these should be read in conjunction with BPP, C.3182: 34, *I*, Inquiry into complaints of Mnyamana against Hamu, pp. 41–4.
28 GHZ 677: encs. in Osborn to Colley, 24 Jan. 1881.
29 Referring to his memoranda on Wolseley's settlement; see above, pp. 80–1.
30 NA, Sir T. Shepstone collection: box 18, Osborn to T. Shepstone, 22 May 1880. In the same letter Osborn thanks Sir Theophilus 'for all the good things you said about me in high quarters'.
31 ZA 21: Osborn to Colley, 10 July 1880 and the reply, 27 July 1880.
32 NA, Sir T. Shepstone collection: box 18, Osborn to T. Shepstone, 27 Sept. 1880.
33 BPP, C.3182: 87, minute by Osborn to Colley, 4 Sept. 1880. (Also in GHZ 677.)
34 NA, Sir T. Shepstone collection and GHZ 677: T. Shepstone, memo. on Osborn's minute of 4 Sept. 1880.
35 CO 179/135: 19893, minutes on Colley to Kimberley, 20 Nov. 1880.
36 GHZ 677: Osborn to Colley, 7 Dec. 1880 and encs., in particular enc. D, Message to Hamu, 6 Dec. 1880.
37 GHZ 677: Osborn to Colley, 24 Jan. 1881, enc. 6, message from Osborn to Zibhebhu and Ndabuko, 23 Jan. 1881.
38 Most of the records of the inquiry and related correspondence were published in BPP, C.3182: 34. The complete records can be found as minutes and enclosures in CO 179/137: 13855, Wood to Kimberley, 23 June 1881. There is an Usuthu account in Colenso, series 2, pp. 281–2. Because

Osborn had undertaken these inquiries before he had received authority,
they are not dated. Internal evidence suggests that the inquiry into the dispute between Mnyamana and Hamu took place in the second week of Dec.
1880, and that between Ndabuko and Zibhebhu on 26 Jan. 1881.

39 BPP, C.3182: 34, *I*, Inquiry into complaints of Mnyamana against Hamu,
p. 49.

40 Ibid.

41 BPP, C.3182: 34, *K*, Inquiry into complaints of Ndabuko and Ziwedu
(Usiwetu) against Zibhebhu.

42 Ibid., statement by Ziwedu, p. 52.

43 Malimade or Malimathe – Osborn's Zulu name, derived from Melmoth.

44 Colenso, series 2, p. 282.

45 BPP, C.3182: 34, Inquiry into complaints of Ndabuko and Ziwedu against
Zibhebhu, p. 59.

46 Ibid., p. 51.

47 Ibid., p. 52.

48 Colenso, series 2, p. 282.

49 ZA 36: Osborn to Wood, 6, 11, and 12 April 1881.

50 CO 179/137: 6611, Wood to Kimberley, 13 April 1881 (teleg.). This portion
was omitted when the telegram was published in BPP, C.3182. Punctuation
added.

51 Ibid.: minutes and reply.

52 NA, Sir T. Shepstone collection: box 18, Osborn to T. Shepstone, 8 Oct.
1880.

53 NA, Sir T. Shepstone collection: box 18, Osborn to Shepstone, 22 May
1880.

54 CO 179/137: 6611, Wood to Kimberley, 13 April 1881 (teleg.).

55 BPP, C.3182: 34, minute, Osborn to Wood, 30 May 1881, p. 36.

56 Ibid.

57 Ibid.

58 BPP, C.3182: 34, minute, Osborn to Wood, 31 May 1881.

59 BPP, C.3182: 34, Osborn to Wood, 1 June 1881. The three defiant groups
were said to be the Qulusi, the Egazini lineage of Hlezibane, and the
Mbatha of Dilikana.

60 It is impossible here to analyse the Sitimela incident in any depth. This
highly condensed narrative is based on the official correspondence, Colenso's
analysis and critique of this based on newspaper accounts and reports from
the Usuthu. There are a number of references to Sitimela in the Stuart
Papers (KC), and Ch. 45 of A. T. Bryant's *Olden Times in Zululand and Natal*,
London, 1929, is devoted to the incident. In discussions I had with people in
the area in 1970 no one had any doubt that Sitimela was an impostor.

61 Derived from 'steamer'. The railway between Durban and Pietermaritzburg
had been opened six months previously.

62 ZA 36: Osborn to Wood, 28 July 1881.

63 H. Rider Haggard, *Cetywayo and his white neighbours*, London, 1896, p. 41.
Osborn and Haggard were corresponding at the time, and although
Haggard's narrative is based on the Blue Books, it is almost certain that he
drew on Osborn's letters as well.

64 An old Resident in Zululand [the missionary Robertson] says that John

Dunn carried off all the cattle taken on this occasion, and that the Zulus gnash their teeth when they speak of 'the red cattle of the Umtetwa tribe' in his clutches. Colenso, series 2, p. 64.

65 Old Mlandela later reported that after his defeat Sitimela 'rode through the sea on Elephants carrying with him tusks of ivory with which he ransomed Cetywayo, and he is bringing Cetywayo into Zululand on those Elephants...' CO 179/140: 8426, Bulwer to Kimberley, 6 April 1882, enc. 1, Osborn to Officer administering the Govt, 18 Feb. 1882.

66 BPP, C.3182: 84, encs., in Osborn to Wood, 14 Aug. 1881; GHZ 677: Osborn to Wood, 19 Sept. 1881, statements 2–10; Colenso, series 2, pp. 15–16.

67 Perhaps Osborn told Dunn when they met over the Sitimela affair, and the information reached Zibhebhu either through Dunn, or Colenbrander.

68 BPP, C.3182: 13, Wolseley to Colonial Office, 5 April 1881, enc., Dunn to Wolseley, 21 Feb. 1881, Proposition from Dunn to make the Zulu country self-supporting.

69 BPP, C.3182: 78, enc., memorandum by Osborn, 6 Aug. 1881, p. 128.

70 CO 179/139: 14390, Wolseley to Kimberley, 12 Aug. 1881.

71 And the telegram ended with the words '... be very cautious in all you do, so as not to commit [the] Govt.' CO 179/138: 14521, Wood to Kimberley, 14 Aug. 1881 (teleg.).

72 CO 179/138: 14810, Wood to Kimberley, 17 Aug. 1881 (teleg.).

73 NA, Sir Evelyn Wood collection: III/2/10, Kimberley to Wood, 25 Aug. 1881.

74 Following instructions, the chiefs at the meetings were asked their opinion on the appointment of sub-residents, the levy of a hut tax, road tolls, a border police and industrial schools. These questions were based on Dunn's proposals to make Zululand 'self-supporting'. Although the officials were to discuss at great length the apparently indifferent attitude of the Zulu to these suggestions, events in Zululand never allowed their implementation.

75 ZA 36: Osborn to Wood, 12 Aug. 1881.

76 In a cold snap, just before the Nhlazatshe meeting, Wood's party lost 320 oxen valued at £4 480, in other words the equivalent of four years of Osborn's salary. A few months later the Colonial Office balked at authorising funds to build Osborn a house at Nhlazatshe, although he claimed that his health was suffering as a result of primitive living conditions.

77 F. Dixie, *In the Land of Misfortune*, London, 1882, p. 378.

78 Journalist, traveller, controversialist, daughter of the 9th Marquis of Queensbury, and aunt of Lord Alfred Douglas. A full account of her activities in southern Africa can be found in B. Roberts, *Ladies in the Veld*, London, 1965, and in her own book, *In the Land of Misfortune*. For her subsequent role in Zulu politics, see below, p. 134.

79 Magistrate of the Klip River District and Natal civil servant of long standing.

80 See the illustration in Dixie, *In the Land of Misfortune*, facing p. 380. The official account of the meeting was published as No. 65, Wood to Kimberley, 31 Aug. 1881 in BPP, C.3182. This perfunctory account in no way reflects the mood of the meeting. Osborn appears to have made no record and failed to write a report; as far as he was concerned the less said about this

disaster the better. The Usuthu reported to Colenso immediately after the meeting and their accounts show the shock they felt at what had occurred. See Colenso, series 2, pp. 14–16 and Colenso's analysis of the official report on pp. 245–51.

81 Colenso, series 2, p. 15.
82 Ibid.
83 Cetshwayo.
84 Colenso became involved in a lengthy controversy over whether the word *ishinga* was used or not; on balance it would appear that it was.
85 Colenso, series 2, p. 15.
86 Ibid.
87 Colenso, series 2, p. 64.
88 CO 179/138: 21667, Wood to Kimberley, 14 Nov. 1881, statement by twenty-five wives of Cetshwayo on 18 and 19 Oct. 1881, in Osborn to Wood, 29 Oct. 1881.
89 Colenso, series 2, p. 60.
90 GHZ 677: Osborn to Wood, 19 Sept. 1881, statements 8–17. These statements give a vivid account of the immediate aftermath of the Nhlazatshe meeting. Significantly, they do not seem to have been forwarded to London, but they confirm, in their essential features, the account given to Colenso by Fokothi, leading member of the Mandlakazi *ikhohlo*, in Colenso, series 2, pp. 33–5.
91 Ibid., p. 33.
92 GHZ 677: Osborn to Wood, 19 Sept. 1881, statement no. 16, 14 Sept. 1881.
93 BPP, C.3182: 75, enc., Osborn to Wood, 23 Sept. 1881, statement by Sikumbana and Ungarbu, 5 Sept. 1881.
94 Ibid., statement by Untambo, 23 Sept. 1881.
95 It was alleged that Osborn's chief *induna*, Sotondose, was implicated in the violence that followed, and that he was subsequently dismissed 'because . . . he had a great deal to do with Hamu's slaughter of the abaQulusi'. Colenso, series 2, p. 60.
96 This account of the Ngenetsheni/Qulusi battle is based on a letter by Nunn, 15 Oct. 1881, in the *Natal Mercury* of 14 Nov. 1881, reprinted on p. 54, series 2, by Colenso, and analysed with additional information from official and Usuthu sources on pp. 295ff. Official reports can be found in BPP, C.3182: 88 and 101 and encs. Some estimates place the number of Qulusi casualties far higher. The Ngenetsheni lost a handful of men.
97 BPP, C.3182: 83, enc., Osborn to Wood, 9 Oct. 1881, statements and messages.
98 W. Campbell, *With Cetywayo in the Inkandhla, and the present state of the Zulu question*, Durban, 1883, p. 16. This statement is corroborated by one made at the time by some of Ndabuko's people, in BPP, C.3182: 83, enc. 1, statement by Untyotyo, p. 137.
99 B. H. Kemp, 'Johan William Colenbrander' (PhD thesis, University of Natal, 1962), i, Ch. 6. Here the Mandlakazi hold the Usuthu to be the aggressors.
100 BPP, C.3182: 83, Osborn to Wood, 7 Oct. 1881, p. 139. This private letter must have been published inadvertently.
101 BPP, C.3182: 93, enc., Osborn to Wood, 16 Oct. 1881.

102 NA, Sir Evelyn Wood collection: III/2/15, Osborn to Wood, 16 Oct. 1881 (private).

103 He did write privately to Wood that Mnyamana had 'acted very fairly throughout'. Ibid.

104 Colenso, series 2, p. 53, quoting from Nunn's letter, see Note 96 above.

CHAPTER EIGHT

The exiled king re-enters Zulu politics

Cetshwayo in Cape Town

The story of Cetshwayo's exile and his struggle to be allowed to return to his country is an absorbing and tragic one. Although the king was illiterate, did not speak English, and had never left his country until his deposition, he adapted to his new environment with extraordinary skill. His understanding of the political world in which he had now to operate and the success he had in recruiting supporters to his cause demonstrate this. In spite of the restrictions imposed on him by his detention in Cape Town, he managed to publicise his point of view both in southern Africa and in Britain, and he persuaded a large number of people, some of great importance, that he had suffered a great injustice and that Britain should make amends for this.

An important factor in his success was that physically Cetshwayo was a most impressive man. At the time of his capture the public had accepted the idea that Cetshwayo was the gorilla-like monster depicted in the popular illustrated papers and whose barbarities had been so well described by Frere in official dispatches. Wolseley was therefore surprised to discover that the man he dragged out of the Ngome forest in August 1879 was 'quite the King in bearing & deportment'.[1] By the time Cetshwayo had been imprisoned in the Castle in Cape Town his imposing presence and appearance had been commented upon widely. Frere was hard-pressed to explain away the difference between the king as he appeared in reality, and the creature that his propaganda had done so much to create. Frere wrote:

> Long habit of uncontradicted command gives great dignity to his general manner, and takes in the casual observer with the belief that he is a very superior being; but you will look in vain for kingly attributes, as we understand them, apart from those associated with superior force and cunning.[2]

But many of those who met Cetshwayo after his capture disagreed, and they were to ensure that his petitions and protests reached the British public and the authorities, and also that he made contact with his supporters in Zululand.

From the start Cetshwayo objected to being regarded as a curiosity. Once in Cape Town he insisted on wearing European clothes and being treated with the deference due to a head of state. Whenever possible he made known his conviction that he had been unjustly attacked by the nation with which he and his forebears had the closest links. At the time when he replied to Colenso's telegram offering sympathy[3] the king received permission to send a message to Queen Victoria:

> Ketchwayo begs permission to be allowed to send his humble respects to the Queen; he is staying here awaiting the Queen's pleasure and will willingly and cheerfully go wherever the Queen directs. At the same time he is living in the hopes that at some future time he may be pardoned.
>
> He feels greatly honoured to hear that his portrait is going to the Queen, whom he has always looked up to as his 'mother' and still regards her in that light.[4]

This was the first of many pleas for clemency that Cetshwayo was to make to Queen Victoria. At this time, however, it stood no chance of success. The authorities busied themselves with the legal and financial problems raised by the king's detention while Cetshwayo and his interpreter occupied themselves with writing a history of Zululand and the recent invasion.[5]

Just as the Liberal victory in April 1880 raised Colenso's hopes of a change in policy towards Zululand and its exiled king, so it persuaded Cetshwayo to renew his pleas for pardon. Wolseley received a letter from him, and Frere was asked to forward another message to the Queen asking that Cetshwayo might be pardoned, and returned to Zululand as a private individual. The king also suggested that his son, Dinuzulu, should be sent to the Cape to be educated and to act as a hostage for his father's good behaviour.[6] Although these petitions were again rejected it became apparent that this was being done with some regret and that Cetshwayo was raising a degree of sympathy in England. Frere was concerned about this and wrote to Sir Theophilus Shepstone asking him for a letter which he could use 'which may prevent any act of sentimental folly such as would undo all your labour of a lifetime & ruin Natal & its neighbours in time to come. . . .'[7] Shepstone supplied the required memorandum and in it he expressed the opinion that the Zulu power was 'weakened not broken' and the return of the Zulu king would lead to its revival. 'Just what I wanted to finish Dr. Colenso and Solomon', Frere wrote in acknowledgement.[8]

In November 1880 Bishop Colenso and Harriette visited Cetshwayo in

the Castle at Cape Town.[9] It was a significant event in the lives of all
parties concerned. The Bishop and the king had not met for twenty-five
years and it was the first and only time that Harriette was to have personal
contact with the man whose cause she was to defend for many years to
come. Cetshwayo listened eagerly to the news from Zululand, of his
wives and children, and the visit of his brothers to Natal and their
political objectives. The conversation moved on to the policy which had
led to the war. Cetshwayo found it difficult to believe that it was Frere who
was largely responsible for the invasion. He had found him 'a very kind,
friendly man. He sat and spoke with me just as you are doing. His voice
was as kind as yours is.' Colenso felt it necessary 'to dispel his pleasing
illusion as to Sir Bartle Frere's friendliness. . . .'[10] And as they discussed
the war and the allegations used to justify the invasion, Cetshwayo's
knowledge of recent southern African history increased significantly. He
was soon to use Colenso's view that the war was brought on primarily by
officials in southern Africa who, by misrepresenting Cetshwayo and the
nature of his rule, misled the British Government into supporting the
invasion of the Zulu kingdom.

During these conversations the possibility of Cetshwayo being returned
to Zululand was discussed. Colenso suggested that as an initial step
towards restoration it might be a good strategy to obtain permission to go
to England and petition personally the authorities there. It appears as if
Colenso was confident that such a visit would convince both the British
public and the authorities of the king's innocence and his ability, and
thereby place him in a better position to persuade the British Government
to return him to his country. Although Cetshwayo was terrified of the sea
he agreed to consider such a plan, and the Colensos, for their part, did all
they could to keep Cetshwayo's name before the public and the authorities.

At the same time Colenso and Cetshwayo planned a way in which it
could be demonstrated to the Zulu that the king was still alive, and enable
him to regain some influence over events in his country. The Bishop
persuaded the authorities in the Cape to allow the exchange of Cetshwayo's
adviser and loyal associate, Mkhosana, for his *imbongi* and hairdresser,
Dabuka.

Mkhosana arrived in Zululand at the end of February 1881. The mere
fact that the man who had been 'killed together with the king' had
returned caused a stir throughout the country.[11] Mkhosana had been
instructed to arrange that certain trusted *izinduna* be ordered to travel to
the Cape to share Cetshwayo's exile,[12] and also apparently to visit Zibhebhu and attempt to heal the breach between him and the royal brothers.[13]

It is difficult to assess the impact of Mkhosana's return. It was reported that many people attended the meeting at Ndabuko's homestead, kwa-Minya, where Mkhosana gave an account of his experiences. At the same time there are hints of a certain reserve on the part of the Usuthu. This might have been partly due to intimidation – Zibhebhu punished certain individuals who attended the meeting with Mkhosana. It is also very likely that at this stage, just a few months after Osborn's investigation into the disputes between the Usuthu and the appointed chiefs, the Usuthu leaders felt that it was wiser to await the findings of the official inquiry than to resort to a programme of open demonstration in support of the deposed king which would be disapproved of by the officials, and possibly provoke further violence from Zibhebhu and Hamu. It was said that Mnyamana and Ndabuko refused to allow Mkhosana to go to Zibhebhu to deliver the king's message.[14] Only three of the six *izinduna* Cetshwayo asked for agreed to go to Cape Town,[15] and they were hindered in their objectives by Osborn and the officials at the office of the Secretary for Native Affairs in Pietermaritzburg.[16]

But if the king's strategy had only limited success in Zululand in 1881 before the Nhlazatshe meeting, he did have a number of successes in the Cape which were soon to be of great importance in his bid to return to his country. In January 1881 Cetshwayo was moved from the Castle in Cape Town to Oude Moulen, a farm on the Cape Flats to which the exiled Hlubi chief, Langalibalele, was also taken. Residing with the king was a new interpreter, R. C. A. Samuelson, the son of a Norwegian missionary, who had grown up in Zululand and just left school. Samuelson and his family had received many kindnesses from Cetshwayo and the royal family while they lived in Zululand, and they had a genuine respect and affection for the king. Although Samuelson grew to hate the atmosphere at Oude Moulen he stayed at his post out of concern for the king, and also because he hoped that if the king did go to England he could accompany him.[17]

With someone he could trust as interpreter and secretary, Cetshwayo spent much of his time composing petitions and letters which were dispatched to people of note in southern Africa and in England. These documents worked, for the most part, strongly in Cetshwayo's favour, and he was very aware of their importance. As he was to say, they were 'now his only assegais'.[18]

In these letters Cetshwayo complained of the way he had been treated by the British, he attacked the men he saw as his enemies, and appealed for clemency. Much of the effectiveness of the letters lay in their powerful figurative language, for which the king must take the credit; but it was also their simple, ungrammatical and artless style which, while in accord with the popular conception of how an African king would express himself in English, in fact owed more to Samuelson's educational short-comings than naivety on the part of Cetshwayo. At the same time these unstructured and informal transcriptions of the king's ideas were frequently, one suspects, a more accurate reflection of his thoughts than the ordered formulations a more sophisticated interpreter might have attempted to write.

For example, Cetshwayo suffered a personal loss when his ex-custodian, Major Poole, was killed in the first South African war, and Cetshwayo wrote to the High Commissioner to 'express my deep sorrow at what has happened to the troops of Her Majesty the Queen'. Cetshwayo pointed out that:

> Although the Boers have slaughtered these men they have gained no advantage, the English troops will soon give them their deserts.
> Let the Queen cheer up; the Boers will soon flee before the British soldiers. The Boers ought to be punished for not obeying the Queen. It will be a happy day for the black people of South Africa when the English are South Africa's sole rulers. The Boers are fond of lawlessness and taking away land from the dark races. The Queen is fond of justice, and treats her captives very kindly.[19]

Samuelson and Cetshwayo soon set to work on a petition which would make known the king's version of the events which led to the war and defend the policy he had adopted. His intention was given in the opening remarks:

> I am writing to you, Sir Hercules Robinson, Governor of this land, to ask why my case is kept quiet even now, seeing that the Boers have sued for peace and their affair is quieted. I think now is the right time to hear and learn about the grounds on which the arguments for killing me ... were based. I wish now to lay my case, as clearly as possible, before this Parliamentary Assembly, but specially before the Parliament in England, and the Queen.[20]

The petition ended with a request that he be returned to Zululand.

The letter made its mark in London, and Kimberley sent it to Gladstone saying:

> I send herewith a very curious and interesting letter from Cetywayo. It is a painful document to send for one who like myself believe the Zulu war to have been unjust and unnecessary.[21]

But, the Secretary of State for the Colonies continued, nothing could be done for the king, for the moment at least. By May Cetshwayo had not received a reply to his petition, and he decided to take up Colenso's suggestion and formally requested to be allowed 'to proceed to England to state my case before the Queen and have it settled there'.[22]

In June Cetshwayo persuaded Samuelson to forward certain of his letters directly to Bishopstowe, instead of handing them over to the authorities to be vetted as was required.[23] By writing directly to Colenso, Cetshwayo was able to escape the official censor and make clandestine contact with his supporters in Zululand.

But in spite of this important advance Cetshwayo became increasingly despondent and fell into moods of deepening despair as 1881 advanced. Although he was allowed a number of visitors, was taken on the occasional trip into Cape Town, and he and Langalibalele hunted together on the farm, the atmosphere at Oude Moulen was oppressive. The king was troubled by strange dreams in which Jesus and Queen Victoria appeared. The warders drank and squabbled, and Samuelson quarrelled with everyone except the Zulu. The news from Zululand was deeply disturbing to Cetshwayo and the detainees were morose and unhappy.

In July, Dambuka, Cetshwayo's attendant, hanged himself. It was alleged that he had attempted to assault one of Langalibalele's wives.[24] Samuelson believed that he was innocent of the charge, but, because Dambuka thought that an inquiry would inevitably cast a slur on the king, he committed suicide.[25]

A few days later the Acting-Governor of the Cape, General Smyth, visited Cetshwayo to deliver Kimberley's rejection of the king's petition[26] of March. He reported that he found Cetshwayo in

> a very depressed condition, and he told me he would rather die than remain as he was at present. That he was like a bird in a cage, and that he would follow the example of his follower and commit suicide. He repeated the statements so often made that he was a friend of the English, and had always been so, and that he would never have attacked them had they not invaded his country. That he thought if he were allowed to go to England that he could show how sincere he was, and how readily he would obey any injunctions Her Majesty might be pleased to place upon him. . . . It was a painful interview, for Cetywayo was in great mental distress, and his dignified and gentlemanlike deportment always inspires sympathy.[27]

The news of the suicide, and Cetshwayo's threat of suicide, reached the Colonial Office at a crucial moment – just when Wood's dispatch of 23 June which reported Osborn's inquiry into the Usuthu dispute with the appointed chiefs was circulating among the officials. These documents seemed to indicate that Wolseley's settlement might be breaking down. Fairfield wrote that if Cetshwayo did kill himself there 'will be a great outcry', and he wondered whether,

> If the Zulu Settlement breaks down through rebellions and disturbances, the 12 nobodies who have 12 of the 13 divisions might be superseded by John Dunn with Cetywayo as his suzerain.[28]

Here we have the first hint at what was to become a major British initiative in Zululand. Courtney picked up Fairfield's suggestion:

> Should Cetywayo commit suicide the scandal would be extreme, and I do not see why the possibility of visiting England should not be entertained. His restoration to Zululand is for the time being out of the question. . . . We may wait the breakdown of the present organization, with which John Dunn might disappear. . . . I should seize every opportunity of interesting and amusing him [Cetshwayo] with preparations for a visit to England and a visit afterwards, always with a view to his possible return under altered circumstances.[29]

Kimberley was however reluctant to go this far, but he wrote to the High Commissioner urging him to try to 'relieve the irksomeness of [Cetshwayo's] detention . . . and remove from his mind the sense of injury from which he is suffering . . .',[30] and asked his opinion on Cetshwayo's request to visit England.

But Robinson could do little to comfort the king.

> Do you kill me like this because I am a black man? [Cetshwayo asked Kimberley in a letter.] My country would not have been destroyed and I would not have been taken captive if the Zulu matters had been from the very first properly looked into by the Imperial Parliament.

He stressed once again the close relations that had existed between the Zulu and the English:

> Who could be a greater friend of the English than I, who remained quiet in my country till I was attacked and taken captive. I fought when I was attacked, just to ward off a falling tree, as it were, even as any other person would do. I request you to look to my case and not to my colour, and not leave me to die here while my family is being scattered and is dying off on the hills.[31]

While in detention Cetshwayo had had the opportunity to broaden his knowledge on imperial affairs. He contrasted the manner in which the Boers, the Afghans, and the Basotho had been treated, with the British policy towards Zululand. Gladstone was asked

> why [do] you keep quiet and do not talk for poor sufferers like me. . . . If you could split my heart and understand it, I am sure I would be here no longer, but in my native land. Put me back with good and discreet men to look after me and direct me.[32]

Kimberley was suspicious of these letters suspecting 'European inspiration', but he noted that it was going to become increasingly difficult to ignore the exiled king, and furthermore that, in the week before the Nhlazatshe meeting,

> there are marked symptoms of Wolseley's settlement breaking down, and the feeling here in favour of Cetywayo is strong & likely to grow stronger.[33]

Gladstone was considerably affected by Cetshwayo's letters. Kimberley wrote to Gladstone that he shared his feelings as to Cetshwayo,

> and am quite ashamed to be obliged to be his gaoler. He was, as you say, most villainously used.
>
> I am disposed on the whole to let him visit England. I believe that we shall ultimately have to let him go back to Zululand, and it would be a decided advantage to us that he should form some notion of what the power of this country really is.[34]

Thus, on 14 September 1881, Cetshwayo was informed that Her Majesty's Government was 'disposed to entertain Cetywayo's request to visit England'.[35]

In these minutes and letters we see the first hesitant movements towards a policy which was eventually to lead to the king's return to his country. The Colensos at Bishopstowe had done what they could to publicise Cetshwayo's virtues, and there was a genuine sympathy for Cetshwayo among members of the Liberal government. There was also the fear of public outcry if he took his own life. Cetshwayo's letters were a significant factor, especially the one to Gladstone of 15 July 1881. But, it must be emphasised that from the very start the possibility of restoration was only considered because it was felt that Cetshwayo might have a role to play in the plans that would have to be devised should Wolseley's settlement break down to such an extent that British interests in southern Africa were threatened.

And as 1881 progressed it seemed as if that time was approaching rapidly. As Kimberley noted after his subordinates had written long inconclusive minutes attempting to formulate a reply to reports of the Nhlazatshe meeting:

> By the (as I think) uncalled for and most impolitic Zulu war, & by the dethronement of Cetywayo we have involved ourselves in extreme difficulties. Had we left Cetywayo on the throne, or annexed the country, we should in either case have taken an intelligible course. As it is, we neither control the affairs of Zululand, nor are we free from responsibilities for them.[36]

Then came the news of Zibhebhu's post-Nhlazatshe attacks, Hamu's massacre of the Qulusi, and the arrival of Osborn's despairing letter to Wood of 7 October.[37] The Colonial Office began to cast about for some solution which would avoid responsibility and expense but would create some sort of order in Zululand. There was no answer in trying to shift responsibility on to Natal: as Fairfield pointed out,

> This would be all very well if we are going to keep Natal as a Crown Colony, or if Natal, being self governing, was strong enough, like the Cape, to take on its shoulders a great slice of adjoining Native Territory. But neither condition

is likely to be fulfilled. . . . We shall then have the most unsatisfactory of all tasks on hand, the task of governing a Native Territory through a semi-independent Colonial government.[38]

When John Dunn suggested that he be appointed 'supreme chief' in Zululand Kimberley minuted that

annexation, John Dunn and Cetewayo present three paths open to us; and that it must follow the first as little as possible. The Resident in his report gives weighty and, to my mind, conclusive reasons for thinking that John Dunn could not be accepted as Supreme Chief, but the difficulty of getting rid of him is extreme. Cetewayo promises to be the most amenable to advice, if returned, and I do not doubt that through him we could exercise the strongest influence without incurring the responsibilities of Annexation, and we should have a chance of re-establishing a self supporting Zulu nation. . . . Supposing we could manage to keep things as they are, or at least to prevent them from becoming worse [?] for twelve months more.[39]

This was what London attempted: Cetshwayo's anxiety was to be stilled by the promise of a visit to England, and his supporters in Zululand by the possibility of some change in the settlement. Meanwhile it was suggested that the new Governor of Natal, Sir Henry Bulwer,[40] should also be Special Commissioner for Zululand. According to his instructions he was to investigate the situation in Zululand, and if it warranted it, he should facilitate the return of Cetshwayo to re-establish himself as head of a political system which would not involve the British exchequer in expense, but over which Britain would have some control.

Far from calming Cetshwayo, the news that he was to be allowed to go to England only increased his frustration. He was by now seriously disturbed by the news of the violence which followed the Nhlazatshe meeting. And when colonial Natal protested against the news that Cetshwayo was to go to England, the king responded by attacking the Natal press, John Dunn and his 'nominee and friend', Zibhebhu. He implored the authorities to honour their responsibilities by protecting the Zulu royal family who were suffering under Britian's appointees. And, he wrote,

I know myself that the mouths of the Zulus are shut, and their feelings suppressed by the Natal people. The same plans are now used to keep me in misery as were used when my country was invaded. I never received the Ultimatum, and now the Natal people say that the Zulu nation does not wish me back although they do.[41]

Cetshwayo had plans to overcome the misinterpretation of Zulu feeling by the officials and the colonial press, who continually put forward the view that the Zulu people were opposed to Cetshwayo and his return to their country. A secret message was passed to Colenso for transmission to the Usuthu in Zululand. It went:

Wau! Have you really been on the alert, since Lukuni[42] . . . has already started for England (before me)? I say this because the voice of Zululand is stifled for those in England to whom you belong, so that they in England speak quite differently from what is the real fact, they do not know the hearts of the Zulu People!

Now what I say is that since they . . . are stopped by Malimati . . . & Mr John Shepstone . . . you should send to Maduna, & to Mnyamana, to Seketwayo, Ntshingwayo, Sitshaluza, Somkele, Siwunguza, Faku, Mgojana, Somopo, & Palane, a messenger with these words which I am going to write. Send on your own account, that no one may know, that it may be a surprise when they arrive in Maritzburg. . . .

I – I, Cetshwayo – am alive, I greet you, I say, you do not speak (as you ought to). It depends upon you, upon your asking for me, whether you will ever see me again. I say to you Mnyamana, Ntshingwayo, Seketwayo, Maduna, Gather together all who lament for me, & go! Hasten to make your prayer in Maritzburg! Stop your ears to those who are deceiving you; no harm will happen to you (for going). Start up like one man, & go to pray for me at Maritzburg. Make haste, since I am now going to pray for myself to the English & to their Queen. I have been told that the English are waiting for you to pray for me, upon which they will send me home. . . . Do this without appearing to be directed by me. Don't say publickly 'the King says so & so' but let those who will pray for me tell one another.

Cetshwayo ka 'Mpande

If Malimati refuses to let you go to Natal, just go! No harm will come to you. They are deceiving you, John Dunn, Malimati, and others who wish me to die here.[43]

This message was received by the Usuthu when their attempts to obtain redress from the authorities had failed, the appointed chiefs had redoubled their harassment, and many Usuthu had been expelled from their homes and were living with relatives and supporters. Three months after Cetshwayo's message arrived in Zululand two thousand Zulu began to walk towards the Natal border, on their way to Pietermaritzburg to express their desire for the return of Cetshwayo to his country.

Bulwer, Bishopstowe, and the 'Great Deputation'

The arrival in Pietermaritzburg of what the Colensos called the 'Great Deputation' had important consequences, both for the Usuthu, and for their allies and opponents in Natal. Positions became more clearly defined, the debate between colonial and metropolitan interests became a public one, and the factions in Zululand began to prepare for further conflict.

By the beginning of 1882 the Colensos were quite satisfied with the situation. They had established secret contact with Cetshwayo and through them his messages were reaching Zululand. Cetshwayo was to travel to England to put his case. As Harriette Colenso told some visiting Usuthu, 'the ground seems well tilled, & the crop is coming up nicely, & we shall get a good harvest – if we have rain!'[44]

But Harriette was over-optimistic and the movement for the restoration of Cetshwayo suffered a series of setbacks early in 1882. The Bishop had recruited the eccentric and adventurous Lady Florence Dixie to the Usuthu cause when she visited southern Africa in 1881, and she began placing pro-Cetshwayo articles in the *Morning Post* in London. However, neither as honest nor as astute as Colenso or Cetshwayo, she wrote a paragraph attacking the Shepstones, and interpolated it in a letter written by Cetshwayo, which she then published. In the uproar that followed the king denied having expressed such views, Samuelson's activities as a private letter-writer for Cetshwayo were exposed and he was dismissed, and the undercover link between the king, Bishopstowe, and Zululand thus broken. For many observers the incident confirmed their belief that the movement for Cetshwayo's restoration was the work of unscrupulous whites who took advantage of, and worked on, the unsophisticated Zulu for their own ends.

But even more serious than the consequences of the Dixie incident was the fact that in December 1881 Sir Henry Bulwer was offered the post of Governor of Natal and Special Commissioner for Zululand. It seemed a good choice; Bulwer had had over four years' experience in the colony as Lieutenant Governor; although he had signed the Ultimatum which preceded the invasion he had done so reluctantly and under pressure from Frere. Furthermore he had refused to be browbeaten by either Frere or Chelmsford during the war and had done his best to protect the interests of Natal, and Natal Africans, while the invasion was being prosecuted.[45] He was a hard-working, intelligent man and, within the colonial context, an official of integrity.

However, although Bulwer had criticised Frere's policy and had never believed that the Zulu intended invading Natal, he had little sympathy for Cetshwayo or his mode of government. Moreover it was his memoranda to Wolseley in 1879 which had provided the framework for the settlement, and he approved of the arrangement in that it avoided annexation and therefore left the land in the possession of those people for whose welfare the war had been fought. To allow the king to remain in Zululand would nullify the important freedoms gained for the Zulu people by the British invasion. No matter what restrictions were placed on Cetshwayo, Bulwer believed that he would never be willing, nor able, to avoid working towards establishing the old order again with himself at its head; 'the rehabilitation of the Zulu King', Bulwer wrote in 1880, 'after all that had happened . . . [would] be a mistake as grave as could well be committed.'[46]

Bulwer had not moved from this position at the beginning of 1882 when, before taking up his post, he was called to the Colonial Office for discussions on Cetshwayo's future. Moreover he disapproved strongly of the manner in which Cetshwayo and Colenso were agitating for restoration. The tone of the king's letters was 'not consistent with his position' and he was

> anxious that the visit to England should not take place & suggests for consideration whether it might not be got rid of on the ground that he [Bulwer] is going out with special instructions to consider the whole question.[47]

But the Colonial Office was not convinced by Bulwer's objections. Thus Bulwer went out to Natal, to carry out a policy devised in London and with which he disagreed. As a result he acted reluctantly, dragging his feet at every step, determined to obstruct restoration if possible, and if it did take place, to make it clear that it was the result of calm deliberation and in the interests of all southern Africa's people, and not the result of a hurried attempt to appease a vocal pressure group. Whatever the settlement's faults, Bulwer argued, it had set up various authorities in Zululand and certain forms of procedure which had to be followed. These, Bulwer was to argue, the Usuthu and their allies ignored, and this he found unacceptable.

Throughout Bulwer's term of office, during which the situation in Zululand changed from one of tension and minor clashes to bloody civil war, he and Colenso were in bitter dispute. But whatever their differences over matters of detail, their quarrel was rooted in completely different interpretations of events in Zululand since the war. Colenso would not have quarrelled with the emphasis that Bulwer placed on the need to follow correct administrative procedures and to obey regulations. The Bishop's point was that the local officials had themselves deliberately ignored these procedures, leaving the Usuthu no choice but to by-pass men like Osborn, and the officials in the office of the SNA, in order that the Governor, the authorities in London, and the public might learn the truth about events in Zululand and the feelings of its people, the truth that local officials were determined to suppress.

Bulwer never came near to understanding or sympathising with the Colensos' viewpoint. For him they were misguided humanitarians whom objective conditions turned into agitators. And while much of his criticism of the Usuthu and Bishopstowe was based on their apparent refusal to work through constituted channels, his concrete suggestions show that he followed closely the ideas and the policies of local officials, especially those of the retired SNA, Sir Theophilus Shepstone.

It is somewhat strange that a man of Bulwer's intelligence and integrity should have accepted so uncritically the advice of Sir Theophilus, a man with whom he had been so dissatisfied only a few years previously,[48] and that he depended so heavily on John Shepstone who he had good reason to believe was neither honest nor efficient.[49] Although this must have been due, in part, to the obvious need for any administrator to gain the support of his subordinates, it was also the consequence of the peculiar position of the colonial governor who had to depend on local advice in the 'esoteric, difficult and potentially hazardous field' of African administration.[50] Moreover, long before he arrived in Natal, Bulwer knew that he disagreed with London over its attitude to the future of Cetshwayo; he could not have sustained this position on his own and he had to draw on support in Natal, and the Shepstones and their allies were only too willing to give this to him.

As a result Bulwer accepted without apparent hesitation many highly doubtful interpretations of recent events in Zululand. For example, he never realised that the Usuthu had attempted to work with the officials to bring about reform of the settlement. He accepted Osborn's view that Ndabuko and Ziwedu had been guilty of 'rebellious conduct' towards Zibhebhu and, as a result, that the appointed chief had been forced to expel them from his territory. He also never questioned the view that Osborn had made a fair inquiry into the origins of the disputes in northern Zululand, or that the various Usuthu parties had visited Natal, not to petition the authorities, but to make contact with Colenso to agitate against the settlement.

But Bulwer was to go further than putting forward the misconceptions of the local officials as established facts. In his lengthy first report on Zulu affairs he demonstrated that he was prepared to advance, as first principles, settler mythology on such subjects as the 'native mind'. Thus he argued that the aims of the Usuthu could not be a spontaneous reflection of Zulu views, for the African was incapable of arriving independently at new ideas: in a statement on African psychology, a classic expression of colonial prejudice, ringing with Shepstonian overtones, Bulwer proved that the Usuthu movement was inspired from outside Zululand:

> Those best acquainted with the native races and tribes of South Africa, with their history, their habits, their customs, their ways of thinking, and their modes of procedure, know very well that the idea of asking for the restoration of a Chief who has been taken in war or has been deposed by a superior power

would never so much as occur to a native mind. To them a Chief who has ceased to rule, who has been removed from them, becomes, for all purposes, to his people as one that is dead. For the tribe or people to send a deputation to the power or Chief by whose act of conquest this has been effected, in order to ask for the restoration of their Chief would be at variance with the very nature and constitution of the native mind, which accepts the fortune of war and the inexorable logic of facts, and does not attempt to argue with either. If, therefore, Undabuko and Tshingana came into Natal in May 1880, with an intention of asking for the release of their brother, their intention, we may be sure, never contemplated more than the return of the brother to the family as a member of the family. It never contemplated his restoration as the Chief of his people. . . .

In such matters as these the native mind, if left to itself, depends entirely upon the will and direction of the power which it recognises as its superior, whether by natural right, by act of conquest, or otherwise. It is not habituated to have any wish of its own in such matters, or, if it has one, it refrains from expressing it. It leans upon the will of the power whom it considers to be its master . . . to agitate for any object . . . is so absolutely foreign to the nature of the people with whom we are concerned, that the idea of doing such a thing would never, of itself, enter into their minds. . . .[51]

Soon after his arrival in Natal, Bulwer called Osborn from Zululand for consultation on the Zulu question. On 15 April 1882 while he was in Pietermaritzburg he was approached by Zulu messengers who informed him that a Zulu deputation was nearing the city and wished to be introduced to the new Special Commissioner.[52] Osborn lost his temper 'and became excited, and flew out at them'.[53] The presence of two thousand Zulu in Natal, without permission, was obviously very embarrassing for the Resident. At the same time he could not afford to alienate the deputation to such an extent as to lose all control over its members and allow them to march through the streets of Pietermaritzburg to Government House. Moreover he knew by now that everything he said to the Usuthu would reach Colenso and possibly be made public. Thus, after his initial outburst, Osborn became more conciliatory. He promised to report their request to the Governor, pointing out that, no matter how he felt personally, the question of whether or not they would be allowed to make their petitions lay with the Special Commissioner. Then, after having given the impression to the Usuthu that responsibility lay with Bulwer, Osborn advised Bulwer not to give official recognition to the Zulu's illegal action by granting them an interview.

After hearing nothing from Osborn by 21 April the Zulu began to move towards Pietermaritzburg. Osborn hurried out to stop them. He asked again for the object of their visit, took down the names of the leaders, and promised to inform the Special Commissioner. On 24 April he met them again and asked them to put their request to him officially.

So as to act in accord with official wishes, it was the representatives of three appointed chiefs who spoke first and they gave a similar message:

> Our chiefs said we are to ask you to help them in their prayer for Cetywayo and to enable us to approach the Governor to prefer the prayer.
>
> They say when a man beats his child he afterwards wipes his child's tears.[54]

The Usuthu then gave an account of their history under the settlement.[55] Their sufferings at the hands of Hamu, Zibhebhu and Dunn were recounted fully and vehemently: the Zulu had been 'eaten up' on the grounds that they had concealed royal cattle; there had been demands for tribute; their appeal to the Resident had been rejected and as a result of his intervention their sufferings at the hands of Zibhebhu and Hamu had only increased. To them it appeared as if Osborn had misled them and not considered their complaints. As Ziwedu said:

> Before we go on, Sir, you should tell us what has become of the report which you wrote when you heard us and Zibebu together, since you told us that you had reported then. But Zibebu sent to tell us that 'we need not think that *our* words had gone in that letter, for that you, Sir, had deceived us, and had sent his words only'.
>
> And then we were called to meet Lukuni (Sir E. Wood), and then indeed it appeared that Zibebu's words had come true. It is of no use for us to speak here to you on the hill-side, since you yourself say that you cannot bear witness for yourself. But take us, Sir, to the Governor, and let the whole business be made plain, since the persecutors all say that it is your doing.[56]

As we have seen in Chapter 7 these are very reasonable inferences to be drawn from the events which led up to the Nhlazatshe meeting. And there is no reason to doubt that the appointed chiefs shifted a good deal of the responsibility for their actions onto the British Resident. To Bulwer, however, the fact that the Usuthu even questioned the Resident's veracity and good faith was intolerable. He wrote, no doubt on Osborn's advice, that Ndabuko and Ziwedu had adopted an 'exceedingly disrespectful and overbearing' tone and had charged Osborn

> with not reporting their words to the Government. They demanded that his letters to the Government about them should be laid open before their assembly in the presence of the Governor. They said that they would not talk over matters in the veldt with him, but *would* go into Town, and see the Governor, and talk before all the great men in town. They had come to do this and would do it.
>
> The behaviour of these men towards the Resident on this occasion accords well, I am told, with their general character and the pretensions to which, as brothers of the ex-king, they lay claim, Undabuko, especially, being well known for a most overbearing disposition, and it will be remembered that it was their rebellious conduct towards the appointed chief Usibebu which led to their being obliged to leave his territory.

Their behaviour towards the Resident on Monday last was without excuse, and the distrust which they affected to feel of his good faith in reporting truly to the Government was an audacious attempt to gain their ends, and to discredit any unfavourable account he might have to give of them by discrediting his trustworthiness. . . .[57]

Not wishing to expose the Resident to further treatment of this kind, and more determined than ever not to see the Zulu deputation, Bulwer asked John Shepstone, the Acting SNA, to order them to return to Zululand. On 27 April the representatives of the deputation were told to leave Natal and put their case to Osborn in Zululand. Shepstone reported:

These men were most respectful in their behaviour, and paid particular attention to what was said to them, and accepted the instruction to return home without demur. . . .[58]

Their departure was, however, delayed by the arrival in Pietermaritzburg of John Dunn. Bulwer decided not to lose this chance of examining, in the presence of their chief, the members of the Usuthu deputation from Dunn's territory, and they appeared before the Special Commissioner on 2 May.[59] In a long inconclusive wrangle the Usuthu accused Dunn of stating that the taxes he collected were for the government when they were in fact used by him personally, and of imposing fines and seizing royal cattle unjustly. Dunn either denied the charges or held that he was merely exercising the authority granted him by the settlement. Bulwer felt that the charges made against Dunn were not substantiated; the Usuthu returned to Zululand saying that Dunn had been 'thoroughly beaten'. The meeting ended with a long speech from Bulwer in which he admonished the Zulu for leaving their territory without Dunn's permission, and he urged them to obey their appointed chief. Dabulamanzi promised to consider what the Governor had said and returned two days later to tell him that he and the other chiefs refused to remain under Dunn any longer. Bulwer informed the Colonial Office that Dabulamanzi had probably been advised to take this course at a meeting he had with Bishop Colenso at Bishopstowe.[60]

For the Colensos, the visit of the Zulu party to Natal was the ultimate proof that 'all Zululand' desired the restoration of the king. For Bulwer it was an overbearing, unrepresentative pressure group, instigated by the Colensos with the intention of forcing the Special Commissioner's hand. The deputation had made the journey to Natal, Bulwer believed, not primarily to see the Special Commissioner, but to give Colenso the ammunition he needed to work on public opinion and the British Government, and make it appear that there was a general wish for Cetshwayo in Zululand. Moreover these agitators spread reports in Zululand of the king's impending return, thus calling in question the authority of the appointed chiefs, upsetting the working of the settlement, and making it extremely difficult for Bulwer to conduct his investigation into the Zulu situation and make recommendations about the country's future. He therefore suggested that Her Majesty's Government 'postpone [the] visit of [the] —— ex-king until [his] future is decided or for some time'. Reluctantly Kimberley agreed, but at the same time he urged Bulwer to visit Zululand and make his report on the country's future as soon as he could.[61]

An examination of the backgrounds of the leaders of the deputation gives a fairly clear idea of their motives and intentions. Of the two thousand Zulu, 646 were said to be chiefs and headmen. There were five sons of Mpande present, but the core of the deputation was made up of men from the northern districts who, in the two and a half years since the invasion, had suffered from the attentions of Zibhebhu and Hamu. They included the two *abantwana*, Ndabuko and Ziwedu, the leaders of the Mandlakazi *ikhohlo*,[62] Msushwana of the Mdletshe, and representatives of men of rank and status whose homesteads were in the southern portions of Zibhebhu's district, like Mbopha and Mfinyeli. From Hamu's territory came Tshanibezwe, chief son of Mnyamana. Mahubulwana of the Qulusi was back in Natal again, and two more royal sections, the Sebeni and Mphangisweni were represented, as well as the Egazini lineage of the Zulu under Hlezibane. Men like these were the driving force behind the Usuthu; frustrated at Nhlazatshe they were motivated by anger, resentment, and the desire for retribution, and a very real fear for their survival.[63]

Shingana, Sitheku and Dabulamanzi were all sons of Mpande who had lost authority by the settlement, like Somhlolo the unrecognised chief of the Biyela. There were also the representatives of three appointed chiefs, the minor lineage head Faku of the Ntombela, and the important *izikhulu* Sekethwayo of the Mdlalose, and Somkhele of the Mpukunyoni, both of whom had given unequivocal support to the Usuthu and were now demonstrating it publicly. Thus, although dominated by men from the northern districts, members of the deputation of 1882 were not confined to the districts of Hamu and Zibhebhu. A few other appointed chiefs had gained confidence during 1881 and were asserting their authority, and thereby provoking a reaction. Some members complained of the actions of Mfanawendlela, Siyunguza, and Mgitshwa and the party from Dunn's district was particularly strong. It was led by Dabulamanzi, and many of the major chiefs were represented. One of Dunn's 'magistrates' reported that there were Zulu represented from every district within the territory.[64] Although Dunn's energetic collecting of royal cattle and his imposition of hut tax were resented, his rule does not seem to have been particularly oppressive if compared to that of Hamu and Zibhebhu. But the five-shilling hut tax was doubled in 1881[65] and by this time it had become clear that the tax was not imposed by most of the appointed chiefs, and that it was for Dunn's personal use.

Other Zulu joined the deputation for less obvious reasons. In 1882 many wild rumours were current in Zululand. Reports of the king's impending visit to England, and his possible restoration were passed on in garbled form by traders from Natal, together with snatches of information from Zulu who had attended the king in Cape Town. These became exaggerated and confused as they passed from homestead to homestead. Many Zulu, worried by these reports, and in need of first-hand information, sent representatives with the Usuthu party to gather information, and no doubt to keep on the right side of the royal house in the event of restoration.

The political aims of the organisers of the Zulu party were two-fold. First, they were acting on the king's order that they should go to Natal and demonstrate their support for him and ask for his restoration. It would be naive however to see the visit (as the Colensos tended to do) purely as a selfless show of loyalty to the deposed monarch. Cetshwayo's return was requested for a number of reasons, the most general being the hope that it would bring about political change in Zululand which would recognise the power of the deposed political officers, reduce that of the appointed chiefs and force them to make amends for their actions. Secondly, those Zulu who had been expelled from their homes wished to return and the restoration of the king would facilitate this. Their position was becoming increasingly desperate. Ndabuko, Ziwedu and the Mandlakazi *ikhohlo* had been driven from their homes in the spring of 1881 and had been unable to utilise the crops of the preceding year or plant for the coming one. Their friends and supporters had given them shelter and food, but a midsummer drought in the 1881–2 season had caused widespread crop failure. As the winter of 1882 drew nearer it became increasingly obvious to the expelled men that if they did not have land to cultivate in the 1882–3 season they would be in serious difficulties. Thus for many of those present in the Usuthu party, their journey to Natal was more than a political move to expedite Cetshwayo's return and the end of the 1879 settlement. It was also a move made in desperation by people who saw that, if there was no change in the coming months, their survival as members of viable social entities would be seriously threatened.

For Dunn, Hamu and Zibhebhu, the deputation was another example of the Usuthu determination to flout their authority and to threaten their positions as appointed chiefs. As the deputation travelled back to northern

Zululand, Dunn reported that Dabulamanzi and Ndabuko were calling up their followers in his territory and women and children were seen moving from Zululand towards the Thukela and Natal for safety.[66] Dunn ordered the headmen in his district to 'confront' those who had been to Natal, but few responded to his call.[67] Dunn also asked Bulwer for permission to take 'steps' against Ndabuko and his followers who were inciting his people. Bulwer told Dunn to obey the terms of his appointment and exercise 'moderation and forbearance',[68] and he reported to London that Ndabuko and Dabulamanzi were fomenting disturbances although he could not yet tell whether they would go beyond 'intrigue and agitation, and . . . passive quasi rebellion'.[69]

As it turned out, Ndabuko and his supporters soon passed through Dunn's territory on their way to the northern districts. But before they arrived they heard that Hamu had sacked three of Mnyamana's homesteads and that Zibhebhu had seized property from the members of the Mandlakazi lineage represented on the deputation.[70]

Mbopha's Hlabisa and Msushwana's Mdletshe abandoned their homes, sending their non-combatants into Somkhele's territory while the fighting men gathered in the forests near where the Hluhluwe game reserve is today. They alleged that they took this extreme measure because they had heard that Zibhebhu was about to attack them.[71] Zibhebhu stated that they had left their homes in preparation for an Usuthu invasion of his district.[72]

By this time the *abantwana* and Osborn had arrived at Nhlazatshe from Natal and the reports of these events reached them there. Osborn tried to intervene but failed to improve the situation. The Usuthu armed and gathered on the Sikhwebezi river near Mnyamana's homesteads. The Mdlalose and the refugee Qulusi raided Hamu's territory and were joined by the Egazini, Mphangisweni and other Qulusi. The Emgazini under Mabhoko and the 'Thonga' groups to the north and north-east of Zibhebhu mobilised.

The officials alleged that rebellion had broken out and that the Usuthu were about to move against Hamu and Zibhebhu after which they would overthrow Dunn 'with the ultimate intention of Undabuko making himself master of Zululand'. Bulwer accepted Osborn's interpretation that

> The ostensible object of the party . . . is to bring about Cetywayo's restoration, but their real motives in creating the present disturbances are . . . personal interests and revenge.[73]

On the other hand, Usuthu messengers told Colenso that the trouble had begun before the Usuthu leaders had arrived back in Zululand.

Their followers had heard of an impending attack by Zibhebhu and Hamu, and taken defensive action.[74] Far from planning to overthrow the settlement the Usuthu leaders on their return held their people back and attempted to bring the situation under control.

There is strong circumstantial evidence to suggest that there was no truth in the allegation that these disturbances were the initial stages of a 'rebellion'. Osborn was eventually able to persuade the Usuthu to disband their forces, once they had been assured that Hamu and Zibhebhu would do the same.[75] Mnyamana was personally approached by Bulwer to use his influence for peace and he did so willingly and with real effect informing Bulwer that at last he felt that he was

> not cast away, and have hope that I shall live. . . . Who am I, that I should make war upon anyone? What I did was self-defence . . . [and I send you] one of my principal men . . . as proof of my sincerity, and that I now feel that I am known to the Government.[76]

Nonetheless Osborn persisted in stating that Mnyamana was determined to establish himself as an independent chief and the rule of 'Chaka's dynasty' over the whole country. Osborn's extraordinarily prejudiced and hostile attitude towards Mnyamana may well have been the result of a deliberate effort to discredit Mnyamana in Bulwer's eyes. It is significant that Bulwer had made contact with Mnyamana independently of the British Resident, and one must suspect that by discrediting the Special Commissioner's informant, Mnyamana, Osborn was protecting himself from any evidence of his own shortcomings that might have reached Pietermaritzburg.[77]

At the heart of the disturbances lay the mutual mistrust and fear that existed between Hamu and Zibhebhu on the one hand, and the Usuthu party on the other. When the deputation returned to Zululand rumours of an imminent attack on the appointed chiefs were widespread, but so were rumours of an attack by Hamu and Zibhebhu on the Usuthu; no doubt members of both parties had made many threatening statements at one time or another. As it happened, it was Hamu who made the first move when he raided Mnyamana's homesteads, and this gave rise to mutual arming and mobilisation. But although the situation of those Usuthu who had been driven from their homes and lost their land was grave, and in spite of their real grievances and fears, the Usuthu leaders felt that their best chance still lay in attempting to co-operate with the officials: they were not yet prepared to take the momentous step of trying to depose the Queen's appointees, and to brave the unknown consequences. Moreover a crucial consideration in Usuthu thinking was the reports of Cetshwayo's possible restoration. They had after all made the trip to Pietermaritzburg to demonstrate Zulu support for the king, and to provide him with ammunition when negotiating with the authorities in England. There was little point in their throwing away all chances of negotiation in Zululand before Cetshwayo had been given an opportunity to bring about reform by appealing above the heads of the local officials.

But although a major clash was averted in the winter of 1882 peace was not attained for many years. The sporadic local violence which had taken place between the appointed chiefs and the Usuthu in northern Zululand since the end of the war was now gaining an impetus of its own. Minor border clashes between Zibhebhu's men and those expelled from his districts continued. The Hlabisa and Mdletshe who had fled from their up-country homes in Zibhebhu's district suffered from diseases they contracted in the lowlands of Somkhele's district where they had taken refuge. Their cattle died and they suffered from malnutrition. Osborn was to receive a stream of complaints and petitions asking that they might be allowed to return to their homes. The suffering of these exiled groups and the legacy of resentment it left was to play a significant part in fuelling the violence that was soon to overwhelm the country.

Notes

1 A. Preston (ed.), *The South African Journal of Sir Garnet Wolseley, 1879–1880*, Cape Town, 1973, p. 103, entry for 31 Aug. 1879.

2 J. Martineau, *The Life and Correspondence of the Right Hon. Sir Bartle Frere*, London, 1895, ii, p. 345.

3 See above, p. 93.

4 CO 879/16, 204: no. 230, enc., message from Cetshwayo to Queen Victoria, 27 Oct. 1879.

5 'Cetshwayo's story of the Zulu nation and the war', in *Macmillan's Magazine*, Feb. 1880. Colenso reprinted most of this article in series 1, pp. 705–32, and was critical of certain passages which he believed owed more to the king's captors than Cetshwayo himself.

6 BPP, C.2695: 20, enc. 2, Cetshwayo to Frere, 8 May 1880.

7 NA, Sir T. Shepstone collection: box 15, Frere to Shepstone, 17 May 1880 (private and confidential).

8 Ibid., 24 June 1880. Solomon, the publisher and Cape Parliamentarian assisted Colenso in his attempts to help both Cetshwayo and Langalibalele; see W. E. G. Solomon, *Saul Solomon, 'The Member for Cape Town'*, Cape Town, 1948, pp. 167ff. and 293–4. Shepstone's memo was dated 4 June 1880 and can be found in BPP, C.2695; 30, enc. 2.

9 For an account of the visit see Colenso, series 1, pp. 749–60.

10 Ibid., pp. 751–2.

11 For accounts of Mkhosana's return see Colenso, series 2, pp. 230–1.

12 According to Maphelu, who was Mkhosana's son (KC, Maphelu, p. 15), they were Ngobozana, Mavumengwana, Ngcongcwana, Maqhoboza, Phosile,

Hayiyana, and Mabedla. Maphelu's account of events at this stage is useful but raises a number of problems as there is a major confusion in chronology.

13 Ibid., p. 53.

14 Ibid., p. 53.

15 Ngobozana, Ncongcwana and Phosile.

16 They were also the subject of lengthy controversy between Bishopstowe and the officials. See Colenso's analysis of the official documents in series 2, pp. 216–51 which reveals cross-cultural confusion, misunderstanding, intimidation, an obstructive attitude on the part of local officials, evidence of a conscious evasion on the part of Osborn, and a certain disingenuousness on the part of Colenso.

17 In his important, but naive and eccentric autobiography, *Long, Long Ago*, Durban, 1929, Chs 13–15, Samuelson gives an account of his life with Cetshwayo in Cape Town. His diary, on which much of this is based, is in KC.

18 See below, p. 149.

19 BPP, C.2866: 95, enc., Cetshwayo to Robinson, 1 March 1881, p. 185.

20 BPP, C.2950: 42, enc. 2, Cetshwayo to Robinson, 29 March 1881, p. 129.

21 BM, Add. MSS, 44226: Kimberley to Gladstone, 3 June 1881.

22 BPP, C.3247: 1, enc., Cetshwayo to Robinson, 2 May 1881.

23 See Samuelson's covering letter to Colenso, in KC, Colenso collection: folio 26, Z185, Samuelson to Colenso, 16 June 1881; also the Bishop's account of this new departure in the same collection, Z187, J. W. Colenso to Chesson, 2 July 1881.

24 CO 48/501: 13862, Smyth to Kimberley, 12 July 1881, encs. and minutes.

25 Samuelson, in *Long, Long Ago*, p. 99, appears to confuse the names of the various Zulu at this point.

26 See above, p. 128.

27 BPP, C.3247: 1, Smyth to Kimberley, 15 July 1881, p. 1.

28 CO 48/501: 14062, minute by Fairfield, 9 Aug. 1881.

29 Ibid., minute by Courtney, 9 Aug. 1881.

30 BPP, C.3247: 2, Kimberley to Robinson, 11 Aug. 1881, p. 2.

31 BPP, C.3247: 3, enc. 2, Cetshwayo to Kimberley, 15 July 1881, pp. 2–3.

32 Ibid., enc. 1, Cetshwayo to Gladstone, 15 July 1881, p. 2.

33 BM, Add. MSS, 44226: Kimberley to Gladstone, 26 Aug. 1881.

34 Ibid., Kimberley to Gladstone, 2 Sept. 1881.

35 BPP, C.3247: 4, Kimberley to Robinson, 14 Sept. 1881 (teleg.).

36 CO 179/138: 15682, minute by Kimberley, 6 Sept. 1881.

37 See above, p. 116.

38 CO 179/138: 17877, minute by Fairfield, 14 Oct. 1881.

39 CO 179/138: 19985, minute by Kimberley.

40 Bulwer had been Lt Governor of Natal from Sept. 1875 to April 1880, and returned as Governor, and Special Commissioner for Zululand, in March 1882.

41 BPP, C.3247: 17, enc., Cetshwayo (to Robinson), 21 Dec. 1881, p. 13.

42 Name given to Sir Evelyn Wood. 'Ulukhuni' means not only 'wood' but someone of a 'hard, unyielding' character.

43 I have been unable to trace most of the clandestine correspondence between the king and Bishopstowe. This fragment is in AS papers: 131/118; it is undated but headed: '(This letter shews the confidence which Cetywayo had in the attachment of his people for him.) NB *This letter, of course, must not be*

published. Copy of letter from Cetshwayo to the Bp. of Natal.' It seems to have been provided for the information of Colenso's biographer, G. W. Cox.

44 KC, Colenso papers: Z223, J. W. Colenso to Chesson, 28 Dec. 1881.

45 See above, p. 57.

46 BPP, C.2584: 66, enc., Bulwer to Wolseley, 4 Feb. 1880, p. 143.

47 CO 48/501: 976, minute by Herbert, 26 Jan. 1882.

48 See for example, the entry for 13 April 1880, in *Wolseley's Journal*, p. 270, which begins, 'In talking of Sir T. Shepstone whom Sir H. Bulwer dislikes very much . . .'

49 See above, p. 84.

50 D. Welsh, *The Roots of Segregation: native policy in colonial Natal*, Oxford, 1970, p. 202.

51 BPP, C.3466: 42, Bulwer to Kimberley, 30 June 1882, p. 74.

52 This account of the visit to Pietermaritzburg is drawn largely from the official record in BPP, C.3247: 78 and encs.; also C.3270; No. 1 and encs. Although the Zulu deliberately avoided obvious contact with Bishopstowe, the Colenso family was kept fully informed of what occurred. The original reports by the Usuthu can be found on pp. 189–215 of Colenso, series 2, and the narrative constructed from these was published in BPP, C.3466: 18, APS to CO, 7 July 1882, enc., Account of the Great Zulu Deputation from a Zulu point of view.

53 Colenso, series 2, p. 198.

54 BPP, C.3247: 78, enc. 2, Osborn to Bulwer, 24 April 1882, notes of interview between British Resident and Cetshwayo's brothers and Zulu Chiefs, p. 70.

55 When one considers the problems in transcribing and translating the long statements of the members of the deputation, and bears in mind that the Usuthu messengers who reported to Colenso had to memorise the proceedings, the official and the Bishopstowe versions of this interview are, in the main, surprisingly similar. There are, however, important inconsistencies. The most significant is the difference in tone: in the Bishopstowe account the Usuthu are firm but respectful; in the official version they are violent and antagonistic, particularly Ndabuko.

56 Colenso, series 2, p. 204.

57 BPP, C.3247: 78, Bulwer to Kimberley, 29 April 1882, pp. 65–6.

58 Ibid., enc. 3, J. Shepstone, memo of interview, 28 April 1882, p. 74.

59 BPP, C.3270: 1, enc. 1, notes taken at an interview, 2 May 1882.

60 This allegation evoked a written denial from Colenso and the ensuing correspondence illustrates the antagonism which developed between him and Bulwer. See for example, BPP, C.3247: 89, Bulwer to Kimberley, 12 May 1882, and C.3466: 60, enc. 1, Colenso to Bulwer, 22 July 1882.

61 GHZ 844: Bulwer to Kimberley, 9 May 1882 and the reply, 10 May 1882 (telegs.).

62 Hayiyana, eldest son of Maphitha, and Mahu and Fokothi.

63 This section is based on BPP, C.3247: 78, enc. 1, Osborn to Bulwer, 21 April 1882, list of chiefs and headmen present at an interview with the British Resident near Pietermaritzburg, 21 April 1882.

64 GHZ 678, F. Galloway to Dunn, 6 May 1882, forwarded in Dunn to J. Shepstone, 8 May 1882. Of the most important chiefs, Qethuka, Hlongolwana, Nobiya, Zokufa and Ndwandwe were represented.

65 Dunn informed the authorities that he collected £2 468 in 1880 and £5 101 in 1881. See BPP, C.3466: 83, enc., Osborn to Bulwer, 2 Aug. 1882.

66 BPP, C.3270: 4, enc. 1, Dunn to SNA, 16 May 1882 (teleg.) and enc. 5, Border Agent to SNA, 17 May 1882.

67 Colenso, series 2, p. 315.

68 BPP, C.3270: 4, enc. 2, SNA to Dunn, 16 May 1882 (teleg.).

69 Ibid., Bulwer to Kimberley, 20 May 1882.

70 An Usuthu account of these incidents can be found in Colenso, series 2, pp. 324–9. The official report and an Usuthu statement can be found in BPP, C.3466: 20, Bulwer to Kimberley, 10 June 1882, statement A, 17 May 1882, and statement B, 26 May 1882, both by Umbozisa, brother of Mnyamana.

71 BPP, C.3466: 58, annexure, statement by Ndabuko, 28 June 1882, statement by Msushwana, 29 June 1882.

72 Ibid.: 69, enc. 1, Osborn to Bulwer, 12 July 1882, statement by Sikota and Unhlanhla, 11 July 1882.

73 Ibid.: 28, Bulwer to Kimberley, 17 June 1882, p. 55.

74 Colenso, series 2, p. 328.

75 BPP, C.3466: 41, enc. 1, Osborn to Bulwer, 23 June 1882.

76 Ibid.: 53, enc., statement by Kilane and Ungalonkulu, 11 July 1882, p. 89.

77 For Osborn's comments see BPP, C.3466: 52 and 58, and GH(Z) 679, Osborn to Bulwer, 30 June 1882.

CHAPTER NINE

The partition of Zululand

Cetshwayo in London: July to September 1882

For Bulwer the visit of the Usuthu deputation to Pietermaritzburg in April 1882 and the violence which broke out in Zululand on its return were manifestations of the agitation taking place at Bishopstowe and the intimidation carried out by the Usuthu. Bulwer did what he could to persuade London to assist him in bringing it to a halt. His attacks on the Colensos and the Usuthu during the following months were long, detailed and frequent. From Sir Theophilus Shepstone he obtained the anthropological data to back the argument that the Zulu were psychologically incapable of protesting against an arrangement devised by their conquerors, unless disturbed by ideas of external origin. With this *a priori* position it was not difficult to show that the Zulu unrest was the consequence of agitation from outside, disturbing the essential passivity of the African mind. Melmoth Osborn, the British Resident, supplied Bulwer with evidence of the determination of the Usuthu leaders to upset the settlement and seize power. John Shepstone turned his hand to obtaining evidence on the activities of the Colensos. African informers and spies attached to the SNA's office went to Bishopstowe, drank beer, and exchanged stories with Natal Africans and visiting Zulu, gathering extraordinary tales of sedition and exhortations to violence which, in time, arrived in London as enclosures in confidential dispatches.[1]

But any success Bulwer had in discrediting the Colensos and the Usuthu was necessarily limited as long as it was public knowledge that Cetshwayo was soon to visit England to put his case. In May Bulwer successfully persuaded Kimberley to postpone Cetshwayo's journey.

When Cetshwayo was told the news it was thought from his reaction that he had suffered a heart attack. After he had recovered and it was explained to him that the postponement was thought necessary to avoid bloodshed in Zululand he burst out:

There has been more bloodshed since I have been a prisoner than during the whole of my reign. The bloodshed in my reign was, to the bloodshed since, as an ant in a pond of water. . . . What crime have I committed? I have never done wrong! Why am I a prisoner? My wives and daughters – the women of the Great House – have been taken and distributed amongst my enemies in Zululand. Sibebu has taken five of the women of the Great House as wives, and has given the others to his chiefs and headmen. The thought of this is eating into my heart. It will kill me.[2]

Once again it was feared that Cetshwayo might take his own life. Orders were given to keep him under close observation and clumsy attempts were made to distract the king's thoughts from Zulu affairs by keeping him occupied. It was suggested that he express himself in letters to his friends. The king, it was reported, said 'smiling . . . that letters are now his only assegais'.[3]

But, although they had bowed to Bulwer's demand that the visit of the king be postponed, the Colonial Office officials were becoming increasingly uneasy over the Special Commissioner's attitude to Zulu affairs. Bulwer's long dispatches concentrated on attacking Bishopstowe and discrediting the Usuthu as agitators but they did little to suggest what steps should be taken in Zululand. London found Bulwer negative and procrastinating, and it was felt that he should 'address himself to the practical points' raised by the possibility of the king's restoration and accept eventual restoration as a fact, rather than rail against the difficulties it raised. Kimberley agreed and commented:

> Rather too many 'ifs'. No doubt '*if*' every one would abstain from agitation &c &c this would be the best possible of worlds for Government and Governors. As there is not the slightest chance of the Governmental millennium, we must accept the facts and deal with them accordingly.[4]

In June 1882 Kimberley pointed out that the news of the postponement had not had any apparent effect on the 'disturbances' in Zululand and he forced Bulwer to agree to Cetshwayo visiting London immediately. The knowledge that Cetshwayo was going to negotiate directly with the British only persuaded Bulwer and his advisers to intensify their attacks. Fairfield minuted:

> These Reports are intended to prove that the agitation in favour of Cetywayo is fictitious and fostered by terrorism. Exactly the same information was supplied about the agitation among the Boers for independence; but the absolute unanimity of the Boers in fighting the English Govt. proved how utterly worthless the official information was.

Anthony Ashley, the Under-Secretary for the Colonies, agreed. It was, he said,

> The sempiternal error that, because an agitation can be shown to have

leaders, who stir and conduct it, therefore it is fictitious and unreal! Every movement, however deep seated it may be, must have leaders and advisers. The larger the movement the more necessity there is for a few directing hands.

Kimberley then remarked that it 'is the same old & very dangerous delusion, which has been the ruin of more governments than perhaps anything else'.[5]

By the end of July, with Cetshwayo due to arrive in England within a few days, Bulwer had still not visited Zululand to discover the 'real feelings' of the Zulu as he had been instructed, let alone made recommendations on the country's future. Kimberley was forced to demand that Bulwer telegraph his 'main conclusions',[6] and five days later Bulwer replied: Cetshwayo could return to Zululand if he was placed in authority over only a portion of the country, and territory had to be set aside for those Zulu unwilling to come under the king's rule and this territory should be proclaimed a protectorate.[7] A flurry of telegrams from Kimberley ascertained that Bulwer believed that this area excluded from the king's authority should become a 'special native territory under Natal Government rule', but failing this, should be proclaimed a British protectorate.[8]

Kimberley would have none of it. He ordered Bulwer to proceed on the principle that Cetshwayo was to be restored to that part of Zululand which would accept his authority, and that a territory should be assigned to those chiefs who were not prepared to remain under Cetshwayo. No part of Zululand was to become 'British territory either under [the] Natal Government or otherwise. . . .'[9]

It was decided that Cetshwayo should be informed of these basic principles while he was in London. Once he had accepted them the details of the arrangement could be worked out later. As Kimberley told Gladstone, some initiative had to be taken and he was

> anxious to set Bulwer in motion. He is very procrastinating and the state of Zulu affairs will not bear further delay.
>
> We must leave him discretion as to details as much must depend upon the temper of the chiefs.[10]

On 12 July Cetshwayo left Cape Town on board the R.M.S. *Arab*. His party included Sir Theophilus' son, Henrique, as interpreter, companion and guide. Henrique had been out of a job since the retrocession of the Transvaal and was given the post in spite of Lady Florence Dixie's clumsy attempt to obstruct his appointment.[11] There were two other interpreters: Lazarus Xaba from Edendale near Pietermaritzburg, an African assistant of Sir Theophilus for many years, and R. E. Dunn (who was not related to John). Cetshwayo had three chiefs with him: Mkhosana of the Zungu, Ngcongcwana of the Zulu, and Ngobozana. By this time these Africans were well-versed in white manners and customs, and their behaviour evoked patronising admiration from their fellow passengers. An elderly woman spent her time knitting socks for the king, and it was reported that the nephew of Shaka and the victor at Isandlwana admonished a sailor for throwing a cat overboard. Even Shepstone, who had to deal with Cetshwayo's personal needs and found him spoilt and petulant, could not fault the way in which the king conducted himself publicly.[12]

But Cetshwayo did not let either the novelty of the journey or his fear of the sea interfere with the political objectives of the mission. Soon after leaving Cape Town he asked for a meeting with Henrique Shepstone, apparently with the object of sounding him out and winning him to his side if possible.

Cetshwayo had already decided that, whatever he felt personally about Sir Theophilus Shepstone and his treachery before the invasion, he could not afford to continue the dispute with Somtsewu or his family while he was prisoner. Sir Theophilus and his brother and sons were too influential, and if Cetshwayo could get it, he needed their support.[13] The meeting therefore opened with an explanation of the king's attacks on Henrique's father at the time of the invasion and they discussed the role Colenso played in Zulu matters. The king did not speak against Colenso but he did make the point that Sobantu was inclined to act impulsively. After further fencing Cetshwayo asked what tactics he should use in London. Shepstone replied that he should not try to 'justify himself & set the English wrong' but rather

> appeal to their feelings of mercy saying that he was a child who had been punished by its Father for doing what his Father thought was wrong, that a Father never punished with a view of destroying his child but only for correction & warning as to his future conduct &c.[14]

Cetshwayo and his three Zulu advisers listened carefully and did not question this advice. When the time came to meet the officials in London however, Cetshwayo did not follow it.

Cetshwayo's impending visit caused a considerable stir among the public in London. A special train was ordered to take the party to London, and to avoid the crowds at Paddington station, Cetshwayo was taken off the train at Westbourne Park to the house in Kensington where he was to stay. Curious crowds gathered outside hoping for a glimpse of the Zulu monarch and he had to appear every few hours on the balcony to acknowledge their cheers.

One of the purposes of the visit was to impress the king with the power and might of the British nation; thus Woolwich Arsenal and the London Docks were placed on the king's itinerary. The visit to the London Zoo was by all accounts a great success, and a tour was made of the Houses of Parliament.

Cetshwayo met many notable figures in British public life. He argued with Gladstone over whether he or John Bright was the greatest orator in the House and he mistook the Prince of Wales' wife for his daughter. He played his public role with skill and charm. Gifts, including a stag from Lady Florence Dixie which none of the Zulu would touch, poured into their London house together with a variety of letters. They included an application for a job as a wizard in Zululand, and an acrostic from the Brighton Workhouse:

C etewayo! Zulu King!
E ngland thee is welcoming
T hy misfortune through sad war
E nglish hearts have watched afar
W hen returned to Afric's shore
A fter thy brief visit o'er
Y oung and old hope thou again
O ver Zululand may'st reign![15]

But once he was out of the public eye the king was not so easy to please. Uppermost in his mind were the political objectives of the visit and he brooded over the possibility of failure. He was often quarrelsome and jealous of favours shown to his attendants. He was also nervous of going out, and of the crowds that mobbed him in the streets, fearing that a relative of someone killed in the war might attempt to assassinate him. He did not leave the house at night if it could be avoided. When on one occasion his Zulu councillors tried to go out, some girls broke from the waiting crowd, embraced and kissed them; according to the horrified Shepstone 'they bolted inside as there were a lot of other girls & they were afraid that they might attack them also'.

Cetshwayo's first interview with Kimberley took place at the Colonial Office on 7 August 1882. It was an informal meeting and Cetshwayo was invited to make 'any statement as to his case that he desired'.[16] The king replied that he wanted to know why the British had punished him, but Kimberley refused 'now to go into the past'. In a rather shapeless discussion various topics came up including reports which had reached England of Cetshwayo's 'cruelties'. Cetshwayo said he could not reply to 'mere general accusations', and asked for specific charges so that he could justify himself. None were forthcoming. The meeting finished with an

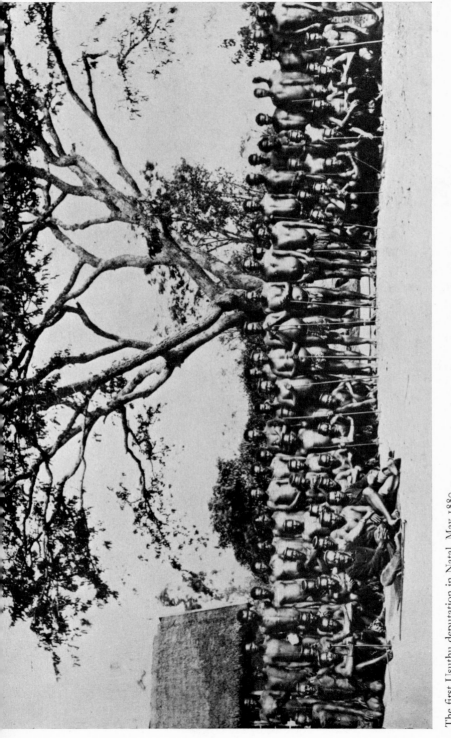

The first Usuthu deputation in Natal, May 1880

The leaders of the deputation are identified by numbers on this historic photograph as follows:

1 Ndabuko: Only full brother of the king: from Zibhebhu's territory; 2 Shingana: son of Mpande: from Faku's territory; 3 Ngcongcwana: member of the Zulu lineage: from Hamu's territory; 4 Makhoba: son of Maphitha and member of his *ikhohlo*: from Zibhebhu's district; 5 Ndabezimbi: member of the Mandlakazi, cousin of Zibhebhu; 6 Nyosana: member of the Emgazini lineage, son of Masiphula: from Hamu's district; 7 Nkungane: brother of Cetshwayo's mother, of the Zungu: from Zibhebhu's district; 8 Mkhosana: brother of Cetshwayo's mother, of the Zungu: from Zibhebhu's district; 9 Mhlolo: *induna* of the Ekubaseni royal homestead: from Zibhebhu's district; 10 Mahubulwana: chief *induna* of the Qulusi: from Hamu's district; 11 Magadeni: chief *induna* of the Isixepe *ikhanda*: from Ntshingwayo's district; 12 Dlambula: *imeku* to Cetshwayo: from Zibhebhu's district; 13 Mqobe: son of Mbopha of the Hlabisa: from Gawozi's (Siyunguza's) territory; 14 and 15: *izinceku* to Shingana; 16 Mgwazeni: brother of Cetshwayo's mother, of the Zungu: from Zibhebhu's district; 17 Ngatsha: *induna* of the Ekubaseni royal homestead: from Zibhebhu's territory; 18 Madlenya: son of Masingana, representing some of the Emgazini

Zulu king in exile: Cetshwayo kaMpande in London, August 1882

appeal by the king for the support of the British Government and the Queen.

'Let the Queen not take him merely by the hand', he said. 'If you take a man merely by the hand, he may slip from you. Let Lord Kimberley rather grasp him by the arm, and let the Queen take him by the waist, for then will they hold him fast.'[17]

They met again on 15 August 1882 for a formal interview. The Secretary of State was present together with Ashley, the Under-Secretary, and Meade and Bramston, Assistant Under-Secretaries, together with the Zulu delegation, and the three interpreters. Full records were kept.

Kimberley opened the meeting by informing the king that the British Government 'have determined to consider the possibility of making arrangements for his return to Zululand' under certain conditions:

First, a portion of the country, to be hereafter defined by Her Majesty's Government, will not be placed under his rule, but will be reserved for other purposes. . . .
Secondly, a Resident will be appointed by the Queen to advise him and report to Her Majesty. . . .
Thirdly, he will be required to enter into engagements with Her Majesty for the just and peaceful government of his people, similar to those by which the thirteen Chiefs are now bound.[18]

Cetshwayo was deeply disturbed – 'a portion of the country . . . will not be placed under his rule, but will be reserved for other purposes' – it was this condition upon which everything depended. Although soon after the war Cetshwayo had asked to be returned as a private individual his hopes had been raised since then. He had good reason to expect that he might be restored as ruler of the country and now he heard for the first time the suggestion of partition as a condition for his return. At the same time he knew the weakness of his bargaining position and he did not wish to appear dissatisfied or ungrateful; the obvious retort to an expression of protest, or even disappointment, would have been a reminder that it was only British magnanimity which gave him a chance to return to Zululand at all. Shaken, but fearing that a straightforward expression of protest would be seen as presumptuous, the king fumbled for an adequate response, saying

that after hearing what has just been said to him it stops him from making any reply now. He says, 'I might have spoken, but I am now quite unable to speak.'

He conferred privately with the chiefs, and then said that:

these words of your Lordship are pressing hard upon him. He says, 'If I had anything to say in my heart I would mention it, after I have had a "resting time to breathe".'

The Earl of Kimberley. – Tell him that it is very right and proper that he should have time to breathe, and that I have no desire to take any advantage of him by hurry. . . .

Mr. Dunn. – He says, what part of the country would you allow him.[19]

This was of course the vital question and Kimberley could not answer it: Bulwer had still to report on the feeling of the Zulu to the king's return and make recommendations on where the boundaries of the alienated territory should be drawn. However, the Secretary of State expressed his willingness to hear of

any particular portion of the territory about which he has any strong feeling, and that we have no wish to take anything that is not necessary.

But the meeting ended with the king expressing his great concern about the removal of any part of Zululand from his jurisdiction, and Kimberley trying to persuade him from taking too gloomy a view saying 'he should wait to see how much country will be reserved'.[20]

The final meeting took place two days later on 17 August. Cetshwayo informed Kimberley that he accepted without complaint all the conditions read to him on 15 August, except the one about the land which was to be reserved.

He says that after the kind way in which he has been met and the conditions being so satisfactory, he feels as if he had been raised up from the dead . . . and felt that he was to be seated again. But the land which belonged to his father is now very small . . . and the idea of another piece of land being taken from that little country has buried him up to his knees again. . . . He had been encouraged to speak to the English nation the feelings of his heart, and he asks that his feeling with reference to this piece of land, that his representations and feelings here, may be made known to the Government, and also to Her Majesty the Queen, with respect to this piece of land; and in that matter he throws himself on Her Majesty's mercy, and also hopes for the favourable consideration of Her Majesty's Government.[21]

Cetshwayo suspected that the portion of land to be removed from his rule might be that awarded to Dunn in 1879, and he asked to make a statement about the white man who 'came to me empty handed, and I picked him up . . . I took care of him, and he grew great under my fostering care . . .', but who acted treacherously towards his benefactor

'On the one side, he took my words, he came to me, and, as I thought, as my friend, took my words, got at the feelings of my heart, and turned my words on their back.'

Cetshwayo accused Dunn of plotting against him before the war, of taking his property after it, and obstructing the Zulu under him when they asked for their king's return.

'Who was John Dunn? who is John Dunn? what was John Dunn? and who would he have been if I had not raised him up? The English would never have heard of him; and I feel that it is placing an assegai by my side to let John Dunn be near me. He took my property and my cattle away from my children, and caused my people and my children to suffer hunger. . . . Who would stay with a rat in his hut that ate his food?'[22]

Kimberley's reply only exposed the weakness of Cetshwayo's position:

Say it is quite right that he should make his representation, but that the Government will expect the fulfilment of the conditions. He must respect the border limits which we may draw, and keep the peace, and I can add no word to that; and that if he is not willing to comply, the arrangements might become impossible.

Cetshwayo had no defence against this threat, and could only ask that the matter be reconsidered:

There may be a talk over-night, and a man lie on one side and lie on the other, and by the next morning he may see that another course might be taken or an improvement made. That is all I ask.[23]

The meeting drew to a close. Mkhosana, Cetshwayo's trusted adviser, assumed his usual role of the staid respectful councillor to the younger, more excitable king when he asked Kimberley to remember that

the child in speaking out as it has done has simply spoken to its father. . . . There is no self-will in the child in any way, but it simply wishes to represent its feelings to its father.[24]

Cetshwayo finished by pledging his allegiance and asking for continued support:

'I cannot take your hand alone; I take your arm, and I ask your Lordship to lay on one side and the other' (Cetywayo here took his Lordship's hand and right arm to indicate his pledges of friendship.)
The Earl of Kimberley – Say that, whether I am in office or not, I will always listen to his words if he acts well.
Mr Fynney[25] – 'I have gratefully accepted all that has been given to me, and in addition now I say, "My Lord, watch me." '[26]

On 14 August 1882 Cetshwayo and his party travelled to Osborne for an audience with the Queen.[27] The meeting was not an easy one. Shepstone was very nervous and the Queen, influenced by the military men who had led the 1879 invasion, had been opposed to Cetshwayo's visit to England.[28] Nevertheless she told the king that she had respected him as a brave enemy and trusted that he would now be a firm friend and the short audience closed with the Zulu visitors giving their royal salute.

On 1 September the Zulu party, with their large collection of gifts and purchases, sailed for Cape Town, to await the announcement of the details of the conditions under which Cetshwayo was to return to Zululand.

The partition of Zululand: September 1882 to January 1883

A few days before Cetshwayo left London, Bulwer dispatched his long-awaited report, entitled 'Settlement of Zulu Country'. It has to be remembered that the main points raised by Bulwer in the report had already been rejected in London in the telegram of 8 August.[29] The Special Commissioner was therefore writing with the knowledge that his most important suggestions were unacceptable to the Colonial Office. This is perhaps one reason why Bulwer, in this public dispatch, urged Kimberley to assume direct responsibility for at least a portion of Zululand with such vigour. Moreover, whatever positive aspects the report might have had, these were hopelessly outweighed by Bulwer's misconceptions about Zulu society and his acceptance of the notion that the majority of Zulu were eagerly seeking the security implicit in white rule.

In the report Bulwer dismissed the Usuthu interpretation of the history of the 1879 settlement; for him the basic weakness in the arrangement lay, not in the oppressive actions of certain appointed chiefs and the widespread desire for the king's return, but in

> the misunderstanding that exists as to the extent of the power that is vested in the appointed chiefs, and in the weakness arising from the want of a duly recognised and adequate paramount authority.[30]

The British held that authority lay with the appointed chiefs; the Zulu believed that it lay with the British by right of conquest. It therefore followed that this misunderstanding 'which strikes at the root of all authority' must be resolved and the settlement had to be altered. Any new arrangement

> must establish in some form that paramount and supreme authority, which is an essential condition of the Government of any native race.[31]

This could best be done by direct annexation to the Crown, but as Her Majesty's Government refused to consider this course, and because it insisted that Cetshwayo should play some part in the new arrangement, another solution had to be found. Any arrangement, Bulwer argued, had to take into consideration interests other than those of the Zulu royal house; the communities on Zululand's borders for example, and of those Zulu (particularly the appointed chiefs) who might be opposed to Cetshwayo's return.

Moreover Bulwer felt that unrestricted restoration could lead to the resuscitation of the Zulu dynasty and its concomitant, the Zulu military system. In a passage couched in Shepstonian mechanistic metaphor, Bulwer warned that while the military system might be a dormant, inactive power . . . at the present moment, but it exists – a perfect organisation, such as it has been from the time of Chaka. The system which was then established has, during a period of more than half a century, taken a deep root in the Zulu nation. It is part and parcel of the Zulu life, and its extinction would be the work of many years. The organisation is there, the material is there, the machinery is there. And as a time-piece, which has been suffered to run down and lies in disuse, is silent, but no sooner is the action of its mainspring restored than, complete in all the parts of its mechanism, it begins to tell again the hours and moments of time, so with the wonderful mechanism of the Zulu military system, it needs only to be touched by the master hand of whoever is recognised by the Zulu people as their supreme chief, and straightway the whole machinery is put in motion.[32]

Bulwer did not hide his opposition to Kimberley's plan to return Cetshwayo without at the same time accepting any responsibility for the country as a whole. With no enthusiasm he suggested his compromise solution, the restoration of Cetshwayo to part of Zululand only.

The portion of the country which was to be alienated from Cetshwayo's rule would serve as a place of refuge for the Zulu who objected to being placed under the king. It was absolutely essential that the British take this under their 'authority and protection'. But this tract of Zululand was to be more than a place of refuge for anti-royalist Zulu; it should also be open to Africans from Natal

who, being Zulus by birth, may be fairly considered to have an equal claim to live on Zulu soil with the Zulus who have remained in Zululand, and whose repatriation therefore and occupation of some portion of Zulu soil would not be an encroachment upon the rights of the Zulu people.[33]

This suggestion demonstrates the influence on Bulwer's thinking of the ex-Secretary for Native Affairs, Sir Theophilus Shepstone, and the manner in which he intended to use the return of Cetshwayo to subordinate the Zulu to Natal's interests.

Although in June 1880 Shepstone had attacked the idea of Cetshwayo's return, Bishop Colenso was surprised to learn, a year later, that Somtsewu was speaking in favour of it.[34] But the Colensos were soon to hear rumours that this change in attitude was the result of a larger plan in which Shepstone hoped to link the return of the king with the opening of part of Zululand to Natal's 'excess native population'. Colenso informed Chesson that Shepstone's

idea is that an outlet should be made for the redundant native population of Natal – redundant, that is, in the idea of colonists, & perhaps the Govt., who want land, now occupied by natives, for the use of white settlers – by allowing any people that choose to migrate into the southern belt of Zululand. . . .[35]

The Bishop's source of information proved to be reliable.

As we have seen,[36] Shepstone's desire for more land for the colony of Natal had a long history and by the mid-1870s he believed that the shortage of land available to the colony's black population was creating a situation which threatened the safety and security of all in Natal. Since then Zululand had been invaded but, to Shepstone's bitter disappointment, the country still remained beyond the colony's reach. Furthermore, Natal's Crown Lands, on which many Africans lived, had been placed on the market. Sir Theophilus, from retirement, urged the British Government to attend to the imminent crisis in Natal and the possible solution that lay in Zululand. He wrote that it had to be 'always borne in mind that the question of managing the Zulus in Natal, and that of managing those in Zululand, separated as they are by only a stream of water, is essentially and practically one'.[37] The settlement of 1879 had not only failed to recognise this but 'thrown away' £40 000 – £50 000 a year which might have been had 'for the asking' if a hut tax had been introduced.[38] In December 1881 he wrote a memorandum in which he stated that the crisis, to which he had drawn the attention of the authorities many times, was now fast approaching. The increasing African population and the decreasing amount of land available to them was leading to a 'catastrophe'. The sale of Crown Lands would affect 80 000 blacks and some solution had to be found. Shepstone continued:

> The Zulu country is the only direction in which relief can be looked for; it was the domestic policy of that country that forced its inhabitants to take refuge in, and so to seriously incommode Natal; when the Zulu settlement was made the needs of Natal in this respect might have been satisfied, for they had been often enough brought to notice and were patent enough; but they were not. It may have been supposed perhaps that this arrangement which supplanted Cetywayo's rule would have induced the Natives in Natal to emigrate to Zululand; but no greater mistake could have been made; no such emigration had taken place, or is likely to take place, because the Natives of Natal distinguish too clearly between steady effective authority and its shadow, and they decline to trust themselves to the uncertain conditions of residence in Zululand under its present system of Government.
>
> In the event of Cetywayo being allowed to return to Zululand, a contingency which, under the circumstances I cannot help regarding as probable, another opportunity will present itself of doing something to avoid the agrarian difficulty that is so rapidly coming to a head among the natives in Natal; and as far as I can see it will be the last.
>
> As compared with Natal Zululand is but thinly populated, and there is, I believe, ample room for the accommodation of the present Zulu population north of the Umhlatuze River; and if the strip of country between that River and the Boundary of Natal could be set apart for the redundant population of Natal, or more correctly, for that portion of the population of Zululand that has from time to time been driven by the past barbarism of Zulu rule to seek

protection in Natal, the dangerous tension that now exists in this Colony would at once be relieved, and a source of safety be created that no other measure could accomplish.[39]

But Bulwer knew that in spite of lengthy arguments and protests London was deeply suspicious of Natal's attempts to expand and that Kimberley was unlikely to be impressed by any plan which sought to bring a portion of Zululand into the orbit of colonial Natal, to serve the settlers' interests as perceived by the retired Secretary for Native Affairs. At the beginning of September Bulwer set off to Rorke's Drift to confer with Osborn and Zulu leaders about the coming changes. His mood is reflected in a passage from the Report:

> . . . we are in a position which is beset on all sides with difficulties and objections. Out choice lies between them. It is not a question of choosing between advantages and disadvantages. The whole situation is made up of disadvantages, and we have to make our choice out of them.[40]

Once he had arrived at Rorke's Drift Bulwer found himself under pressure from another local interest which would be threatened if Cetshwayo was to return to rule all Zululand: Zibhebhu of the Mandlakazi. Of all the Zulu he met on this occasion, Bulwer informed Sir Theophilus, he was the

> only one who made a favourable impression on me. He speaks openly and to the point. . . . He strikes you as being honest and straightforward; on the whole as a man to be depended upon.
>
> He can never come again under Cetywayo he says. He wd. become a fugitive & where cd. he go! His name, his people, all wd. be broken up. He was very strong on the point of being left where he is, independent of Cetywayo. He is confident of his ability to hold his own provided only the govt. gives him the right.
>
> He is . . . certainly the only one of the appointed chiefs that could do this. His people are a confident people, all devoted to him . . . not merely as their hereditary chief, but also personally on acct. of his great goodness and kindness to them. Beloved by his own people, he is also popular with the Zulus generally. He is a man of energy, courage, and strength of mind. He can bring into the field not less than 3,000 fighting men and probably more.[41]

Osborn, from whom Bulwer must have obtained this information, gave Zibhebhu the strongest backing in his plea for independence. The British Resident had already made this suggestion in the previous month but Bulwer had rejected it on the grounds that it would only lead to violence when the king returned.[42] However, when faced with Zibhebhu and Osborn personally, Bulwer was persuaded to accept the view that Zibhebhu, as an independent chief, would act as a 'check' on Cetshwayo, whereas to bring him under Cetshwayo's rule would drive him to 'one of two courses':

. . . either he will accept the fate and become out bitterest enemy, in which case we may look out for trouble; or he will resist Cetywayo's authority and we shall have civil warfare at once.[43]

As a result of these pressures Sir Henry Bulwer drew up a plan which partitioned Zululand, arguing that Cetshwayo could only be returned if two vast tracts of territory were alienated from his rule. In his final report the Special Commissioner recommended that Zibhebhu be left independent but that his boundaries should be adjusted so as to exclude his major Usuthu opponents who would then come under Cetshwayo; in return for this loss of territory Zibhebhu should be awarded the territory given to Mgojana in 1879. Cetshwayo should be placed over the territories previously held by Hamu, Somkhele, Mlandela, Mgitshwa, Mfana-wendlela, Ntshingwayo, and portions of those under Zibhebhu and Sekethwayo. The southern district, to come under white 'protection and authority' would comprise the districts awarded in 1879 to Siyunguza, Hlubi, Faku and Dunn, and part of Sekethwayo's district. (See Map VII.)

For Bulwer the success of the plan lay in the form of government established in the southern district. It was here that any Zulu could seek protection from the royal house, and it was here that the virtues and advantages of white rule could be demonstrated.

There is only one authority which the Zulu population [living in the southern district] would accept or have confidence in, and that is our authority. It is only by the establishment of this authority in the protected territory that we can hope for a stable condition of things, and it is absolutely necessary, therefore, for all the purposes which we have in view, that this territory should be placed both under our protection and under our authority.[44]

Again Bulwer wrote:

The truth is that all turns on this matter of our authority. In that authority the Zulu people from one end to the other of the protected territory will have confidence. They will welcome it, they will rejoice in it, they will unite supporting it. It is the keystone of the fabric of government to be established in the protected territory.[45]

The need for 'a clearly defined authority' in Zululand had been Theophilus Shepstone's cry since the end of the war. Indeed no one could disagree that it was necessary. But once this abstraction was made concrete by Bulwer it was clear that it was simply a form of colonial overrule which would have the effect of forcing the Zulu into Natal's economic orbit. Bulwer recommended that the area should be 'a native independent territory under British protection and authority . . . for the exclusive use and purposes of people of Zulu origin'. A Resident Commissioner would have the 'power to issue, proclaim and enforce all regulations that may be

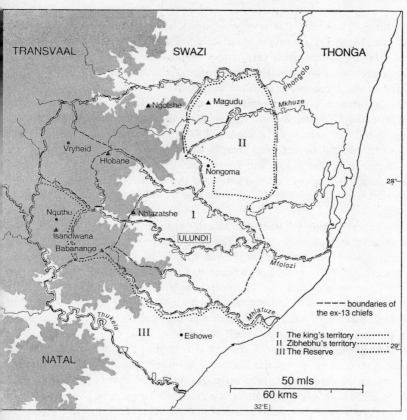

Map VII The Partition: 1883

necessary for the good government and order of the protected territory', and the

> government of a territory shall, in the first instance, be by the duly recognised and constituted chiefs and headmen, exercising direct authority over their respective tribes, peoples, and followers, subject to the paramount authority of the protecting government.

The Resident Commissioner would have the power to call up all males for military service, and the expenses of the administration would be defrayed by means of a hut tax, fees and licences. Bulwer estimated that the revenue raised in the first year would reach £11 000. This would cover the cost of establishing the administration, and therefore after an initial advance from the Treasury the territory would become self-supporting.[46]

But a scheme of this sort was just what London wished to avoid. Kimberley had no intention of either sanctioning such sweeping proposals or delaying Cetshwayo's return to Zululand any longer by engaging in argument with Bulwer. He congratulated the Special Commissioner on his 'able and comprehensive' reports and then proceeded to emasculate the recommendations contained in them.[47] While he was prepared to accept that Zibhebhu had to be left independent of Cetshwayo, he reminded Bulwer that the Colonial Office had decided that 'no more country should be reserved than is necessary to enable us to fulfil our obligations to the chiefs and people unwilling to remain in Cetywayo's territory'. For this reason the extent of the southern district was reduced so that it consisted only of the territories awarded to Dunn and Hlubi in 1879.

Kimberley ignored Bulwer's lengthy arguments on the need for 'real authority' in the southern district, and refused to allow the term 'protected territory' to be used; he suggested that it be called the Zulu Native Reserve.[48] Nor were Bulwer's recommendations on the administration of the Reserve accepted. Sir Henry was told that these matters could be finalised when it was known how many chiefs moved into the Reserve to escape the king's rule, and Bulwer was ordered to proceed immediately with arrangements for the king's return.[49]

Angry and despondent, Bulwer was forced to take action. Whereas he had hoped to lay down the boundaries, inform the Zulu of the arrangements, and then allow them to move into the district of their choice before the king's return, Bulwer was not allowed the time for this. He was therefore forced to spend the last month of 1882 hurriedly trying to prepare Zululand for the restoration.

Osborn was ordered to inform the appointed chiefs that they had been deposed;[50] J. Eustace Fannin[51] was appointed to demarcate the crucial boundary between Zibhebhu and Cetshwayo's districts.[52] John Shepstone was to be the Reserve's first Resident Commissioner and was ordered to proceed to the territory, meet the chiefs and headmen and 'invite them to declare their wishes and intentions with respect to their remaining in the reserved territory or otherwise'.

> All those who desire to accept and recognise the authority of the British Resident Commissioner as representing the paramount authority shall . . . be constituted as Chiefs and headmen over their several tribes, peoples and followers. . . .
> Those who desire to be under the re-established authority of Cetywayo you will allow to remove freely. . . . You will make and keep a record of all the Chiefs and headmen who wish to remain in the reserved territory, and whom you may decide to recognise as duly constituted Chiefs and headmen.[53]

Henry Francis Fynn[54] was appointed British Resident with Cetshwayo. Sir Theophilus Shepstone was appointed to meet Cetshwayo at Port Durnford on the Zululand coast, and from there escort him to a suitable place where an installation ceremony could be held.[55]

In Cape Town on 7 December Cetshwayo and his advisers met the High Commissioner, Sir Hercules Robinson, who informed him of the conditions under which he would be allowed to return to Zululand. The king was profoundly shocked. The impression he had gained from Kimberley that a small portion of land was to be removed from his jurisdiction to house irreconcilable enemies had proved false; two massive tracts in northern and southern Zululand were to be alienated from his rule, one of them to be handed over to the man who had taken advantage of his exile to despoil the royal house.[56]

Apart from his personal disappointment the king realised immediately the dangers implicit in the proposed division of Zululand; that this partition would only perpetuate civil strife and that the social links which spread throughout the territory could only be severed by violence. Moreover, the king knew that if he was party to an arrangement by which certain Zulu would be forced to live under an authority which they resented, and which threatened others with eviction, then he would be held responsible. As he said later,

> Here was I alone and being saddled with . . . laws applying not only to myself, but to the Zulu nation at large. The nation's heads were not present; they were absent and ignorant of all this, and when I went to them with it they would be surprised indeed.[57]

After the revised conditions of his restoration had been read to him Cetshwayo replied,

> I have heard all you have to say and I thoroughly understand it, I also understand what was said to me by Lord Kimberley in England and I know the replies I gave him. I thoroughly understand all you have said to me . . . but I do not wish to make any reply till I get back to the Zulu country. I will meet all my great men there and shall know all those who would like to leave the country that is set apart for me to govern. When I hear what my great men have to say then I will make a reply.[58]

Cetshwayo was told this was impossible and that his acceptance of the proposals was a precondition to his return. The king capitulated immediately and agreed to sign. Such an obvious surrender, however, was not satisfactory, and Robinson urged Cetshwayo to consider the conditions carefully before signing. Cetshwayo was not taken in by this attempt to make it appear that he had a choice in the matter.

'Of course I have no chance of making any reply,' he said, 'my mouth is closed. . . . I would be willing to write my name to-day if you asked me to do so.'[59]

Robinson insisted that he study the conditions and Cetshwayo left, urging the High Commissioner to ask the British Government to reconsider the matter.

Four days later the king returned, as he said, 'merely . . . to put my name on the paper'. So different was the final arrangement from the proposals outlined in London that Cetshwayo was convinced that his 'enemies in Natal' had once again intervened between the Zulu and 'the Queen', thereby prejudicing the British against him. But his adviser in Cape Town, Saul Solomon, advised him to 'accept under protest and get back to [his] country, and that constitutional means would be found to set things right'.[60] Whether Cetshwayo thought this a possibility or not, he knew he had little choice but to put his name to the paper; attempts to alter the terms of his return to Zululand would have to be considered when he reached his country.

Thus on 11 December Cetshwayo signed the conditions; in doing this he agreed to respect the borders of the Reserve and Zibhebhu's district and not to attempt in any way to interfere with any of the people living in those territories and to grant an indemnity for any acts committed in the country during his absence. Early in January 1883 he boarded the *Briton* and sailed for Port Durnford and Zululand.

Notes

1   See for example CO 179/140: 11837, Bulwer to Kimberley, 30 May 1882 (conf.), statements by Umkuba alias Tom and Umzungulo, together with information on these men supplied by the SNA in GHZ 678; CO 179/141; 12612, Bulwer to Kimberley, 16 June 1882 (conf.), statements by Umtungwana and Siboro. See also the statement by Umkuba to J. Shepstone on 13 July 1882, the attached report and subsequent minutes, in GHZ 679, in which Bulwer tried to obtain evidence that the Colensos overcharged their tenants.
2   BPP, C.3247: 84, notes of interview, 14 May 1882, p. 81.
3   Ibid.: 92, enc., Lister to Native Affairs Department, 15 May 1882, p. 90.
4   CO 179/141: 11854, minute by Kimberley.
5   CO 179/141: 14117, minutes on 11 and 12 Aug. 1882.
6   GHZ 844: Kimberley to Bulwer, 24 July 1882 (teleg.)
7   Ibid., Bulwer to Kimberley, 29 July 1882 (teleg.).

8 Ibid., Bulwer to Kimberley, 2 Aug. 1882 (teleg.).

9 Ibid., Kimberley to Bulwer, 8 Aug. 1882 (teleg.).

10 BM, Add. MSS, 44227: Kimberley to Gladstone, 2 Aug. 1882.

11 See above, p. 134.

12 The most detailed and intimate information on Cetshwayo's visit to London can be found in Henrique Shepstone's letters to his father, and related documents, in NA, Sir T. Shepstone collection: boxes 20 and 23. F. E. Colenso's account in *The Ruin of Zululand*, London 1885, ii, is also useful.

13 Sir Theophilus had met Cetshwayo once since the war. This was in Cape Town in April 1880. It must have been a deeply disturbing experience for both men, but Shepstone's account of the meeting, despite its apparent frankness is, one suspects, ultimately disingenuous and larded with half-truths. See a photocopy of a typescript in NA entitled 'Memorandum of Sir T. Shepstone's interview with Cetywayo', 10 April 1880.

14 NA, Sir T. Shepstone collection: box 20, H. Shepstone to T. Shepstone, 20 July 1882.

15 Ibid.: box 23, Albert Sayers, The Workhouse, Brighton.

16 The record of Cetshwayo's three meetings with the officials can be found in BPP, C.3466: 61, enc. 1, notes of Cetshwayo's interview with Kimberley at the Colonial Office, 7 Aug. 1882, 15 Aug. 1882, 17 Aug. 1882.

17 Ibid., p. 106.

18 Ibid., p. 107.

19 Ibid., p. 108.

20 Ibid., p. 109.

21 Ibid., p. 110.

22 Ibid., p. 111.

23 Ibid., p. 112.

24 Ibid.

25 Another interpreter who arrived later than the rest of the party.

26 Ibid., p. 113.

27 G. E. Buckle (ed.), *The Letters of Queen Victoria*, London, 1928, series II, iii, p. 326, entry for 14 Aug. 1882.

28 BM, Add. MSS, 44227: Kimberley to Gladstone, 3 June 1882 and 10 June 1882.

29 See above, p. 150.

30 BPP, C.3466: 79, enc., Report by Bulwer, Settlement of Zulu Country, Aug. 1882, p. 138.

31 Ibid., p. 142.

32 Ibid., pp. 144–5.

33 Ibid., p. 150. This argument contains all the elements used so often in South African history to justify appropriation in terms of 'ethnic' origin. For Colenso's rejection of these ideas see Colenso, series 2, pp. 550–5.

34 KC, Colenso papers: folio 26, Z190 and Z192, J. W. Colenso to Chesson, 10 and 24 July 1882.

35 KC, Colenso papers: Z323, J. W. Colenso to Chesson, 5 Feb. 1882.

36 Ch. 3 above.

37 CO 879/16, 204: no. 168, T. Shepstone, Memorandum on Wolseley's scheme 23 Aug. 1879.

38 CO 179/136: 830, T. Shepstone to Sec. of State for Colonies, 17 Jan. 1880.

39 CO 179/140: 1848, Mitchell to Kimberley, 2 Jan. 1882, memorandum by T. Shepstone, Dec. 1881. This document was written by Shepstone after a conversation he had with Wood, and it was shown to Bulwer before he left London for Natal in 1882.

40 BPP, C.3466: 79, enc., Report by Bulwer, Settlement of Zulu Country, Aug. 1882, pp. 149–50.

41 NA, Sir T. Shepstone collection: box 13, Bulwer to T. Shepstone, 20 Sept. 1882.

42 For Osborn's recommendations see CO 179/141: 18468, Bulwer to Kimberley, 19 Sept. 1882 (confidential), memorandum by the British Resident in Zululand, 26 Aug. 1882. The territorial divisions suggested by Osborn here were almost the same as those finally accepted.

43 NA, Sir T. Shepstone collection: box 13, Bulwer to T. Shepstone, 20 Sept. 1882.

44 BPP, C.3466: 106, Bulwer to Kimberley, 3 Oct. 1882, p. 205.

45 Ibid., p. 204.

46 Ibid., pp. 206–9.

47 BPP, C.3466: 114, Kimberley to Bulwer, 30 Nov. 1882.

48 Henceforth referred to as the Reserve.

49 BPP, C.3466: 115, Kimberley to Bulwer, 30 Nov. 1882.

50 BPP, C.3466: 139, enc., Bulwer to Osborn, 4 Dec. 1882.

51 Previously a Natal border agent, and member of the 1881 Natal Native Commission.

52 BPP, C.3466: 153, enc. 1, Bulwer to Fannin, 21 Dec. 1882.

53 BPP, C.3466: 154, enc., Bulwer to J. Shepstone, 22 Dec. 1882, p. 275.

54 Son of the famous settler of the same name. Since 1876 he had been a magistrate in the Natal civil service.

55 BPP: C.3466: 155, enc., Bulwer to T. Shepstone, 28 Dec. 1882.

56 For these interviews and the telegraphic correspondence leading to them, see BPP, C.3466: 138, Robinson to Kimberley, 11 Dec. 1882 and encs.

57 W. Campbell, *With Cetywayo in the Inkandhla, and the present state of the Zulu question*, Durban, 1883, p. 8.

58 BPP, C.3466; 138, enc. 2, minutes of interview held on 7 Dec. 1882, pp. 244–5.

59 Ibid., p. 247.

60 Campbell, *With Cetywayo in the Inkandhla*, pp. 8–9.

CHAPTER TEN

The return of the king

Port Durnford to Emthonjaneni: January 1883

Cetshwayo was brought ashore at Port Durnford on the afternoon of 10 January 1883. He was met by Sir Theophilus Shepstone who had been brought out of retirement to supervise the restoration. Ten years before, Shepstone had travelled to Zululand to recognise Cetshwayo formally as successor to Mpande over a region which stretched from the Thukela to beyond the Phongolo and Lubombo; now he was to place him in charge of the strip of land which lies between the Mhlatuze, the upper reaches of the Phongolo and the lower reaches of the Black Mfolozi.

Shepstone was accompanied by a detachment of British troops who were to escort the king out of the coastal bush, across the dense thorn of the Mhlatuze valley, up to the Emthonjaneni heights, some 70 km inland and 1 000 m above sea level, overlooking Emakhosini (the place of the kings, where the ancestors of the Zulu kings were buried), and 25 km from the burnt remains of the Ulundi homestead.

Since his crushing disappointment in Cape Town, when he was told of the partition, Cetshwayo had worked out his future strategy. He had decided that every effort had to be made to convince London that the great majority of Zulu wished to return to his rule, and to hold Kimberley to his statement that only sufficient territory to settle those who opposed the king would be alienated. Therefore demonstrations in his support and against the new arrangements had to be organised. The lines of communication between the Usuthu and Bishopstowe had to be kept open to ensure that reports of these demonstrations were not blocked by the 'Natal Agencies' who had devised the terms of his restoration and, he believed, were determined to destroy him. The Zulu had to be informed of the discrepancies between what Cetshwayo had been promised in London and what he had been told in Cape Town and the way in which he had been forced to sign the conditions. And they had to be persuaded that there was a possibility of the partition being abandoned if the Zulu demonstrated their support for him, their king, and the news of this reached Britain.

On landing on the Zululand coast Cetshwayo declined the offer of a cart to take him to the camp-site and managed, while walking on the beach, to pass a message to the Zulu now in the Reserve telling them

> to disregard the alleged curtailment of his territory; that he had heard nothing in England of the Umhlatuzi river being the boundary; that it was only a Natal device, which he would defeat.[1]

Furthermore Cetshwayo was convinced that the arrangements made for the partition of his country were so ignorant and misconceived that they would on their own accord demonstrate their inadequacy. As he told Shepstone:

> 'After all the whole country is yours; you will yourselves see the inconvenience which your arrangements cause and remove it yourselves; I still hope.'[2]

The journey from the coast to Emthonjaneni took a week, and the party then had to wait twelve days for the Usuthu leaders to agree to participate in the installation ceremony. It was a tense and unpleasant period for all concerned. Shepstone found the king 'peevish', 'rude and overbearing', and reported that he was already disregarding the solemn pledges he had made in Cape Town not to interfere with the Zulu living outside his territory. The camp was disturbed by rumours of impending violence from different quarters. The Usuthu alleged that Zibhebhu had threatened to attack their homes when they left to welcome Cetshwayo. The king asserted that he feared assassination and asked for a bodyguard of his own men. Assegais were hidden in the bedding rolls of the Zulu coming into the camp and discreet precautions were taken by the troops for the defence of the camp.

The four thousand Zulu who, it was said, visited the camp during this period to greet the king were those living along the route he took from the coast. Apart from members of the king's family few Usuthu leaders were to be seen, and officials and journalists attached to the party were inclined to interpret this as evidence that there was no general support for Cetshwayo's return to his country.[3] However, although most of the Usuthu leaders did not show themselves at the camp before the installation ceremony, this is not to say they were not taking an intense interest and positive political steps during this period; in fact, a consistent line of policy on the part of the Usuthu can be followed from the moment they discovered that Cetshwayo's return would mean the partition of Zululand.

By the time Cetshwayo landed on the Zululand coast the Usuthu had long suspected that there would be an attempt to link Cetshwayo's return with the alienation of a portion of Zululand. News of recent developments that reached the Colensos were passed into Zululand; Agnes Colenso had written proudly at the end of 1882, 'We are "intriguing" vigorously & have Zulus here always, in fact several work here as day labourers while they wait for news.'[4] Thus when in August 1882 it was officially announced that Cetshwayo was to be returned but that a tract of land of undetermined size was to be removed from his rule, this important piece of information was passed to the Usuthu.[5] As a result, when Bulwer arrived at Rorke's Drift in September to announce to the Zulu that the king was to return,[6] and so to attempt to settle the northern districts by persuading the appointed chiefs to allow the Usuthu they had expelled to return to their homes, the Usuthu were highly suspicious and on their guard when they met the Special Commissioner. Bulwer failed to understand the reason for this and he was not helped by his adviser on the Zulu, Melmoth Osborn, the British Resident. Bulwer informed Shepstone that his

> direct experience of Zulu character during my stay here has somewhat appalled me. I cannot conceive anything much more unpleasant than to have dealings with such men, so great is the habit of falsehood, lying, treachery, and evil nature in them. It is the result, says yr brother, of the Zulu system.

Mnyamana, although intelligent, had a 'restless crafty look'.

> In all that he said he shewed a good deal of readiness, ability & diplomatic finesse; but subtle as he was he cd. not disguise his subtlety. He was easily tripped up but it did not appear at all to disconcert him when he cd. not get out of the toils of a lie.

Ndabuko appeared to Bulwer to be a 'vain, violent bad man, and I shd. think destined to a violent and bad end'.[7]

From reports reaching Colenso of these meetings it is clear that the Usuthu believed that 'falsehood, lying, treachery' were being practised on *them* by Bulwer, Osborn and John Shepstone and, far from being part of the 'Zulu system', were part of the colonial one. They suspected that an attempt was being made to divide the Usuthu leadership (for they were interviewed individually) and trap them into participating in some scheme to divide the country.[8] Thus Mnyamana refused to point out the territory occupied by his people.[9] Ndabuko and Ziwedu did the same, one of their party asking how they could 'speak of boundaries, when the Sutu country stretched even beyond Zibebu?' and another, 'How can I divide the land, when it is all the land of Tshaka?'[10]

In their public dispatches Bulwer and Osborn chose to interpret this reluctance of the Usuthu to participate in the official attempt to settle the northern districts prior to the king's arrival as evidence that they had been insincere both in their complaints of oppression against the appointed chiefs and in their appeals for Cetshwayo's return.[11] The officials failed to appreciate the degree to which their motives were understood by the Usuthu, and saw them as a handful of disgruntled, self-interested men, who had succeeded in 'humbugging' the Bishop and winning him and his band of sentimental humanitarians to their side.[12]

Usuthu suspicions were confirmed when, in the first fortnight in January, Fannin began to mark out Zibhebhu's new boundaries. The Usuthu boycotted the proceedings refusing to witness the new beacons. But Mnyamana's spies soon brought back the news that although Zibhebhu's 1879 boundary on the Black Mfolozi had been moved to the north, and his western boundary on the Ivuna to the east, many important Usuthu lands and homesteads still remained under Zibhebhu. These included the homesteads of those who had taken the full force of Zibhebhu's harassment since the war: Mbopha, Msushwana, Hayiyana and the Mandlakazi *ikhohlo*, the people of the Gqikazi homestead, and many of the homesteads under Ndabuko and Ziwedu. Furthermore Zibhebhu had been given the territory placed under Mgojana in 1879. This was occupied by the powerful Emgazini, who had been only marginally involved in the Zibhebhu/Usuthu disputes up to then, but now found to their consternation that they were under the Mandlakazi chief. Moreover a number of Mandlakazi had taken refuge from Zibhebhu among the Emgazini; now they were under Zibhebhu once again. With arrangements like these it is little wonder that the Usuthu could accuse the officials of deliberately 'killing them' once again.

Once they had confirmed that Cetshwayo had reached Zululand the Usuthu leaders, Mnyamana, Ndabuko and Ziwedu at their head, began to move towards Emthonjaneni. But instead of scaling the heights they remained in the valley a few miles away at Emakhosini – the place of kings – and camped here while the leaders made contact with the king on the subject of future political action. Cetshwayo visited them secretly one morning soon after his arrival at Emthonjaneni.[13] While much of the discussion must have been on political affairs certain religious ceremonies were carried out as well. Emakhosini was the most sacred place in Zululand; it was here that the great national ceremonies had been performed, and it was only the king who could invoke the aid of the shades of his ancestors buried in the valley.[14] The implications of Cetshwayo's return for the spiritual life of the Zulu are difficult to assess, but certain ceremonies appear to have been thought necessary as soon as possible after he arrived. Mnyamana asked Shepstone to postpone the formal installation so that the Zulu might 'celebrate a dance at the burial place of Cetywayo's ancestors'.[15] At least one Zulu was finally convinced that the king was returning to his country when he heard that Shaka, in the form of a snake, had swum the Thukela on his way to Zululand.[16]

There were of course some Zulu who expressed opposition to the king's return, particularly among the chiefs appointed in 1879 for whom restoration meant a definite reverse in fortunes. Wolseley's attempts to revive the pre-Shakan chiefdoms had had virtually no success, but a few appointed chiefs did express themselves in terms of opposition to the Zulu lineage which had deprived them of their independence over sixty years before. Mlandela, chief of the Mthethwa, said:

> I will have nothing to do with Cetywayo. I live on ground belonging to the Umtetwa tribe on which my forefathers lived. I was conquered by the English . . . and I will now live for them and not for any Zulu Chief.[17]

Mgojana, grandson of Shaka's great enemy Zwide of the Ndwandwe, said to Osborn that he did 'not belong to the Zulu nation'.[18] Mfanawendlela of the Zungu, who had returned to his homesteads on the site of Ulundi, and was soon to be turned off when Ulundi was rebuilt by Cetshwayo, told Osborn that he

> would not object to the return of the King if the Government placed him in charge of his own tribe only, the Zulu, and leave me and other hereditary Chiefs in charge of our own tribes. . . . The Zulu Chief conquered our tribes and he again was conquered by the English. If he is restored over his tribe only, it would be all he is entitled to. . . .[19]

At the same time one should not make too much of these expressions of independence. None of the chiefs mentioned above carried their chiefdoms with them, and important individuals within each group committed themselves unequivocally to the royal house.

Mgitshwa and Siyunguza, whose people lived on either side of the Mhlatuze, told Osborn they intended to remain 'under the English' and they would move into the Reserve. Ntshingwayo said he would have nothing to do with the 'house of Chaka'[20] and Dunn protested vigorously against his deposition. Hamu, who had every reason to fear the return of the king, told Osborn that he would not return to Cetshwayo's rule. The remaining appointed chiefs either accepted the news of the king's return without complaint or thanked the officials for it.

Zibhebhu was the one appointed chief who had been fortunate enough to persuade the officials that he should be left independent. On 27 January twelve mounted men rode unexpectedly into the camp at Emthonjaneni to shouts of abuse from the royal women. The mounted squadron was led by Zibhebhu who had made a swift dash through the Mfolozi valley to pay his respects to Osborn and Shepstone. He stayed an hour and then 'rode away in sight of all as if into the very jaws of death', Shepstone wrote in his diary.

Perhaps no incident illustrates more clearly the difference between the situation of Cetshwayo and Zibhebhu. The Mandlakazi chief was based in a compact and comparatively remote district in north-eastern Zululand. With the tacit support of the officials he was able to gather round him white traders who supplied him with horses and firearms. He was able to move swiftly and unobtrusively across the country at the head of a small group of mounted men – he was the first leader in Zululand to make use of the horse in this way. Cetshwayo, however, was returned to a territory deliberately sandwiched between two districts in the charge of men hostile to him. He was the leader of a large cumbersome traditionalist party, drawn from all parts of the country and representing a number of conflicting interests. Many of its members were deeply disappointed with the terms under which the king had been returned and felt that by accepting Cetshwayo they had been tricked into accepting the division of their country and loss of independence. Cetshwayo was watched carefully by white officials who were unsympathetic to him personally,[21] and from the moment he arrived it was said that he was ignoring the conditions to which he had solemnly assented in Cape Town and on which the peace of Zululand depended. Moreover the king had returned to Zululand a comparatively poor man; he had lost many of his cattle to the very men now favoured by the officials, and cattle were an essential part of political power in Zululand.

Sir Theophilus Shepstone installs Cetshwayo kaMpande

By 28 January 1883 Shepstone and his party had been at Emthonjaneni for eleven days and the leading Usuthu had still not presented themselves. Shepstone informed Cetshwayo that he intended leaving the following day; the ultimatum had the desired effect and on 29 January Mnyamana, Ndabuko, and Ziwedu came to the camp together with many of the most important Zulu sympathetic to the king.

The installation ceremony was held in the afternoon.[22] Fearing trouble, Shepstone ordered that only head-ringed men should attend. It was estimated that there were between five and six thousand Zulu present. Shepstone opened the proceedings by announcing the changes that were to be made in Zululand. Then the conditions to which Cetshwayo had agreed in Cape Town were read out and Shepstone asked the king to state whether he had 'understood and assented' to them. Cetshwayo attempted to explain the predicament in which he had found himself in Cape Town when he agreed to the conditions, but Shepstone silenced him by demanding a 'simple answer'. Cetshwayo acknowledged that he agreed to the conditions, and was then officially 'installed' as chief of the central territory.

The Zulu reply, as Bulwer had feared,[23] took the form of a long, well-planned protest which had been organised by Cetshwayo and the Usuthu leaders while Shepstone had been waiting at Emthonjaneni and the Usuthu camped in the valley below. The organisers intended that newspaper correspondents present should give the protest publicity, and they knew that an official report would have to be written of the proceedings. Then as long as Colenso was kept fully informed,[24] Cetshwayo's sympathisers could correct any distortions and, if any attempt was made to suppress the protest, they could give it publicity.[25]

As chief minister to Cetshwayo, Mnyamana replied first.[26] He began diplomatically:

'I thank, Sir, that you have restored my child to me. I thank for your kindness, since you have come to restore him to his country. He comes to-day from his mother (the Queen), and is now the son of the Queen, not of me. I thank you for bringing him back, for bringing back the Bone of Senzangakona.'

Mnyamana then moved on to the attack, setting the tone of protest taken up by the rest of the speakers:

'But, if you now speak of cutting off the country, and of leaving him stripped of his cattle – . . . what is to become of him?'[27]

Hemulana, *induna* to Mnyamana, and an orator of repute, followed his chief.

'We thank you, son of Sonzica, for bringing back the "Bone" of Senzangakona. But even to-day in bringing him back you are killing him, killing him, I say, as you have done all along! Did you not set-him up at first and then destroy him for nothing? Did you not take him to his Mother (the Queen) and bring him back, and now do you cut off the land, saying "it is for those dissatisfied"? Where are they? You have taken the King's and the people's cattle, and given them to those Chiefs whom you set up! You have taken the royal girls and have given them to those Chiefs of yours! The Government left them, all the cattle [after the war]; but you to-day have taken them! You have taken these our children, and given them to common people! You have taken these our cattle, and given them to common people! And do you to-day set up these Chiefs of yours, and give them the King's property? What is he to live upon? We thought that this King was now a child of the Queen. Do you mock us in saying that you are restoring him? We thought that you would go back to the appointment of the 13 Chiefs, when it was ordered that they should not shed blood, but should govern the land quietly, since he, "the shedder of blood", as you called him, was removed. We thought that you would inquire how those Chiefs came to do as they have done, killing our people, and seizing our daughters, and eating up our cattle. What sort of settlement is this, Sir! We do not call it a settlement at all. We say that you are killing us also to-day as you did before.'[28]

Hemulana continued in this strain until Shepstone interrupted him:

'Do you say that I am his enemy'? Said he [Hemulana] 'Yes! You are his enemy from the beginning! You are the author of all our troubles! Why don't you inquire about those kinglets of yours, those murderers? You have sent them away and allowed them to keep all the King's property! How will you deal with us? We shall arm, and seize the cattle, and stab those who try to keep them! For we have learned that with the Government one who spills blood is not blamed; on the contrary he is praised, and is given the women, and the cattle, and the land of the peaceable ones!'

About forty speakers followed Hemulana;[29] it was a formidable display which included speeches from some of the greatest men of the nation. Some of their statements were short, merely thanking the authorities for returning the king but complaining of the conditions under which he was returned, while others took the form of prolonged protests and attacks on the authorities and the appointed chiefs. For the most part Cetshwayo kept aloof from the protests, merely calling Shepstone's attention to points he considered to be of special significance: the king wanted it to appear that the protest sprang unprompted from the Zulu themselves. Some speakers, like Ziwedu, were 'moderate' in their statements, others followed Hemulana and were aggressively outspoken. Dabulamanzi, for example, spoke with such vehemence that Shepstone felt obliged to silence him. Although Shepstone reported that he felt an 'immediate and unqualified rebuke' was required because the speech was 'calculated, if not intended [?] to excite hostility to Usibebu and contempt for Her Majesty's Government, and especially for that of Natal', Somtsewu's anger was in fact caused by Dabulamanzi's accusation that 'you [Shepstone] are killing him still as you did before, when you first made him King, and then killed him'.[30] Years later James Stuart was told by a man present:

I saw Somsewu's face turn red. 'You, Mpande's boy! This, Sonzica's house[31] what has it done to you? Are you then saying it is this house that is killing you? The soldiers that came and finished the Zulu country, did they belong to Sonzica? Were all the cattle that were eaten up from the Zulus taken to Sonzica? Did they not go to the authorities? Mpande's boy! Your manner of speech is not new. You speak without respect. I am stepping aside now, you can speak on your own with the Queen.'[32]

These personal, public attacks on the man who had cast himself in the role of protector of the Zulu and guardian of its king were a bitter humiliation. Shepstone's motives for wanting to bring the southern districts of Zululand under the informal control of Natal were clear; but we can only speculate on the reasons why he agreed to conduct the ceremony formally announcing the return of the king, and thereby exposing himself to attack, rather than remaining in Pietermaritzburg and working behind the scenes as he had done up to then.

From the evidence it would seem that Shepstone was genuinely ignorant of the feeling of the Zulu towards him. When he spoke with Cetshwayo in Cape Town in 1880 he absolved himself of the charge of treachery towards the king and his nation by arguing that Cetshwayo had rejected his guardianship at the 1877 Blood River meeting[33] and as a result he was no longer able to intervene on the king's behalf and protect him from the developments which followed. For Shepstone, the fact that the Zulu had refused to allow him to hand their borderlands over to the Boers, and accused him of treachery when he suggested it, put them beyond the pale and was tantamount to a declaration of war. Shepstone had come to believe in the myth he had created of himself as the Great White Chief, who not only understood African needs and African thinking, but represented and protected their true interests. As a result he went to Zululand in 1883 blinded by his egoism and unable to comprehend how the Zulu felt towards him. His misconceptions can only have been confirmed by Cetshwayo's requests from exile that he assume responsibility once again for Zulu affairs; Shepstone failed to realise that this was to a large extent a diplomatic move on the king's part, for Cetshwayo knew too well the advantages of having the house of Sonzica on his side, and the overwhelming disadvantages of alienating it. Thus Shepstone went to Zululand, it would seem, confident that Cetshwayo appreciated his intervention which had assisted his return to his country, and also that he could use his diplomatic and oratorical skills to persuade the Zulu to accept the partition. Moreover there were practical reasons why he had to undertake the task: he was obliged to assist Bulwer who had drawn so heavily on his advice, and we know that he felt that the future of Natal, and his reputation for posterity, depended on a successful partition of Zululand.

He was of course seriously mistaken. The verbal attack made on him at Emthonjaneni at the installation ceremony was more severe than that made at Blood River five years previously, and Shepstone, in protecting himself and the policy he had done so much to devise, took terrible revenge on Cetshwayo and the Usuthu.

Once the four-hour installation ceremony was over Shepstone was angry and upset. He gave orders to strike camp immediately and moved across the Mfule river.[34] Fynn, Cetshwayo's new Resident, hurried to

Shepstone just before he left with news of a clash in the northern districts. Shepstone told him that this was not his but Fynn's problem and rode off after the troops.[35] That evening Sir Theophilus telegraphed Bulwer: 'Installation took place this afternoon. Everything most satisfactory.'[36]

But everything was not satisfactory and Shepstone knew it. However, he refused to admit this and with remarkable skill shifted the responsibility for any future violence from the authorities to the Zulu, and also effectively nullified any effect the Usuthu protest might have had with the officials in London. As soon as he arrived in Natal, Shepstone reported to Bulwer, who telegraphed London:

> Much anxiety in Zululand on Cetywayo's return, great relief at hearing prohibition of military service, summary executions, revival of old charges against individuals and of claims respecting royal girls and cattle.

(There is no evidence that this was a significant response to Cetshwayo's return.)

> Ultra Usutu party declaimed against curtailment of powers and territory; this party now much weakened their conduct has alienated many.

(Shepstone never produced any substantial evidence to back this statement.)

> On landing Cetywayo was overbearing and aggressive . . . [but] became more moderate on discovering feeling of people; ultimately at the installation assumed submissive bearing.

(This 'submissive bearing' was possibly Shepstone's interpretation of Cetshwayo's decision to let the Usuthu protest at the installation ceremony while he assumed the role of passive onlooker.)

> All inhabitants of Reserve territory that Sir T. Shepstone saw congratulated themselves on being within it. They said their headmen might go if they chose but they would remain where they felt safe and free.

(In this way Shepstone protected the authorities from future criticism; some of the Reserve's most important leaders had spoken for the king and against the partition at the installation ceremony, and Shepstone, without producing any satisfactory evidence, here alleged that there was a division between chiefs and commoners.)

> . . . with regard to removals [to and from the] Reserve I can as yet give no information. Crops being in the ground and food scarce removals not likely till winter. Much will depend on Cetywayo's behaviour, much also on assurance of people as to our intention that Reserve territory will not be under Cetywayo. Too soon to form impression as to results but my opinion is that, if Cetywayo will keep conditions and if outside party of agitation will only leave things alone all will be well, otherwise we must expect troubles.[37]

In February Shepstone expanded on this interpretation of events in his official report on the installation. It is a remarkable document. When writing it Shepstone was well aware that it would be scrutinised by Colenso, compared with newspaper reports and with Usuthu accounts, and possibly be shown to the king for comment. Thus Shepstone did not shy away from information which, considered in isolation, might seem to be embarrassing for the authorities. The criticisms and protests made by the Usuthu at the installation for example are quite adequately summarised (although Shepstone could not bring himself to report that he had been attacked personally). But, by innuendo,[38] by emphasising the views expressed by those few chiefs who were openly opposed to the king, or by unidentified Zulu, and by casting doubt on the veracity of any Zulu statement unless it was interpreted by those few initiates with a knowledge of the native mind,[39] and by burying the basic points at issue in a mass of detail, Shepstone succeeded in convincing the officials in London that, if violence did break out in Zululand, then it would be the work of Cetshwayo and his band of reactionary supporters.

Shepstone dwelt at some length in his report on conversations he said he had with Zulu people as he passed through the newly proclaimed Reserve territory. Here the 'common people' told him of their joy at being released from the duties they had previously owed to the Zulu king. He was struck by the progress the inhabitants had made since the overthrow of the old order. Groups of young men, anonymous and therefore impossible to trace, told him how they appreciated the destruction of the military system. Whereas they had once thought it 'a good thing',

> 'Now ... we see differently. We find that we can go and work and earn money, and buy what we want, and marry and become heads of families while we are yet young.'[40]

During Cetshwayo's absence, Shepstone wrote,

> they had, to a great extent, adopted European articles and fashion of clothing; they spoke of the facilities for their young men earning money by labour in the Colony, as a new and great privilege, and such it undoubtedly was; they had learned that 'shillings were better weapons than assegais where-with to capture property'; they had, as a rule, enjoyed the sweets of liberty and comparative security to a very considerable extent, and these were blessings which they did not feel inclined to lightly part with. Ten years ago all this would have been looked upon as revolutionary, and punishable, and would have been sternly repressed. It was impossible to withhold sympathy from men in such a condition of mind, and at the moment of such a serious crisis to them, or not to be impressed with a sense of the heavy responsibility that would rest upon us if, by any arbitrarily imposed measure, we should blight all these new-born aspirations in the minds of, in many respects, a noble people, and thrust them back into the barbarism from which they were just beginning to emerge.[41]

At first sight this seems to be a fine example of the penetration of capitalism into Zululand; however, although these statements increase one's understanding of Shepstone's ideals and objectives, one cannot accept them as a fair reflection of what was happening in Zululand. Shepstone gives us neither the names nor the districts where he met these 'common people' and 'young men' who were so enamoured of their new way of life. It is quite possible that such groups did exist by this time; after all Dunn had imposed a hut tax in southern Zululand for the last two years. Nonetheless, given the subsequent history of the Reserve territory it is far more likely that Shepstone, if he wasn't lying, was exaggerating. This passage is in fact a plea for the granting of stronger colonial authority in the Reserve; these signs of progress, he is suggesting, will only survive if Britain commits herself to the territory and establishes an active administration to counter the forces of barbarism beyond its border. These progressive young men, giving stimulus to the Natal economy as they travel so willingly to work for the shillings they need to dress themselves in European clothes, were being dangled before the eyes of the London officials as signs of what was to come if Britain would only commit herself to the Reserve. If she did this, Shepstone argued, the scheme for the partition of Zululand could not fail, for it

> contains so many self-adjusting balances, all the springs of which, in the case of Cetywayo, as in that of the people, are put into operation by the instincts of self-preservation and self-interest, that if only time enough can elapse to enable the people to acquire such confidence in the intentions of Her Majesty's Government, as will encourage them to resist the efforts which Cetywayo and the ultra Usutu party will, it is to be expected, make to overbear them, this self-adjusting machinery will act in the direction of ultimately securing peace to the country, and will grow stronger by such action; but it must not be forgotten that the foundation of the whole scheme is the retention and firm rule of the Reserved Territory. . . .[42]

Cetshwayo had said in Cape Town that letters were now his only assegais. Nobody, however, knew the power of 'letters' better than Shepstone, and this one, his report on the installation and related events, was particularly effective. When the document arrived in London the officials hardly questioned Shepstone's interpretation of events. Telegraphic reports of widespread violence had already been received and it seemed indeed as if Cetshwayo had gone back to Zululand never intending to abide by the conditions he had accepted in Cape Town, and he had joined with the Usuthu to overthrow the partition by force. The Usuthu protests made at the installation ceremony were ignored. Moreover in December 1882 Lord Derby had replaced Kimberley as Secretary of State for the Colonies, and whatever influence Kimberley's personal sympathy for the king had on British policy was now lost. Most of the officials felt fortunate that they had been able to draw on Shepstone's knowledge and experience of Zulu society and felt that he had clearly demonstrated 'the difficulty of dealing with Zulus, and the shiftiness' of their king.[43] And when, only six months after Cetshwayo's return, the northern part of the country had been devastated by Hamu and Zibhebhu, the leading men of the nation were dead, the king wounded and in hiding, the general feeling, among whites in Natal and in official circles in England, was that Cetshwayo had only himself and his white advisers to blame.

Sir Theophilus Shepstone's *imbongi* felt differently however when he declaimed the praises of 'Our white man in the Town of Pietermaritz-burg . . .'

> Our own eagle with the sharp talons,
> That accounted for certain men;
> For it accounted for Cetshwayo son of Mpande,
> It took him in its claws
> And threw him across the sea to England;
> It destroyed him, then gave him a respite,
> And eventually spat him out.[44]

Notes

1 BPP, C.3616: 31, enc., T. Shepstone to Bulwer, 27 Feb. 1883, p. 42. This enclosure contains Shepstone's official report of the installation and henceforth is referred to as T. Shepstone, Report.

2 T. Shepstone, Report, p. 45.

3 Information on events in Zululand in the weeks following Cetshwayo's arrival can be found in T. Shepstone, Report, and in Colenso, series 2, pp. 349*b*–64*b* and pp. 365–433 where the Bishop compares Usuthu reports with Natal newspaper accounts. Bulwer's important letters to Shepstone can be found in Box 13 of the Sir T. Shepstone collection (NA). There is an error in the pagination in Colenso, series 2 at this point. I have therefore cited the section beginning on p. 349 with the words 'So the *Natal Mercury* . . .' and ending on p. 364 with '. . . let them mark that there is no blood on his'. as pp. 349*a*–364*a*. The section opening with the words 'The following account . . .' and ending '. . . move his cattle, to begin' on p. 364, is referred to as pp. 349*b*–364*b*.

4 AS papers: box 5, Agnes Colenso to Sophie [Mrs Frank] Colenso, 11 Dec. 1882.

5 Colenso, series 2, p. 349*a*.

6 See above, p. 159.

7 This important private letter is in NA, Sir T. Shepstone collection: box 13, Bulwer to T. Shepstone, 21 Sept. 1882.

8 It is significant that no official record was kept of these meetings. As in the case of the Nhlazatshe meeting, the officials seem to have had something to

hide, and on both occasions the Usuthu believed that they were being led into a trap.

9 Colenso, series 2, statement by Mtokwane, p. 434.

10 Colenso, series 2, statement by Batakati (Mnyamana's son), p. 436.

11 BPP, C.3466: 134, Bulwer to Kimberley, 24 Nov. 1882 and encs.

12 Osborn told Shepstone that he had to comment officially on Colenso's accusations 'and I believe that I have in *every* case beaten "Sobantu" hoplessly. He is of course a very clever man, but cleverness cannot avail much where truth is disregarded.' NA, Sir T. Shepstone collection: box 18, Osborn to T. Shepstone, 18 Nov. 1882.

13 T. Shepstone, Report, p. 46.

14 See A. T. Bryant, *The Zulu People, as they were before the white man came*, Pietermaritzburg, 1967, pp. 503–4, 514–15, 524–5; and E. J. Krige, *The Social Systems of the Zulu*, Pietermaritzburg, 1957, p. 233.

15 T. Shepstone, Report, p. 49.

16 '. . . on reaching Mgamule's we found that the news must be true, for the (*amadhlozi*) ancestral spirits had returned to the country, a very large snake having been seen crossing the Tugela the day before, which was recognized as Tshaka'. Colenso, series 2, p. 353*b*. Shaka was buried south of the Thukela.

17 BPP, C.3616: 54, enc. 1, J. Shepstone to Bulwer, 13 March 1883, statement by Mlandela, p. 102.

18 BPP, C.3466: 158, enc., Osborn to Bulwer, 28 Dec. 1882, reply by Mgojana, p. 287.

19 Ibid., reply by Mfanawendlela, p. 286.

20 Ibid., reply by Ntshingwayo, p. 287.

21 Fynn, the king's Resident, was an exception, but he was totally ineffectual.

22 My account of the installation is derived from three major sources: T. Shepstone, Report, pp. 51–7; Colenso, series 2, pp. 403–22 where the Usuthu version is compared with newspaper reports; and Ch. 31, 'Ukubuya Ku Ka Cetshwayo, e Buyiselwa kwa Zulu uSomsewu', in J. Stuart, *uKulumetule*, London, 1925.

23 In Pietermaritzburg during January Bulwer was in an agony of apprehension fearing, quite correctly, that the installation would be turned into a protest meeting by the Usuthu; see NA, Sir T. Shepstone collection: box 13, Bulwer to T. Shepstone, 26 Jan. 1883. These letters from Bulwer to Shepstone, which exist only for periods when one of the parties was away from Pietermaritzburg, are important for they demonstrate the intimacy between the two men, and suggest (unless evidence is found to the contrary when Bulwer's papers are made accessible to researchers) that for the most part the relations between the two men took place through personal contact in Pietermaritzburg.

24 Colenso's role in the development of Usuthu strategy seems to have been an important one. Consider this advice given when the conditions of restoration were made known:

> It is your affair, therefore, to speak out & say who do – & who do not wish for him. Cetshwayo will not be able to speak for you in this matter, because his mouth will be shut by his promises. You must speak for yourselves to Somtseu, & this will be your last opportunity for speaking.

KC, Colenso papers: folio 26/2, Z411, J. W. Colenso to Chesson, 16 May 1883.

25 Messengers were sent two days after the meeting to give an account to Colenso. He was also asked to 'send a telegram in our name – in the name of the headmen of the Zulu People – to protest to the Queen against all this being done in her name'. Colenso, series 2, pp. 423–4.

26 In this reconstruction of the installation ceremony I have tended to follow the Usuthu version; it is the fullest, the best translated, and of course emphasises the points the speakers themselves wanted to make. There are many differences in the various versions, but, as Colenso wrote, they are of 'no consequence to the main point'.

27 Colenso, series 2, p. 408.

28 Colenso, series 2, p. 409. I have quoted at length from Hemulana's speech; not only is it eloquent and impassioned but it makes nearly all the points repeated by later speakers, although the tone is more aggressive than that used by some of the speakers who followed him.

29 They included Melelesi, Matshana kaSitshakuza, Mavumengwana, Ntuzwa (brother of Sekethwayo), Msushwana, Hayiyana, Magonondo, Mlumbi (brother of Mbopha), Ndabuko, Ziwedu, Sitheku, Somkhele (although Stuart's informant stated that he was not there), Sigananda, Nobiya, Qethuka, Godide, Mkhosana. Siyunguza and Mgitshwa also spoke, but appear to have defended their actions as appointed chiefs; the Usuthu messengers reported that they had spoken for the king.

30 Ibid., p. 411.

31 The house of Shepstone's father.

32 Stuart, *uKulumetule*, p. 176 (translation). It is instructive to compare this statement, made long after the event, with the Usuthu version, taken down by Colenso only weeks afterwards:

> Said Somtseu 'What, my boy *Dabulamanzi*! Is it you that say it is the house of Sonzica which is destroying you? Can I return answer to you, a mere boy?' He was plainly angry.

Colenso, series 2, p. 411.

33 For the Blood River meeting see above, pp. 46–7.

34 NA, Sir T. Shepstone collection: box 9, Diary 1883, entry for 29 Jan. 1883.

35 KC, Stuart Papers; evidence of Henry Francis Fynn, in Life of T. Shepstone.

36 BPP, C.3616: 17, enc. 1, T. Shepstone to Bulwer, 29 Jan. 1883 (telegram).

37 GHZ 844: Bulwer to Derby, 10 Feb. 1883 (telegram – some punctuation added).

38 Consider for example the following extract on p. 44 of the Shepstone Report:
> [Cetshwayo] then went on to speak very gratefully of what the English people had done for him, and wished that it might be his good fortune to find an enemy to the English within his reach; how gladly he would fight for them he said, and mix his blood with theirs. He spoke warmly on this subject, forgetting probably that the conditions which forbade his re-establishing the Zulu military system would deprive him of the power of showing his gratitude in this way.

39 For example, Shepstone alleged that some Zulu publicly welcomed the king and protested at the terms of his restoration, and yet spoke privately to him of their opposition to Cetshwayo. If indeed there were such men, there is nothing mysterious in hedging one's bets. But for Shepstone (Report, p. 43) these 'puzzling phases of Zulu conduct'

. . . are the natural result of the perpetual sense of insecurity and uncertainty which has been the experience of every unfortunate Zulu in
Zululand from childhood to the present moment; but which add very
much to the difficulty of dealing with these people, and compel recourse
to knowledge, other than that to be gathered from their professions, to
form a correct estimate of their real feeling.

40 T. Shepstone, Report, p. 57.
41 Ibid., pp. 58–9.
42 Ibid., p. 58.
43 Co 179/145; 5573, minutes on T. Shepstone, Report.
44 T. Cope (ed.), *Izibongo: Zulu Praise-poems*, Oxford, 1968, p. 198, given
incorrectly as p. 189.

CHAPTER ELEVEN

The end of the Zulu Kingdom

From the installation to the battle of Msebe: February and March 1883

After the installation ceremony Cetshwayo, his wives, attendants and a large number of his supporters moved into the valley of the White Mfolozi on to the Mahlabathini plain where Ulundi was to be rebuilt. Soon more Zulu began to arrive to pay their respects to the king.

Cetshwayo was attended by men of the highest rank, from all parts of the country. Many of them were the elderly contemporaries of Mpande, the *izikhulu,* members of the highest council of the land. They included Mnyamana, Sekethwayo, Mbopha, Sitshaluza, Somkhele, Dilikana, Qethuka, Godide and Nobiya. Other Zulu of note who attended the king soon after his return were Sigananda, Hayiyana, Msushwana, Ntuzwa, Ngcongcwana, Hemulana, Somhlolo, Mgamule and Sihayo, and of course the *abantwana.* Most of the major groups in Zululand were represented and permitted their followers to visit Ulundi and give service by rebuilding the royal homesteads, while others sent tribute in grain and cattle.[1]

There were some obvious and significant absentees from Ulundi. Hamu, Zibhebhu and Dunn did not visit the king; neither did Mgojana of the Ndwandwe nor Mlandela of the Mthethwa. Two other ex-appointed chiefs, Siyunguza and Mgitshwa, remained in the Reserve. Both Mfanawendlela and Ntshingwayo attended Cetshwayo at Ulundi but they had objected to his return and as a result suffered insult and intimidation from the Usuthu. Ntshingwayo was one of the very few *izikhulu* who did not support the king's return and there was talk that he had appropriated royal cattle.[2] Mfanawendlela had planted his crops around Ulundi and the young men assisting in the rebuilding of the homesteads helped themselves to his crops. Soon reports were appearing in the Natal press that 'Cetshwayo is at his old tricks again, and has already commenced the eating up process. . . .'[3]

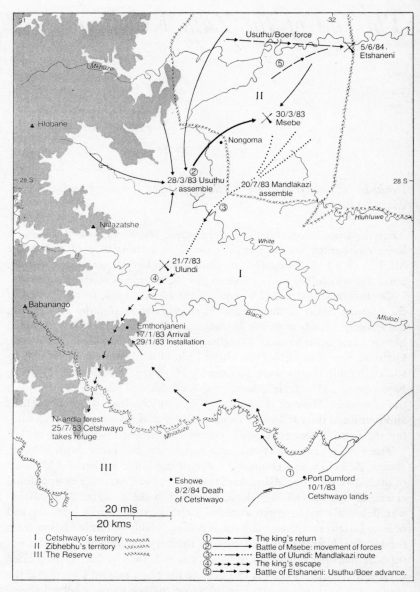

Map VIII The Civil War in Zululand: January 1883–June 1884

The second Usuthu deputation of
April-May 1882: Shingana
kaMpande (right) and Dabulamanzi
kaMpande (below)

return of the king, 1883. Above: Sir Theophilus Shepstone (centre) with his staff and members of the British escort; below: the Installation, Emthonjaneni, 29 January 1883

The young Dinuzulu kaCetshwayo, possibly taken on 21 May 1884, when he was proclaimed king of the Zulu by the Boers; Zibhebhu, sketched the day after the battle at Ulundi, 21 July 1883

Cetshwayo appears at this stage to have still been convinced that any attempt to overthrow the authorities in the alienated territories by force would be disastrous for him. He continued with his tactics of sending protests, petitions, and evidence of Zulu support to London to hold the British officials to their promise that only sufficient land to support those who opposed the king would be alienated from his rule, and thereby foil the local influences which had altered 'the Queen's words'.

For a number of reasons this policy of protest proved an extremely difficult one for the king to follow. Perhaps the greatest obstacle was that by 1883, in parts of the country, the material base upon which social continuity depended was beginning to break down. The fragile, pre-capitalist Zulu social formation, which lacked forms of storeable wealth apart from cattle, depended for its continued existence on unhindered access to land for cultivation, and pastures for grazing. Six months of war in 1879 had been followed by three years of disturbances, raiding and violence in certain districts. Many Zulu in the northern regions had lost their homes, cattle and grain stores, and were being denied access to arable land by Zibhebhu. People in the north-western districts were now living in caves from which they scavenged and stole when they had the opportunity. Some lived on Hlobane, the Qulusi drifted back and forth across the border of the Transvaal, from stronghold to stronghold, living by their wits. A group of Qulusi attacked some of Hamu's homesteads a few days before the installation took place.[4] And the months that followed the king's return were characterised by numerous minor clashes between Hamu's Ngenetsheni and Zulu identified with the Usuthu from this region like the Qulusi, Ndabankulu's followers, the Egazini under Hlezibane and those Mdlalose who lived near Hlobane.[5]

The colonial press and the officials held Cetshwayo responsible for the violence. But as the Usuthu messengers pointed out to Colenso:

'how is it possible that there should not be trouble in Hamu's district, since the country is still full of abaQulusi, homeless, bereft of parents, brothers, wives, or children, or, at any rate, plundered of their cattle . . .?'[6]

Or as the king himself said later to those who accused him of ignoring the conditions he had accepted and attempting from the start to overthrow the settlement: 'I did not land on a dry place. I landed in the mud.'[7]

The same difficulties existed in the north-east in the vicinity of Zibhebhu's new chiefdom. The alteration of Zibhebhu's southern and western boundary still left many Usuthu homesteads within his borders, including some of Ndabuko's, and those of Mgamule, Mfinyeli, Mbopha Msushwana, Ziwedu, the Ekubazeni and the Gqikazi and those of the

Mandlakazi *ikhohlo*. Many of the owners of these homesteads were refugees in Cetshwayo's territory, some of them living in the unhealthy lowlands towards Lake St Lucia. Their desire for revenge was intense, as was their need for food, and as they tried to salvage grain from their old homesteads they clashed with the Mandlakazi.[8]

This tense and potentially dangerous situation was made even worse by the officials' extraordinarily stupid move of compensating Zibhebhu for the territory taken from him in the south and west, with the district given to Mgojana in 1879. In this large territory between the Mkhuze and Phongolo lived the powerful Emgazini under Mabhoko and Sitshaluza, sections of the Buthelezi under Bantubensumo, and Mandlakazi refugees. Reports reached Ulundi in March saying that Zibhebhu was demanding that they acknowledge his authority or move from their homes.[9]

While Cetshwayo was trying to gain some control over the northern districts he was faced with a different, but just as difficult, set of problems to the south in the Reserve. Nominally this territory was in the charge of John Shepstone who had been transferred temporarily from the office of the SNA in Natal, to oversee the establishment of the Reserve for the first three months, before Melmoth Osborn, his post as British Resident now abolished, took up the post of Resident Commissioner.[10]

John Shepstone arrived in the Reserve about a fortnight before Cetshwayo's return with orders to prepare the inhabitants of the district for the coming changes and to set up the new administration. At this time the constitutional status of the Reserve had still to be decided. Bulwer's detailed proposals had not been approved by the Colonial Office which refused to go beyond giving authority for the Reserve to be 'proclaimed independent native territory' under a British Commissioner. Such subtleties were lost on John Shepstone. Escorted by a Natal African 'police' and some favourite 'indunas' from the office of the SNA who had been promised land in the Reserve, Shepstone blustered his way through the Reserve. He wrote of the territory as 'ours', and divided its inhabitants into those who were 'staunch to us' and the 'intriguers'.[11]

Soon after his arrival he called meetings at Entumeni and Eshowe where he informed leaders of the coming changes. Two independent Zulu accounts confirm that for John Shepstone the Reserve had come under the *de facto* rule of Natal and that he had no conception of the British Government's attitude towards the territory. A Zulu remembered John Shepstone telling the Reserve chiefs:

'Au! Men, I have called you because I want to tell you that Cetshwayo is coming back. The country has been divided, the Mhlatuze river being the boundary. The country on this side of the Mhlatuze will be controlled by the

Government (Hulumeni)[12] and will pay a fourteen shillings hut tax. I am now telling you to choose. Those who choose Cetshwayo and those who choose the Government should indicate their choice and in the winter, after the crops are reaped, they should cross to his territory. The others should remain. Even if you all choose Cetshwayo this is no concern to the Government for it has many people who need a place to live.'[13]

But the Zulu refused to 'indicate their choice'. The majority of the headmen continued to visit Cetshwayo at Ulundi, and many of the younger men crossed into Cetshwayo's territory to give service to the king. Occasionally, in private correspondence, Bulwer came close to recognising that the public justification for the exclusion of the Reserve territory from Cetshwayo's rule was based on an invalid interpretation of Zulu feeling. He wrote to John Shepstone towards the end of January:

> The prospect indeed, looks bad if it is the case as you say that all the Chiefs & Headmen of the Reserved Territory, with the exception of four have gone to meet Cetywayo without consulting you.
>
> Well then we must have been all wrong & they must really desire his rule, unless it is that they distrust us and believe that the whole country will be under C.[etshwayo] in wh. case it wd. [be in] their interest to be on good terms with him.
>
> At any rate it seems to me it will be difficult to rule the country if all the Chiefs & Headmen desire to be under C: or at heart are loyal to him & disloyal to us.[14]

But this momentary, tentative admission, that perhaps the basic assumption underlying the partition of Zululand was invalid, was never admitted publicly. John Shepstone was determined to obtain evidence that the reluctance of the Zulu to commit themselves to him and the Reserve was the result of Usuthu intimidation and false reports that the Queen would soon restore all Zululand to the king. Bulwer had in fact urged him to gather information to support this view; it is *'absolutely necessary'*, he wrote, 'you shd. be able to shew that you have Chiefs & Headmen on yr. side. If you can not shew this I know not what will happen.'[15]

Thus, using violent language,[16] John Shepstone ordered all Zulu leaders from the Reserve to return to their homes and submit to his authority or take up residence in Cetshwayo's district. He then began a tour of the Reserve to collect the names of those 'loyal' to his authority. On 21 February at Qudeni John Shepstone lost his temper and ordered his Natal 'police' on to the Zulu. A general fracas broke out and soon messengers were arriving at Bishopstowe with accounts of the incident and descriptions of the wounds received.[17] He continued his tour of the Reserve threatening, intimidating, and fining Zulu who did not attend his meetings. Little wonder that the lists of 'loyal' chiefs and headmen who had accepted the Resident Commissioner's authority are of little value and were contradicted by Cetshwayo, whose lists of Zulu from the Reserve who pledged themselves to him contained many of the same names.

Cetshwayo saw the trap that was being sprung and protested vehemently at the alternatives being presented to the Zulu in the Reserve:[18] if they demonstrated their loyalty to their king they were to be evicted from their homes; if they were to retain possession of their lands they had to submit to John Shepstone's authority and would be classed as Zulu who opposed Cetshwayo's rule, and this would be used to justify the partition.

Once publicly committed to the theory that the Zulu were reluctant to give their allegiance to the authorities in the Reserve because Cetshwayo was spreading the idea that in time the Queen would return southern Zululand to his rule, the next step, to the officials' way of thinking, was a show of force to counteract Usuthu intimidation. So in January Bulwer received authority to provide John Shepstone with a detachment of British troops to give him 'more of those outward ceremonies & forms which go for so much with the mass'.[19] Next Bulwer persuaded the Colonial Office to permit Shepstone, not merely to represent the British Government, but also to exercise 'paramount authority' in the Reserve, and to impose a hut tax 'as an outward and visible sign' of white power.[20] Soon permission was obtained to place 'Government men' (that is, Natal Africans) armed with rifles on the boundary of the Reserve to keep a check on who was crossing into Cetshwayo's territory.[21] In April Bulwer sent a mounted squadron of twenty-two Africans recruited in Natal into Zululand. Under two white officers these men were to form the core of the Zululand Native Police, the notorious *Nongqayi*.[22]

Thus by April 1883 the Reserve had moved a long way from being the haven for Zulu opposed to the king which Bulwer had originally proposed. In the name of the welfare and real interests of the Reserve's inhabitants Bulwer had acquired the instruments of coercion needed to break their resistance to the full implications of colonial rule. And the Zulu in the Reserve were soon to react to the authoritarian actions of the Resident Commissioner, taxation, granting land to official favourites, and compulsory military service against Zulu in other parts of the country.[23]

Throughout February and March messengers from Cetshwayo arrived at Bishopstowe with information on conditions within the country and letters from the king urging Colenso to

> send all these words of mine across the Sea, to Mr Gladstone, and to Lord Kimberley, and to him who has entered on Lord Kimberley's office. And let the Parliament know, and let the Queen herself be told, that she may interfere to protect me in this my misery.[24]

Cetshwayo stressed that the Bishop should carry out these injunctions privately, and not as a representative of the king, so that he should not appear to be flouting his Resident who had been given a number of protests to be forwarded through official channels. In these messages the king complained of John Shepstone's intimidation of the Zulu in the Reserve and of his insulting language; of the cattle lost to Zibhebhu, Huam and Dunn during his exile; of the boundary laid down between his and Zibhebhu's territory which cut off many of his most loyal followers. And he reiterated that the promises made to him in Downing Street had been broken when the final terms were read to him in Cape Town.[25]

But these protests made very little impression in London: the determined attack mounted by the Natal officials and the colonial press was accepted with very little criticism. Weary of contradictory reports and the incessant controversy surrounding events in Zululand, and with a new, notoriously cautious, Secretary of State,[26] the officials turned their backs on the man they had welcomed to London and had returned to southern Africa with such high hopes only nine months before. To Bulwer, the Shepstones and Osborn all that was needed for peace in Zululand was for Cetshwayo to keep his Cape Town promises. The violence in the north and John Shepstone's difficulties in the Reserve were blamed on Cetshwayo's refusal to accept his new role. Bulwer wrote:

> . . . there need be, and would be, no trouble if Cetywayo himself would only rest quietly and contentedly and keep faithfully the conditions to which he pledged his word.[27]

Cetshwayo had already answered this inadequate, simplistic injunction:

> 'The conditions, clause by clause, say "I will", &c., as if I had made these conditions. It should have been, "We, the English stipulate you, Cetywayo, and Zulu shall," &c.; and to these my replies, I see, are not added; this is like a knife having only a sharpened edge on one side; I wish to do what is correct and pleasing to the English Government, but the difficulties are great I have to contend with – the division of the people, which has led to great complications.'

(Cetshwayo spoke of the Nhlazatshe meeting where the Zulu were prohibited from informing Wood of their desire for the king's return, and of the meeting at Rorke's Drift in September 1882 where an attempt was made to divide the Zulu.)[28]

> '. . . now there is no union, which is necessary for the preservation of peace . . . had the Chiefs been all assembled and openly interviewed there would have been no secrecy, which secrecy of interviewing each Chief alone made them suspicious of something in the background. The severing of my personal adherents in the Reserve, Transvaal, and Usibebu boundaries will unavoidably

bring about bloodshed through rivalry and the smallness of the country now allotted to me.'[29]

Although he was personally sympathetic to the king, Henry Francis Fynn, the British Resident with Cetshwayo, was of no assistance to him. He was not sure what his official role was in Zululand, he misunderstood Bulwer's instructions to him, and his dispatches were so badly written that Bulwer was unable to send them to London as they stood and often had to paraphrase them himself. On Bulwer's instructions Fynn called two meetings in March, to explain to Zulu leaders the new order set up by the authorities. From the large number of Zulu present and the great distance which many had travelled, it appears as if an announcement of some importance was expected. But judging from Fynn's report, his statements to the Zulu can have only seemed irrelevant and foolish. It is sufficient to consider Fynn's own account of his reply to Msushwana, whose people had been harassed by Zibhebhu every year since the war and were still in exile suffering from disease and starvation:

> Upon a respectful remark of Umsuthshwana's, that they had lost all they had, I replied, – that was not the way to go on. When a man's hut was burnt down he did not sit in the middle of the cinders watching them, grumbling because they did not grow into a hut again; but he at once built a new hut where he chose to put it, and before the cold and rainy season. [Fynn urged the gathering to obey the law and keep the peace, saying]
> . . . that their ruler the child of Chaka may grow great by his and their good acts of peacefulness and to the pleasure of the Queen of the world. Farewell, and all of you help me to do my duty to the country I belong. Farewell.[30]

It was only a matter of time before the sporadic raids and skirmishes in the northern districts led to a widespread outbreak of violence. It happened, predictably, in Zibhebhu's territory, in that part which lay between the Mkhuze and the Phongolo over which he had just been appointed and where the Emgazini of Mabhoko lived together with a number of Mandlakazi refugees. Zibhebhu had already threatened these people with expulsion and on 23 March he moved troops into the vicinity of Mabhoko's homesteads. No attack was made but the men helped themselves to the growing crops.[31]

According to one commentator, 'The effect was electrical.'[32] The Usuthu leaders like Ndabuko, Mnyamana and Tshanibezwe (Mnyamana's chief son) came from the same region and had experienced similar actions by Zibhebhu repeatedly since the end of the war. For them Zibhebhu was continuing to harass and evict all in his territory who did not recognise his authority, regardless of status and rank. Tshanibezwe and Ndabuko were at Ulundi when the news of Zibhebhu's actions reached them and they left immediately for the northern districts to organise a force which would invade Zibhebhu's territory and put an end to his pretensions once and for all.

According to Cetshwayo they went without his authority saying 'they might as well die at once: what were the people to eat, if all their crops were destroyed'.[33] The officials later alleged that these stories were part of a carefully laid Usuthu plot to destroy Zibhebhu without implicating the king directly, even though he had full knowledge of it. It is impossible to say with certainty what Cetshwayo's role was in this, although it seems to me unlikely that, even by the end of March, Cetshwayo had abandoned completely the non-violent tactics he had decided upon after the Cape Town interviews and that he had embarked on a plan to overthrow Zibhebhu by force – a strategy which he knew would be extremely hazardous for him personally and should only be adopted as a last resort.[34]

The Usuthu army was mobilised by company and not by regiment which meant that they marched and fought by chiefdom and local group rather than age-set.[35] Ndabuko was in charge of the followers and dependants of the royal house. Mabhoko led the Emgazini, and Tshanibezwe the Buthelezi, while Makhoba mobilised the detachment of Mandlakazi which opposed Zibhebhu. It was said that the force numbered five thousand men and that Zibhebhu could not raise more than fifteen hundred to defend his territory.[36]

Confident in their superior numbers and eager to settle scores and regain their cattle, the army mustered near Mnyamana's homesteads on the Sikhwebezi river on the afternoon of 28 March 1883. The next day it crossed the Ivuna river, climbed the Nongoma heights and moved across the open undulating plains to the north-east until it had penetrated well into Zibhebhu's territory. Homesteads were burnt and grain stores plundered while the inhabitants fled with their cattle before the invading force. Camp was made late in the afternoon when the Usuthu were surprised to see Zibhebhu, mounted on a white horse, ride to within shouting distance. He abused the invaders, fired a few rounds, and then disappeared. The next morning small parties of horsemen were seen by the Usuthu, but they fled towards the valley of the Msebe stream (near the present Nongoma-Banganomo road) pursued by the invading army.

Here in the Msebe valley, Zibhebhu had laid an ambush. His infantry was hidden in the broken, eroded sides of the valley, and they sprang upon the Usuthu while Zibhebhu and his squad of horsemen with firearms attacked the Emgazini who were on the left. The Usuthu were caught completely by surprise; they were not in fighting order and the unarmed baggage-boys were still among the troops. The Emgazini broke, followed by the Buthelezi, and without making any concerted stand the Usuthu began to retreat, pursued by Zibhebhu's foot-soldiers while his well-trained mounted men used rifle-fire to break up any group which attempted to rally. The open plain across which the Usuthu had to retreat offered little cover or protection. The Emgazini tried to hive off to the north towards cover and their homes, but Zibhebhu's mounted force turned them back. Zibhebhu was particularly active and demonstrated his skill as a marksman. At one stage his mounted men succeeded in out-stripping the retreating force and attacked the Usuthu leaders who had been in a place of safety at the rear. Makhoba and Mgwazeni, associated from the start with the movement for the king's return,[37] were killed, together with five sons of Ndabuko, and ten of Mnyamana's.[38] J. Y. Gibson, who worked in the area a few years later, stated that 'probably in no battle had the Zulus ever suffered greater loss of life'.[39] Ndabuko, Ziwedu and Tshanibezwe survived, although the defeat was to weigh heavily on Ndabuko for many years. Towards the end of the day the survivors had reached Nongoma leaving thousands of bodies marking their line of retreat. Below them, in the valley of the Black Mfolozi and along the streams coming down from the Ngome forest lay the homes of many of the invading force.

But the Usuthu's difficulties were not yet over. That night Hamu heard of the defeat of his enemies and the Ngenetsheni swept out of their strongholds and moved towards the Black Mfolozi, attacking the Mphan-gisweni and Ndabankulu's people on the way. Another section of Hamu's army moved to the north to attack the Buthelezi living, or retreating, in the direction of the Phongolo. Hamu's forces then joined with Zibhebhu's and their path could be traced by the smoke of the burning homesteads. One of the Usuthu baggage-boys recounted years later that the Ngenet-sheni

> formed themselves into squads to carry out economic warfare. Their task was to burn all stored grain in the province before leaving it, and to demolish growing mealies and corn in the lands. Nearly every land was visited and plants destroyed.[40]

There was now no turning back. The supporters of the king had not only suffered a terrible defeat in the field but their homes had been destroyed and their food stocks plundered. It would be eight or nine months before they had the chance of reaping again, and until then they had to find some means of subsistence. Zibhebhu had emerged as the most formidable power in the land, his army inflicting thousands of casualties on the Usuthu while suffering only a handful of losses itself. To neighbouring whites he appeared as an heroic and loyal ally, the 'Napoleon of North Zululand' who was

> really fighting the battle of South Africa, and championing the cause of civilization and order, in the stubborn and so far successful resistance he has offered to the hostility and intrigues of Cetshwayo.[41]

The royalists fled in different directions; some crossed into the Transvaal, others south towards Ulundi or the Reserve. The Buthelezi, Qulusi, Mdlalose, Mphangisweni and other groups from northern Zululand retreated into strongholds in the Ngome forest or the Hlobane range. Here Hamu made a series of attacks to dislodge them or seize what cattle they had with them. Then in mid-April, the Mandlakazi and Ngenetsheni swept through the northern districts once again, burning and plundering any homesteads previously overlooked and coming within a few miles of Ulundi itself.[42]

> Cetshwayo has found his louse a hard one to crack, [crowed Hamu's white man, Herbert Nunn] Numbers of old men, women, and children are coming in. What will thousands eat this year? No cattle to purchase! A fine time to gather these refugees together here, and send them out to work on the Natal Govt. railways or sugar estates! Wages ought to come down 100 per cent.[43]

From Msebe to the battle of Ulundi: 30 March 21 to July 1883

April was a cruel month for the Usuthu living north of Ulundi. Their homes had been burnt, their cattle looted and their grain destroyed. Women and children had been seized and the bodies of thousands of their menfolk lay unburied on the plain that stretches east of Nongoma. A few homesteads like those of Mgojana and Mfanawendlela remained standing, exposing their occupants as Mandlakazi sympathisers, and marking them out for future Usuthu vengeance. The total defeat of the large royalist army by the smaller Mandlakazi force left the Usuthu survivors demoralised and their leaders discredited; Zibhebhu emerged as a formidable military leader and a real power in Zululand, and his victory allowed Hamu's Ngenetsheni to dominate the area in the north-east.

After the Msebe defeat and the April attacks, the northern Usuthu retreated into the broken, mountainous terrain and the forests north of the Black Mfolozi. Here they prepared themselves for the struggle which they knew must follow – not only against Zibhebhu and Hamu but against starvation and complete social disruption. Maphelu described the occupation of *nqaba*, the caves which were used as strongholds within the forests. These had not been used by large numbers of people since Shaka's time and wild animals had to be driven out, stone defences built, and the entrances camouflaged before they could be occupied. Some were so large that they housed not only women and children and their defenders, but livestock as well. The stronghold at Ngotshe, which Hamu was to make use of so effectively, was said to be the most formidable.[44]

The Qulusi, Mdlalose, the Egazini under Hlezibane, and Ndabankulu's Ntombela found refuge in or near the Hlobane and associated mountain ranges. Others moved (at considerable cost) with their cattle into the Transvaal. The Mphangisweni hid near the sources of the Black Mfolozi and the numerous Buthelezi under Mnyamana retreated into the Ngome forest. They were joined by adherents of Ndabuko, Ziwedu, Hayiyana and others who had been driven from Zibhebhu's territory. Bantubensumo's Buthelezi, those Ndwandwe who had not followed Mgojana when he joined Zibhebhu, and a portion of the Emgazini retreated to the Dlomodlomo range, while the majority of the Emgazini (under Mabhoko) either crossed the Phongolo out of Zululand with other Usuthu, or prepared to defend themselves on Magudu mountain.[45]

Interspersed among the Usuthu groups were Hamu's Ngenetsheni, although they tended to concentrate on the northern slopes of the Ngome range, where it falls to the Mkhuze. They had strongholds on the Ngotshe, and another north of the Mkhuze. From these retreats they harassed the Usuthu, and disrupted communications between them.

There was no need for Zibhebhu to use defended strongholds at this time; his victorious followers were in possession of large herds and looted grain, and as a result of his policy of expelling dissidents the Mandlakazi occupied a contiguous territory whereas the Usuthu had their Ngenetsheni enemies living among them.

At one level, the period which followed the Msebe battle was characterised by a continual series of minor clashes and skirmishes between different sections of the Usuthu and their enemies. In order to obtain food, parties left their retreats to scavenge and raid; at other times attempts were made to avenge previous defeats or drive opposing groups from a particular area. Communication in the northern districts broke down; the white officials, the Natal newspapers, and even the Usuthu headquarters at Ulundi received a stream of confused and often contradictory information, which frequently found its way into print, and which tends to obscure the fact that the Usuthu leaders were trying to impose order and discipline on their dispersed followers, and to evolve a broad overall strategy by which they could defeat their enemies.

The essence of Usuthu strategy lay in trying to ensure that the Mandlakazi and Ngenetsheni would be unable to launch a combined attack.

Hamu had to be dealt with first, and this would allow a massed attack on Zibhebhu without the fear that the Ngenetsheni would mount an attack or harass unguarded Usuthu in the rear. An Usuthu attack early in May drove Hamu and his people into their strongholds where they were besieged, and their unprotected homesteads and stock were plundered.[46] But despite this the Usuthu were unable to dislodge the Ngenetsheni from their defended positions and from which they launched attacks and raids which were, on balance, successful.

After Msebe, Cetshwayo abandoned all efforts to convince the officials that he was trying to obey the impossible conditions under which he was restored. He told the authorities that by their actions Zibhebhu and Hamu had forced him to gather his people together and defend themselves. He openly refused to accept the role of a chief in a divided Zululand, and he asked Fynn, how it was 'that they [Hamu and Zibhebhu] should presume to retaliate, knowing him to be their king and ruler?'[47] Or as his chiefs protested to Colenso, through an African convert who had been living with Dabulamanzi:

> With the Queen Cetshwayo ate food prepared for him; here, through you, he eats water only. Make it known in all the lands, O English! how you are treating Cetshwayo this year. Cetshwayo's dogs are given his Kingship, and are making sport of it in the public road![48]

And after one of the many arguments the king had with Fynn, during which the Resident had demanded that the king keep within his boundaries and Cetshwayo refused to accept that they were his boundaries, he turned on Fynn saying,

> 'Oh! you, Gwalagwala![49] . . . who tell us to remain quietly here! Oh! you English people, while our women and children are being killed and our cattle taken, let us go free to protect our families, let us black people fight it out between ourselves!'[50]

Through May and June, while the northern Usuthu were occupied with the Ngenetsheni, Cetshwayo remained at Ulundi from where he called on Zulu from other parts of the country to come and defend him. He had considerable success in this and, from the end of April, Fynn saw thousands of soldiers parading, training, and undergoing military ceremonies at the royal homestead. Osborn, who on 1 April replaced John Shepstone as Resident Commissioner in the Reserve, protested strongly against the presence of royal messengers in the Reserve[51] and fined those Zulu people resident in the Reserve who crossed into Cetshwayo's territory, demanding that they leave their homes and live under the king.[52] Cetshwayo in turn protested that Osborn was 'killing' him by obstructing those Zulu who wished to defend him from his enemies.[53]

The troops at Ulundi were mobilised according to regiment although they never reached their full complement. They were used not only to protect the king but also as reinforcements to assist the northern Usuthu when they were hard-pressed. The Usuthu forces were concentrated at two points – around Cetshwayo at Ulundi, and in the upper reaches of the Sikhwebezi around Mnyamana's homesteads. But the broken, wooded terrain made communication between the scattered Usuthu difficult and they found it hard to co-ordinate their movements. Thus on 11 May the Egazini were surprised and defeated when they mistook an approaching Ngenetsheni force for their Qulusi allies, and Hlezibane was killed.[54]

Moreover the Usuthu were unable to produce a military leader who inspired confidence and gained the support of all the royalist groups. The leaders of the army were mostly old chiefs who had served Mpande. Ndabuko had been discredited by the defeat at Msebe, and while Mnyamana played an important role as leader of the Buthelezi and the northern Usuthu, he was now well over seventy and was forced to spend most of his time near the Ngome, unable to abandon his people to lead the royalists as a whole. Dabulamanzi did take a force from Ulundi against Zibhebhu at the end of June but the Usuthu refused to fight when the Mandlakazi appeared.[55]

The king himself was tied to Ulundi; his presence there was vital to Usuthu recruitment and their morale. Moreover Cetshwayo was physically unable to provide the type of leadership needed. What the Usuthu wanted was a leader like Zibhebhu: a man able to obtain rifles and fresh mounts from Natal through the agency of white traders and mercenaries, an active soldier in the field who led his troops personally, using new tactics which took advantage of the horse's mobility and accurate rifle fire. Cetshwayo suffered many disadvantages and his tactics were essentially defensive as he tried to create a situation where he could deploy his greatest advantage – numbers. The royal homestead soon included about a thousand huts, and associated royal homesteads were rebuilt on the Mahlabathini plain. The Emangweni royal homestead was also revived; its strategic position was crucial, lying as it did between Dunn and Zibhebhu, and soon reports from there indicated that modern rifles and ammunition were passing along the coast to Zibhebhu, and on to Hamu.

In Natal, Sir Henry Bulwer and Bishop Colenso received news of events in Zululand from their different sources and were horrified at the reports of death and destruction. Bulwer sent Henrique Shepstone to the country with instructions to mediate between the warring factions but the mission was unsuccessful.[56] Bulwer informed the Colonial Office:

The whole mischief lies in the inability of Cetywayo to accept and abide loyally by the conditions which limited his territorial restoration, and which he says he signed under protest, and with the hope held out to him that all the remainder of the country would be restored to him.[57]

Bulwer feared that Cetshwayo would ultimately succeed in defeating Zibhebhu in the north, and would then turn on the Reserve. He urged his superiors in London to grant him the authority to establish 'with a strong and firm hand our authority and protection in the Reserve',[58] for the Reserve was

the only means we have of meeting our obligations towards the Zulu people, and the only obstacle that opposes itself to the great danger which, after all has happened, will threaten the Colony of Natal from any rehabilitation of Cetywayo's power as it was before the year 1879.[59]

Once again the Colonial Office did not question the analysis of their man on the spot, especially when it received formal support from Sir Theophilus.[60] Nonetheless London was still reluctant to assume direct responsibility.[61] An attempt was therefore made to make it appear to the Zulu that the British would defend the boundaries of the Reserve if the Usuthu crossed them; Bulwer was given permission to move troops towards the Reserve, but not into it, if Cetshwayo's men violated the boundary.[62]

Bishop Colenso also tried to intervene more directly in Zulu affairs. He had long felt that Cetshwayo should have with him a 'respectable, trustworthy whiteman at his side to conduct his correspondence with the Resident & the Natal Govt. *in writing* so that there may be no chance in future of his communications being misinterpreted'.[63] The Bishop chose an ex-Zululand trader and Durban storekeeper, William Grant, whose firm had recently gone bankrupt, leaving Grant, his wife and ten children destitute.[64]

Nothing is more indicative of Colenso's sense of isolation and his need for support than his friendship with Grant. The bankrupt trader lacked the personal qualities needed for the task that Colenso expected him to fulfil. He required constant recognition both on a personal and official level. When it was necessary to work unobtrusively he informed the press of his activities, and when there were secret tasks to be carried out, he approached the authorities for official sanction. Frances Colenso discerned some of his faults earlier than the rest of her family. She wrote that his correspondence was permeated with a tone of 'insufferable assumption'; 'He writes as tho' he were the King of Zululand himself.'[65] For Harriette Colenso recognition of Grant's shortcomings took longer, and was infinitely more painful. In 1884 Grant was a signatory to one of the documents ceding Zulu territory to the Boers.[66]

Colenso's support for Grant, which proved to be such a serious error of judgement, must be seen in the light of Colenso's weariness, profound disappointment and his desperate need for sympathetic supporters and allies. Ever since the return of Cetshwayo, colonial Natal had held Colenso largely responsible for the bloodshed. The attacks made on him were vicious: the 'monomaniac' Bishop was said to be motivated by the need to keep his name in the public eye, now that his Biblical criticism was no longer attracting attention. As a result a thousand Zulu had died and

> Not a word has been said by the Bishop of Natal, the one man who, forsaking his high calling for politics, has been the main instrument of this bloodshed.[67]

And one anonymous correspondent of the *Times of Natal* saw ominous forces at work in Natal and Zululand:

> At times like these, when we find men deliberately stirring up troubles with the natives, we are justified in suspecting that, if not fools and dupes, they are agents of those many socialistic societies of Europe who preach rebellion, plan wholesale assassinations, or work one way or another for that one common object – weakening the hands of all Governments, especially that of England, by means of a reign of terror which is to destroy civilization. Let no man imagine that these societies have not extended their work over Africa. . . . Let no one imagine that any man is so high in position as thereby alone to be beyond suspicion.[68]

Colenso was finding it more and more difficult to counter these attacks, and to publicise the Usuthu interpretation of events in Zululand. Indeed he had little to show in practical terms for the decade during which he had led the offensive against colonial policy towards Africans in Natal and Zululand. Langalibalele was still in exile and his people dispersed; the return of the king was developing into a disaster for the Zulu people; and the man who Colenso believed was primarily responsible still had the ear of the government. Indeed Colenso now had 'a sort of superstitious dread' of Somtsewu '& his influence'.[69] Apart from attending to his episcopal duties the Bishop, who was now nearly seventy, worked vigorously collecting and distributing information in an effort to promote the Usuthu cause. But by now the work was taking its toll and at the end of 1882 he had written that the last

> two years pretty full of anxious care and hard work, in respect of various matters, have taken, as I feel, a good deal of strength out of me. . . . My body and soul are crying out for *rest*, before I go hence.[70]

In June 1883 Colenso fell ill. On the 17th, unable to write, he dictated his comments on Zulu affairs for Harriette to pass on to Magema Fuze, the Bishopstowe printer. The next day he asked her not to read the editorials 'so full of abuse' in the Natal newspapers. It was clear that the Bishop's illness was not just the consequence of overwork; he became delirious, imagining that he was preparing a statement for the Aborigines' Protection Society or talking about Zulu affairs with Grant or Statham. On Wednesday, 20 June, he died.

To his family he died a martyr and they pledged that they would continue his work, fighting for the causes he had taken up. Frances wrote to Chesson:

> He died for the cause in which he has fought so long, the cause of justice, truth, and mercy, for truly it was overwork in that cause, and the sorrow of seeing it still trampled under foot, that wore away his strength and took him from us.[71]

In later years Africans spoke of him as the 'last of the race of true white man friends'.[72]

An Usuthu messenger then at Bishopstowe was taken to see Colenso's body before carrying a letter to Cetshwayo which read:

> This worn-out-garment of his which he has left with us, we have allowed Melakanya to see, as your eyes, because you too are Sobantu's son.
> Listen well to these words of mine, my brother, knowing that I come from him, that it is not I, but Sobantu who speaks to you saying 'Do not despair, my son.'[73]

In his reply Cetshwayo wrote of his shock and distress, and also his hope in Sobantu's children:

> I have taken heed to your word saying that I must not despair, and my trust is now in you. I will agree that it is his garments only which are buried, and that he himself is still there, since you are there and all the company of your friends who have been working together with my Father.

Shingana then paid tribute to the Bishop:

> The thing which we admired in Sobantu was that he resisted the devices of Satan for deceiving other people, for eating up their strength, and oppressing them that they may become like dogs for ever.[74]

Not only did Cetshwayo lose his most trusted white ally in June but his plans to defeat Hamu were unsuccessful. Mnyamana, supported by regiments from Ulundi, made a concerted attack on Hamu's stronghold in the middle of the month, but the Falaza regiment[75] which led the storming party was so severely mauled that the attack was abandoned. Hamu was apparently assisted by about ten companies of Mandlakazi who had crept through the Usuthu cordon and joined the Ngenetsheni.[76] Dabulamanzi then tried to relieve the pressure on the forces besieging Hamu with an attack on Zibhebhu; it was on this occasion that he led a force of three regiments from Ulundi which, when confronted by the Mandlakazi, refused to fight.

Thus after two months of bitter skirmishing the situation was still one of stalemate; both sides knew that this had to be resolved before the spring rains, and it was now mid-winter. Early in July the Usuthu decided upon a change of tactics and the force besieging Hamu was suddenly withdrawn[77] when it was decided that it was impossible to dislodge the Ngenetsheni from their strongholds and that an attack should be made on Zibhebhu.

For months Cetshwayo had been in contact with Usuthu supporters, sympathisers and potential allies in the area surrounding Zibhebhu's territory. To the south-east of the Mandlakazi district lay Somkhele and his Mpukunyoni, staunch supporters of the royal house; to the south again Cetshwayo had rebuilt the Emangweni homestead, mobilising point for the Emangweni section. Samlbane of the Nyawo, and 'Thonga' who lived on and beyond the Lubombo, guarded that line of retreat for the Mandlakazi. North of the Phongolo, in the wedge of Transvaal territory which split the Zulu from the Swazi, lived Usuthu sympathisers, whose services were apparently much in demand because of their Swazi links which made them expert in warfare waged from and against caves and mountain strongholds. In the same area there were a number of Mandlakazi and Emgazini refugees from Zibhebhu. To the east of Zibhebhu's district were his most intractable enemies, the northern Usuthu. A co-ordinated offensive by these groups against Zibhebhu, together with an attack by the regiments gathered at Ulundi would have forced the Mandlakazi to fight on different fronts against overwhelming numbers.

Zibhebhu alleged that such an attack was being prepared and the authorities were convinced that this was so.[78] At the same time the Usuthu alleged that Zibhebhu was preparing for an attack on Ulundi and that it was necessary for them to take precautions against this.[79] Bulwer declared that Zibhebhu had neither the strength nor the desire to attack the king.[80] Throughout July tension was high as both sides watched and waited for the predicted clash. On the 14th a group of Buthelezi raided Zibhebhu's territory and killed a number of Emgazini who supported the Mandlakazi chief. At this point Zibhebhu decided that he must take the initiative. On 20 July Zibhebhu met with his allies at the Ekuvukeni homestead in the south-west portion of his territory. In all they mustered about three thousand men, one-quarter of whom followed Hamu. Information of this gathering reached Ulundi but Cetshwayo and the chiefs with him decided that it was a move against Mnyamana and

Ndabuko, and no special precautions were taken. A report reached Mnyamana and Ndabuko, however, that the Mandlakazi were preparing to attack Ulundi. Mnyamana made contact with leaders of the northern Usuthu forces and it was decided that they should march, as a single body, towards Ulundi and intercept the Mandlakazi should they attempt to reach the royal homestead.[81]

As evening fell on 20 July, Zibhebhu moved his men along the flanks of the Qongqo hill towards the Black Mfolozi and began the 50 km night march which brought them, just as it was getting light, to the low hills to the east of Ulundi. People were beginning to stir at the royal homesteads and it was when the first wood-gathering and water-collecting parties were going out that the alarm was given. There was confusion as the surprised Usuthu hurriedly tried to form up in regiments. In the king's homestead itself were the *izikhulu*, the leaders of the army, trusted councillors and notable officials from all parts of the country. Most of them were elderly men, and they gathered round the king, some demanding that the regiments make a stand around the royal homestead, and others that they go out and meet the enemy. In the end, on their own initiative rather than under explicit orders, the Usuthu soldiers began to move towards the Mandlakazi force, in the king's words,

'in a most disorganised state, they were only just awake, and in no state for fighting: they ran towards the attacking force but did not make any stand. There was no real fighting, for my men at once began to run.'[82]

Beyond making an attempt to stop the Mandlakazi charge with long-range firing the Usuthu made no stand but fled across the Mahlabathini plain, past Ulundi towards the White Mfolozi. Left virtually unprotected in the royal homestead were Cetshwayo, his most senior officers and the women of the royal household. At first the king refused to leave Ulundi, but the brother and emissary of the Swazi king, Mbandeni, brought him a horse and Cetshwayo was persuaded to flee. With Sihayo leading the small and rather decrepit animal, Cetshwayo left his homestead through a gate in the rear as Zibhebhu's men put Ulundi to the torch.

The Mandlakazi met with little resistance. The powerful force of northern Usuthu had failed to reach Ulundi. Instead of obeying Mnyamana's orders and proceeding with haste to Ulundi the force had split up; there had been differences between Ndabuko, Tshanibezwe, and the Qulusi, and they had camped for the night instead of pressing on for the Mahlabathini plain.[83] On the plain itself the Mandlakazi cut down fleeing Usuthu, slaughtered or captured women and children, and set fire to the dry winter grass. Three of Cetshwayo's wives and three of Mpande's were killed and Cetshwayo's youngest son was speared in his mother's arms. Many women and children were burnt to death in their huts. Zibhebhu's white men, Darke, McAlister and Eckersley, watched the looting of the king's possessions; within a few days presents given to Cetshwayo in London, including some from the British royal family, were exhibited in Natal stores.[84]

By the time Cetshwayo reached a small stream on the northern bank of the White Mfolozi his horse had been brought to its knees on the rough ground, and the king was exhausted. He moved to the protection of a small thicket; some of his party passed on so as not to draw attention to the king, who sat down to rest. Here a band of young men from Zibhebhu's force found him and four assegais were thrown, two of which wounded him in the thigh. Cetshwayo called out to them:

'What! Do you, my own people, stab me with assegais?' The young men who had thrown the assegais asked one another 'Who is it?' Halijana, one of their indunas, said 'It is the King! Do you not hear that it is the King?' Said they 'We thought that it was Ziwedu,' and these four turned and fled. Halijana and Mzikiza, and a good many others approached a little and sat down . . . and spoke to the King, saying 'Yes Sir! . . . Why did you cast off Zibebu, who fought for you against the English and before too at Ndondakusuka . . .? Why, on your return from England, did you not at once summon us the Mandhlakazi to you, instead of trusting to the iziGqoza . . .?[85] All this would then never have happened.' The King made no reply, and after a while they all went quietly away. Then he said 'Come, children, let us be going.' And he and the two girls, the only ones with him who were left alive, went their way also unmolested.[86]

For the Usuthu the tragedy of Zibhebhu's attack on Ulundi lay not so much in the magnitude of the slaughter – although that was terrible enough[87] – but in the number of Usuthu leaders who were killed. For at the time of the attack the king had gathered round him the most important and loyal of his supporters. Many of them were old, contemporaries of his father, men of experience and with great influence in the country. As Darke, one of Zibhebhu's white mercenaries, wrote

All the principal headmen were killed. . . . Being all fat and big-bellied, they had no chance of escape; and one of them was actually run to earth and stabbed by my little mat-bearers.[88]

They included Sekethwayo of the Mdlalose, the hereditary chief whose father had been appointed by Shaka to establish Zulu influence in the north-western districts; Godide, son of Ndlela and hereditary chief of the Ntuli; Hayiyana, Maphitha's eldest son and head of the Mandlakazi *ikhohlo*; Mbopha, *isikhulu*, closely related to the royal house by marriage, was killed together with his son; Sihayo, chief of the Qungebe, who before he died ensured that the king had left Ulundi in safety; Vumandaba, a royal favourite and Mpande's personal attendant; Dilikana, elderly chief of the Mbatha, the man who had appealed for the return of the king at Nhlazatshe,[89] and his son Simukanaye ('we go together'); and Ntshingwayo, who had led the Zulu army and was an appointed chief in 1879, although he had become involved in a dispute over cattle with the Usuthu and had never shown any enthusiasm for the king's return. And so the list of important men killed continues: Ngcongcwana who was on the first Usuthu deputation and had accompanied Cetshwayo to London; Ndwandwe, chief of the Langeni from the Reserve; Nobiya, chief of the Sibiya, also of the Reserve; Mnqandi, the *isikhulu* and chief of the Sibisi, father of Sitshitshili (who had ensured that Dinuzulu escaped unhurt from Ulundi); Blankhede of the Biyela, and Siqhoto of the Egazini whose brother Hlezibane had been killed a few weeks before.

Fynn gave a list of fifty-nine 'important men' killed.[90] Gibson, who took an interest in Zulu history and worked in Zululand a few years after the battle, found that many traditions were difficult to collect because so many knowledgeable men had lost their lives at Ulundi in 1883.[91] Zibhebhu's praise poem gives a dramatic insight into the immensity of the tragedy:

> Shield of Shaka and Jama:
> He devoured Godide son of Ndlela
> Amongst the Zulu bodyguard;
> He destroyed Ndwandwe son of Mdlaka
> Amongst the Zulu bodyguard;
> He ate up Sihayo son of Xhongo,
> He ate up Sekethwayo son of Nhlaka,
> Of the great men of Zululand;
> He destroyed Mtokwe son of Mdamba
> Amongst the Zulu bodyguard;
> He devoured Ntshingwayo son of Mahole
> He ate up Siqhoto son of Mkhanyile,
> He ate up Dilikana son of Hlakanyana,
> He devoured Mnqandi son of Mtshana,
> Amongst the Zulu bodyguard;
> He ate up Bulangethe son of Magidi,
> He devoured Vumandaba son of Ntethi,
> Amongst the Zulu bodyguard.
>   He devoured So-and-So of So-and-So,

> I don't like to mention his name,
> If I named him there would be an outburst of wailing;
> [This triplet is repeated in total eight times]
>   He who stalked forth in broad daylight,
> For he entered Ondini not when it was dark,
> But when it was clear and they saw him,
> He finished them off entirely,
> Destroyer of the enemy assembly.[92]

When Cetshwayo gave the names of those men of note killed at Ulundi in 1883, he was stopped after he had reached fifty-two. He said,

'every name I have given you is that of a man of influence, a man with a following; men who say let it be so, Zulu, and it is so in accordance. Ah! but they are gone, and I feel alone. They were men, many my seniors, and favourites of Mpanda, my father, and many of my own age who had grown up with me, belonging to the same regiment, and our life in boyhood and manhood has been one. But they are not. They have been finished. Count my headmen who have been killed?' asked the King. 'Easier far to count those who have escaped – the few who are still left to me – left with me to hold our mouths in wonder at the way our own Zulu (nation) is being spilt.'[93]

If one has to find an historical moment to mark the end of the old Zulu order, then it is this Mandlakazi attack on the royal homestead on 21 July 1883 when Zibhebhu succeeded where Chelmsford had failed in July 1879. The British commander had left the political hierarchy of Zululand virtually untouched: Zibhebhu decimated the Zulu leadership, killing the great men of the country upon whose authority Usuthu dominance depended. In 1879 the Zulu turned from war to seek out their cattle, and prepare their lands for the spring rains: in 1883 the upholders of the Zulu royal house had lost their cattle and were unable to turn to the urgent tasks required by the agricultural cycle and were forced to seek refuge beyond their borders or were driven further into the forest, caves and mountain strongholds.

The death of the king

Once again, as they had done after the battle of Msebe, the Mandlakazi and their allies devastated the territory north of the Black Mfolozi, only this time they were able to extend their operations further and burnt and plundered the inland districts up to the borders of the Reserve. Most of the force which had escaped from the royal homestead fled into the Reserve. The Mdlalose, further to the west, escaped into Hlubi's area where he gave them protection – at a price – while the Qulusi retired to the Hlobane range or across the Bivane into the Transvaal.[94] Mnyamana and the Buthelezi and the rest of the northern Usuthu withdrew once again into the Ngome forest and other strongholds. When the looting was over the Ngenetsheni and Mandlakazi destroyed the foodstuffs they could not carry, excreting or putting human and animal corpses into the grain stores. Boers from the Transvaal moved through the north-western districts loading unspoiled grain they found in deserted homesteads on to their waggons.[95] Women and children were captured and taken to Mandlakazi homesteads where they joined others seized at Ulundi. Fire spread through the dry winter grass of northern Zululand and it was reported that 'everything is in a most fearful state of desolation, the whole country burnt off a dismal black'.[96]

After the central districts had been plundered and its inhabitants scattered, Zibhebhu turned his attention to other areas. His dispute with Somkhele was one of long standing[97] and had been revived during the Sitimela incident and by the refugees from Mandlakazi territory who had fled to Somkhele for protection. In mid-August Zibhebhu launched an attack on the Mpukunyoni. The conflict spread when Sokwetshata took advantage of the general disruption by attacking the Emangweni section and he then assisted Zibhebhu against Somkhele, before turning on the Emangweni again.[98] Colenbrander, McAlister, Darke and two other whites participated and Bulwer suggested that 'cattle lifting' was the most important element in these attacks.[99] Somkhele fled to the fever-ridden swamps and forests of Dukuduku and the flats around St Lucia lake, while the Emangweni took refuge in the reed-beds on the margins of the Enseleni and Mhlatuze rivers. In all parts of Zululand the Usuthu were on the retreat, and those Zulu associated with Zibhebhu and Hamu, like Mfanawendlela and Mgojana, or those men who had co-operated with the authorities in the Reserve like Dunn and Hlubi, seemed to have emerged as the heirs of the deceased Zulu kingdom.

It was widely believed that Cetshwayo had been killed at Ulundi. He was in fact in hiding near the White Mfolozi, resting his injured leg while the few attendants with him went out at night to get food from nearby homesteads. His whereabouts were reported to Shingana, and, together with Mahanana, and Sigananda and Luhungu of the Chube, he came to the king with a horse,[100] and they took him south to the Nkandla forest.

The Nkandla forest runs for some 20 km along the crown and the south-western slopes of a ridge which lies above the Mhlatuze and Thukela rivers. It has developed as a result of high precipitation, and the streams which rise in the forest have cut deep gorges which drop sharply into the

Nsuze river which runs along the base of the ridge. These gorges are separated by steep narrow ridges, which are grass covered at lower altitudes before the forest is reached. Throughout Zulu history the Nkandla forest has been a place of mystery, the home of supernatural beings, and a formidable stronghold and place of retreat. The Chube are the iron-workers associated with the Nkandla and they were never conquered by Shaka; it has always been the last retreat of the Zulu from Shaka's time to that of Bambatha in 1906.[101]

Cetshwayo's stronghold in 1883 was situated high on the Mome stream, about 4 km from where it enters the Nsuze. Surrounded by forest and cliffs the only practical access route lay up the steep narrow grass ridge. Within the forest in a clearing the Enhlweni homestead was built by Luhungu for the king. From Enhlweni a narrow tunnel, complete with blind alleys and dead ends, was hacked through the forest to caves above a waterfall where Cetshwayo had his hideout.[102]

From here, in the company of bands of survivors, and a few *izinduna*, Cetshwayo sent messengers to his supporters in the north, and also to the authorities to inform them that, as he had predicted, his enemies had attacked while he was 'sitting still', and he appealed for British intervention on behalf of the man they had restored to Zululand.

Such appeals were fruitless. Osborn demanded that Cetshwayo place himself under his protection at Eshowe where he had established his Residency. When Cetshwayo refused Osborn alleged that the king intended

> to establish himself in a position of supreme power at the Nkanhla; . . . that he means to make the Nkanhla his permanent headquarters, and from thence endeavour to rule the territory to which he was restored, and that he will entirely ignore the existence of the Reserve as forming a distinct and separate territory.[103]

Whatever Cetshwayo would have liked to do it is obvious that, with his followers scattered and in hiding, he did not have the means to implement any such grandiose scheme. Nonetheless Bulwer felt that such a threat was real, and obtained authority to send a detachment of troops to the Reserve, not for active service but 'as a moral support for the purpose of reassuring the people in the Reserve as to our intentions, and for defence'.[104]

When the troops entered Zululand Cetshwayo believed for a moment that they had come from 'the Queen', at last moved by his appeals that England should honour the promises made to him in London.[105] His hopes were soon dashed, first by Grant, and then when Zibhebhu, interpreting the movement of troops as the first step in an attempt to force

Cetshwayo from his retreat, moved to the borders of the Reserve and sent threatening messages which reached the Usuthu in the Nkandla.[106]

Frightened by the threat of military action, Cetshwayo at last realised that he could do nothing to consolidate his position while in the Nkandla. Moreover the spring rains had arrived and if his people were to survive, some solution had soon to be reached. As he said to Osborn

> The planting season is advancing, and unless my people can cultivate with some sense of security, the additional misery of starvation will be added to their troubles.[107]

The king sent a secret message to Osborn (which Osborn neither answered nor treated privately):

> I ask you, my father, to take my territory into your hands and to rule it for me. A hut tax could be collected from all my people in it, and all the tax received shall be yours for the trouble you will have in managing the affairs of my country. You will greatly help me and my people if you will consent to do this.[108]

Cetshwayo had finally realised that he could not protect his people or reassert himself in Zululand without the support of local officials. On 17 October 1883 Cetshwayo placed himself under the Resident Commissioner's protection at Eshowe.

Cetshwayo was lodged in a small homestead near the Residency. Here he was visited by his family and his closest followers. It was a time of wretched misery for Cetshwayo. From the north came stories of death and desolation. Osborn accused the king of using the safety of the Reserve to attempt to build up his power once again, and the king alleged that the restrictions Osborn had placed on his followers visiting him constituted unnecessary harassment and exposed him to attack by his enemies.

London received requests from all sides to intervene and impose order in the territory and stop the slaughter. But the Liberal government refused to make any decision, either about Cetshwayo or his territory's future. As the Secretary of State for the Colonies, Lord Derby, said to his Prime Minister, after pointing out the drawbacks to intervention and the possible dangers of continued inactivity,

> In any case, though unpleasant complications may follow, we have half the Zulu nation against him, so that there is no question of a war like that of 1879.[109]

Early in February, however, the situation was suddenly and dramatically changed. On the 8th of that month Osborn was called urgently to the king's hut. On his arrival he was informed that Cetshwayo had collapsed in his hut and died.[110] The *abantwana* present refused to grant permission for a post-mortem to be performed, but the medical officer who examined the body decided that he had died of a heart attack. The Zulu believed, and do today, that he was poisoned.

The available evidence remains inconclusive. A medical examination made in Cape Town found that Cetshwayo was suffering from a heart complaint[111] but another, undertaken in London, found the king's heart to be sound.[112] Initially Harriette Colenso believed that he had died as a result of the callous persecution he had suffered. She wrote to her brother:

> . . . they have just tortured him to death as they did his Father [Bishop Colenso] 7 months ago, only that he has been able to endure it longer, being younger & stronger. He said, when he heard of Sobantu's death, that it was his own death-warrant; then came Ulundi & since then blow after blow, indignity upon indignity, has been heaped upon him – it is difficult not to say with the intention to break his heart.[113]

The Zulu believed that Cetshwayo, like Sobantu, had been poisoned; they told Harriette that he was 'dragged from the Nkandhla in order to be killed'.[114] It had been done, they believed, by one of the local officials such as John Shepstone or Osborn, or by Zibhebhu. Harriette Colenso rejected the idea of poison because

> So many & so minute are the precautions on this point wh. habitually surround a Zulu king. His clothes, his food, his very sticks all have their own carefully chosen guardians . . . all this was habitual etiquette.[115]

This does raise the possibility of assassination from within the group of men closely associated with Cetshwayo, and this was suggested at the time and again in the years to come.[116] Usuthu policy did take a radical change in direction after the king's death when the Usuthu allied themselves with Transvaal Boers; Cetshwayo might have been obstructing this. However, explanations along these lines are still rejected indignantly and with expressions of shocked disbelief.

But, even if we can only speculate on the precise cause of the king's death, what is certain is that the officials who had devised the partition, and those who authorised it, bear a heavy responsibility. And although the Natal officials and the majority of the settlers placed the blame on the actions of Cetshwayo himself and those who had agitated for his return, and most of the men in London accepted this explanation, one young Colonial Office official was able to perceive the reasons for Cetshwayo's death more clearly; he wrote that when, in 1881, it had become clear that Wolseley's settlement was breaking down,

> Her Majesty's late Government conceived that the only alternatives lay between assuming the responsibility of government or restoring Cetywayo, and they chose the latter course as an experiment, and not, it may be remarked, for the sentimental reasons to which the step has been generally attributed.

That experiment might possibly have succeeded, if Cetywayo had been left free to maintain order in his own former drastic fashion; but this was felt to be impossible. He was forbidden to re-establish his military system. He was put under the control of a resident, and a strip of territory, in which the chief strength and wealth of his adherents lay, was withheld from him. His enemy, Usibebu, was under no similar disabilities, and was therefore easily able to crush him. Thus not only did the late Government reverse by a very conspicuous proceeding the action of the preceding one, but it failed to back its own man, and allowed him to be so used by the Natal Government and his enemies as to give him no chance of success. His own criticism on the transaction was that the Government had thrown him down in the grass to be murdered by his enemies.[117]

But in its attempt to use Cetshwayo in its plans for southern Africa, and then bowing to Natal demands, the Colonial Office had done more than contribute directly to the king's death; the men through whom he ruled were also killed and, more fundamentally, it had broken the continuity of production upon which Zulu self-sufficiency and strength depended. Consequently the people who only five years before had defended their land and way of life with so much success now lay exposed and vulnerable to the forces which for so long had been waiting on Zululand's borders for this moment.

Notes

1 This reconstruction of events in Zululand after the king's return is based on Colenso, series 2, and various reports in BPP, C.3616, supplemented by some of Fynn's reports in GHZ 683.
2 KC, Maphelu, p. 13. Other reports said he had some of Mnyamana's cattle.
3 *Times of Natal,* 17 Feb. 1883, in Colenso, series 2, p. 453.
4 See above, pp. 175–6 where this event is reported to Sir T. Shepstone.
5 For examples of these clashes see BPP, C.3616; 25, 37, 45 and encs., and also statement by Shingana and others in Colenso, series 2, pp. 461–3.
6 Colenso, series 2, p. 462.
7 W. Campbell, *With Cetywayo in the Inkandhla, and the present state of the Zulu question,* Durban, 1883, p. 11.
8 BPP, C.3616: 42, enc. 1, Fynn to Bulwer, 22 Feb. 1883; KC, Stuart papers: 30055, Native habits and customs in war, evidence of Mpatshana.
9 BPP, C.3616: 56, enc. 1, Fynn to Bulwer, 14 March 1883; Colenso, series 2, pp. 452–500 *passim.*
10 Osborn thanked Sir Theophilus Shepstone for 'advocating my interests' in regard to this appointment. NA, Sir T. Shepstone collection: box 18, Osborn to T. Shepstone, 6 Jan. 1883.
11 See for example BPP, C.3466: 159, enc. 3, J. Shepstone to Bulwer, 6 Jan. 1883. Bulwer had already referred to the Reserve as 'our portion' in a private letter to Sir Theophilus; see NA, Sir T. Shepstone collection: box 13, Bulwer to T. Shepstone, 20 Sept. 1882.

12 By using 'Hulumeni', Shepstone can only have meant the Natal Government. See Note 13.

13 J. Stuart, *uKulumetule*, Ch. 31, 'Ukubuya Ku Ka Cetshwayo e Buyisel wa kwa Zulu uSomsewu', p. 181 (translation). Compare this account with a contemporary one, received by Colenso through a 'reliable channel', in Colenso, series 2, p. 355*b*;

> 'I have also to inform you that the Umhlatuze is now to take the place of the Tugela, and that all the land south of it now belongs to the (Hulumente) Natal Government. White people will not be allowed to go there, but Natal natives in want of land may settle in it, and the Missionaries are to remain. You need not, however, move at present, and I have not come to separate you from the King. Your mealies are not yet ripe. You may stay and gather in your crops, and then in the winter time those who prefer to be under Cetshwayo can move over to him, while those preferring to remain here can do so. But, if they stay, they must understand that they will have to pay taxes to the Natal Government according to our custom.'

14 NA, John Shepstone collection: box 3, Bulwer to J. Shepstone, 24 Jan. 1883.

15 Ibid., 19 Jan. 1883.

16 Or so it would seem from Fynn's remark to J. Shepstone: 'I did not tell him [Cetshwayo] what you say you will do to them or their people or his messengers if they don't comply' BPP, C.3616: 35, enc. 1, Fynn to Bulwer, 15 Feb. 1883, Fynn to J. Shepstone, 8 Feb. 1883, p. 64.

17 This incident caused a scandal in Natal when Colenso passed the information from the Usuthu to F. R. Statham, editor of the *Natal Witness*, who published it and was sued for libel by John Shepstone. Statham lost the case, and it does not seem as if Shepstone personally assaulted any Zulu, but he did set his police on to them for being 'disrespectful'. See Henrique Shepstone's letter to his father, Sir Theophilus, based on an eye-witness account, in NA, Sir T. Shepstone collection: box 20, 27 May 1883.

18 See for example BPP, C.3616: 35, enc. 1, Fynn to Bulwer, 15 Feb. 1883, statement by Cetshwayo, 8 Feb. 1883; Colenso, series 2, Cetshwayo ka Mpande to J. W. Colenso, letters I–III, pp. 625ff.

19 NA, John Shepstone collection: box 3, Bulwer to J. Shepstone, 12 Jan. 1883.

20 BPP, C.3466: 143, Derby to Bulwer, 18 Jan. 1883, summarises the telegraphic correspondence. Minutes on Bulwer to Derby, 12 Jan. 1883, in CO 179/145; 614, show the officials pondering on the problem of how to establish 'paramount authority' without committing themselves to what would be virtual annexation. It was eventually decided that there 'is no *via media* between keeping for a time some sort of order in this territory, and abandoning it, either directly to Cetywayo, or to lawlessness'.

21 BPP, C.3616: 29, Bulwer to Derby, 24 Feb. 1883 and encs.

22 Originally the Reserve Territorial Carbineers. For the formation of the *Nongqayi* see CO 179/145: 8556, Bulwer to Derby, 23 April 1883.

23 See below, p. 231.

24 Colenso, series 2, Letter V, Cetshwayo to J. W. Colenso, 6 April 1883, p. 631.

25 BPP, C.3616: encs. in 36, 41, 42, 53, 67, 68.

26 Lord Derby, for whom 'inactivity was a principle of policy'. For an analysis of Derby's term of office see D. M. Schreuder, *Gladstone and Kruger: Liberal Government and Colonial 'Home Rule' 1880–85*, London and Toronto, 1969, Ch. 6.

27 BPP, C.3616: 67, enc. 7, Bulwer to Fynn, 29 March 1883, p. 118.

28 See above, p. 113ff. and p. 169ff.

29 BPP, C.3616: 41, enc. 1, Fynn to Bulwer, 21 Feb. 1883, p. 74.

30 BPP, C.3616: 70, Bulwer to Derby, enc. 1, Fynn to Bulwer, 17 March 1883. See also, BPP, C.3616: 86, which is based on minutes numbered 47 and 49(a) in GHZ 683.

31 BPP, C.3616: 77, enc. 2, Fynn to Bulwer, 25 March 1883; Colenso, series 2, p. 523, statement by Mtokwane and Melekanya.

32 J. Y. Gibson, *The Story of the Zulus*, London, 1911, p. 247.

33 Colenso, series 2, p. 574.

34 The official view that Cetshwayo was deliberately trying to provoke a clash can be found in a minute written by Osborn, 22 March 1883, on Fynn to Bulwer, 14 March 1883, in GHZ 683. A son of Mnyamana, captured by Zibhebhu, alleged that Cetshwayo had ordered the Usuthu to say that the attack had been planned by Ndabuko and Makhoba. See BPP, C.3705: 3, enc. 1, Osborn to Bulwer, 11 April 1883, statement by Nsaba, 10 April 1883. See also a trader's view in BPP, C.3705: 39, Bulwer to Derby, 11 May 1883, and the enc., Fynn to Bulwer, 27 April 1883.

   However the two detailed Zulu accounts made long after the event both deny that Cetshwayo knew about the attack. See KC, Maphelu, p. 30, and A. Xaba, 'Before and after Umsebe battle' in Competitions, Zulu essays, 1942.

35 They mobilised as *amaviyo* which is usually translated as 'companies' and averaged about fifty soldiers.

36 This account of the battle of Msebe is based largely on an extract from the *Natal Mercantile Advertiser*, 7 April 1883, reprinted in Colenso, series 2, pp. 534–5; an extract from the *Natal Mercury*, 28 April 1883 (written by Herbert Nunn), in Colenso, series 2, pp. 562–8; Colenso, series 2, statement by messenger from Cetshwayo, pp. 574–6; Letter V, Cetshwayo to Colenso, 6 April 1883, pp. 630–1. There is useful information in BPP, C.3705: 3, enc. 1, Osborn to Bulwer, 11 April 1883, statement by Nsaba, 10 April 1883; C.3864: 9, enc., statements by messengers from Zibhebhu; also enclosures in BPP, C.3705: 28 and 39; A. Xaba, 'Before and after Umsebe battle' cited above; Gibson, *Story of the Zulus*, pp. 246–9.

37 See above, pp. 88 and 100ff and Plate 13.

38 H. E. Colenso, 'The Eshowe Trials – No. VII', *Women's Penny Paper*, 1889 [?], in a collection of cuttings made by A. Werner, 1915 (13682) in KC.

39 Gibson, *Story of the Zulus*, p. 249.

40 A. Xaba, 'Before and after Msebe battle', cited above.

41 *Natal Mercury*, editorial, 30 April 1883, reprinted in Colenso, series 2, p. 570.

42 BPP, C.3705: 28, enc. 2, Osborn to Bulwer, 24 April 1883.

43 Extract from a 'diary' of H. Nunn, entry for 3 April, published in the *Natal Mercury*, 28 April 1883, reprinted in Colenso, series 2, p. 567.

44 KC, Maphelu, pp. 37–8.

45   This description and the accounts of the skirmishes which follow are drawn
     from Colenso, series 2, pp. 608–761, *passim*; and BPP, C.3705: 12, 16, 44,
     49, 51, 55, 57, 60, 83; C.3864: 5, 13, 26, 29. Maphelu's account (KC) is also
     most useful.
46   BPP, C.3705: 57, enc. 2, Fynn to Bulwer, 25 May 1883.
47   BPP, C.3705: 44, enc. 4, Fynn to Bulwer, 9 May 1883, p. 77.
48   Colenso, series 2, statement by Nomahobodiya, p. 651.
49   Fynn's Zulu name, after the loerie, the feather of which Fynn wore in his hat.
50   BPP, C.3705: 51, enc. 1, Fynn to Bulwer, 10 May 1883, p. 86.
51   BPP, C.3705: 4, encs. 4 and 6, Osborn to Bulwer, 12 and 13 April 1883.
52   ZA 38; see the lists of fines imposed from April to July jotted down in the
     back of the Letter Book.
53   BPP, C.3705: 58, enc. 2, Osborn to Bulwer, 1 June 1883, and Cetshwayo to
     Osborn, 23 May 1883. This letter was written by Simon Mini, son of Chief
     Mini of Edendale and first of the Natal Africans to serve as a secretary to the
     Zulu royal house.
54   See encs. in BPP, C.3705: 51 and 55; and Colenso, series 2, p. 654.
55   BPP, C.3864: 29, Bulwer to Derby, 16 July 1883.
56   For H. Shepstone's instructions see CO 179/147: 9426, Bulwer to H.
     Shepstone, 4 May 1883; for his report, BPP, C.3705: 51, enc. 3, H. Shep-
     stone to Bulwer, 13 May 1883. See also Henrique Shepstone's letters to his
     father in NA, Sir T. Shepstone collection: H. Shepstone to T. Shepstone,
     16 May 1883.
57   BPP, C.3705: 51, Bulwer to Derby, 21 May 1883, p. 83.
58   BPP, C.3705: 42, Bulwer to Derby, 12 May 1883, p. 71.
59   Ibid.
60   BPP, C.3705: 48, T. Shepstone to Colonial Office, received on 19 June
     1883.
61   BPP, C.3705: 61, Derby to Bulwer, 12 July 1883.
62   Ibid.
63   KC, Colenso papers: folio 26/2, J. W. Colenso to Chesson, 17 July 1882;
     and AS papers: 131/194, J. W. Colenso to Chesson (first page missing).
64   For Grant's background, and his activities subsequent to his involvement
     in Zulu affairs, see Evidence of W. Grant, pp. 481ff., *Report of the Transvaal
     Labour Commission*, Johannesburg, 1903.
65   AS papers; 130/141, Frances Colenso to Chesson, 30 Sept. 1884.
66   See above, p. 233.
67   Editorial from the *Times of Natal*, 30 April 1883, reprinted in Colenso,
     series 2, p. 572.
68   Colenso, series 2, Letter to the *Times of Natal*, 2 April 1883, p. 526.
69   KC, Colenso papers: folio 26/2, Z406, J. W. Colenso to Chesson, 28 April
     1883.
70   G. W. Cox, *The Life of John William Colenso D.D., Bishop of Natal*, London,
     1888, ii, J. W. Colenso to the Dean of Grahamstown, 10 Sept. 1882,
     pp. 593–4.
71   Ibid., p. 631.
72   G. A. Shepperson and T. Price, *Independent African: John Chilembwe and the
     origins, setting and significance of the Nyasaland native rising of 1915*, Edinburgh,
     1958, p. 71.

73 Colenso, series 2, letter from H. E. and R. J. Colenso to the Zulu king, 23 June 1883, pp. 739–40.

74 Colenso, series 2, pp. 740–2, Cetshwayo to H. E. Colenso, 5 July 1883, pp. 740–2.

75 A young regiment, renamed 'Falaza' (the rubbish talkers) after Cetshwayo's return 'because the Zulus had lost the ability of talking commonsense', according to R. C. A. Samuelson, *Long, Long Ago*, p. 244.

76 BPP, C.3864: 36, Bulwer to Derby, 21 July 1883.

77 For these incidents see BPP, C.3864: 26, 29 and 36, and C.4037: 11, Bulwer to Derby, 11 Jan. 1884, pp. 7–8 where Bulwer analyses letters from Grant covering this period.

78 BPP, C.3864: 29, enc., Fynn to Bulwer, 5 July 1883, Eckersley to Fynn, 30 June 1883; BPP, C.3864: 49, encs. 11 and 16, Osborn to Bulwer, 4 and 9 August 1883, statements by Zibhebhu's messengers.

79 Colenso, series 2, statement by Mtokwane, p. 764.

80 BPP, C.3864: 26, enc. 2, Bulwer to Fynn, 7 July 1883.

81 This account of the attack on Ulundi is based on BPP, C.3864; 38, encs., 3, 9, 12, 13, 14, 16; C.3864: 39, enc., Osborn to Bulwer, 25 July 1883; and C.3864: 71, enc., Fynn to Bulwer, 23 Aug. 1883. KC, Maphelu, pp. 30–3 contains useful information. See also KC, Competitions, Zulu essays, 1942: A. Xaba, 'Before and after Umsebe battle'; J. Stuart, *uKulumetule*, 'Impi ka Zibebu Yasondini, Nokwavela Ngemva Kwayo'. Information from Natal newspapers, and from the Usuthu themselves can be found in Colenso, series 2; see especially Walton's account, pp. 780–3, Darke's account, pp. 815–20, the Usuthu account, pp. 820–2 and Cetshwayo's account, pp. 823–5.

82 Colenso, series 2, statement by Cetshwayo to Grant, 22 Sept. 1883, p. 823.

83 KC, Maphelu, p. 32.

84 Colenso, series 2, p. 818, n. 538.

85 Mbulazi's faction in the civil war of 1856.

86 There are a number of accounts of this incident, differing in detail but in general terms corroborative. This version was told to the Colensos early in August by an Usuthu messenger, Kukula; see Colenso, series 2, p. 822.

87 'Mr Fynn computes the total number of people who were killed . . . at 500 persons . . . very few of these were young men, who in flight would naturally have the best chance of escaping. . . .' BPP, C.3864: 71, Bulwer to Derby, 10 Sept. 1883.

88 Colenso, series 2, p. 819.

89 Some accounts have it that he was killed later in the day at his home north of Ulundi, after refusing to be carried to safety, believing that the king was dead.

90 BPP, C.3864: 71, enc., Fynn to Bulwer, 23 Aug. 1883, list of important men killed on 21 July 1883, p. 156.

91 J. Y. Gibson, *The Story of the Zulus*, p. 258.

92 T. Cope (ed.), *Izibongo: Zulu Praise-poems*, pp. 204–7. I have adapted the translation very slightly.

93 W. Campbell, *With Cetywayo in the Inkandhla*, p. 23.

94 KC, Maphelu, p. 33. See also the journal of Mubi Nondenisa (one of the Bishopstowe printers), Colenso, series 2, pp. 833–42 *passim*.

95 BPP, C.3864: 166, enc. 2, Fynn to Bulwer, 26 Dec. 1883.

96 BPP, C.3864: 44, enc. 2, Fynn to Bulwer, 25 July 1883, p. 79.

97 Campbell, *With Cetywayo in the Inkandhla*, p. 35; BPP, C.4037: 14, enc. 4, extracts from a letter of a Zulu trader, 7 Jan. 1884.

98 BPP, C.3864: 59, enc. 2, Osborn to Bulwer, 20 Aug. 1883, and 66, enc. 5, Osborn to Bulwer, 23 Aug. 1883.

99 BPP, C.3864: 92, Bulwer to Derby, 1 Oct. 1883.

100 NA, Colenso collection: box 119, W. Grant, 'Journal of a visit to Cetshwayo', entry for 22 Sept. 1879.

101 For a description of the Nkandla and its history see J. Stuart, *A History of the Zulu Rebellion, 1906*, London, 1913, pp. 204–11.

102 KC, Stuart papers: Evidence by Mageza kaMkantshwana, 21 Feb. 1909, Papers and Articles. In April 1970 I visited this part of Zululand above Mome gorge and was taken into the forest and shown the remains of the encampment built for the king in 1883. The Enhlweni homestead is still in existence and the descendants of the Chube (or to use the *isibongo* – Shezi) who protected the king still reside there. Luhungu's grandson, Hambayedwa Shezi, is in charge of the district and Sinandenkosi Shezi, great grandson of Sigananda is *mnumzana* of Enhlweni; their assistance in reconstructing the events of 1883, and their hospitality, is here acknowledged.

103 BPP, C.3864: 59, enc. 1, Osborn to Bulwer, 20 Aug. 1883, p. 115.

104 BPP, C.3864: 33, Bulwer to Derby, 21 Aug. 1883, pp. 54–5.

105 NA, Colenso collection: box 119, W. Grant, 'Journal of a visit to Cetshwayo', entry for 12 Sept. 1883.

106 Ibid., entry for 25 Sept. 1883.

107 BPP, C.3864: 92, enc. 4, Osborn to Bulwer, 22 Sept. 1883, Cetshwayo to Osborn (per Grant), 20 Sept. 1883, p. 197.

108 Ibid., message from Umlambo and Sibatya, 22 Sept. 1883, p. 198.

109 BM, Add. MS, 44141: Derby to Gladstone, 26 Sept. 1883 (private).

110 BPP, C.4037: 43, Bulwer to Derby, 15 Feb. 1884 and encs.

111 BPP, C.3247: 33, Robinson to Kimberley, 11 March 1882 (teleg.).

112 See the extract from the *British Medical Journal* printed in the *Natal Mercury*, 3 April 1884, and cited in Appendix E, 'The Death of Cetshwayo . . .', in C. T. Binns, *The Last Zulu King: the life and death of Cetshwayo*, London, 1963.

113 KC, Colenso papers: folio 28BB, H. E. Colenso to Frank Colenso, 10 Feb. 1884.

114 Ibid.

115 AS papers: C130/198, H. E. Colenso to Chesson, 19 Feb. 1884.

116 *The Natal Witness*, 17 June 1886.

117 Colonial Office Memorandum, 1885, E. Fairfield, 'Vacillation in policy in South Africa', reproduced as Appendix IV, in D. M. Schreuder, *Gladstone and Kruger*.

PART III

'Kwafa inyoni enkulu kwabola amaqanda'

('When the great bird died the eggs became rotten')*

I see a terrible future for S. Africa not very far ahead – the spread of a Boer empire over the whole, & the establishment of a horrible slavery of the blacks. As things are going what is to prevent it? See how the Boers are creeping on, on every side!

. . . Our little English colonies are struggling for 'independence'. Once they get it they will make common cause with the Boers for all evil, & I firmly believe that, as things are going now, three or four generations more will see a race of Boers with a mixture of the sort of British Colonist who fraternises best with the Boers, independent of Europe, establishing a slavery before the horrors of which the recollections of the Southern States of America will pale.

Frances Colenso, 1884

* R. C. A. Samuelson, *Long, Long Ago*, Durban, 1929, p. 244. A Zulu saying which according to Samuelson, refers to the death of Cetshwayo and the events which followed.

CHAPTER TWELVE

The defeat of the Mandlakazi

The Usuthu face extinction: July 1883 to April 1884

The Zulu king was dead, but if the Usuthu were to maintain their influence and status in the country they had to ensure that the Zulu kingship lived on. Furthermore it was imperative that the *abantwana* avoid that recurring theme in Zulu history, a disputed succession. Thus, three days after Cetshwayo's death Ndabuko, Dabulamanzi, Shingana, Ziwedu and Mahanana appeared before Osborn and told him that on the morning that Cetshwayo died he had called his brothers together and, feeling that death was near, he asked them to pass on the following statement to the authorities:

'I say that when Mageba died he left the country to Punga; Punga, on his death, left it to Undaba; Undaba, on his death, left it to Jama; Jama, on his death, left it to Zenzangakona; Zenzangakona, on his death, left it to Chaka; Chaka, on his death, left it to Dingane; Dingane, on his death, left it to Umpande; Umpande, my father, left it to me, Cetywayo; I, Cetywayo, leave the country to my son Dinuzulu for him to have when I am no longer here.

I have become the son of the Queen; when I die there is my son Dinuzulu, who I leave in my place. I say my words and my writings are with my mother, the Queen, and when I die I shall not be altogether dead, as my son Dinuzulu will live. The questions about my country are not ended yet. They exist still, and will remain until the Government settle them; and about the people having stabbed me – I wish the Governor to settle those questions even when I am no more as if I were still present. Take these, my words, to Mr. Osborn, and ask him to send them to the Governor, with the request that he would send them to the Queen.'[1]

Bulwer called for an investigation into the circumstances under which this statement was made, and discovered many inconsistencies in the evidence of those who were with the king when he died.[2] As he suggested, it does not seem very likely that the statement on succession was made by the king, and it was probably formulated by the *abantwana* after Cetshwayo's death. However the question of the validity of the statement, as a dying wish of Cetshwayo, is not of major significance. For the authorities it was not a matter of who should succeed Cetshwayo, but whether there should be a succession at all. And for the *abantwana* and their allies the statement indicates their determination to continue working for the recognition of the royal lineage and the need to place on record an unambiguous statement vesting the succession firmly in Cetshwayo's son. Dinuzulu at the time of his father's death, had not by Zulu standards reached an age when he could be expected to enrol in a regiment,[3] let alone the age when he could assume political responsibilities. He remained under the guardianship of Ndabuko, his father's full brother, and Mnyamana, still the most influential and respected man in the land. By proclaiming Dinuzulu successor to Cetshwayo, the royal brothers gave their actions, taken in the name of Dinuzulu and the royal lineage, legitimacy in the eyes of the Zulu people. At the same time Dinuzulu was too young to seriously challenge their position or their activities as leaders of the royalist movement. In doing this the *abantwana* successfully brought forward a strong claimant to the Zulu kingship without showing divisions in their own ranks and thereby further weakening the Usuthu at a time when the royalists were under severe threat.[4]

For by the time Cetshwayo died early in 1884 the Usuthu were facing the possibility of extinction. After the burning of Ulundi seven months before, Zibhebhu and Hamu had moved through the northern districts attacking pockets of Zulu they alleged had royalist sympathies.[5] The Usuthu fled into neighbouring territories or withdrew to defensive positions in forests, caves and swamps. Once he had defeated the coastal Usuthu,[6] Zibhebhu's forces dominated all the territory north of the Mhlatuze. In October 1883, near Babanango, they killed old Mahubulwana, *induna* of the Qulusi, and staunch supporter of the royal house, who had been on all the Usuthu deputations to Natal to ask for Cetshwayo's return.[7] Two days after Cetshwayo arrived at Eshowe, Zibhebhu wrote a letter through Colenbrander informing Osborn that he demanded all Usuthu cattle in the Reserve, and claimed by right of conquest supreme authority over the district from which he had driven Cetshwayo.[8]

But most serious of all for the Usuthu in the northern districts was the fact that the spring rains had come and they had been unable to plant their crops. Many of them had exchanged the cattle they had left for grain; they were now threatened with complete disaster unless they could gain access to arable land to sow their crops.

Mnyamana approached Zibhebhu asking for a truce so that planting could be carried out. According to Usuthu sources, Zibhebhu refused, saying that he intended to exterminate Mnyamana and his people.[9] A trader described seeing Mnyamana's followers in

> the rocks and caves, where they were living in a most deplorable state, dying in dozens from deprivation and dysentery, children perishing at their mother's breast for want of nourishment, and each person covered with the itch and otherwise emaciated, and if nothing is done to relieve them before the winter sets in there will be scarcely a soul alive, for all their crops were then cut and trodden by Usibepu's forces.[10]

Large tracts of open country were deserted, the homesteads burnt and the grain plundered or despoiled. From caves and strongholds Usuthu launched raids and attacks on isolated targets. Social order had broken down as the Usuthu fought for survival. Typical of these marauding bands were two near the Black Mfolozi who were 'under no headmen or control, and they issue from these places during the night to steal cattle, and commit other depredations. . . .'[11] White farmers, traders and adventurers sold food, arms and ammunition to the Zulu but it was becoming increasingly unsafe for them in the northern districts, as the Usuthu 'were beginning to find out that all their troubles were caused by the white man, and they were determined no one should pass' through their territory to Hamu or Zibhebhu.[12] And, as the Usuthu became increasingly brutalised by their wretched existence in the caves, so the nature of their raids became more callous. The same trader asked some Usuthu in the Buthelezi district why they did not put an end to their suffering by submitting to Zibhebhu and was told that

> they would all die first, and that when all the king's followers are dead Usibepu and Oham may become owners of the country, but not before, and in the meantime neither Usibepu or Oham shall sleep soundly.[13]

Not only Zibhebhu and Hamu had their sleep disturbed by the Usuthu. Mfanawendlela was one of the most important of the Zulu who had tried to remain neutral after the king's return. As a result his homesteads had been spared when Zibhebhu attacked the king in July. But, when the Mandlakazi and Ngenetsheni forces withdrew to their homes in the north, Mfanawendlela was exposed to the wrath of the Usuthu. In a number of eloquent pleas he tried to draw the attention of the authorities to the dangerous position he was now in as a result of his attempts to fulfil the obligations the British had demanded of him. He stated that he had not been an enemy of Cetshwayo but had accepted the position of appointed chief and as a result he and his followers were subjected to 'constant and gross insult' from the Usuthu. He asked the authorities

> to send an English Chief into the country to exercise supreme rule; unless this is done, there will be still greater troubles for the people to endure.

Among other things famine will result next year, as because of the unsettled state of the people, they cannot put in crops, and the planting season is now set in. All the Chiefs and people are expecting the Government to come and establish order, as there is now no head in the country. The chiefs and people have until now kept quiet because of the messages you sent them conveying the Governor's word desiring them to sit still, but if something more be not done soon, we shall think we are abandoned by the Government, and the stronger will attack the weaker.[14]

Further messages followed but nothing could be done as the British Government refused to grant the authority needed for any positive act of intervention. In December Mfanawendlela with his family and close followers abandoned their homes in the face of Usuthu threats and made a dash for Zibhebhu's territory. On 14 December 1883, on the banks of the Black Mfolozi, they were attacked by a band of Usuthu and all killed.[15]

The attack was led by Mankulumana of the Ndwandwe and Ndabazimbi son of Tokotoko (a brother of Zibhebhu's father, Maphitha). Like Maphelu of the Mdlalose, Ndabankulu of the Ntombela, and Mehlokazulu of the Qungebe, they were members of the new Usuthu leadership which emerged after the defeat of Cetshwayo and the killing of the older generation of Zulu leaders at Ulundi in July 1883. They were much younger[16] and had direct experience of the white man and his world. Mehlokazulu had moved easily in white society for years, his father being one of the few 'progressive' Zulu.[17] Maphelu had a white 'friend' who kept him supplied with arms, ammunition and horses, and he was involved in gun-running and cattle-raiding, moving across political boundaries when under pressure. He was also accused at the time of plundering a German mission in northern Zululand and killing the missionary. Ndabankulu, since his appearance on the Usuthu deputation to Natal in May 1880, had been Osborn's 'policeman' but was now back in the Usuthu fold.[18] They were good horsemen, adept with gun and rifle, and their experiences since 1879 had left them with a ruthless cynicism uncommon in the older generation of Zulu leaders. Their grievances against Zibhebhu and Hamu were deep, and they were uncompromising in their desire to destroy them.

Mnyamana, one of the few older Usuthu of major importance left alive, adopted a different approach, and placed saving his own people from destruction above the need for immediate revenge. In 1881 and 1882 it was largely through his influence that full-scale hostilities in the northern districts were avoided, but in 1883–4 he was finding it increasingly difficult to control his followers, driven by the terrible exigencies imposed on them by war, disease and starvation. Thus in December 1883, Mnyamana appealed to the authorities to work with him for peace in the country north of the Reserve. He suggested that

> an *order* should have been sent to him [Mnyamana] to assemble all the heads of the people, and to require them to desist from killing each other and to return to their kraals, for at present . . . they are all scattered about in rocky and other fastnesses.

Then, confidentially, Mnyamana's messengers added that their chief

> begged the Government not to delay any longer in establishing order authoritatively in the country as it was impossible to endure the present state of lawlessness. 'If the Government,' said Umnyamana, 'does not take action soon all the people will be destroyed and it is not in my power to prevent this as the people no longer regard my orders or advice.'[19]

This type of request confirmed Bulwer and Osborn's belief that the only solution to the problem lay in extending colonial rule over the whole country. Bulwer realised however that London would never agree to formal annexation and suggested a number of variations on that theme.[20]

In London Bulwer's suggestions were mulled over at some length. But at that time the British Government was more concerned about the state of the Transvaal's western border, and the presence in London of a deputation from the Transvaal which was urging Britain to review the terms of the Pretoria Convention. Some officials at the Colonial Office complained bitterly of the new Secretary of State's approach; Lord Derby, it was said, 'never can be got to make up his mind' and was 'for letting everything drift, [and] is always trying to evade responsibility. . . .'[21] When Derby was asked to consider establishing a protectorate beyond the Reserve his reply was concise: 'I don't want more niggers.'[22]

Thus, at the time of Cetshwayo's death in February 1884, a destructive stalemate had been reached. Zibhebhu and Hamu had devastated the northern districts, driven the Usuthu into the caves and forests and, unable to destroy them by direct attack, were attempting to starve them into submission. The Usuthu, while they were unable to organise a concerted attack on their enemies, were able to harass selected targets in all parts of Zululand. All parties realised that this situation could not continue much longer, and that the essential productive processes would have to be restarted soon and without restriction if the Zulu were to survive. The officials in Natal believed that this deadlock could be broken if white authority was established beyond the borders of the Reserve, and some Zulu felt such a move was the only way to save their people. But the British Government would not give their representatives authority to intervene; slaughter and starvation among the people living north of the

Mhlatuze did not seem to pose any immediate threat to British interests in southern Africa.

Etshaneni: June 1884

It was the younger Usuthu leaders who took the initiative and broke this deadlock. The policy they adopted was dangerous in the extreme but they felt that they had little choice. Early in 1884 an agreement was reached with certain whites living on the Transvaal border to raise a force which would assist the Usuthu in their battle with Zibhebhu and Hamu.

The intrusion of white fire-power into northern Zululand swung the balance away from the Mandlakazi and Ngenetsheni, and the Usuthu were able to take the initiative once again. At the same time the active involvement of whites led by Transvalers marks the beginning of a period of obscurity and darkness in Zulu history. Both parties were aware that, while they might be able to co-operate against Zibhebhu, their long-term interests were incompatible. As a result, both sides consciously tried to influence the historical record so that it would reflect favourably on their motives and actions if it came under scrutiny at a later date.[23] Furthermore Usuthu communication with the Natal Government and with Bishopstowe was stopped and the reflected light that this cast on Zulu affairs was extinguished.

The Usuthu who led the movement which brought whites into Zululand were said to be two of the younger men, Mehlokazulu and Ndabankulu.[24] The Transvaal borderers who, it was reported, initiated the movement included Coenraad Meyer, who had long been involved in Zulu affairs; Jacobus van Staden, who was given the task of informing local Transvaal officials of their intentions; and Rudolph Wilhelm, a storekeeper, who was sent to Durban to head off any plans William Grant might have had for influencing humanitarian pressure groups in England against the white movement – something Wilhelm did with great success.[25] The general idea was that, in the name of peace and order, Dinuzulu should be recognised as successor to Cetshwayo and his rule imposed over the Zulu with the backing of Boer guns.

The extent to which the *abantwana* were initiators of the movement is difficult to ascertain, but they appear to have accepted it as necessary once Cetshwayo had died, and they gave the movement their support. Once the statement vesting the Zulu succession in Dinuzulu had been made in February, the young son of Cetshwayo was hidden in the Nkandla. The *abantwana* then returned to Eshowe and began a long dispute with Osborn about the time and place of Cetshwayo's burial. Osborn had by this time antagonised many Zulu in the Reserve with his tax-collecting activities, and feared an uprising, with the king's burial as the pretext for the gathering together of a large number of Usuthu.[26]

All parties involved realised that if their plan was to succeed it should have the support of Mnyamana. The Buthelezi chief, however, was too aware of the consequences of directly involving whites from the Transvaal in Zulu affairs. Some sources indicate that Mnyamana still felt that the Usuthu would be able to defeat Zibhebhu without help from outside, and we know that at this time Mnyamana was trying to persuade the British to intervene and break the deadlock in the northern districts. Osborn was still in contact with Mnyamana, and the Buthelezi chief reacted cautiously but positively to his suggestions. Then suddenly this attempt at co-operation came to an end. At the end of March two of Osborn's Zulu messengers, returning from the Ngome where they had been sent to see Mnyamana, were murdered.[27] Immediately after this Osborn was unable to make contact with the Buthelezi chief, and messengers were told he was ill, dead, or that his people had hidden him away.[28]

The murdered messengers had arrived at Ngome just at the time when Meyer and van Staden were visiting Mnyamana to urge him to allow Dinuzulu to be taken to the Transvaal. It seems quite possible that these messengers had information which, if passed on to the authorities in Natal, might have jeopardised the proposed Usuthu/Boer alliance. It is significant that a year later Mehlokazulu threatened an adversary by reminding him of one of the messengers' fate.[29] The killing of these men was unprecedented in Zulu history, as messengers always had immunity. And it successfully isolated Mnyamana and put an end to any possibility that might have existed of British intervention in affairs north of the Reserve during April and May when the Boer/Usuthu initiative was being planned.

Soon after this Dinuzulu was removed from the Nkandla and, in the face of objections from Mnyamana, taken to the Transvaal.[30] The *abantwana* hurriedly buried Cetshwayo's body at the Nkandla, and made their way to the northern districts, leaving Dabulamanzi in the Reserve to protect the Usuthu against Osborn, who chose this moment to demand Usuthu submission there. As April advanced rumours of a coming Boer/Usuthu alliance began to spread through the country,[31] creating insecurity among those Zulu who had opposed the royalists and giving confidence to the Usuthu, who began to move out of their strongholds and their retreats beyond Zululand's borders, and make their way to northern Zululand. At the end of April a white force, bringing with it Dinuzulu, entered Zululand and established a laager in the north-west of the country. As they did so, Hamu and Zibhebhu drew back on to their strongholds.

Once in Zululand, the Boers and the Usuthu began to try to work out the terms on which they were to co-operate. The Boers wanted to formally install Dinuzulu as Cetshwayo's successor, and then demand Zibhebhu and Hamu's submission. The Usuthu felt that Zibhebhu must be crushed, and then an agreement could be negotiated. Mnyamana disagreed with both approaches and at a meeting of Usuthu and Boers he said:

> 'I still object to your interference in our war with Zibhebhu . . . we shall fight Zibhebhu singlehanded and we shall also speak for ourselves with the English. You should give way, let us alone! Go back to your homes. You have come to spoil our land.'[32]

But Mnyamana could not carry the bulk of the Usuthu with him and the debate which followed reveals with terrible clarity the Usuthu's predicament. Hemulana, who had opened the attack on Shepstone at the installation ceremony in the previous year, now spoke against Mnyamana, and the points he made were telling ones. While he agreed that the Usuthu were still numerically superior to the Mandlakazi, they were physically weak as a result of their long sojourn in the caves. And he rejected Mnyamana's argument that they would lose their land if they co-operated with the Boers against Zibhebhu; as the position stood at the moment, with the Usuthu having to eke out an existence in caves and forests, they were not in possession of their land.[33]

But although Mnyamana was unable to convince the majority of the Usuthu that they should reject the Boer offer of assistance, the Usuthu in turn were unable to persuade the Boers to attack Zibhebhu before reaching a formal agreement. On 21 May the sixteen-year-old Dinuzulu was proclaimed King of the Zulu by the Boers; two days later Dinuzulu allegedly put his mark on a document by which the Boers bound themselves to bring 'peace, law and order' to Zululand in return for a tract of land as large as they 'may consider necessary for establishing an independent self-government'.[34]

These agreements and proclamations should not obscure the primary motives of the participants. The Boer leaders felt that they had to tread carefully if they were to avoid adverse diplomatic consequences,[35] and did all they could to obtain documents which could be used to give their actions a semblance of legal and constitutional respectability. The Usuthu tried to avoid putting their signatures to documents or committing themselves publicly. But both sides had to make concessions if they were to obtain their prime objectives: land on the one side, firepower on the other.

Zibhebhu for one had no doubt about this. In April one of his messengers told Osborn:

> The chief Usibebu desires me to say that he is under the British Government and would like help from that quarter. The Boers think they may frighten Usibebu into giving up his country to them, but they will be disappointed, for he will fight them first. . . .[36]

When Bulwer and Osborn failed to respond, his appeals became more urgent:

> Usibebu says he is not afraid of encountering his black enemies, but what chance of success has he got when they are joined by white men. . . . He fears that with this help given by the Boers he will be beaten by the Usutus who will spare none. He has always been obedient to the Governor, and now he finds himself obliged to ask the Governor to help him against his enemies. He never did anything to the Usutu to provoke their enmity, his only fault in their eyes being that he accepted the chieftainship given him by the English who conquered the whole country, and has hitherto maintained his position. He prays the English will help him.[37]

Bulwer urged London to take some action for, if Zibhebhu was attacked by the Boers and the Usuthu,

> He will be destroyed, and his destruction will involve that of his people, the finest and bravest people of Zululand. His destruction will be wholly undeserved. . . . His destruction will be altogether unmerited, and I do not hesitate to say it will be the greatest misfortune to the Zulu country. A great portion of the country will pass away from the Zulu people, and the remainder, with the exception of the Reserve, will, under the Usutu dynasty, come sooner or later under the domination of the Boers.[38]

But the British Government was not to be moved. Derby and Gladstone made public statements which made it impossible for Bulwer and Osborn to intervene, and gave added encouragement to the Boers. Gladstone said in the House of Commons that his government would not intervene militarily outside the Reserve and this was published in Natal on 21 May.[39] By the end of the month the Usuthu/Boer force was moving towards Zibhebhu's territory.

Zibhebhu found himself without most of his white supporters. Colenbrander, who had been in Natal trying to raise a troop of white mercenaries, was unable to force his way through the Emangweni section, guarding the coast road to the north. And Zibhebhu admonished another associate of long standing, John Dunn, for throwing him away when 'the odds are great and the Boers are very good marksmen'. Osborn was told that the Mandlakazi chief intended 'to fight . . . and die a British subject'.

> The Chief begs me to say that he blames you very much for not helping him in his trouble. He has fought against his own nation for the British Govern-

ment, and now that the Boers are coming you will not help him. . . . The Chief begs me to say come and see the place I die in, as this is the last hope of getting a message through and of instructing you to come and assist him against the combined Boer and Usutu force.[40]

The Usuthu army reached the Ivuna river on 2 June and spent the next night at Msebe.[41] There was no ambush laid now however and Zibhebhu and his people retreated before the Usuthu and moved to the east down into the thorn country. When the invaders reached Zibhebhu's homestead at Bangonomo they found it deserted. The Mandlakazi were making for Etshaneni where the Mkhuze river flows through a narrow gap in the Lubombo mountains. Here with their backs to the mountain range the Mandlakazi prepared to make their stand. The women, children and old people were hidden among the bushes, caves and boulders on the northern side of the Mkhuze. Zibhebhu's 3 000 fighting men situated themselves in the bush on the southern side of the river, in broken terrain where the Boers would find it difficult to use their horses.

On 4 June at about four in the afternoon the Usuthu force, perhaps double the strength of its opponents and supported by about two hundred Boers, came upon the Mandlakazi. The attack was made using the traditional horns and chest formation. The Mandlakazi left stood up well to the charge and was beginning to drive the Usuthu back when Boers opened fire over the heads of their allies, causing heavy casualties, driving the Mandlakazi back and allowing the Usuthu to recover the initiative. Most of the Mandlakazi casualties occurred on the river bank or as they were trying to cross to the northern side.

In the little time they had before the sun set the Usuthu and the Boers began rounding up Mandlakazi cattle and driving the women and children out of their places of refuge. Zibhebhu and Eckersley escaped by climbing the Lubombo where Zibhebhu looked down onto the battlefield below, and admitted defeat. 'I have had my day . . . I wonder I have lived so long', he said to the trader, 'but oh, my poor children.'[42]

The next day the Usuthu and Boers continued their search for booty while Zibhebhu did what he could for the safe-keeping of survivors. He then made the hazardous journey to Eshowe in a final, but unsuccessful, attempt to persuade 'the English' to save his people 'before they are all exterminated by our enemies'.

Unless this help be given we must die; all our cattle and property have been taken from us, and the people have nothing to subsist upon. As it is, I believe weak persons and young children will, by this time, have perished for want of sufficient food.[43]

Bulwer, when reporting the battle of Etshaneni and Zibhebhu's pleas for help, told London that it was 'impossible to regard without feelings of the greatest pain and concern the ruin that has thus been brought upon the Chief Usibebu', who 'has always shown himself a loyal friend to the Government'. However, the British had chosen to let the country north of the Reserve 'take its chance'. This had brought 'this most undeserved fate on the head of a Chief who has proved himself to possess as chivalrous and gallant a nature as the history of the Zulu nation can show'.[44]

Derby was still not persuaded. He informed Bulwer that Zibhebhu was wrong to assume 'the attitude of an ally from whom aid, to which he is justly entitled, has been withheld. . . .' Neither in 1879 nor in 1883 had the British pledged themselves to support Zibhebhu. The Secretary of State informed Bulwer:

> The condition of Zululand since 1879 has been one of chronic war, carried on by barbarous reprisals, and opinion is hopelessly divided as to the degree of blame to be assigned to each chief or party. Usibebu at least has often acted on his own responsibility; his recent defeat was the consequence of his victory of 1883, and his ambitious projects of the present year, and Her Majesty's Government has never entered into any engagement to aid or defend him. All, therefore, that he is entitled to is an asylum in the Reserve. . . .[45]

For the men who had supported and encouraged Zibhebhu, his defeat was a bitter blow. Neither Dunn nor Colenbrander had been able to aid their trading partner. For Osborn the defeat was a personal humiliation; he had persuaded Bulwer to recommend that Zibhebhu be set up as an independent chief to counterbalance the influence of the restored king. In September 1884 he had to watch the remnants of the Mandlakazi take refuge in the Reserve. In the same month Zibhebhu managed to guide about one-third of his people south into the Reserve. General Smyth watched them enter the territory and described the sight as

> one of the strangest and saddest . . . imaginable. They numbered 5 or 6,000 souls; the men as lean as greyhounds; sleeping mats and blankets on their heads; all fully armed with assegais and shields, but with few guns; the women with enormous loads on their heads, weary and tired; children of all ages to the infant at the back. They had also a great many cattle. How such a host could have managed to pass through a large extent of hostile territory unmolested is a mystery.[46]

After five years, during which they had suffered first insult, harassment and then bloody civil war, the Usuthu had had their revenge. But at the moment of victory they turned to face a more formidable enemy: in the southern part of the country a colonial regime buttressed by Usuthu enemies, and in the north an ever-growing number of armed whites who were demanding land for the services they had given in defeating the Mandlakazi.

Notes

1 BPP, C.4037: 44, enc. 1, Osborn to Bulwer, 12 Feb. 1884, statement by Dabulamanzi and others, 11 Feb. 1884.
2 BPP, C.4037: 67, Bulwer to Derby, 17 March 1883, and statements in enc.
3 Before the invasion a boy reported for enrolment in the army after his first nocturnal emission. In Dinuzulu's case this was to occur in November 1884; see AS papers: 131/92, Grant to Chesson, 4 February 1885.
4 There were divisions among the *abantwana*, particularly between Ndabuko and Dabulamanzi, but these only came to the surface later, with tragic results, culminating in Dabulamanzi's assassination by Boer gunmen.
5 See for example, BPP, C.3864; 136, Bulwer to Derby, 20 Nov. 1883 and encs.
6 See above, p. 205.
7 See Plate 18.
8 BPP, C.3864: 116, enc. 1, Osborn to Bulwer, 21 Oct. 1883, and Colenbrander (for Zibhebhu) to Osborn, 19 Oct. 1883.
9 NA, Colenso collection: box 119, W. Grant, 'Journal of a visit to Cetshwayo', entry for 20 Sept. 1883.
10 BPP, C.4037: 104, encs., A. Moore to SNA, 9 April 1884, p. 104.
11 BPP, C.3864: 152, enc. 1, statement by messengers from Zibhebhu, 25 Nov. 1883, p. 294.
12 BPP, C.4037: 104, encs., A. Moore to SNA, 9 April 1884, p. 105.
13 Ibid, p. 104.
14 BPP, C.3864: 80, enc., Osborn to Bulwer, 5 Sept. 1883, statement by Mfanawendlela, 3 Sept. 1883, pp. 163–4.
15 BPP, C.3864: 161 and 165, Bulwer to Derby, 24 and 31 Dec. 1883 and encs.
16 Note that in Plate 18 neither Ndabazimbi nor Maphelu have head-rings, and in the photograph of Mehlokazulu in D. R. Morris, *The Washing of the Spears*, he is also without a ring. The head-ring was worn after permission had been received from the king to marry.
17 See above, p. 16.
18 Colenso, series 2, p. 484.
19 CO 179/151: 2478, Bulwer to Derby, 15 Jan. 1884 (conf.).
20 BPP, C.3864: 142 and 145, Bulwer to Derby, 26 Nov. and 30 Nov. 1883.
21 Quoted by D. M. Schreuder in *Gladstone and Kruger*, p. 385. Schreuder examines the decision-making process in the British Government on southern African affairs at this time in scrupulous detail.
22 Ibid., p. 393.
23 South Africa's past weighs heavily on the present, and the concerns of those whites involved in the movement into Zululand in 1884 have become the concerns of contemporary white South Africans. Thus M. C. van Zyl has subjected the records to close analysis in order to discover whether the Zulu invited the Boers into Zululand or not, and discovered that they did. Yet this legalistic search for documentary evidence of an 'invitation' is ahistorical; it denies the long-standing, changing nature of the relationship between the Zulu and the Boers on their border; it ignores the fact that the Usuthu were but a faction of the Zulu, and were themselves divided on the question of co-operation with the whites; and obscures the fundamental motives of both

parties. See M. C. van Zyl, *Die Koms van die Boere na Zoeloeland in 1884: Genooides of Indringers?*, Pretoria, 1962.

24 KC, Maphelu, on p. 42, states categorically that Ndabankulu and Mehlokazulu were working with the 'Boers'; once this statement is accepted a large number of scattered and initially obscure references to these men become significant. See for instance BPP, C.4191: 65, enc. 1, Fynn to SNA, 6 June 1884; GHZ 689: Fynn to SNA, 2 June 1884; BPP, C.4587: 72, Bulwer to Derby, 3 April 1885, encs; Colenso, series 3, statement by Melakanya, 13 Jan. 1885, pp. 3–4.

25 This section is based largely on a series of confidential documents forwarded by the Colonial Office to Bulwer's successor, Sir Arthur Havelock, when he took office. They were the result of investigation undertaken by Osborn and Bulwer who gathered information from the alleged initiators of the movement when, for various reasons, they had withdrawn their support from it. See GHZ 699: Herbert to Havelock, 11 March 1886 (conf.).

26 For Osborn's fears see, for example, BPP, C.4037: 85, Bulwer to Derby, 4 April 1884.

27 BPP, C.4191: 9, enc., Osborn to Bulwer, 25 April 1884.

28 BPP, C.4037: 102, enc. 1, Osborn to Bulwer, 9 April 1883, statement by Socwasha and Mpengula, 9 April 1884.

29 KC, Shepstone papers: folder f, Magema Magwaza to SNA, 5 June 1885.

30 Colenso, series 3, statement by Melakanya, 13 Jan. 1885. The exact nature of events in Zululand at this period became the subject of intense controversy later. I cannot enter into these debates here.

31 BPP, C.4037: 65, Bulwer to Derby, 12 April 1884; BPP, C.4191: 8, enc., Osborn to Bulwer, 22 April 1884, statement by Zibhebhu's messengers, 21 April 1884.

32 KC, Maphelu, p. 51. Maphelu's account is an extremely important source for this period in Zulu history.

33 Ibid., p. 48.

34 C. T. Binns, *Dinuzulu; the Death of the House of Shaka*, London, 1968, pp. 29–32.

35 The London Convention by which the Government of the South African Republic was bound to 'do its utmost to prevent any of its inhabitants from making any encroachments upon lands beyond . . . [its] boundaries' was only three months old.

36 BPP, C.4191: 16, enc. 1, Zibhebhu (through Eckersley) to Osborn, 29 April 1884, p. 24.

37 Ibid., enc. 2, message from Zibhebhu to Osborn, 2 May 1884, statement by Rozana, p. 25.

38 BPP, C.4191: 12, Bulwer to Derby, 6 May 1884, p. 19.

39 See BPP, C.4037: 110 and 112, Derby to Bulwer, 16 May 1884 and 17 May 1884 (teleg.); and the telegram published in the *Natal Witness*, 21 May 1884.

40 BPP, C.4191: 46, enc. 1, Zibhebhu (through Eckersley) to Dunn, 19 May 1884 and enc. 3, Zibhebhu (through Eckersley) to Osborn, 19 May 1884, p. 70.

41 In this account of the battle of Etshaneni I have made use of KC, Maphelu, pp. 56–9; BPP, C.4191: 70, enc., Osborn to Bulwer, 13 June 1884, statement by Zibhebhu, 13 June 1884; CO 179/166: 2617, petition of Gros-

venor Darke. See also accounts in Binns, *Dinuzulu*, pp. 34–8; H. P. Braatvedt, *Roaming Zululand with a Native Commissioner*, Pietermaritzburg, 1949; J. Y. Gibson, *The Story of the Zulus*, London, 1911, pp. 270–2.

42 *The Natal Witness*, 19 June 1884, account from Darke's diary.

43 BPP, C.4191: 70, enc., Osborn to Bulwer, 13 June 1884, statement by Zibhebhu, 13 June 1884, p. 109. There were apparently nine traders with Zibhebhu, two of whom died of exposure after the battle, while others reached safety 'broken down, starved, ragged and ruined'.

44 BPP, C.4191: 66, Bulwer to Derby, 16 June 1884, p. 98.

45 BPP, C.4191: 82, Derby to Bulwer, 19 Aug. 1884, p. 138.

46 BPP, C.4274: 10, enc., Smyth to Sec. of State for War, 19 Sept. 1884, p. 16.

CHAPTER THIRTEEN

Conclusion

Aftermath

With the defeat of Zibhebhu and the occupation of northern Zululand by the Boers in the winter of 1884 Zulu history enters a new context. The unity and self-sufficiency which existed before 1879 was gone; the regiments, both the product and the guardian of Zulu independence were broken, the people deeply divided politically, and neither warring faction had escaped crippling losses and defeat in battle. And as the Zulu entered this state of material weakness, social chaos and political fragmentation, the colonial authorities in the south and the armed whites in the north demanded radical changes in the Zulu way of life.

In the Reserve Osborn imposed a 14-shilling hut tax. This was a fundamental departure tied directly to the productive capacity of any community, for the 'hut' was the production unit and if cash was not available then cattle were taken instead. The money raised was used to support the administration of the Reserve, and in this manner the Zulu covered the costs of their own coercion. The hut tax, together with the cattle seized as fines, the licence fees paid by traders, shopkeepers, prospectors and those exploiting the Reserve's timber resources, raised over £30 000 during the four years the Reserve was in existence.[1]

The Usuthu resisted the imposition of a hut tax in 1884 and fell back on the Qudeni and the Nkandla, cut communications between Osborn at Eshowe and Hlubi and the sub-commissioner at Nqutu, and raided cattle from 'loyal' Zulu. Osborn tried to put them down with a show of force by the detachment of British troops with him, and direct action by the *Nongqayi*, his African police from Natal, and Zulu loyalists, particularly those associated with the ex-appointed chiefs. Hlubi was especially useful, with his 150 mounted men supported by 200 on foot. After a number of violent clashes the troubles subsided with the onset of the spring rains. Osborn knew that he could not deploy troops in the broken country of the Nkandla during the wet season, and the Usuthu for their part had to leave the forests and start planting; as a result they were allowed to 'submit' to Osborn's authority.[2]

But the disruption of 1884 had already done serious damage to the material life of the Zulu of the Reserve and this was compounded by drought which led to shortages in many parts of Zululand. In the Reserve Natal traders brought in grain and took out cattle. Osborn offered relief for those who laboured on the road he was driving through the Nkandla to connect the Reserve's administrative centres.[3] In the more remote areas the women collected grasses, bulbs and roots for their starving families.

As 1885 progressed Osborn began to feel more secure. The anarchy north of the Reserve assisted him by sending a steady flow of Zulu into the territory who felt that even his regime was better than the chaos in the northern districts where the Boers were demanding farms. Soon eight of the unfortunate thirteen chiefs Wolseley appointed in 1879 were in the Reserve, where they gave the Resident their support. In March 1886 five men were hanged on the new Eshowe gallows, the remaining nine accused receiving in instalments a hundred lashes with a cat-o'-nine-tails.[4] Licences were granted to storekeepers, and prospectors began working the gold-bearing strata at Nondweni and in the Thukela valley.[5] Men left the Reserve and travelled to Natal to look for work.[6] Osborn was not only able to balance his budget but show a surplus.

Although the new rule in the Reserve was oppressive it did give a degree of security that was absent in the northern districts. And this moment of Zulu vulnerability in the mid-1880s coincided with a general intensification of white expansion throughout southern Africa. To the west of the Transvaal, Boers had set up the 'robber republics' of Stellaland and Goshen. And, just as commercial interests in the Cape Colony felt that these republics should be cleared from the access route to the far interior of the sub-continent, so Natal protested that an Afrikaner republic in northern Zululand would deprive the colony of its rightful heritage – the land and labour of the Zulu, together with access to the gold fields of the eastern Transvaal and the fabled wealth of the African interior.[7] Furthermore, southern Africa was experiencing at this time what has been described as the worst slump of the nineteenth century.[8] The original band of Boers who had fought with the Usuthu against Zibhebhu were now joined not only by more Boers looking for farms in northern Zululand, but colonial riff-raff, adventurers, speculators, concession-seekers and bankrupts. Harriette Colenso identified so many representatives of Natal commercial houses among these whites that she insisted on calling them filibusters, not Boers.[9] Nonetheless the political leadership of the whites looking for booty in northern Zululand remained in the hands of Afrikaners from the Transvaal.

The Usuthu leaders did what they could to avoid signing another concession, but in August 1884 Dinuzulu and William Grant put their marks to a proclamation which awarded the whites 1 355 000 morgen (2 710 000 acres) and the 'right to establish there an independent republic, called the New Republic'.[10] Surveying teams began to mark out farms and early in 1885 they had reached the Indian ocean.

The situation became more complicated and urgent when, in 1884, Germany unexpectedly made claims to the coast of south-west Africa. Later in the same year 'German agents' were reported to be at work in Zululand.[11] As a result the African territories lying between the Transvaal and the Indian ocean, hitherto largely the objects of attention of neighbouring settler communities, acquired some importance in the eyes of the imperialist powers.

Desperately the Usuthu tried to find allies among the multiplicity of white groups now occupying Zulu territory or hovering on the boundaries. They were unable to use force and so they attempted to divide New Republicans from the border Boers who initiated the movement, colonial Natal from metropolitan Britain, and to gain assistance from the 'Germans'. But the Usuthu leaders, Mnyamana, Ndabuko, Shingana and Dinuzulu, concentrated on the strategy they used before their alliance with the Boers and petitioned the British Government for assistance through its representatives in Natal. After a period of exclusion from Zulu politics the assistance of Bishopstowe was again requested and the burden now fell on Harriette. Bulwer rejected their petitions with scorn:

> To intrigue against the forbearance and lenity of English authority in the Reserve Territory was an easy thing to do; but to resist the acts done on behalf of 800 Boers with rifles in their hands, who are not troubled by ideas of constitutional government or leniency or forbearance, is another thing.[12]

And later he wrote that the Usuthu had only themselves, and their white advisers to blame: they had defeated Zibhebhu

> ... but at what a cost! – at what a cost to the Zulu people, to the generation of to-day and to the generations of the future! The price of blood is a hard price; and to compass the destruction of Usibebu the Usutu leaders bartered away the best part of the inheritance of the Zulu people, an inheritance, let it be remembered, which was left untouched by the British Government after the war of 1879.[13]

Beyond reasserting her rights to St Lucia Bay and its environs Britain was still reluctant to assert herself north of the Reserve, but at the end of 1885 the New Republicans overstepped the mark. On 26 October they proclaimed the boundaries of the New Republic. The Natal officials calculated that the Boers claimed five-sixths of the Zulu territory beyond the Reserve. London felt obliged to move and warned the Boers formally that a claim of this extent would injure British interests in the region.[14] The Boers took their revenge on the Usuthu. The leaders were called to a meeting, their appeals for British intervention read from the latest Blue Book, they were accused of treason, and attempts were made to terrorise them into signing a new document by threatening them with hanging or the firing squad. Fines were imposed on the leaders and hostages taken. It was a bitter humiliation for the Usuthu; a flood of appeals were sent to Natal reporting what had happened, and messengers were told to 'impress' on the authorities,

> the Zulu people are sinking away; they are dying; their trust is in the English and unless the English come between them and the Boers soon, at once, they fear it will be too late. . . . Tell the Governor and the other Chiefs of the Queen that Umyamana, the Zulu chiefs and people are in great trouble and they call loudly to the English to whom they and the country belong, not to delay, but to come at once and save the Queen's people and land from the Boers.[15]

Bulwer advised intervention, for the Zulu people and for Natal, repeating at length Sir Theophilus Shepstone's argument:

> The outlet for the native question of Natal lies in Zululand; and I will go further and say that the outlet for every native question in that part of South Africa lies through Zululand and the native territories that adjoin it to the vast African continent beyond the region of European occupation.
> That way lies a golden bridge for the native questions of the future. But let that outlet be closed, let that golden bridge be destroyed, and there will remain, pent up within our limits, unable to escape, the elements of burning questions which, for want of their natural outlet, must some day be kindled into flames in our very midst.[16]

Bulwer's term of office ended in 1885 and early the following year in London he recommended that his successor open negotiations with the New Republicans, and that Britain's interests be secured in the area by attempting to limit them to the western portions of northern Zululand, while the coastal districts be left to the Zulu.

It fell to his successor, Sir Arthur Havelock, to carry out these decisions. He soon came under the influence of the Shepstone family.[17] He warned the Usuthu messengers who came to greet him not to 'expect to escape the effects of their own acts'.

> The utmost that, in my opinion, the British Government may be induced to do is to bring about an agreement with the Boers, by which a portion of land may be secured for the Zulus; and this I will be prepared to recommend. If the Queen's Government will consent to do this much, the Zulus should be thankful.[18]

But the Boers drove a hard bargain. The line that was eventually demarcated excluded nearly all the highland grazing, and the valuable mixed veld in the upper reaches of the major river systems, and the strongholds of the Ngome. Much of the remaining territory towards the coast was tsetse area and where malaria was endemic. It cut off the main homesteads of Mnyamana, Ndabuko and Dinuzulu in the north, together with a huge segment between the Mkhuze and the Phongolo which excluded many homesteads of the Qulusi, Sebeni, and Mphangisweni sections, as well as the Mdlalose, Ndabankulu's Ntombela, Hamu, many Buthelezi, and the Emgazini of Masiphula. In the southern area (including the 'Proviso B' district – excluded from the New Republic but where the whites were given property rights) the homesteads of Shingana, Ngobozana, Sitheku, Faku and Qethuka fell under the Boers. The highland pastures around Babanango were lost, and so was the most sacred part of the country – Emakhosini – where the pre-Shakan kings were buried. (See Map IX.)

The Usuthu could only protest. They did this vehemently and at length:

> We are your children yesterday, to-day, and to-morrow, and for ever. We cry to you as children who have been injured. (We cry) in the name of the Zulu people. We bear earnest witness that this cutting off of the Zulu country, without our having been given a single opportunity of answering or being listened to, we do not willingly accept. We desire that these words may not be obliterated, but always remain known forever and ever.[19]

Harriette Colenso wrote:

> The English and Dutch are conspiring together to finally crush out the Zulu and to divide the spoil. And, if the Zulu make an attempt to stand for their liberty, they will be mercilessly butchered by either or both of these civilized & Christian nations. And I want you to understand the real nature of the transaction, & the cruel injustice of thus wiping out the national existence of the Zulu people, by robbing them of their country. . . .[20]

Harriette's sister, Frances, reacted more strongly to the news of the partition:

> Whether the robbers & tyrants are called Shepstone, Osborn, Natal Colonists or Boers is 'only' a difference of degree not of kind, & personally I think it would be better for our poor friends to die to a man, than to be made subject to any rule by colonists, or that brings them into contact with the colonists. There are many worse things than death.[21]

Frances was writing this from a sanatorium, only a few months from death herself. Harriette, to whom the Zulu still turned for advice, was almost overwhelmed by the responsibility:

> when grey headed men put their case earnestly to me, & ask what can be said against it, I can only cover my eyes & admit that there is no answer – no real honest answer.[22]

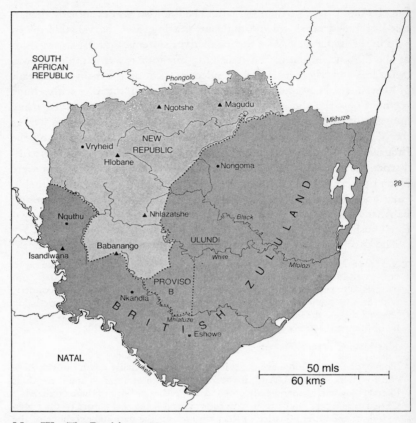

Map IX The Partition: 1887

Harriette was fully aware that petitions and pleas for justice had little chance of assisting the Zulu regain their land and that

> my very existence as my Father's daughter tended and *still tends* to hold them back from resorting to force . . . wh. might – (who can tell) . . . 'have been their best chance. . . .'
>
> I could not advise them to fight because I could not share the responsibility or the consequences – because I could not sufficiently judge of their chance of success, because as an Englishwoman I had no right to believe that England would not in the end – when she had heard – do right.[23]

Frances, however, had no such doubts:

> Better to die to a man, as the brave men they have always shown themselves [to be], fighting for their rights, than to die out slowly as a degenerate race in the wretched unhealthy worthless corner left to them.[24]

But the majority of Zulu were still not prepared to take this path. It is difficult to generalise about Zulu opinion as a whole at this time but Harriette Colenso probably made a valid observation when she wrote:

> It is, no doubt, true that since the English have permitted *no government* in Zululand – since 1879, many of the people welcome anything settled, anything which checks Zibhebhu's raiding propensities, & allows them to plant and eat. But this by no means implies that they *prefer* white chiefs & laws to their own. . . .[25]

But the Zulu were not to be allowed even this. In June 1887 the area outside the New Republic was joined with the Reserve and the establishment of British Zululand was announced at Eshowe. The Governor of Natal was to rule by proclamation as Supreme Chief. The Resident Commissioner and Chief Magistrate was Melmoth Osborn, and the establishment of local magistracies, the imposition of the new colonial order and the collection of hut tax was placed in the hands of Assistant Commissioners, many of them young men from Natal who soon gained a deserved reputation for ignorance and brutality. From the start they were determined to put an end to the pretensions of the Usuthu leaders, in particular Ndabuko and Dinuzulu; every attempt was made to interfere with, and reduce, the authority they exercised among their people. In order to impress upon the Usuthu chiefs that they were no longer independent they were harassed and fined; in November 1887 Havelock himself travelled to Zululand and told the assembled Zulu that

> Dinuzulu must know, and all the Zulus must know, that the rule of the House of Chaka is a thing of the past. It is dead. It is like water spilt on the ground. The Queen rules now in Zululand and no one else. The Queen who conquered Cetywayo has now taken the government of the country into her own hands. The Governor is sent to represent the Queen, and to maintain her

authority in Zululand. Let Dinuzulu and Undabuko and everyone know that
the Governor is determined to do this. The Queen has taken the rule of the
country out of kindness for the Zulu nation. The Zulus can no longer stand by
themselves. If they were left to themselves they would fight among themselves,
and others would come and take the whole country down to the sea. . . . It is to
save the Zulus from the misery that must fall upon them if they were left to
themselves that the Queen has assumed the Government of the country.[26]

But Havelock did not travel to Eshowe merely to admonish the
Usuthu. To the shocked meeting he announced that the new Government
had decided that Zibhebhu should be allowed to leave the Reserve and
return to his old lands. Osborn and Theophilus Shepstone had been
pressing Havelock for this throughout 1887. Osborn had a real commitment to the man whom he had supported but been unable to save in 1884.
Shepstone pointed out the practical benefits implied by his return to
British Zululand; he wrote,

the real and effective coercive force of the country must be furnished by
its own population under the direction of the Government. . . .
   The return of Sibebu to his people will at once throw the balance of Zulu
power into the hands of the Government.[27]

Within a fortnight of the announcement Zibhebhu was marching back
to the Mandlakazi territory. Soon reports reached Havelock that he was
taking possession of his old lands by force, driving the Usuthu from their
homesteads.

The Usuthu retired to their strongholds once again, and in June 1888
Dinuzulu led an attack on the Mandlakazi and defeated them under the
guns of the British at Nongoma. But when British troops advanced on
their positions the Usuthu leaders dispersed their forces. Ndabuko,
Dinuzulu and Shingana were eventually captured and in 1889 found
guilty of high treason and exiled to St Helena.

This final despairing attempt by the old Zulu leadership to assert its
independence and protect itself from the men whom the Natal authorities
used to undermine their power, was a political expression of the basic
changes that had been brought to Zululand and the Zulu by external
forces. In the southern districts the imposition of the hut tax, the support
given by the colonial authorities to certain 'loyal' Zulu and the harassment
of the Usuthu, together with the establishment of Natal Africans in the
territory, had already caused substantial changes. In the north the partition
of the country between the British and the Boers had disrupted the life of
all inhabitants, forcing them either to flee to the north, become labour-
tenants on their own land which was now in the possession of Boers, or
accept British rule, with its hut tax and the administration of their affairs

by white magistrates. The attempt to force the Usuthu to accept this by returning Zibhebhu had caused major disruption and, apart from the political consequences, had serious economic ones. 1889 was yet another year of shortage; the Zulu people had the experience of having the shortfall in their harvests made up with American grain. The following year large numbers of Zulu men were looking for work building the Natal Government railway which was forcing its way to the north towards the recently discovered gold mines on the Witwatersrand. These mines were already absorbing Zulu labour, and many of the men who had fought in Cetshwayo's army against the British were now selling their labour in Johannesburg. Bad harvests, cattle disease, and smallpox introduced from the mines caused much suffering in Zululand during the early years of the 1890s. But it was reported that the effects of the shortages in Zulu agricultural production were not too severe because of the large amount of cash circulating in the country, obtained by Zulu labour outside, and now used to buy food stocks from storekeepers and traders. By 1894 Zululand was described as one of the chief sources of the native labour supply on the Rand. The people who in 1879 had stood proudly independent, and fought the British to save their self-sufficient kingdom and its political system, had now entered the mainstream of southern African history.

The significance of the Zulu civil war, 1879–1884

When British forces invaded Zululand in 1879 they intended to end the independent existence of the Zulu kingdom with a sudden sharp blow. They failed in this, but the imperial power had to hide this fact, and Wolseley's settlement was built on this deception. As a result the arrangement failed to take into account the fact that material and social continuity in Zululand had not been broken by the invasion, and it excluded from authority men of status and power in the country, the representatives of the old Zulu order. Consequently few of the thirteen chiefs appointed by Wolseley could exercise the authority granted to them in 1879. However, four of them did attempt to impose their will over the people in their new territories: John Dunn and Hlubi, as aliens, did so with some discretion; Hamu and Zibhebhu acted without caution, singling out for harassment members of the royal house and its supporters as their most obvious rivals and men whose power and pretensions had to be reduced.

Both Hamu and Zibhebhu were closely related to the dominant lineage of the Zulu royal house but this relationship, while important, was not a fundamental motivating factor. Far more crucial was the fact that, unlike most Zulu, both these men had substantial connections with the colonial world. In Hamu's case these were largely political; he was the only important Zulu to defect to the British in 1879, and he was given his chieftainship as a reward for this. But his links were also economic; Hamu was a habitual gin drinker, had established trading connections, and had a resident white trader.

Zibhebhu's trade links were extensive and stretched from Natal, through Zululand, and then far to the north. The difference in his manner, his way of life and the skills he had acquired and those of the vast majority of Zulu was obvious to outsiders. He was a horseman, could count and tell the time in the western manner, and was personally aggressive, energetic and self-confident. His partner in trade and labour-recruiting was John Dunn. And it was Hamu and Zibhebhu who, through their appropriation of the property of the men placed under them in 1879, created the tension in northern Zululand which culminated in civil war.

But they must not be held solely responsible for the civil war; widespeead violence broke out only after British officials had become involved in the disputes and thereby given Zibhebhu and Hamu the confidence to move against their opponents. The most important of these officials were Melmoth Osborn, British Resident in Zululand, and Sir Theophilus Shepstone in Pietermaritzburg. Their general attitudes can be seen as reflections of the colonial situation in which they had grown up and worked, and their specific motives discovered in the needs of the Colony of Natal as they perceived them. For these men the Zulu king was the 'representative of the sentiment . . . and of all those that cherish it in South Africa, that is opposed to civilization, Christianity and progress', and an independent, united Zulu kingdom would deny Natal the land and the labour the colony needed for security and for progress.

The numerous recommendations made by Osborn and Shepstone for the future of Zululand pointed in one direction: the subjugation of the country to Natal's interests through a system of colonial overrule, to be achieved with the assistance of men like Hamu, Dunn and Zibhebhu, who had profited by the king's misfortune, and who could be trusted to oppose him and his allies.

Initially the Zulu who had been excluded from authority by the settlement and who had suffered directly at the hands of the appointed chiefs were still prepared to co-operate with the colonial authorities and seek redress through them. Osborn was seen as the representative of the conquering power which, although it had inflicted terrible suffering on the Zulu and dismantled the centralised political system, had left them in possession of most of their land. But in August 1881, at Nhlazatshe, they realised their error. In the face of overwhelming evidence of oppression and the misappropriation of property the officials not only excused the men responsible for these injustices, Hamu and Zibhebhu, but punished the injured parties, Mnyamana, Ndabuko and Ziwedu. The appointed chiefs, now confident of official support, drove home their advantage; the Nhlazatshe meeting was followed by evictions, violent clashes, and a major battle which left a thousand men dead.

The Zulu who had suffered as a result of this official intervention now adopted different tactics. It was decided that an appeal should be made to the British Government, recounting their grievances, and asking for the restoration of the king to Zululand. The ground for this had already been well prepared, both by Cetshwayo himself working from exile, and his white sympathisers who were led by the Bishop of Natal and his family. The Usuthu – the supporters of the royal house as represented by Cetshwayo kaMpande – re-emerged as a political force within Zululand, attracting to its ranks the disaffected in the country, and also the hostility of the local officials.

Much has been written about the 'fiercely glowing faith in British rule and British justice' held by Africans in southern Africa in the late nine-teenth and early twentieth centuries. At first sight Cetshwayo's letters and the Usuthu petitions might appear to be excellent examples of this; but once one goes beyond the formal conciliatory phrases and the rhetoric, they can be seen to be based on sound political strategy which exploited the difference between the interests of settler Natal and metropolitan Britain. Natal saw Zululand as a potential source of land and labour, the control of which would also give the colony access to the north. For Britain, in these years before the discovery of gold on the Witwatersrand altered the situation, Zululand's importance was largely strategic. The country lay between the Transvaal and the sea and its prime role was to block Afrikaner expansion to the east, and secure the coastline. A strong secure government was needed in Zululand and its internal structure was, at this particular point in time, of lesser importance. Thus the immediate interests of the Zulu royal house and those of Britain were to a large degree compatible; those of colonial Natal and the royal house were in direct opposition.

The original intention of the British was to return Cetshwayo to Zululand so that he could set up a self-supporting system of government over the people occupying this block of territory and the coastline. The cost to Britain would be slight and the country would be susceptible to informal British influence. Settler Natal found these proposals intolerable.

The African did not appreciate 'magnanimity'; it would be interpreted as weakness if Cetshwayo was restored, and would encourage blacks throughout southern Africa to resist progress. Natal officials had already established interest groups in Zululand and these had to be protected against the royal house. But, most important, a united self-sufficient Zulu kingdom would exclude Natal, and for the officials the only answer to the colony's economic difficulties lay in Zululand. Thus the Natal officials recommended in the strongest terms the partition of the country, and the British Government, lacking the confidence to go against the advice of a man like Sir Theophilus Shepstone when it came to native affairs, did not oppose the recommendation.

As a result Cetshwayo returned to a deeply divided country and immediately war broke out between those who had worked for his return and those who had opposed it. The Natal officials represented the violence as the result of the activities of an atavistic minority, spurred on by misguided humanitarians, and led by a wily king who had duped the officials in London. It was in fact the result of the active encouragement and support given by the officials to individuals within Zululand who opposed the king and the Usuthu, in order to destroy any chance of the re-emergence of a united independent Zulu kingdom.

The Usuthu tried to defeat Zibhebhu; the cumbersome traditionalist army was destroyed by fine leadership and modern weapons. Driven from their homes, the Usuthu were attempting to launch another offensive when Zibhebhu forestalled them by a surprise attack on Ulundi which virtually annihilated the leaders of the old political order, and drove the king into hiding. It is this battle, the second battle of Ulundi, in July 1883, which marks the end of the Zulu kingdom, not the face-saving demonstration of British fire-power at Ulundi four years before. In 1879 Wolseley persuaded the Zulu to lay down their arms by offering them their land; in 1883 the Usuthu's enemies drove them into the forest and denied them access to their land.

The very success of the Zulu kings in protecting the kingdom from colonial intrusion had the effect, after the invasion, of making its people more vulnerable to the consequences of civil war. The Zulu homesteads, scattered throughout the country were the production units of the nation. There had been no need to site them near strongholds or in terrain which lent itself to defence. Herds of cattle were extremely difficult to guard for they could only spend a limited amount of time away from natural grazing and water-points. The Zulu were not traders; forms of non-perishable foodstuffs were not produced in the country and few Zulu were in possession of storeable wealth or significant amounts of cash or coin. Thus the influence of the cycle of the seasons on all aspects of Zulu life was direct, and social continuity depended on uninterrupted access to grazing and arable land.

In parts of northern Zululand groups lost their grain and their cattle nearly every season from 1879 to 1882. Their suffering was considerable but alleviated with the help of relatives and associates, or by moving into other districts. In 1883 Zibhebhu and Hamu deliberately destroyed the foodstores and seized the cattle of most of the people living north of the Mhlatuze, and then denied them access to productive land.

Contemporary officials and observers, and later commentators, have failed to understand the restrictions that the pre-industrial economy of the Zulu imposed on the society's leaders during the civil war. The political acumen of such men as Cetshwayo, Mnyamana, Shingana, Hemulana and Mfunzi, and their tragic awareness of their situation cannot be doubted. But, because they worked within a society whose economy demanded the resolution of conflict every spring, the range of choices open to them was severely limited.

This is most clearly demonstrated in the alliance between the Usuthu and the Boers. It is true that there was a deep desire for revenge on Zibhebhu. But an even more telling factor in the minds of the Usuthu – then living in caves, forests and swamps, their children starving, their grain and their cattle gone – was the realisation that, unless Zibhebhu was crushed, they faced either death by starvation, or social extinction.

In essence the struggle which took place in Zululand between 1879 and 1884 was between representatives of the pre-capitalist and the capitalist social formations; between representatives of the old Zulu order working for the revival of the kingdom, and those trying to ensure political division as a prerequisite for subordination to capitalist production. And although the story told here is only a fragment of Zulu history which itself is only a small part of the history of southern Africa, it does illustrate a fundamental historical event, one manifested on widely different time-scales and in a multitude of forms: the separation of producers from their means of production and the products of their labour; the dissolution of the pre-capitalist social formation.

Of course historical events are never neatly self-contained; the pre-capitalist Zulu social formation was showing signs of the changes to come long before 1879, and pre-capitalist features continued to exist. But there was a fundamental difference between the life of the Zulu before 1879 and their way of life after 1884. In the former period they were in possession of their land and largely in control of their labour and its products:

after 1884 they were losing this possession and control. These changes were initiated by external invasion and perpetuated by civil war.

There has been a tendency to interpret the civil war solely in terms of conflict within Zulu society. It is suggested that many groups which made up the Zulu kingdom were deeply divided and once the authoritarian rule of the king was removed these rivalries emerged in violence. Holders of this view then go on to condemn Britain for her 'irresponsibility' in failing to intervene to save the Zulu from themselves.

This standpoint is in my opinion inadequate. Three dominant historical forces can be discerned in the events in Zululand between 1879 and 1884: one with its origins in Zulu society, another in the settler communities bordering on Zululand, and the third from metropolitan Britain. Between and within these groups were factions moving towards capitalist domination of Zululand, and factions attempting to revive and retain the pre-capitalist system. It was the tension between these factions that drove the Zulu into civil war and the destruction of the old order.

Thus the story told here is a particular example of a universal historical phenomenon and the suffering of the men and women who fought the civil war has been shared by millions of others, at different times and at different places throughout the world. And they were tragically conscious of what they were fighting for and what they stood to lose. One does not have to accept the idea of a Zulu Arcady, that life was essentially egalitarian, or that the social structure was in any way 'organic', to understand that the pre-1879 Zulu social formation created in its people a self-sufficiency and a sense of totality which they knew was intrinsically valuable and was absent in the manner of existence that their enemies wished to force on them. The division of labour in the Zulu kingdom was not highly developed. Once mature the great majority of Zulu were entitled to land and they worked it themselves, retaining a good proportion of its produce for their use. The destination of the surplus that was extracted was known, and the purpose to which it was applied included their own security. Men and women remained in close proximity to the instruments and means of production, and were involved in the labour process from start to finish. When disasters occurred there were a number of social devices to pull any individuals who had lost access to the means of production back into the productive process.

The contrast between this way of life and that of the colonial African who was selling his labour or his produce was immediately discernible, and surely in the 'Amakhafula' of neighbouring Natal – those who had been spat out – we have the Zulu conception of alienated man. The Zulu who received the Ultimatum which demanded the destruction of the military system saw immediately that the intention was to turn them into similar creatures, or as they expressed it, from dry, healthy maize, to maize that was rotten; from maize with a potential for self-sustained growth to corn which had softened and lost that quality.

Both sides in the civil war expressed their opposing concepts of man and society in the imagery they used. Thus Shepstone tended to fall back on mechanistic metaphor when describing Zulu society. He conceived the independent kingdom as a steam engine, and the military system as its boiler about to explode with disastrous consequences both to the engine itself and all in the vicinity. Zulu society after 1879 was likened to a watch that had been allowed to run down. The exiled king was the key. If he was restored, the officials alleged, the mainspring would regain its tension, the cogs would turn, and the Zulu regiments would assemble again to threaten the peace of southern Africa. And in his arguments for the partition of Zululand Shepstone revealed that, in spite of his reputation as the man who had acquired the secret of African government, he was in fact a captive of the imagery and ideology of nineteenth-century European capitalism: thus he proposed for the Zulu a scheme which

> contains so many self-adjusting balances, all the springs of which . . . are put into operation by the instincts of self-preservation and self-interest.

Against this statement we must place the Zulu image of the king as a bird giving protection and ensuring the fertility of its eggs without regard for individual self-interest – the eggs which were left to rot when the great bird died in 1884.

The 1880s saw the physical destruction of the Zulu kingdom. And yet the kingdom is still a potent element in African life and politics in southern Africa. The memory of the kingdom, its history, its victories as well as its defeats continue to influence events in a transformed situation. The survival of the kingdom into the last quarter of the nineteenth century meant that it existed within the lifetime of many of the men who articulated and organised the first social and political protests against colonial rule in Natal. Searching for an acceptable programme, alienated by their colonial backgrounds, and closely related to the Zulu, they identified readily with the kingdom and its long history of independence. The House of Shaka has had an emotional appeal which remains an important factor in African thinking.

Even as the civil war was being fought, the African convert William Ngidi wrote of the policy of setting Zulu against Zulu which was being implemented 'by the cunning of white men, who want to eat up their land. My heart is very full of grief, I cannot find words to express it, for this splendid old Zulu people.'[28] In 1897 Zululand was formally incorporated into Natal and early in the twentieth century much of its land opened to white settlement. In spite of protests from the Natal officials the Zulu continued to look to the royal house for leadership. In the rising in Natal and Zululand in 1906 it was a 'centralising device' which gave assistance and inspiration.[29] The nature of the royal house profoundly affected the structure and development of the independent African churches in the region.[30] The first nationalist leaders identified with the Zulu royal house and supported it in their writings and speeches. The complex relationships between the Zulu royal house, African political leaders and white politicians are now being explored and analysed within the southern African context.[31] In 1973, during the Durban strikes, the cry of the black workers was 'Usuthu',[32] a slogan which originated as a reference to raided cattle, in a homestead of the Zulu prince Cetshwayo kaMpande more than 125 years previously. The Zulu nationalist movement today, whose leaders are in many cases the direct descendants of the men who fought the civil war, and who draw consciously on the Zulu past, is a force which will still affect the course of southern African history.

Notes

1 BPP, C.4645, Appendix.
2 See especially BPP, C.4274: 10, enc., Smyth to Sec. of State for War, 19 Sept. 1884, also 6, enc. 1, Osborn to Bulwer, 20 Sept. 1884, together with Bulwer's reply, enc. 3, Bulwer to Osborn, 29 Sept. 1884.
3 BPP, C.4587: 66, Bulwer to Derby, 27 March 1885 and encs.
4 CO 879/25, 329: no. 43, Havelock to Granville, 15 March 1886 and encs.
5 CO 179/156: 1974, Bulwer to Derby, 3 Jan. 1885 and enc.
6 NA, Colenso collection: box 126, H. E. Colenso to Chesson, 9 June 1885; GHZ 694: Osborn to Bulwer, 11 June 1885.
7 BPP, C.4587: 21, Bulwer to Derby, 12 Jan. 1885.
8 M. Wilson and L. Thompson (eds), *The Oxford History of South Africa*, Oxford, 1971, ii, Ch. 1, D. Hobart Houghton, 'Economic Development, 1865–1965', p. 12.
9 NA, Colenso collection: box 139, H. E. Colenso to Jorissen, 25 March 1886.
10 C. T. Binns, *Dinuzulu, The Death of the House of Shaka*, London, 1968, p. 54.
11 CO 179/154: 865, Bulwer to Derby, 16 Dec. 1884 (conf.).
12 BPP, C.4587: 40, Bulwer to Derby, 23 Feb. 1885, p. 42.
13 BPP, C.4913: 1, Bulwer, Memorandum on the situation in the Zulu Country, 6 Jan. 1886, p. 8.
14 BPP, C.4645: 49, Stanley to Mitchell, 4 Jan. 1886.
15 GHZ 696: Osborn to Special Commissioner, 17 Feb. 1886, statement by messengers sent by Dinuzulu, Ndabuko and Mnyamana to Resident Commissioner, 16 Feb. 1886.

16 BPP, C.4913: 1, Bulwer, Memorandum on the situation in the Zulu Country, 6 Jan. 1886, p. 10.
17 NA, Sir T. Shepstone collection: box 16, Havelock to T. Shepstone, 7 March 1886.
18 BPP, C.4913: 25, enc. 2, reply by Havelock, 22 March 1886.
19 BPP, C.4980: 62, enc. 10, M. Luthuli (for Shingana and others) to Her Majesty the Queen, 11 Nov. 1886, p. 132.
20 NA, Colenso collection: box 126, bk II, H. E. Colenso to Prof. Ruenen, 7 Nov. 1886.
21 AS papers: 130/70, F. E. Colenso to Chesson, 18 Dec. 1886.
22 AS papers: 131/71, H. E. Colenso to Chesson, 8 June 1887.
23 AS papers: 131/64, H. E. Colenso to Chesson, 20 April 1887.
24 AS papers: 130/73, F. E. Colenso to Chesson, 15 Jan. 1887.
25 AS papers: 131/78, H. E. Colenso to Chesson, 2 Nov. 1887.
26 BPP, C.5331: 37, enc. 2, memorandum by Havelock read to Dinuzulu and Ndabuko, 14 Nov. 1887, p. 64.
27 BPP, C.5331: 9, enc. 4, memorandum by Sir T. Shepstone, 31 July 1887, pp. 28–9.
28 G. W. Cox, *The Life of John William Colenso D.D., Bishop of Natal*, London, 1888, ii, p. 614.
29 S. Marks, *Reluctant Rebellion, the 1906–8 disturbances in Natal*, Oxford, 1970, pp. 114–16 and 336–7.
30 B. G. M. Sundkler, *Bantu Prophets in South Africa*, London, 1961, Ch. 5.
31 S. Marks, 'The Ambiguities of Dependence: John L. Dube of Natal', in *Journal of Southern African Studies*, i, 2, (1975), and 'Natal, the Zulu royal family, and the ideology of segregation', paper presented to the Conference on Southern African History, National University of Lesotho, Aug. 1977.
32 'South Africa: Usutu!' in *Time*, 19 Feb. 1973; and Institute for Industrial Education, *The Durban Strikes 1973*, Durban and Johannesburg, 1974, pp. 96–7.

Appendix

Biographical Notes

These are not comprehensive biographies but have been compiled to assist the reader. The figure following the name is a rough approximation of the person's age in 1879; if in parenthesis it is taken from (F. B. Fynney) *The Zulu Army, and Zulu Headmen*. Words in capital letters can be found elsewhere in the Appendix.

Bantubensumo (45): Buthelezi; lineage head; from northern districts near Dlomodlomo range. 1883 placed under ZIBHEBHU, supported Usuthu.

Bhejane: Cebekhulu; lineage head; *induna* EMANGWENI section; *inceku* to CETSHWAYO. 1879 placed under MLANDELA. Devoted Usuthu supporter, prominent in Zulu councils; the man who angered Shepstone in 1877 by calling him by his Zulu name.

Cetshwayo (Cetewayo, Cetywayo) 53: Zulu king from 1872 to 1879 when he was exiled by the British. Visited London 1882, returned to South Africa 1883 and died a year later.

Dabulamanzi 40: Zulu; son of Mpande; from southern districts. 1879 placed under Dunn. An aggressive man, assassinated 1886.

Dilikana: Mbatha; chief; central districts near Nhlazatshe. Strong Usuthu supporter. Very old. Interrupted proceedings at Nhlazatshe meeting, 31 Aug. 1881, to speak for the king. Killed at Ulundi, 21 July 1883.

Dinuzulu (Dinizulu) 11: son and successor to CETSHWAYO.

Faku (45): Ntombela; lineage head; near Babanango. 1879 appointed chief, but of little significance within the kingdom.

Fokothi: Zulu; MANDLAKAZI lineage; *ikhohlo* branch of MAPHITHA's homestead; near Nongoma ridge. Usuthu supporter.

Gawozi (60): Mpungose; chief; *isikhulu*. 1879 appointed chief. Died 5 Jan. 1880.

Godide (70): Ntuli chief; *isikhulu*; 1879 placed under Dunn. Usuthu supporter. Killed at Ulundi, 21 July 1883.

Hamu (Oham, Uham) (45): Zulu; lineage head; genealogical son of Mpande's full brother, biological son of Mpande. Opposed to CETSHWAYO, defected to British. 1879 appointed chief. Headed the NGENETSHENI faction within the kingdom.

Hayiyana (Haiana, Uhayana) (45): Zulu; MANDLAKAZI lineage; eldest son of MAPHITHA and leader of the *ikhohlo* branch of his father's homestead. Leading Usuthu. Killed at Ulundi, 21 July 1883.

Hemulana: Sibiya; *induna* to MNYAMANA; influential position in Usuthu councils and strong supporter. Orator, led attack on Shepstone at installation in 1883.

Hlezibane: Zulu; head of EGAZINI lineage; northern districts. Usuthu supporter, killed 1883.

Mabhoko: EMGAZINI; chief, son of MASIPHULA; northern districts between Phongolo and Mkhuze. 1883 placed under Zibhebhu. Supported Usuthu.

Mahanana (32): Zulu; son of Mpande; *induna* of MPHANGISWENI section; sources of Black Mfolozi. Usuthu.

Mahubulwana: Mdlalose; senior *induna* of QULUSI. 1879 placed under HAMU. Trusted elderly Usuthu supporter. Killed 1883.

Makhoba: Zulu; MANDLAKAZI lineage; member of *ikhohlo* of Maphitha's homestead; Nongoma ridge. Usuthu supporter. Killed at Msebe 1883.

Mankulumana: Ndwandwe, brother of MGOJANA; northern districts. Usuthu supporter who became chief counsellor to DINUZULU. Died 1926.

Maphelu 20: Zungu; son of MKHOSANA; north-western districts. In his old age dictated an account of his life. Usuthu.

Maphitha: died 1872; Zulu; chief of MANDLAKAZI lineage. Most powerful man in Mpande's kingdom. Father of ZIBHEBHU.

Masiphula: died 1872; EMGAZINI; chief. Chief counsellor to Mpande.

Matshana: Sithole; chief; west of the Qudeni. Refugee from Natal.

Matshana: Mchunu; chief; lived south of SIHAYO.

Mavumengwana (45): Ntuli; lineage head; *ikhohlo* branch of Ndlela's homestead. 1879 placed under Dunn.

Mbopha: Hlabisa; lineage head; *isikhulu*; northern districts. 1879 placed under ZIBHEBHU. Related to royal house through MPANDE's mother and a particular favourite. Killed at Ulundi, 21 July 1883.

Mehlokazulu: Qungebe; eldest son of SIHAYO; independent and aggressive Usuthu supporter: killed, Mome, 1906.

Mfanawendlela (70): Zungu; chief; *isikhulu*; central districts. 1879 appointed chief. Killed by Usuthu, Dec. 1883.

Mfinyeli (80): Zulu; *inceku* to Mpande; senior *induna* Gqikazi homestead. 1879 placed under ZIBHEBHU. Usuthu supporter.

Mfunzi: Mpungose; senior confidential messenger to the royal house. Usuthu.

Mfuzi (75): Mdletshe; chief; *isikhulu*; leading officer from north-western district. Died 1879. Father of MSUSHWANA.

Mgamule: Ntombela; lineage head; senior *induna* Ekubazeni homestead. 1879 placed under ZIBHEBHU: leading Usuthu.

Mgitshwa (45): Biyela; son of MKHOSANA's *ikhohlo* section; central southern districts. In 1879 appointed chief, thereby excluding SOMHLOLO, the heir. Anti-Usuthu.

Mgojana: Ndwandwe; chief; northern districts. 1879 appointed chief. Supported ZIBHEBHU. Killed by Usuthu 1888.

Mgwazeni: Zungu; lineage head; *induna* of note within the kingdom. Sent to make contact with Bishopstowe after the invasion. Killed at Msebe, 1883.

Mkhosana (43): Biyela; chief. Killed at Isandlwana 1879.

Mkhosana: Zungu; lineage head. Accompanied Cetshwayo into exile and returned to Zululand as his emissary. Accompanied Cetshwayo to London as his most trusted adviser.

Mlandela: Mthethwa; chief; *isikhulu*; appointed by Shaka. 1879 appointed chief. Of great rank, but old by 1879 and came under Dunn's influence. Died May 1883.

Mnqandi: Sibisi; chief; *isikhulu*; central districts near Nhlazatshe. Killed at Ulundi, 21 July 1883.

Mnyamana (Umyamana) (70): Buthelezi; chief; northern and central districts. Chief counsellor to Cetshwayo, the most powerful man in the kingdom next to the king. Cautious, conservative, politically astute. Died 1892.

Msushwana: Mdletshe; chief; successor to MFUZI. In 1879 his large chiefdom was placed under ZIBHEBHU. Usuthu supporter. Killed in 1888 by ZIBHEBHU.

Ndabankulu: Ntombela; chief; north-western districts. Independent and aggressive. Usuthu supporter.

Ndabuko (32): Zulu; son of Mpande, full brother of CETSHWAYO; Ivuna valley. 1879 placed under ZIBHEBHU and became leader of Usuthu and guardian to DINUZULU. Exiled in 1889.

Ndwandwe: Langa; chief; southern districts. Usuthu supporter. Killed at Ulundi, 21 July 1883.

Ngcongcwana: Zulu; lineage head; northern districts. 1879 came under ZIBHEBHU. Usuthu supporter and adviser to CETSHWAYO in London. Killed at Ulundi, 21 July 1883.

Ngobozana: Mpungose; lineage head; central districts. Adviser to CETSHWAYO.

Ntshingwayo (Tyingwayo) (68): Khoza; lineage head; *isikhulu*; north-western districts. Leader of the army. Killed at Ulundi, 21 July 1883.

Ntuzwa: Mdlalose; brother of SEKETHWAYO; north-western districts. Leading Usuthu.

Qethuka (60): Magwaza; chief; *isikhulu*; southern districts. Leading Usuthu.

Sambane: Nyawo; chief; Lubombo range. 1879 excluded from Zululand, but remained an Usuthu supporter. Died 1911.

Sekethwayo (65): Mdlalose; chief; *isikhulu*; north-western districts. 1879 appointed chief but remained a Usuthu supporter. Killed at Ulundi, 21 July 1883.

Shingana (Tshingana) (40): Zulu, son of Mpande; White Mfolozi valley. Usuthu leader. Exiled in 1889, later banished to Natal where he died 1911.

Sigananda 70: Chube; chief; Nkandla forest. Usuthu supporter. Sheltered CETSHWAYO 1883. Died in a Natal gaol, 1906.

Sigcwelegcwele (53): Ngadini: lineage head: southern districts. Prominent soldier in the Zulu army. Closely associated with John Dunn.

Sihayo (55): Qungebe; chief; Nquthu district; *induna* and favourite of CETSHWAYO. Deposed and banished in 1879. Killed at Ulundi, 21 July 1883.

Sikhobobo: Sibiya; senior *induna* of QULUSI.

Sitheku (43): Zulu; son of Mpande; central districts. 1879 placed under GAWOZI.

Sitshaluza: EMGAZINI; brother of MASIPHULA; northern districts.

Siyunguza: Mpungose; *inceku* to CETSHWAYO; central-southern districts. 1880 appointed chief after the death of his brother GAWOZI. Anti-Usuthu.

Sokwetshata: Mthethwa; son and successor of MLANDELA. Anti-Usuthu leader on the coast.

Somfula: Hlabisa; chief. Too young to rule in the 1880s but supported by ZIBHEBHU against Hlabisa regent, MBOPHA.

Somhlolo: Biyela; heir to MKHOSANA. 1879 excluded from power. Usuthu.

Somkhele (40): Mphukunyoni; chief; *isikhulu*; northern coastal plain. Usuthu supporter and close to royal house. Died 1907.

Somopo: Thembu; lineage head; senior *induna* EMANGWENI section. Personally close to CETSHWAYO, and Usuthu supporter.

Tshanibezwe: Buthelezi; MNYAMANA's son and successor. Frequently represented his father.

Vumandaba (60): Biyela; senior *inceku* to Mpande; southern districts. Usuthu, killed at Ulundi, 21 July 1883.

Ziwedu (Usiwetu) (45): Zulu; son of Mpande; northern districts. 1879 placed under ZIBHEBHU. Became an Usuthu leader.

Zibhebhu (Usibebu, Usibepu) (35): MANDLAKAZI chief; aggressive, independent. 1879 appointed chief, and led anti-Usuthu faction.

Some important groups

Mandlakazi: Zulu lineage, headed by ZIBHEBHU; became identified with Zibhebhu's anti-Usuthu faction.

Emangweni: royal section, founded in Mpande's time, on the coast.

Egazini: royal lineage, headed by HLEZIBANE, north-western districts.

Emgazini: clan, closely related to the Zulu, between Mkhuze and Phongolo rivers.

Mphangisweni: royal section, founded in north-west by Shaka; headed by MAHANANA in 1880s.

Ngenetsheni: HAMU's faction; in the north.

Qulusi: the most important of the royal sections; founded by Shaka in the north-west.

Select Bibliography

Primary sources

This book is based largely on two major groups of sources: the official records of the period published as British Parliamentary Papers on the one hand, and the papers printed at Bishopstowe by the Bishop of Natal, J. W. Colenso, and after his death, by his daughter Harriette. In these papers the Colensos analysed the information published in the British Parliamentary Papers, and other accounts of events in Zululand, and compared them with reports received at Bishopstowe from Zulu sources.

The originals of the published correspondence, together with official minutes and memoranda, were examined in the Public Record Office in London, and in the Natal Archives in Pietermaritzburg. The bulk of the correspondence was published, seldom with any changes.

The privately printed researches of the Colenso family were distributed to interested persons as they came off the Bishopstowe press. I examined collections of them in the Natal Archives, the Killie Campbell Africana Library and the British Museum, and believe that none is complete; some are incorrectly bound, different titles are used, and at least one error in pagination on the Colensos' part had added to the confusion. Harriette Colenso divided them into nine parts, and I have followed her, but identify them as Colenso; series 1–9. The following list is a provisional one; extant copies of these papers need to be examined and classified by a bibliographer.

Colenso; series 1. Compiled by J. W. Colenso. On p. 457, n. 2 of G. W. Cox, *The Life of Bishop Colenso,* II, it appears as if this was originally entitled 'Extracts from the Blue-books' but later it was referred to as 'Digest on Zulu Affairs'. It must be noted however that this title was also extended to cover Colenso; series 2. At least 855 pages.

Colenso; series 2. Copy in KC entitled, 'The course of political events in Zululand, From October, 1881, to 16th June, 1883. Official, Colonial, & Zulu Statements, Analysed and compared by the Bishop of Natal. Printed by Magema at the Bishop's press.' 884 pages, the last 200 produced after the Bishop's death, apparently by Harriette Colenso.

Colenso; series 3. Prints, statements and letters relating to the movement of Afrikaners into Zululand in 1884. 24+ pages.

Colenso; series 4. Concerned with the rights of the Church of England to the KwaMagwaza mission in Zululand.

Colenso; series 5. Documents concerning the Zulu position during the negotiations between the British and the New Republicans which preceded partition and annexation, November to June 1887. 78 pages.

Colenso; series 6–9. Papers on the annexation and the 'disturbances' of 1888 totalling 37 pages.

Additional information was examined in the major collections of material on Natal and Zulu history. The Killie Campbell Africana Library houses files of many of the personalities who took part in the events described and a mass of historical and cultural material, including the typescript of Maphelu kaMkhosana's account of Zulu history and the important James Stuart collection. Since I examined the Stuart papers they have been classified and they are now in the process of being published. The Killie Campbell Africana Library, the Natal Archives, and Rhodes House in Oxford contain important collections of the correspondence of the Colenso family while most of the suriving correspondence of the Shepstone family is in the Natal Archives. For a detailed analysis of the primary material used in this book reference should be made to my Ph.D dissertation.

Secondary sources

A select list of contemporary books and pamphlets

ASHE, W. and WYATT EDGELL, E. V., *The Story of the Zulu campaign,* London, 1880.

CALLAWAY, H., *The Religious System of the Amazulu,* Cape Town, 1970 (reprint).

CAMPBELL, W., *With Cetywayo in the Inkandhla, and the present state of the Zulu question,* Durban, 1883.

CHESSON, F. W., *The War in Zululand: a review of Sir Bartle Frere's policy drawn from official documents,* London, 1879.

CLARKE, W. J., *Notes on Zululand Affairs since the Restoration of Cetywayo*, compiled from the Blue Books, 1898.

COLENSO, FRANCES E. and DURNFORD, E., *History of the Zulu War and its origin*, London, 1880.

(COLENSO, FRANCES E.), *My Chief and I; or, six months in Natal after the Langalibalele outbreak* by 'Atherton Wylde', London, 1880.

COLENSO, FRANCES E., *The Ruin of Zululand; an account of British doings in Zululand since the invasion of 1879*, i, London, 1884.; ii, London, 1885

COLENSO, H. E., *England and the Zulus*, London, 1890.

— *Zululand: past and present*, 1890.

COLENSO, H. E. and FOX BOURNE, H. R., *The Story of Dinuzulu*, London, 1890.

COLENSO, J. W., *Ten weeks in Natal: a journal of a first tour of visitation among the Colonists and Zulu kafirs of Natal*, Cambridge, 1855.

— *Three native accounts of the visit of the Bishop of Natal in September and October, 1859, to Umpande King of the Zulus*, Maritzburg, 1860.

— *First Steps of the Zulu Mission*, London, 1860.

— *St Paul's Epistle to the Romans: newly translated and explained from a missionary point of view*, Cambridge, 1861.

— 'The Missions to the Zulus in Natal and Zululand', a lecture reprinted in the *Social Science Review*, June 1864.

— *Defence of Langalibalele with additional evidence and an appendix*, Bishopstowe, n.d.

— *The History of the Matshana inquiry, with a report of the evidence as taken down by the Bishop of Natal and the Rev. Canon Tönnesen*, Bishopstowe, 1875.

(COLENSO, J. W.), *Langalibalele and the Amahlubi Tribe; being remarks upon the official record of the trials of the Chief and his sons and induna, and other members of the Amahlubi tribe by the Bishop of Natal*, London, 1874.

— *What doth the Lord require of us? A sermon preached in the Cathedral Church of St Peter's Maritzburg on Wednesday March 12 1879*, Pietermaritzburg, 1879.

COX, G. W., *The Life of John William Colenso, D. D., Bishop of Natal*, 2 vols, London, 1888.

DAWNAY, G. C., *Private journal of Guy C. Dawnay, 1872–74* (privately printed), 1894.

DIXIE, F., *A Defence of Zululand and its King: Echoes from the Blue-Books, with an appendix containing correspondence on the subject of the release of Cetshwayo, etc.*, London, n.d.

— *In the Land of Misfortune*, London, 1882.

DURNFORD, E. (ed.), *A Soldier's Life and Work in South Africa, 1872 to 1879: A Memoir of the late Colonel A. W. Durnford, Royal Engineers*, London, 1882.

ESCOMBE, H. and DUMAT, F. C., *A Remonstrance on Behalf of the Zulu Chief, 1889*, Pietermaritzburg, 1889.

FARRER, J. A., *Zululand and the Zulus: their history, beliefs, customs, military system . . .*, London, 1879.

FRERE, B., *Afghanistan and South Africa*, 1881.

FYNNEY, F. B., *Zululand and the Zulus: being an enlargement upon two lectures delivered by Fred B. Fynney under the titles of the Rise and fall of the Zulu nation and our native tribes: their customs, superstitions and beliefs*, Pietermaritzburg, n.d.

(FYNNEY, F. B.), *The Zulu Army, and Zulu Headmen; Compiled from information obtained from the most reliable sources, and published, by direction of the Lieut.-General commanding, for the information of those under his command*, 2nd edn (revised), Pietermaritzburg, 1879.

GREGG, F., *The Story of Bishop Colenso – the Friend of the Zulus*, London, 1892.

GROUT, L., *Zulu-land: or, Life among the Zulu-kafirs of Natal and Zululand, South Africa*, London, 1863.

HAGGARD, H. R., *Cetywayo and his white neighbours; or, Remarks on recent events in Zululand, Natal, and the Transvaal*, London, 1896.

— *The Days of my Life*, London, 1926.

ISAACS, N., *Travels and adventures in eastern Africa, descriptive of the Zoolus, their manners, customs with a sketch of Natal*, Cape Town, 1970 (reprint).

JENKINSON, J. B., *Amazulu: The Zulus, their past history, manners, customs, and language, with observation on the country and its productions, climate, etc., the Zulu war, and Zululand since the war*, London, 1882.

LESLIE, D., *Among the Zulus and Amatongas: with sketches of the natives, their language and customs, and the country, products, wild animals, etc; being principally contributions to magazines and newspapers. . . .*, Edinburgh, 1875.

LUDLOW, W., *Zululand and Cetewayo*, Birmingham, 1882.

MANN, R. J., *The Zulus and Boers of South Africa: a fragment of recent history*, London, 1879.

MARTINEAU, J., *The Life and Correspondence of the Right Hon. Sir Bartle Frere*, London, 1895.

MASON, G. H., *Zululand: a mission tour in South Africa*, London, 1862.

MATTHEWS, J. W., *Incwadi Yami, or twenty years' personal experience in South Africa*, New York, 1887.

Military Report on Zululand, prepared for the General Staff, War Office, London, 1906.

MITFORD, B., *Through the Zulu Country, its battlefields and its people*, London, 1883.

MOODIE, D. C. F. (ed.), *John Dunn, Cetywayo, and the three Generals*, Pietermaritzburg, 1886.

MOODIE, D. C. F., *The History of the Battles and Adventures of the British, the Boers, and the Zulus &c., in Southern Africa from the time of Pharaoh Necho, to 1880, with copious chronology,* Cape Town, 1888.

NORRIS-NEWMAN, C. L., *In Zululand with the British throughout the War of 1879,* London, 1880.

Precis of information concerning Zululand, with a map; Intelligence Division War Office; corrected to December 1894, London, 1895.

SHOOTER, J., *The Kafirs of Natal and the Zulu Country,* London, 1857.

SMITH, J. W., *The Story of the Zulu Agency: an episode in the history of Great Britain's dealings with the Native Races of South Africa,* Pietermaritzburg, 1878.

STATHAM, F. R., *The Zulu Iniquity,* London, 1884.

SWINNY, G. H. (trans.), *A Zulu Boy's recollection of the Zulu War and of Cetshwayo's return,* London, 1884.

TYLER, J., *Forty Years among the Zulus,* Boston, 1891.

VIJN, C., *Cetshwayo's Dutchman: Being the private journal of a white trader in Zululand during the British Invasion,* trans., edited and annotated by J. W. Colenso, London, 1880.

WILMOT, A., *History of the Zulu war,* London, 1880.

Documentary material subsequently published

ARTHUR, G. (ed.), *The letters of Lord and Lady Wolseley (1870–1911),* London, 1922.

BROWN, R. A. (ed.), *The Road to Ulundi: the water-colour drawings of John North Crealock (The Zulu War of 1879),* Pietermaritzburg, 1969.

BUCKLE, G. E. (ed.), *The Letters of Queen Victoria,* London, 1928, series II, vol. 3.

REES, W. (ed.), *Colenso Letters from Natal,* Pietermaritzburg, 1958.

SPOHR, O H.. (ed. and trans.), *The Natal Diaries of Dr W. H. I. Bleek, 1855–1856,* Cape Town, 1965.

(WOLSELEY, G.), *The South African Diaries of Sir Garnet Wolseley, 1875,* ed. A. Preston, Cape Town, 1971.

(WOLSELEY, G.), *The South African Journal of Sir Garnet Wolseley, 1879–1880,* ed. A. Preston, Cape Town, 1973.

A select list of books and articles subsequently published

ACOCKS, J. P. H., *Veld Types of South Africa,* Pretoria, 1953.

ATMORE, A. and MARKS, S., 'The Imperial Factor in South Africa in the Nineteenth Century: Towards a Reassessment', in E. F. Penrose (ed.), *European Imperialism and the Partition of Africa,* London, 1975.

BARNETT, C., *Britain and Her Army*, 1509–1970, London, 1970.

BECKER, P., *Rule of Fear: the life and times of Dingane, King of the Zulu*, London, 1964.

BINNS, C. T., *The Last Zulu King: the life and death of Cetshwayo*, London, 1963.

— *Dinuzulu, the Death of the House of Shaka*, London, 1968.

— *The Warrior People: Zulu origins, customs and witchcraft*, Cape Town, 1974.

BOTHA, C., *Manuscripts and papers in the Killie Campbell Africana Collection*, Johannesburg, 1967.

BRAATVEDT, H. P., *Roaming Zululand with a Native Commissioner*, Pietermaritzburg, 1949.

BROOKES, E. H., *The History of native policy in South Africa, 1830 to the present day*, Cape Town, 1924.

— *White Rule in South Africa, 1830–1910*, Pietermaritzburg, 1974.

BROOKES, E. H. and HURWITZ, N., *The Native Reserves of Natal*, Natal Regional Survey, vii, Cape Town, 1957.

BROOKES, E. H. and WEBB, C. de B., *A History of Natal*, Pietermaritzburg, 1965.

BRYANT, A. T., *A Zulu-English Dictionary . . . including also a . . . a synopsis of Zulu grammar and concise history of the Zulu people from the most ancient times*, Marianhill, 1905.

— *Olden Times in Zululand and Natal, containing earlier political history of the eastern-Nguni clans*, London, 1929.

— *Bantu Origins*, Cape Town, 1963.

— *A History of the Zulu and Neighbouring Tribes*, Cape Town, 1964.

— *The Zulu People, as they were before the white man came*, Pietermaritzburg, 1967.

BUCKLE, G. E., *The life of Benjamin Disraeli, Earl of Beaconsfield*, London, 1920.

BULPIN, T. V., *Shaka's Country: a book of Zululand*, Cape Town, 1952.

BUTHELEZI, G., 'The Past and Future of the Zulu People', *Munger Africana Library Notes*, Jan. 1972.

BUTLER, W. F., *The Life of Sir George Pomeroy-Colley*, London, 1899.

CLAMMER, D., *The Zulu War*, Newton Abbot, 1973.

CLEMENTS, W. H., *The Glamour and Tragedy of the Zulu War*, London, 1936.

COHEN, M., *Rider Haggard, His Life and Work*, London, 1968.

COPE, T. (ed.), *Izibongo, Zulu Praise-poems*, Oxford, 1968.

COUPLAND, R. F., *Zulu Battle Piece: Isandhlwana*, London, 1948.

COWLES, R. B., *Zulu Journal: field notes of a naturalist in South Africa*, California, 1959.

DANIEL, J. B. MCI., 'A Geographical study of pre-Shakan Zululand', *South African Geographical Journal*, lv, 1 (1973).

DE KIEWIET, C. W., *The Imperial factor in South Africa: a study in politics and economics*, Cambridge, 1937.

— *A History of South Africa: social and economic*, London, 1957.

DHLOMO, R. R. R., *uCetshwayo*, Pietermaritzburg, 1956.

— *uDinuzulu kaCetshwayo*, Pietermaritzburg, 1968.

DOKE, C. M., MALCOLM, D. MCK. and SIKAKANA, J. M. A., *English and Zulu Dictionary*, Johannesburg, 1958.

'The Dunn Reserve, Zululand', *Natal Regional Survey*, Additional Report No. 4, Pietermaritzburg, 1953.

FANNIN, N., *The Fannin papers: a pioneer's story of the diamond fields and the Zulu war*, Durban, 1932.

FORTES, M. and EVANS-PRITCHARD, E. E. (eds), *African Political Systems*, London, 1940.

FRASER, B. D., *John William Colenso: a bibliography*, Cape Town, 1952.

FRENCH, E. G., *Lord Chelmsford and the Zulu war*, London, 1939.

(FYNN, H. F.), *The Diary of Henry Francis Fynn*, (eds) J. Stuart and D. McK. Malcolm, Pietermaritzburg, 1969.

GIBSON, J. Y., *The Story of the Zulus*, London, 1911.

GLUCKMAN, M., 'The kingdom of the Zulu of South Africa', in M. Fortes and E. Evans-Pritchard (eds), *African Political Systems*, London, 1940.

— 'The Rise of a Zulu Empire', *Scientific American*, 202, 1960.

— 'The Individual in a Social Framework: The Rise of King Shaka of Zululand', *Journal of African Studies*, i, 2 (1974).

GOODFELLOW, C. F., *Great Britain and South African Confederation, 1870–1881*, Cape Town, 1966.

GORDON, R. E., *Shepstone: the role of the family in the history of South Africa, 1820–1890*, Cape Town, 1968.

GUY, J. J., 'A note on firearms in the Zulu kingdom with special reference to the Anglo-Zulu war, 1879', *Journal of African History*, xii, 4, 1971.

— 'Production and Exchange in the Zulu kingdom', *Mohlomi: Journal of Southern African Studies*, ii, 1978.

HAMMOND-TOOKE, W. D., *The Bantu-speaking Peoples of Southern Africa*, London, 1974.

HATTERSLEY, A. F., *The British settlement of Natal: a study in imperial migration*, Cambridge, 1950.

HERD, N., *The Bent Pine*, Johannesburg, 1976.

HICKS BEACH, V., *Life of Sir Michael Hicks Beach (Earl St Aldwyn)*, i, London, 1932.

HINCHLIFF, P., *John William Colenso, Bishop of Natal*, London, 1964.

Institute for Industrial Education, *The Durban Strikes 1973*, Durban and Johannesburg, 1974.

JUNOD, H. A., *The Life of a South Africa tribe*, 2 vols, New York, 1962 (reprint).

KIERNAN, V. G., *The Lords of Human Kind: European Attitudes towards the Outside World in the Imperial Age*, Great Britain, 1972.

KRIGE, E. J., *The Social System of the Zulus*, Pietermaritzburg, 1957.

LEE, A. W., *Once Dark Country: recollections and reflections of a South African bishop*, London, 1949.

LEHMANN, J., *All Sir Garnet: a life of Field-Marshal Lord Wolseley*, London, 1964.

LLOYD, A., *The Zulu War*, London, 1973.

LUGG, H. C., *Historic Natal and Zululand*, Pietermaritzburg, 1949.

MARKS, S., 'Harriette Colenso and the Zulus, 1874–1913', *Journal of African History*, iv, 3 (1963).

— *Reluctant Rebellion, the 1906–8 disturbances in Natal*, Oxford, 1970.

— 'The Ambiguities of Dependence: John L. Dube of Natal', *Journal of Southern African Studies*, i, 2 (1975).

MAURICE, F. and ARTHUR, G., *The Life of Lord Wolseley*, London, 1924.

MENDELSSOHN, S., *Mendelssohn's South African Bibliography*, London, 1957 (reprint).

MORRIS, D. R., *The Washing of the Spears: a history of the rise of the Zulu nation under Shaka and its fall in the Zulu war of 1879*, London, 1966.

MUTWA, C., *My people*, London, 1969.

Natal Regional Survey, Add. Report No. 4, The Dunn Reserve Zululand, Pietermaritzburg, 1943.

Natal Regional Survey, vol. 1, Cape Town, 1951.

Natal Regional Survey, vol. 13, Cape Town, 1957.

O'BYRNE, S., *The Colony of Natal to the Zulu War, 1843 to 1878*, Cape Town, 1965.

OMER-COOPER, J. D., *The Zulu Aftermath: a nineteenth-century revolution in Bantu Africa*, London, 1966.

PUGH, R. B., *The Records of the Colonial and Dominions Offices*, London, 1964.

READER, D. H., *Zulu Tribe in transition: the Makhanya of southern Natal*, Manchester, 1966.

RITTER, E. A., *Shaka Zulu: the rise of the Zulu empire*, London, 1955.

ROBERTS, B., *Ladies in the Veld*, London, 1965.

— *The Zulu Kings*, London, 1974.

ROBINSON, R. and GALLAGHER, J., with A. DENNY, *Africa and the Victorians: The Official Mind of Imperialism,* London, 1961.

ROTBERG, R. I. (ed.), *Rebellion in Black Africa*, London, 1971.

ROUX, E., *Time Longer than Rope: a history of the Black Man's struggle for freedom in South Africa*, Madison, 1964.

SAMUELSON, L. H., *Zululand: its traditions, legends, customs and folk-lore* Marianhill, reprinted Durban, 1974.

SAMUELSON, R. C. A., *Long, Long Ago*, Durban, 1929.

— *The King Cetywayo Zulu Dictionary*, Durban, 1923.

SCHAPERA, I. (ed.), *The Bantu Speaking Tribes of South Africa: an ethnographical survey*, London, 1937.

SCHREUDER, D. M., *Gladstone and Kruger: Liberal Government and Colonial 'Home Rule' 1880–85*, London and Toronto, 1969.

SHAPIRO, N. and HENTOFF, N. (eds), *Hear me talkin' to ya: the story of Jazz by the men who made it*, London, 1955.

SHEPPERSON, G. A. and PRICE, T., *Independent African: John Chilembwe and the origins, setting and significance of the Nyasaland native rising of 1915*, Edinburgh, 1958.

SIMONS, H. J., *African Women. Their legal status in South Africa*, London, 1968.

SLATER, H., 'Land, labour and capital in Natal: The Natal Land and Colonisation Company, 1860–1948', *Journal of African History*, xvi, 2, 1975.

SMAIL, J. L., *Historical Monuments and Battlefields in Natal and Zululand*, Cape Town, 1965.

— *With Shield and Assegaai*, Cape Town, 1969.

SOGA, J. H., *The South-Eastern Bantu*, Johannesburg, 1930.

SOLOMON, W. E. G., *Saul Solomon, 'The Member for Cape Town'*, Cape Town, 1948.

STUART, J., *A History of the Zulu rebellion, 1906, and of Dinuzulu's arrest, trial and expatriation*, London, 1913.

— *uTulasizwe*, London, 1923.

— *uBaxoxele*, London, 1924.

— *uHlangakulu*, London, 1924.

— *uKulumetule*, London, 1925.

SUNDKLER, B. G. M., *Bantu Prophets in South Africa*, London, 1961.

THOMPSON, L. (ed.), *African Societies in Southern Africa*, London, 1969.

Time, 19 Feb. 1973 ('South Africa: Usutu!').

UYS, C. J., *In the Era of Shepstone: being a study of British expansion in South Africa (1842–1877)*, Lovedale, 1933.

VAN ZYL, M. C., *Die koms van die Boere na Zoeloeland in 1884: Genooides of Indringers?*, Pretoria, 1962.

— *Die Uitbreiding van Britse Gesag oor die Natalse Noordgrensgebiede 1879–1897*, Archives Year Book for South African History, i, 1966.

VILAKAZI, A., *Zulu Transformations: a study of the dynamics of social change*, Pietermaritzburg, 1965.

WALTER, E. V., *Terror and Resistance: a study of political violence with case studies of some primitive African communities*, New York, 1969.

WEBB, C. de B., *A Guide to the Official Records of the Colony of Natal*, Pietermaritzburg, 1965.

— 'Great Britain and the Zulu people 1879–1887', in L. Thompson (ed.), *African Societies in Southern Africa*, London, 1969.

WEBB, C. DE B. and WRIGHT, J. B. (eds), *The James Stuart Archives*, i, Pietermaritzburg and Durban, 1976.

WELSH, D., *The Roots of Segregation; Native policy in Colonial Natal, 1845–1910*, Cape Town, 1971.

WILSON, M., 'Changes in social structure in southern Africa: the relevance of kinship studies to the historian', in L. Thompson (ed.), *African Societies in Southern Africa*, London, 1969.

WILSON, M. and THOMPSON, L. (eds), *The Oxford History of South Africa*, vol. 1: South Africa to 1870, Oxford, 1969.

— *The Oxford History of South Africa*, vol. 2: South Africa, 1870–1966, Oxford, 1971.

WOOD, E., *From Midshipman to Field Marshal*, ii, London, 1906.

WRIGLEY, E. A., *Population and History*, London, 1969.

Unpublished theses and seminar papers

COPE, R. L., 'Shepstone and Cetshwayo, 1873–1879' (MA University of Natal, 1967).

ETHERINGTON, N. A., 'The Rise of the Kholwa in Southeastern Africa: African Christian Communities in Natal, Pondoland and Zululand, 1835–1880' (PhD Yale University, 1971).

GUY, J. J., 'Mandhlakazi and Usuthu: the civil war in Zululand and the reaction of the British officials' (BA Hons. University of Natal, 1966).

— 'An approach to a study of the civil war in Zululand during the 1880s', unpublished seminar paper, African History Seminar, 22 May 1968, Institute of Commonwealth Studies.

— 'Segmentation and Zulu History', unpublished seminar paper, African History Seminar, 10 Feb. 1970, Institute of Commonwealth Studies.

— 'Cattle-keeping in Zululand', unpublished seminar paper, Research group on Cattle-keeping in Africa, late 1970, Language and History in Africa Seminar, School of Oriental and African Studies, London.

— 'Ecological factors in the rise of Shaka and the Zulu kingdom', seminar paper, Conference on Southern African history, Aug. 1977, National University of Lesotho. Published in A. Atmore and S. Marks (eds), *Economy and Society in Pre-Industrial South Africa,* London (forthcoming).

KEMP, B. H., 'Johan William Colenbrander: a history of his times and the people and events with which he was associated, 1879–1896' (PhD University of Natal, 1962).

MARKS, S., 'Natal, the Zulu royal family, and the ideology of segregation', unpublished seminar paper, Conference on Southern African history, Aug. 1977, National University of Lesotho.

SHIELDS, C., 'The Life of John Dunn, with special reference to Zululand, 1879–1897' (MA University of South Africa, 1939).

WOLFSON, F. 'Some aspects of Native Administration in Natal under Theophilus Shepstone, Secretary for Native Affairs, 1875–1875' (MA University of Witwatersrand, 1946).

Index